Stalinism and Nazism

Stalinism and Nazism

History and Memory Compared

Edited by Henry Rousso

English-language edition edited and
introduced by Richard J. Golsan
Translated by Lucy B. Golsan,
Thomas C. Hilde, and Peter S. Rogers

University of Nebraska Press
Lincoln and London

Stalinisme et nazisme: Histoire et mémoire comparées
© Éditions Complexe, 1999
SA Diffusion Promotion Information
24, rue de Bosnie
1060 Bruxelles
Translation and introduction © 2004 by the Board
of Regents of the University of Nebraska
Manufactured in the United States of America
⊗
Library of Congress Cataloging-in-Publication Data
Stalinisme et nazisme. English.
Stalinism and nazism: history and memory com-
pared/edited by Henry Rousso; English-language
edition edited and introduced by Richard J. Golsan;
translated by Lucy B. Golsan, Thomas C. Hilde, and
Peter S. Rogers.
p. cm. – (European horizons)
Includes bibliographical references and index.
ISBN 0-8032-3945-9 (cloth : alk. paper) –
ISBN 0-8032-9000-4 (pbk. : alk. paper) –
ISBN 0-8032-4017-5 (electronic)
1. Totalitarianism.   2. National socialism. 3. Soviet
Union – Politics and government – 1936-1953.
4. Germany – Politics and government – 1933-1945.
I. Rousso, Henry, 1954-   II. Golsan, Richard Joseph,
1952-   III. Title.   IV. Series.
JC480.S8313 2004
320.53'22–dc22
2003026805

Contents

Acknowledgments

I would like to thank Tom Hilde, Peter Rogers, and Lucy Golsan for agreeing to undertake the difficult task of translating this important work. I would also like to thank my colleague Ralph Schoolcraft for carefully reading through the edited translation. All errors, of course, remain my own. Alexis Stewart, an undergraduate student at Texas A&M, was of great help to me in editing the original translation and in locating numerous sources that allowed me to write the introduction to the English-language edition. Thanks are also due to Kimberly Parsons, a graduate student in English at Texas A&M, for preparing the final manuscript. The College of Liberal Arts generously provided support for the translation, and I would like to thank Executive Associate Dean Ben Crouch in particular for his constant willingness to contribute to projects such as this.

In France, Henry Rousso generously agreed to read the introduction to this edition; his insightful comments are much appreciated. He also made available to me his personal archives and those of the Institute for Contemporary History dealing with the *Black Book of Communism*. I wish to thank him for this and for stimulating conversations as well.

Richard J. Golsan

Richard J. Golsan

Introduction to the English-Language Edition

The Politics of History and Memory in France in the 1990s

Henry Rousso's *Stalinism and Nazism: History and Memory Compared* situates itself at the center of a number of important debates that have not only shaped the field of "contemporary history" in France in the last decade but also generated considerable and persistent controversy in the public forum as well.

As its title suggests, this book engages in the first instance with the heated and often ideologically loaded debate surrounding the comparison of Communism and fascism, and National Socialism in particular. Because the comparison of these ideologies in their various expressions inevitably involves discussion of the applicability and viability of the concept of totalitarianism, *Stalinism and Nazism* addresses this subject as well.

As its title also suggests, the collection explores the difficult relationship between history and memory, primarily the history and memory of the traumas associated with the double experience of Nazi and Soviet occupation in several Eastern European countries. While France was of course never occupied by the Soviet Union, the experience of Nazi occupation during World War II, coupled with Vichy complicity in the Holocaust, has left scars on the French national psyche and pitted "history" and "memory" against each other on a number of levels and in several important contexts. Because the competing and often conflicting imperatives of history and memory regarding Vichy have a bearing on the framing of the debates and issues dealt with in this volume, it is important to consider them briefly here.

In his now-classic study *The Vichy Syndrome* (1987), Henry Rousso examines in compelling detail how the memory of the Vichy period has evolved over time since the liberation of France in 1944.[1] Subject to cultural and generational shifts as well as political manipulations, the memory of the Pétain regime and the German Occupation—of *les années noires* (the "Dark Years")—has, in Rousso's view, gone through four distinct phases, the last of which has particular relevance here. Since the late 1970s and early 1980s, the memory of Vichy has been nothing less than a national "obsession," to use Rousso's term, provoking political and judicial scandals and inspiring controversial films and novels. The primary reason for Vichy's remarkable notoriety is that, increasingly, the memory of the period has focused on the regime's involvement with the Nazis' "Final Solution" and on Vichy's own homegrown anti-Semitic laws and policies. For many in France, the memory of these persecutions has required not only a recognition of the nation's racist abuses in the past, along with a variety of forms of commemoration of the victims, but also a belated effort to rectify past injustices by prosecuting perpetrators a half century after the crimes themselves were committed. The prosecutions in question are, of course, the trials for crimes against humanity of the Nazi Klaus Barbie in 1987 and of the Frenchmen Paul Touvier and Maurice Papon in 1994 and 1997–98, respectively. By all accounts these trials constituted the most visible and controversial efforts on the part of the French to come to terms with the abuses of their Vichy past and, in the process, to fulfill a *devoir de mémoire* (duty to memory) toward the victims.

In what way or ways did the memory of Vichy conflict with its history? And in what way or ways did the "duty to memory" interfere with the imperatives and obligations of the historian? In general terms, according to Rousso and others, the predominantly "judeocentric" nature of the memory of Vichy, at least in the public mind, risked distorting a balanced and objectively *historical* understanding of the complex realities of the Dark Years as well as the broader aims, ambitions, and ideology of the Pétain regime itself. Moreover, a near exclusive emphasis on Vichy's persecution of the Jews ran the risk not only of effacing the crucial role played by the Nazis but also of giving the French an exaggerated sense of the *criminality* of their own past, a state of mind hardly conducive to national pride and a sense of optimism about the future.[2] For historians of the Vichy past, the situation was particularly vexed. Solicited by the media to discuss Vichy and its memory in a wide variety of contexts and situations, these scholars were often expected to offer their expertise in a climate that was geared as much to scandalizing the past as it was to establishing the truth. Moreover, on occasion they were called upon to make judgments concerning events and individuals, an activity in keeping, perhaps, with fulfilling a "duty to memory" but highly problematic for the historian in exercising his or her profession in accordance with its own standards and practices.[3]

For Rousso, the "instrumentalization" of history—and of historians—in this fashion reached its zenith in the trials for crimes against humanity of Paul Touvier and Maurice Papon. Because of the nature—and, depending on one's perspective, the perversity—of French statutes concerning such crimes, at his 1994 trial Touvier could only be found guilty if it could be "proven" that in committing his crimes during the Occupation, he had acted essentially as a German, rather than a French, agent.[4] This was unquestionably a distortion of history, but because the "duty to the memory" of his victims—

and public expectations—required Touvier's conviction, the distortion had
to be tolerated. So when he was found guilty of crimes against humanity
for the 1944 murder of seven Jewish hostages, justice may ultimately have
been served and the law satisfied, but only at the cost of violence done to
the historical record.[5]

If the conflicting imperatives of history and memory were apparent in
the Touvier verdict, they also made their presence felt in other contexts in
both the Touvier and Papon trials, especially when distinguished historians
of the Vichy period were called upon to act as witnesses for the prosecution.
First, these scholars were asked to make assessments and judgments less in
the name of establishing an impartial truth—certainly the historian's primary
function—than in providing evidence in order to secure a conviction that
was itself mandated by the "duty to memory." Moreover, offering their assessments on the stand in the context of a criminal trial and not in a scholarly
forum, the historians discovered that their knowledge and expertise could
be challenged and dismissed not on scholarly grounds but as merely the
"opinion" of one witness among others.

It is important to stress again that the conflicting demands of history and
memory as described here, as well as the effect of that conflict on the role
of the historian and the writing of history in contemporary French society,
are not limited in their import to the Vichy past. Rather, the eruption of
these tensions and conflicts—primarily in relation to Vichy, to be sure—has
conditioned other debates in a variety of ways and contexts, including the
ongoing debate over the comparison of Communism and Nazism.

As Rousso notes in his introduction to the present volume, the debate
over the comparison of Communism and Nazism reemerged in France in
the 1990s primarily in relation to the publication of two massive works
dealing, in the main, with the history *and* memory of Communism. The
first of these works was François Furet's *Le Passé d'une illusion: Essai sur
l'idée communiste au XXe siècle*, published in 1995 (translated and published
in the United States as *The Passing of an Illusion: The Idea of Communism in the
Twentieth Century*).[6] Furet's book examines not only aspects of the history of
Communism and the regimes it inspired but also the manner in which its
myths mobilized generations of intellectuals and others in the service of the
Communist idea. Of these myths, among the most inspirational, certainly in
France, was the notion that the Bolshevik Revolution of 1917 was a direct
continuation of the French Revolution, which was itself understood to be
the great liberating experience of modernity. This misperception, according
to Furet, accounts for a good deal of the misguided and even blind support

and devotion Communism enjoyed in many quarters in France even up to after the Soviet collapse of 1989.

In a chapter entitled simply "Communism and Fascism," Furet tackles the thorny issue of the comparison of the ideologies in question and their representative regimes head on while offering his own assessment of the strengths and weaknesses of the totalitarian model. One of Furet's more debated claims, as Rousso points out below, is that Bolshevism, Nazism, and Italian Fascism all shared a common "matrix," or source, in the brutality of World War I. The lessons of trench warfare for all three ideologies and movements were translated into the realm of politics and in large part accounted for the respective movements' successes. These lessons were, according to Furet, a "familiarity with violence, the simplicity of extreme passions, the submission of the individual to the collectivity, and, finally, the bitterness of futile or betrayed sacrifices."[7] Parliamentary democracy, for which Bolsheviks, Nazis, and Fascists all shared a visceral hatred, was simply no match for these war-hardened—and incipiently violent—movements.

The Passing of an Illusion is, in essence, a wide-ranging condemnation of Communism. Moreover, Furet's focus on Communism's vacuity (the "illusion" of the title) and the delusions it fostered, coupled with his own willingness to compare it directly in its origins, methods, and common features to the ultimate evil, Nazism, contributed significantly to the controversy provoked by its publication. As Rousso states in his introduction, the comparison of Communism and Nazism has generally been underdeveloped in France because it has, of course, never found favor with the Parti communiste français (French Communist Party) and the generations of intellectuals it influenced. But with the fall of the Berlin Wall, the opening of the former Soviet archives, and the declining presence and cachet of French Communism and its political organization, the time was ripe to reexamine, or, more accurately, to examine closely for the first time, the history and memory of the *other* great destructive ideology of twentieth-century Europe, Communism, and compare it to Nazism.

If *The Passing of an Illusion* established the precedent of taking a hard look at Communism and the destructive illusions it fostered while comparing it directly with Nazism—in short, of challenging the sanctity of its memory in a comprehensive fashion—the task of *scandalizing* the Communist past and the comparison with Nazism fell to another book, *Le Livre noir du communisme*, published two years later (translated and published in the United States as *The Black Book of Communism*).[8] Representing the combined efforts of six leading historians, *The Black Book* set for itself the hugely ambitious and painful task of writing the history of the crimes of Communist regimes worldwide, from the abuses of the Soviet state under Lenin and Stalin, to those of China under Mao, to the horrors of the Pol Pot regime in Cambodia and the various Marxist dictatorships in Eastern Europe, Africa, and Central and South America. That the crimes of these regimes were not to be soft-pedaled in *The Black Book* was evident in the starkness of the book's subtitle: *Crimes, Terror, Repression.* Moreover, the comparison of Communism's crimes with those of Nazism was evident in the choice of titles. *The Black Book of Communism* echoes the title of Ilya Ehrenbourg's and Vassily Grossman's massive record of the crimes of Nazis against the Jews behind the lines on the eastern front during World War II, *The Black Book of Nazism.*

Despite Communism's diminished presence and influence in 1990s France, the prestige it still enjoyed in some quarters—or the nostalgia it inspired—coupled with its historical role in the antifascist struggles of the 1930s and especially in the resistance to Nazi occupation, meant that a book devoted exclusively to Communism's innumerable crimes was bound to stir controversy. The Parisian daily *Libération* described *The Black Book of Communism* as a "flagstone thrown in the face of history." While many on the Left attempted to do damage control, the right rejoiced. Conservative deputies in the National Assembly, brandishing what appeared to be copies of the book, gleefully called upon then Socialist prime minister Lionel Jospin to justify the inclusion of a party still unrepentant over its "criminal past" in his governing coalition. Those on the extreme right, long on the defensive, took the opportunity to turn the tables on their enemies and in the process make Nazism appear to be, in effect, the lesser of two evils. Referring—with a striking lack of precision—to Communism's massive body count worldwide and comparing it to the number of Nazi victims, the former New Right intellectual Alain de Benoist offered an assessment of the two ideologies on the basis of their respective murderousness. His conclusion was that Communism was worse: "Communism killed much more than Nazism, . . . and for a longer time, . . . and it began to do so before Nazism."[9]

De Benoist's argument in fact draws on one of the major points of Stéphane Courtois's highly polemical introduction to *The Black Book of Communism*, which, in terms of the controversy it provoked, overshadowed the rest of the chapters combined. Unlike the individual case studies that explore the crimes of particular Communist regimes but eschew comparisons with Nazism and its crimes, Courtois makes that comparison the central focus of his introduction. Moreover, he compares Communist and Nazi crimes along quantitative, legal, and moral lines that many found both troubling and ideologically motivated.

Laying the groundwork for the kind of numerical comparison later used by de Benoist, Courtois tallies up Communism's body count, "based on un-official estimates," and concludes that Communist regimes worldwide were responsible for some one hundred million deaths. By comparison, Nazism was less prolific. Courtois then proceeds to a "legal" comparison with Nazism in accusing Communism on numerous counts for crimes against peace, war crimes, and, most significantly, crimes against humanity. Finally, in the context of his legalistic "indictment," Courtois draws a moral equivalency between the Communist crimes and those of Nazism in asserting that "the genocide of a 'class' may well be tantamount to a genocide of 'race,'" and that "the deliberate starvation of a child of a Ukranian kulak as a result of the famine caused by Stalin's regime 'is equal to' the starvation of a Jewish child in the Warsaw ghetto as a result of the famine caused by the Nazi regime."[10]

Courtois's enormous body count of Communism's victims certainly sparked the ire of some of his detractors—including Nicholas Werth, a contributor to the *Black Book of Communism*, who broke publicly with him over several aspects of the introduction, including the fact that Courtois used the figure of twenty million dead at the hands of the Soviets, whereas Werth's own estimate, given in his chapter of that volume, was fifteen million. Moreover, the implicit—and unfavorable—comparison with Nazism on this score was not lost on Werth, who noted in an interview in *L'Histoire* that any tally sheet of Nazism's crimes should include the fifty million dead of World War II, for whom Nazi Germany should be held accountable.[11]

While Courtois's grisly statistics provoked strong reactions from others in addition to Werth, it was undoubtedly the moral and legal dimensions of the comparison of the criminality of the regimes and ideologies in ques-tion that provoked the most heated controversy. To begin with the moral dimension, Courtois's effort to establish a moral equivalency between the death by starvation of a kulak child at the hands of the Bolsheviks and of a Jewish child at the hands of the Nazis was attacked as ludicrous, for as Rousso states in his introduction, "on the level of morality, there is absolutely no reason to hierarchically rank the victims of Nazism, Stalinism, or any other system practicing terror." Moreover, he continues, one should not conclude from such comparisons that "on the level of analysis, all these systems are [therefore] equal. If the sufferings of all the innocent victims of political violence are deserving of equal respect in the name of memory, this certainly does not mean that there is an equivalency of the crimes of the executioners." Nor, for many, of the regimes themselves. To the degree that, in making the comparison, Courtois appeared to suggest the motives and aims of the two regimes were equally murderous and ultimately indistinguishably evil, Werth and others objected on this score as well. Werth and Jean-Louis Margolin, another disaffected contributor to *The Black Book of Communism*, insisted in *Le Monde* that it was crucial to distinguish between the Communist dream of the liberation of the majority of humankind and Nazism's racist ideology, which sought, conversely, to "force most human beings into the shadows." Obviously for Werth and Margolin, Communism was less morally reprehensible because it embodied a noble ideal that tragically was not realized in practice.

To this line of reasoning, Courtois responded pointedly in an essay appearing in *Le Monde* on December 20, 1997: "One has the right to ask in what way the act of killing in the name of 'tomorrows that sing' is more excusable than murder tied to a racist doctrine. And in what way delusions and hypocrisy constitute mitigating circumstances for mass crimes."

Others in fact shared Courtois's perspective in this instance, although they approached the matter differently. In his column in *Le Nouvel observateur*, Jacques Julliard argued, in effect, that if one insists on the "goodness" of Communism, all of the murders carried out in its name are reduced to the status of "accidents."[12] For Alain Besançon the implicit perversity of this perspective—and of Communism itself—was built into its praxis. Comparing Communism to Nazism in moral terms, he concludes: "Communism is more perverse than Nazism because it does not demand of the individual that he consciously embrace the immorality of the criminal and that he exploit the spirit of justice and goodness present in the world in order to spread evil. Each experience of Communism begins in innocence."[13]

While Courtois's dismissal of a moral distinction between Communism and Nazism in terms of their respective ideals and motivations attracted support from other well-known and respected historians and commentators, his efforts to establish the legal equivalency of the crimes of the two political systems attracted no such support. This is not surprising, given that Courtois appears to call—even if in principle only—for nothing less than a Nuremberg tribunal of sorts for the crimes of Communism. Indeed, he summarizes Nuremberg statutes concerning crimes against peace, war crimes, and crimes against humanity and then makes what Rousso describes here as a "muddle-headed attempt" to apply these definitions to numerous crimes committed by Communist regimes worldwide. In each instance he provides no documentary evidence to support his charges and follows no "procedures," legal or otherwise. In short, no "case" is built. Finally, rather than charge individuals, as in done in court, Courtois accuses and condemns entire regimes.

As if these aspects of his approach were not troubling enough, Courtois makes another move in his legal comparison of the crimes of Nazism and Communism that was bound to produce fallout in France, especially in the fall of 1997. After having ascertained the applicability of the Nuremberg statutes to the crimes of Communism, Courtois changes course somewhat in reminding the reader that these statutes, of course, were only intended to be applied to crimes committed "during World War II [*sic*]."[14] In "updating" his indictment, so to speak, Courtois turns to recent French law on the subject and proceeds to a second demonstration of the culpability of Communist regimes for war crimes, genocide, and crimes against humanity.

Given the moment the *Black Book of Communism* appeared and the publicity it garnered, Courtois's evocation of French laws governing genocide and especially crimes against humanity could not have been more provocative. Several weeks earlier, on October 8, the trial for crimes against humanity of former Vichy civil servant Maurice Papon had opened in Bordeaux to enormous national and international media coverage. As already noted, Papon's was the third such trial, and it would prove to be the longest and most contentious.

The Papon trial was intended to be, according to the media at least, the decisive moment of France's legal and symbolic reckoning with its Vichy past as well as a major step in the fulfillment of the nation's duty to the memory of the victims of the Holocaust. But from the outset the proceedings were fraught with difficulties. Like the earlier Touvier trial, this one pitted history against memory in a variety of troubling contexts. The "duty to memory" was tangibly present in the form of large numbers of "memory militants" who kept vigils and chanted outside the court throughout the six-month-long trial. Inside, victims and relatives of victims, suffering from failing memories, provided faulty accounts of what had actually occurred, but given the tragedies they or their loved ones had experienced, lawyers and judges were frequently loathe to contradict them.

The conflict between history and memory was, moreover, not the only pitfall along the path to bringing Papon to justice. The trial also fully exposed the legal fragility of the notion of crimes against humanity and the moral—and other—dilemmas raised by efforts to apply them to individuals. First, was it fair to apply laws retroactively? Statutes governing crimes against humanity in France were not put on the books until 1964, and yet Papon was being tried for actions taken more than twenty years earlier. Was it just to try an individual—and a very old one at that—for crimes he had supposedly committed a half century earlier? How could solid proof of his guilt be established, with so much time elapsed? Finally, given the history of their numerous modifications by various French courts in order to suit the circumstances of the moment (and the demands of competing constituencies), were crimes against humanity so lacking in precision and so discredited by repeated revisions that they had lost all cogency and meaning? For some, the fact that Papon could be tried for crimes against humanity for deporting Jews at the behest of the Nazis but *not* for condoning (ordering, according to some accounts) the brutal beatings and murders of Algerian protesters by Parisian police when he was prefect of police under de Gaulle in October 1961 underscored the degree to which the laws themselves were arbitrary and tailored less to serve justice than political imperatives of the time.[15]

For many, the verdict—guilty, but not of complicity in the deaths of the deportees—and the sentence—only ten years' imprisonment for the most heinous of crimes—summed up not only the inadequacies of French laws dealing with crimes against humanity but also a whole host of other dilemmas attendant upon coming to terms with the crimes of the past. According to Eric Conan, the "verdict of compromise" in the Papon case "illustrate[d] once again the impossibility of reconciling the law, memory . . . and History."[16]

In a context such as this, Courtois's introduction to the *Black Book of Communism* could only further muddy the waters and, in its very conception and execution, make a mockery of both the lengthy and painstaking efforts to bring *one individual* to justice and the legal hairsplitting required to convict him. Moreover, the absolute enormity of Communism's crimes against humanity and acts of genocide—as determined by Courtois—completely dwarfed Papon's (perhaps even Vichy's?) offenses to the point of almost appearing irrelevant. The enumeration of Communism's crimes against humanity and genocides seemed to imply, finally, that Papon had only been the tip of *one* iceberg and that French justice, to be thorough and fair, had a whole *other* criminal past to confront. Given these implications, it is not surprising that Papon's lawyer, Jean-Marc Varaut, attempted to introduce the *Black Book* as evidence. His request was denied.

In retrospect, Courtois's "legal" gambit may well appear crude and deliberately sensationalistic, but there is no doubt that, from his perspective at least, it was integrally linked not only to his own motives for working on the publication project but also to those of his fellow contributors as well. As Courtois explained in the *Le Monde* essay of December 20, 1997, the principal aim of the *Black Book of Communism* was nothing less than to "tear down the 'mental Berlin Wall'" that supposedly prevented the memory of Communism's many crimes from coming to light. The "criminal dimension of Communism" could no longer be "passed over in silence," and the task was therefore to expose the crimes and label them for what they were.

In his introduction Rousso strenuously objects to the notion that the crimes of Communism have been ignored in contemporary France, that they have been cloaked in amnesia, whereas a state of hypermnesia, or excessive memory, prevails where the crimes of Nazism are concerned (as Courtois claims). Rousso stresses that the success of both *The Passing of an Illusion* and *The Black Book of Communism*, itself a bestseller in France with sales reaching almost two hundred thousand copies a year after its publication, confirms that the crimes of Communism are being remembered only too well.[17]

But perhaps surprisingly—in this context at least—Rousso does not express concern for the role Courtois assigns the historian in his essay in *Le Monde*. It could be argued that tearing down "the mental Berlin Wall" and exposing Communism's crimes for what they are falls more clearly under the purview of the "memory militant"—and eventually the prosecutor and judge—than of the historian, and indeed Courtois does not shy away from embracing any—and all—of these roles. In fact in the December 20 article he states that one of the principal aims of the contributors to *The Black Book of Communism* was to pay "legitimate homage to the victims" of Communism, a view that had earlier been articulated in the introduction itself. There, Courtois asserts that the book had been undertaken as both a "work of history" and a "memorial." The latter function was necessary, he writes, because "There is a moral obligation to honor the innocent and anonymous victims of a juggernaut that has systematically sought to erase even their memory." And although he rejects for the historian the role of the figure "entrusted with the vengeance of the people in the face of tyranny" (which he nevertheless invokes), Courtois does argue that the kind of historical knowledge the historian of Communism works with cannot be "seen in isolation from certain fundamental principles, such as respect for the rules of a representative democracy and, above all, respect for life and human dignity." It is in relation to these principles, Courtois concludes, that the historian must "'judge' the actors on the stage of history."[18]

As the preceding remarks suggest, the heated reception of *The Black Book of Communism* in the fall of 1997 certainly succeeded in sensationalizing the history and especially the memory of Communism. Moreover, it further complicated the already controversial role and function of the contemporary historian in France. While the revered specialists of Vichy reluctantly assumed the roles of commentator and witness for the prosecution, the historians of Communism, or at least those associated with the *Black Book* project, willingly assumed the role of memorialist and, in Courtois's case, that of moralist and judge as well.

But at least initially, the *Black Book of Communism* controversy did not greatly facilitate what many, including Courtois, hoped it would: a systematic, objective, and thorough comparison of Communism and Nazism. To be sure, the debate surrounding the book's reception did produce crude comparisons of the enormous number of victims of both systems. It also produced sharp exchanges over the supposed difference in "ideals" of the two ideologies. But in the first instance, as Ian Kershaw and Moshe Lewin point out, comparing through "atrocity tolls" is a hackneyed and politically motivated ploy previously used by "German nationalists and apologists for Nazism" as well as "vehemently anti-Communist Russian nationalists."[19] It does not produce—and is not often intended to produce—meaningful and impartial results. As for differentiating between ideals, while drawing such distinctions is obviously plausible to some, it can also be politically motivated and, equally importantly, dismissed as meaningless in terms of its influence in the real world. To paraphrase Alain de Benoist, what is the difference, after all, between doing evil in the name of good and doing evil in the name of evil? Besides, as Claude Lefort observes in *La Complication*, "was it not the totalitarian model and the opportunities it offered for the creation of a Party-State and a new elite that exerted a formidable attraction on all continents, more so than the image of a society delivered from the exploitation of classes and in which all the citizens would enjoy the same rights?"[20]

If comparing numbers of victims and differences in ideals is ultimately politically suspect or lacking in validity—and a dangerous exercise for responsible historians as well—what forms of comparison between Communism and Nazism can be considered legitimate and impartial? And what is to be gained from the comparison? The debate itself, of course, has a very long history dating back to the interwar years and has most often been conducted in a highly politicized context. Moreover, in general terms the comparison has served "as a device to attack Communism rather than Nazism," even as a means of exculpating the latter in condemning the former.[21] During the "Historians' Debate" in West Germany in the 1980s, for example, Ernst Nolte's infamous claim that the Holocaust was undertaken in imitation of— and as a preemptive strike against—Soviet terror and the Gulag was clearly intended at the very least to reduce Nazi culpability for the Holocaust and at most to suggest that the crime itself could be construed as a legitimate act of German self-defense. To a certain degree that debate has been renewed in France in the 1990s in, among other venues, an exchange of letters between Furet and Nolte, later published under the title *Fascism and Communism*.[22] It has also surfaced in Courtois's recent defense of Nolte's position in his preface to the translation of Nolte's *La Guerre civile européenne*.[23]

But if the comparison of Communism and Nazism lends itself to highly troubling and indeed dangerous claims such as Nolte's, that does not compromise the legitimacy—even the necessity—of the comparison in historical terms. As Ian Kershaw and Moshe Lewin assert, "in some senses, all historical inquiry is comparative," and "refusing to compare leaves us blind to the past—and to the past's implications for the present and future."[24] Moreover, comparing does not only mean "establishing similarities" but also "uncovering differences." The combination of the two activities makes it possible to discern uniqueness. As Kershaw affirms, "Only through comparison can uniqueness be confirmed."[25]

This being the case, what should be the parameters, including the limitations, of historical comparison in this instance? More importantly for situating the present volume, what aspects of the comparison eventually assumed center stage in France during the 1990s?

One important issue that did emerge in the context of the *Black Book of Communism* controversy arose as a result of Courtois's comparison of the numbers of victims of Nazism and Communism. His tally sheet implies that it is legitimate to compare Nazism's crimes to those of *all* Communists worldwide and that, among other things, no geographical, cultural, or chronological restrictions need be imposed on the comparison. Many, of course, found this approach lacking in historical precision, and it was in part to avoid this pitfall that the present volume limits itself to a comparison of Nazism and Stalinism. But for Courtois, the broader and indeed global comparison was justified by the common, determining lineage of all Communist regimes: "Every Communist country or Party has its own specific history, and its own particular regional and local variations, but a linkage can always be traced to the pattern elaborated in Moscow in 1917. This linkage forms a sort of genetic code of Communism."[26]

To the degree that Courtois's "genetic code of Communism" appeared to downplay and essentially marginalize historical, cultural, and geographical specificities in order to emphasize structural commonalities and indeed *identities*, it coincides nicely with the traditional "totalitarian model" approach for analyzing and comparing Communism and Nazism as well as Fascism. In fact, that model has enjoyed a renewed currency in the French debates of the 1990s; Rousso devotes several pages to an astute analysis of its history, virtues, and limitations in his introduction. As he observes, the concept has particular relevance in the Eastern European countries (discussed in part 2) because they experienced both Nazi and Communist tyranny directly.

The totalitarian model also remains useful, despite its limitations, in comparing Soviet Communism and Nazism, if for no other reason than that it allows for a more systematic exposure of the differences between the two systems. In their comparisons of Nazism and Stalinism in part 1, Philippe Burrin and Nicholas Werth rely on variations of the traditional categories of analysis and the defining features of the totalitarian state—the leader, terror, propaganda, and ideology—in comparing the nature of the dictatorship and of the dictator, political violence, and the "social response" of the people to the ideological domination imposed on them.

Generally speaking, Rousso and the authors of the case studies in *Stalinism and Nazism* deal with the totalitarian model to the degree that it can be usefully applied in the particular countries and regimes. Redefining it in theoretical terms is not their aim. But others in the context of the recent debates have sought to redefine or fine tune its constituent elements or even reassess its most salient features. The results of these efforts have not necessarily been groundbreaking, but they certainly testify to a widespread interest in the subject in France in the last decade of the twentieth century.

In *The Passing of an Illusion* and elsewhere, François Furet concerns himself primarily with fine tuning the constituent elements that define a totalitarian state. These are: 1) the absolute rule of the party-state; 2) the cult of the leader; 3) the absence of law; 4) terror; 5) the persecution of churches; and 6) the existence of camps. In an essay entitled "The Totalitarian Experience" published in *L'Homme dépaysé* (1996), Tzvetan Todorov (who grew up in Communist Bulgaria) is also concerned with the building blocks of totalitarianism and argues that three main elements characterize such a regime: 1) it claims to embody an ideology; 2) it uses terror to control the conduct of the population; and 3) the general rule of existence is the absolute defense of one's personal interest and the unlimited reign of the will to power.

Obviously, Furet's and Todorov's definitions overlap most directly on the issue of terror, and although Todorov does not list "camps" as a distinct element, he describes them elsewhere in *L'Homme dépaysé* as a crucial component of state terror. But his definition is less concerned than Furet's with issues such as the persecution of churches while stressing, perhaps more astutely,

the necessity of a common enemy of the people (for examples, Jews, bourgeois) as a scapegoat (in a Girardian sense) to provide a source of social and
ideological cohesion. Todorov also stresses that ideology itself is less central
to "the totalitarian experience" than is commonly assumed. (In fact Kershaw
notes that recent studies of Nazi Germany and Soviet Russia emphasize a
more limited hold of ideology on the peoples in question, a point echoed
by Burrin and Werth here.)[27] Despite these differences, Furet and Todorov
would probably agree with the basic definition of totalitarianism articulated
by Jacques Julliard at precisely the moment the scandal over the *Black Book of
Communism* broke: "Totalitarianism is the previously unheard-of and monstrous alliance of terror and mass crime linked with a state ideology which
presents itself as normal governmental procedure."[28]

For his part Claude Lefort in *La Complication* takes a somewhat different
approach. He argues that a crucial and irreducible feature of any totalitarian
regime is that it is impossible to localize the source of power. (According to
this definition, as Rousso notes in his introduction, Soviet Communism is
more "totalitarian" than Nazism.) Moreover, largely because this is the case, it
is impossible as well in a totalitarian system to distinguish between dominated
and dominator and also what is "political" and what is not. It is therefore
legitimate to conclude that "everything becomes political or nothing is any
longer political" and that all spheres of human activity are therefore affected,
indeed infected.[29]

Todorov echoes these perspectives as well in *L'Homme dépaysé* in his discussion of the Communist system as an embodiment of totalitarianism. While
very much the victim and tool of state authority, for example, what Todorov
labels *l'homo sovieticus* nevertheless identifies with it automatically and completely, thus obscuring the distinction between "dominated" and "dominator" and making power, in effect, "unlocatable." Moreover, with power—
and politics—obfuscated and yet everywhere present, survival and success
within the system is reduced to the simplest and basest political impulses—
denunciation of one's inferiors and subservience to one's superiors.

While the debate surrounding the comparison of Communism and
Nazism, in its various moments and guises, obviously stimulated reassessments
of the concept of totalitarianism, it is not easy to say in precisely what ways
these reassessments affected or inflected the comparison, and conversely, in
what ways the comparison contributed to fine tuning the model. Certainly
one could argue that the renewed discussions of the concept of totalitarianism made it possible to better frame and contextualize a debate that, in
the case of *Black Book of Communism* at least, focused relentlessly on the

murderousness—the *criminality*—of Communism and the equation of that with Nazi criminality. Undoubtedly the broadening of the parameters of the debate made it possible to enrich the comparison itself, and this explains why many leading intellectuals, including Furet, Todorov, Julliard, and Lefort, have chosen to weigh in. As Todorov phrases it in the title of another article on the topic, the time is ripe for "Totalitarianism, one more time."[30]

As for the influence of the *Black Book of Communism*'s revelations on the totalitarian model in particular, one can argue that the extent of Communism's massive criminality and use of terror has made it possible to reprioritize the constituent elements of the totalitarian model or even to add a new, or redefine an old, category. Terror, or perhaps better yet sheer murderousness, should now be placed at the top of the list. This at least appeared to be the view of Alain Besançon in *Le Malheur du siècle*, which was published a year after *Black Book*: "That which ties [Communism and Nazism] most closely together is that they ascribed to themselves the right, and even the duty, to kill, and that both did it using methods that resembled each other, and on a scale unknown before in history."[31]

But as Besançon also asserts, even if murderousness and terror constitute the profoundest links between Communism and Nazism as well as the most crucial building blocks of their respective forms of totalitarianism, "six words" must be spoken before any more systematic analysis is undertaken: "Auschwitz, Belzec, Chelmno, Majdanek, Sobibor, and Treblinka."[32] For Besançon, ultimately, the Holocaust makes Nazism unique, and following a careful comparison of Nazism and Stalinism both in historical terms and as totalitarian systems, Ian Kershaw draws the same conclusion. For him the comparison "demonstrates, above all, the historical uniqueness of National Socialism. Any history of the Twentieth Century needs to acknowledge and explain that uniqueness."[33]

To the degree that the views expressed by Besançon and Kershaw reflect a consensus concerning the debate of the 1990s in France over the comparison of Communism and Nazism (or variations thereon) as well as the viability and applicability of the totalitarian model, that debate has not changed greatly with time. As Rousso notes in his introduction, more than thirty years ago Raymond Aron's comparison of the regimes rejected any final equivalency between Nazism and (Soviet) Communism because of Nazism's extermination of the Jews.

Does this imply then that the *sturm und drang* of the recent debate in France over the comparability of Communism and Nazism and the memory of the crimes of both really accomplished little? In his journal for the year 1997 entitled, appropriately enough, *L'Année des fantômes* ("The Year of the ghosts"), Jacques Julliard expresses serious concern that, in a year that encompassed the *Black Book of Communism* controversy, the appearance of Daniel Goldhagen's *Hitler's Willing Executioners* in French, and the Papon trial, France was succumbing to a morbid fascination with historical monsters. He concludes bitterly, "There is a Jurassic Park side to all of this."[34]

Julliard's view is certainly overly pessimistic, but it does point to the extent to which the history *and* memory of Nazism and Communism—and Vichy—have been sensationalized, politicized, moralized, and conflated in France during the last decade. It is one of the signal virtues of *Stalinism and Nazism: History and Memory Compared* to avoid these pitfalls where the histories and legacies of the two systems are concerned while reconfirming the virtues of comparative—and contemporary—history in the necessary and essential effort to understand what Eric Hobsbawm has aptly labeled "the century of extremes."

Notes

1. Henry Rousso, *Le Syndrome de Vichy* (Paris: Seuil, 1987). For the English translation, see *The Vichy Syndrome: History and Memory in France since 1944* (Cambridge: Harvard University Press, 1991).

2. Rousso has articulated these views in a number of contexts, especially in concert with Éric Conan in *Vichy: An Everpresent Past* (Hanover NH: University Press of New England, 1998).

3. This was especially the case when the newspaper *Libération* organized a roundtable discussion with leading historians of Vichy and the resistance heroes Raymond and Lucie Aubrac in the summer of 1997. At issue were accusations that the Aubracs had betrayed fellow resistance members and misrepresented their actions during the war. The historians found themselves in the uncomfortable roles of interrogators and judges. See Rousso, *The Haunting Past* (Philadelphia: University of Pennsylvania Press, 2000); and Susan Rubin Suleiman, "History, Heroism, and Narrative Desire: The 'Aubrac Affair' and National Memory of the French Resistance," *South Central Review* (forthcoming).

4. French statutes concerning crimes against humanity and the numerous difficulties associated with their application are discussed in detail later in the context of the Papon trial. It is important to stress at this juncture, however, that these laws were not originally intended to be applied to *Frenchmen* but to former Nazis who had operated in France.

5. For a detailed account of Touvier's conviction and its implications, see introduction to Richard J. Golsan, *Memory, the Holocaust, and French Justice: The Bousquet and Touvier Affairs* (Hanover NH: University Press of New England, 1996); and Rousso's and Conan's chapter on the Touvier trial in *Vichy*.

6. For the English translation, see *The Passing of an Illusion: The Idea of Communism in the Twentieth Century*, ed. Deborah Furet (Chicago: University of Chicago Press, 1999).

7. Furet, *Passing of an Illusion*, 163.

8. For the English translation, see Stéphane Courtois, Nicolas Werth, Jean-Louis Panné, Andrzej Paczkowski, Karel Bartosek, and Jean-Louis Margolin, *The Black Book of Communism: Crimes, Terror, Repression*, trans. Jonathan Murphy and Mark Kramer; consulting ed. Mark Kramer (Cambridge: Harvard University Press, 1999).

9. Alain de Benoist, "Le Nazisme et le communisme sont-ils comparables?" *Éléments* 92 (July 1998): 15.

10. Stéphane Courtois, "Introduction: The Crimes of Communism," in Courtois et al., *Black Book of Communism*, 4, 9.

11. "Le Communisme, l'heure du bilan?" *L'Histoire* 217 (January 1998): 8.

12. Jacques Julliard, "Ne dites plus jamais 'jamais,'" *Le nouvel observateur*, November 20–26, 1997, 49.

13. Alain Besançon, *Le Malheur du siècle: Sur le communisme, le nazisme, et l'unicité de la shoah* (Paris: Fayard, 1998), 73.

14. Courtois, "Introduction," 7.

15. For a discussion of this moment in the Papon trial, see Richard J. Golsan, *Vichy's Afterlife: History and Counterhistory in Postwar France* (Lincoln: University of Nebraska Press, 2000), pp. 156–80.

16. Éric Conan, *Le Procès Papon: Un journal d'audience* (Paris: Gallimard, 1998), 314.

17. The figure of two hundred thousand is given in Pierre Rigoulot and Ilios Yannakakis, *Un Pavé dans l'histoire: Le débat français sur "Le Livre noir du communisme"* (Paris: Robert Laffont, 1998), 7.

18. Courtois, "Introduction," 28, 30.

19. Ian Kershaw and Moshe Lewin, *Stalinism and Nazism* (Cambridge: University of Cambridge Press, 1977), 8.

20. Claude Lefort, *La Complication: Retour sur le communisme* (Paris: Fayard, 1999), 16.

21. Ian Kershaw, "Nazism and Stalinism: The Unavoidable but Dubious Comparison," lecture delivered at the German Historical Institute, Paris, November 27, 1995, p. 12. I thank Henry Rousso for providing me with a copy of this essay.

22. François Furet and Ernst Nolte, *Fascism and Communism* (Lincoln: University of Nebraska Press, 2001). The original French version of this book appeared in 1998.

23. Ernst Nolte, *La Guerre civile européenne* (Paris: Éditions des Syrtes, 2000).

24. Kershaw and Lewin, *Stalinism and Nazism*, 2.

25. Kershaw, "Nazism and Stalinism," 9.

26. Courtois et al., *Black Book of Communism*, p. 754.

27. Kershaw, "Nazism and Stalinism," p. 16.

28. Julliard, "Ne dites plus jamais 'jamais.'"

29. Lefort, *La Complication*, 11.

30. Tzvetan Todorov, "Totalitarisme, encore une fois," *Communisme* 59–60 (2000): 29–44.

31. Besançon, *Le Malheur du siècle*, 9–10.

32. Besançon, *Le Malheur du siècle*, 23.

33. Kershaw, "Nazism and Stalinism," 30.

34. Jacques Julliard, *L'Année des fantômes* (Paris: Grasset, 1998), 341.

Henry Rousso

Introduction

The Legitimacy of an Empirical Comparison

Since the collapse of the Soviet system and the subsequent opening of important archives, the renewal of studies of the USSR and of Communism itself has given a new immediacy to the debate over comparing Nazism and Stalinism, most notably in Germany and in central and eastern Europe. In France the discussion was relaunched by the 1995 publication of François Furet's *Le Passé d'une illusion* (The passing of an illusion), a work comprising the latest chapter in the ongoing analysis of the concept of totalitarianism.[1] This is particularly noteworthy because the discussion of totalitarianism, which on the one hand entails a comparison of Nazism and Stalinism (or fascism and Communism) and on the other draws on a specific analysis of these political systems, has never been developed in France to the degree that it has since the 1950s in the Anglo-American and German academic communities. This is so despite the presence of works by Raymond Aron, Claude Lefort, Jean-Pierre Faye, and several others. This lacuna is attributable of course to a number of well-known factors, for example, the influence of the Communist Party on the French intellectual world and the considerable energy invested by the party in legitimizing the largely inaccurate claim that totalitarianism was nothing more than a "Cold War concept."[2] These efforts, moreover, were largely successful.

Since the publication of Furet's work, a large number of French publications on Communism or on the Soviet Union either have directly addressed the comparison with Nazism or have involuntarily encouraged discussions that foreground that comparison. In general terms, however, the same cannot be said of works focusing on Nazism. Whether French or foreign in origin, there are few works on this subject whose principle objective is the assessment of the history of Nazism in relation to the theory of totalitarianism. The one exception is the relatively isolated case of the works of Ernst Nolte.[3] In this sense the debate over totalitarianism, even in its current form, retains many of its original attributes, especially those evident since the 1950s and the discussion of the work of Hannah Arendt. From that time on, the debate sought to understand and to reevaluate the history of Stalinism and of Communism in general terms, while leaving aside the history of Nazism (even though the history of Nazism was the principle object of Arendt's study). Moreover the debate was carried out with political ends in view. Yet these considerations in no way invalidate the scholarly interest, the intellectual necessity, nor even the moral legitimacy of the comparison, regardless of the results obtained.

It is against this backdrop that the present work was conceived. Its principle aim is to reexamine the comparison of Stalinism and Nazism, but along different lines from those followed by previous studies. The book originated in part at a colloquium organized at the Institute for Contemporary History (IHTP; Institut d'Histoire du Temps Présent) in Paris on January 31, 1997, to address the controversy generated by the publication of Karel Bartosek's *Les Aveux des archives* (The Revelations of the archives).[4] Even though Bartosek's book dealt only with the history of international Communist organizations after 1945, some of the polemics it generated, whether supportive or critical of its findings, focused ultimately on the comparison of Nazism and Stalinism, even though this was not the book's aim.

The colloquium at the IHTP had a modest ambition. Its purpose was to gather together a wide variety of specialists on Nazism and Communism and to move beyond the usual polemics in order to ascertain what today constitutes the legitimate as well as the illegitimate bases of comparison. This question has not ceased to challenge historians and social scientists for more than a half a century. Entitled "Parallel Historiographies: Nazism and Stalinism Tested by the Archives," the colloquium's aim was to address the comparison through two precise and limited approaches. The first sought to compare the sources, methods, and tools used by historians of Nazism on the one hand and Stalinism and Communism taken as a whole on the other. The second approach was to examine the memories of Communism and Nazism in the countries of the former Soviet bloc. Despite enormous historical differences, all of these countries share the double experience of having been occupied by or having allied themselves with the Nazis and then of having been subjected to Stalinism and Soviet domination. Hence the title of the colloquium, which referred not so much to a parallelism between the Nazi and Stalinist experiences as such but rather to the manner in which they have been perceived retrospectively.[5]

If the colloquium succeeded in inspiring a good deal of interest, it also aroused objections. The most pertinent, formulated during the debates themselves by the historian of the Soviet Union Yves Cohen, emphasized the fact that both the historians of Nazism and the historians of Communism continued to hoe their own rows, so to speak, while clinging to the respective singularities of the systems they studied. The result was that an empirical comparison based on the most recent findings of historical research was not really undertaken.

The same observation can in fact be made concerning the larger debate in France over the comparison between Nazism and Stalinism. Most of the time this discussion revolves around the political and intellectual legitimacy of the subject, and the outcome inevitably depends on the position of the interlocutors with regard to the question of Communism's intellectual and ideological heritage. This is an obstacle that, for obvious reasons, continues to create problems. For equally obvious reasons the same problem does not arise in relation to Nazism, for there are no defenders of Nazism's "positive heritage" except in certain circles of the extreme right.

On occasion the discussion bogs down in incessant methodological (or supposedly methodological) debates on the question of comparability, that is, of the preestablished positions that would either make possible or preclude comparison, or in controversy over the feasibility of the concept of totalitarianism. These debates often disguise poorly their ideological presuppositions or, conversely, have difficulty making them explicit. Moreover, most of the time, at least among the historians (in principle those best qualified to undertake the comparison), these discussions curiously come to a halt at precisely the moment that a real comparison is about to be undertaken. It is as if such a comparison is superfluous. It is either denounced without further analysis or, conversely, the proximity of the Nazi and Stalinist (or Communist) totalitarian systems, as well as their identical features, are treated as givens. It is striking to see how few analyses exist that examine Nazi Germany and Stalinist Russia with equal profundity and deploy a comparable range of knowledge and methodological approaches in studying both.[6]

This observation is especially true of the debate that accompanied the publication of *Le Livre noir du communisme* (The black book of communism), three of whose authors—Karel Bartosek, Andrzej Paczkowski, and Nicholas Werth—have contributed to the present volume.[7] Without undertaking here an exhaustive critique of this flawed but important book, it is worth noting that a good part of the controversy it produced centered on the legitimacy of comparing Nazism and Stalinism (or Communism taken as a whole) and the manner in which such a study should be conducted. In his widely criticized introduction, Stéphane Courtois alludes on several occasions to the comparison, most notably in a muddleheaded attempt to define the crimes of Communism as crimes meeting the criminal definitions used at Nuremberg and—in an affirmation that caused much ink to flow—in announcing that the respective crimes of Nazism and Communism "were equal," even though the "singularity of Auschwitz" is not challenged. The "genocide of a class" is tantamount to the "genocide of a race": the death by starvation of the child of a Ukrainian *kulak* deliberately subjected to famine by the Stalinist regime "equals" the death by starvation of a Jewish child of the Warsaw ghetto subjected to famine by the Nazi regime.[8]

These connections are not particularly new. They are also in evidence in some of the great testimonies of Stalinist terror, most notably the widely known works of Margerete Buber-Neumann and those of the Russian writer Vassily Grossman, the author of *Vie et destin* (Life and fate).[9] These works have formed a part of the rhetorical arsenal of conservative historiography for quite some time, for example, as in the work of Ernst Nolte, from whom Courtois borrowed the equation of "genocide of race" and "genocide of class." In the introduction to *Le Livre noir du communisme*, which strives to be scholarly, these connections are not proven or demonstrated in the scientific sense of the word. Rather, their value is strictly polemical, although what they call for, in fact, are more-nuanced reactions than those generated in the heat of controversy. On the level of morality, there is absolutely no reason to hierarchically rank the victims of Nazism, Stalinism, or any other political system practicing terror. This in no way means, however, that on the level of analysis, all these systems are equal. If the sufferings of all the innocent victims of political violence are deserving of equal respect in the name of memory, this certainly does not mean that there is an equivalency of the crimes of the executioners. This could only be established if a real inventory of the crimes were carried out.[10] In other words it is not a question here of contesting the legitimacy of the comparison, but of calling into question the necessity of foregrounding it and making it the unifying thread of a work whose principle thrust is not to compare Communism and Nazism but rather to compare almost all the Communist experiments in history to each other. This is already a sufficiently arduous task.

Le Livre noir du communisme is a work exclusively devoted to Communism, to its cost in human lives, to its nature, and to its criminal "essence." It is certainly not a work on totalitarianism, which is understood here as a theory, making it possible to consider together the Nazi regime and the Soviet system as well as other political regimes of the same type. Moreover the historical comparison of the two regimes is absolutely not in the book's provenance. Just the same, the historical comparison [made in Courtois's introduction] has served as a polemical argument, a commercial lever, and a red flag for the media. It has taken on a life of its own. In order to present the new analyses of Communism offered in the book, it was considered necessary to denounce a priori the unequal treatment of the history and above all the memory of Nazism and Stalinism: "The exceptional attention accorded Hitlerian crimes is perfectly justified. It is a response to the survivors' desire to testify, the researchers' need to understand, and the moral and political authorities needed to confirm democratic values. But why is there so little heard in public opinion of testimonies dealing with communist crimes? Why this uncomfortable silence on the part of political leaders? And above all, why this 'academic silence' concerning the communist catastrophe, which, for eighty years, has involved approximately a third of humankind, and on four continents? Why this inability to place at the center of the analysis of communism a factor as essential as crimes, mass crimes, systematic crimes, indeed crimes against humanity? Isn't there here a question of a deliberate refusal to know, of a fear of understanding?"[11]

This position ties in, line for line, with the false symmetry recently promoted by Alain Besançon between, on the one hand, the "hypermnesia" of Nazism in the contemporary public mind and, on the other hand, the "amnesia" of Communism.[12] To these largely unsupported claims we could answer that the considerable success with the general public of Furet's essay, or even more, that of *Le Livre noir du communisme* itself, whose sales in France reached levels of a Goncourt Prize, offers a flagrant denial of this supposed amnesia in the French popular conscience.[13] As Jean-Jacques Becker has aptly pointed out, "One could hypothesize—contrary to what has been generally accepted—that there is widespread anticipation of a putting into perspective of the communist phenomenon."[14] In the same way assertions rightly made by François Furet, Alain Besançon or Stéphane Courtois, which confirm that antifascism continues to prosper despite the fact that its target disappeared more than a half century ago, we could reply that anti-Communism finds itself in an identical situation today, for while there is no real adversary, there is nevertheless a temptation to create one out of whole cloth. Anti-Communism finds itself in an identical situation to the antifascism it condemns, in an imitation so often seen in the long history of fascism and Communism, or of antifascism and anti-Communism.

This tendency is in fact inscribed in a current topos that uses the comparison, not on a historical level but on a politico-memorial one, that sets forth for basically ideological ends not the reality and depth of the similarities and differences between the totalitarian regimes, but the way in which people talk about them today in certain circles and the degree of knowledge the public has of the respective activities of these two regimes, which is a very different matter. The most striking thing about these two adopted positions, even if they contain some truth, is the fact that they make short shrift not only of an actual comparative analysis of Nazism and Communism but also do the same with any concrete history of the memory of Communism, thus transforming perhaps authentic intuitions or generally accepted stories into established truths.[15]

And this leads to a second claim directly linked to the preceding one. Although the comparison has inspired few truly comparative studies in current French historiography, it occupies a place of choice in contemporary international disputes. The fact that this may be of little help in understanding the eventual relationship between the historical experience of Nazism and Stalinism does not alter the fact that this discussion of memory is a cultural and social fact that deserves to be part of the field of investigation of historians who struggle to include all sides of the problem, provided it is not limited to the narrow space of continental France.

The present work uses as a departure these two established methods; even though it does not pretend to exhaust the subject. It proposes, as a start, to create a historical comparison by limiting it to several targeted aspects and then to examine the comparison from the standpoint of memory by describing the situation in the countries of the former Communist bloc, where this comparison takes on a special acuteness.

Even though an enormous amount has been written on these subjects, it remains necessary to specify beforehand the general hypotheses that underlie this project before presenting the broad outline.

The first stumbling block encountered in this type of comparative study is the necessity of defining or clarifying the terms of the comparison, always a perilous undertaking. In his brilliant book Furet continually hesitates, at least in the terms used, to compare "communism and fascism,"[16] "Bolshevism and National-Socialism,"[17] or even "Stalinian communism and German National-Socialism."[18] The difficulty is made even greater by the fact that it is not based simply on opposite terms of comparison but also on the terms used for each of the two together and then separately. Must we speak of "fascism" in general and regard Nazism as a variant of fascism, as in Marxist analysis or in certain "totalitarian-type" approaches? Likewise, should we speak of "Communism," of "Bolshevism," or of "Stalinism"? Here we have terms that cover neither the same political realities nor the same historical groups. For his part Krzysztof Pomian, in his discussion of totalitarianism, rejects the use of the term "Communism," inherited from the nineteenth century, and prefers to speak of "Bolshevism" when the analysis is seen in a comparative perspective, a pertinent argument that has the advantage of situating exactly the historic places of the comparison.[19]

The difficulty is made even greater by the fact that the choice made will always be criticized as ideologically committed. For example, in a rather favorable review of *Stalinism and Nazism: Dictatorships in Comparison*, edited by Ian Kershaw and Moshe Lewin, historian Richard Pipes writes without hesitation that the book as a whole shows "a left-of-center orientation" largely because of the chosen title. In fact, he adds, "the opposite of Nazism is not 'Stalinism' but 'communism.' In eliminating Lenin and the Leninism from the equation, the authors, perhaps consciously, perhaps not, have adopted the post-Khrushchevian outlook of Stalin as an aberration of the historical evolution of the first communist State."[20] If the criticism is unjust in regard to the analyses within the book, the objection itself is worth taking into account. But the reverse method, comparing without any other form of procedure Nazism and all the forms of Communism regardless of time or place, constitutes an intellectual leap even more difficult to justify on a historical level: can one seriously compare Hitler's Germany, the USSR of Nikita Khrushchev or Leonid Brezhnev, and the regime of Fidel Castro? Can one compare unhesitatingly the Nazi Party and the Italian Communist Party? Furthermore, this tendency, even if it raises real questions, also shows a political commitment somewhere to the right of center-right: this is the case in the introduction of *Le Livre noir du communisme*[21] and numerous other works published in its wake.[22]

In the first part of this work, which is an attempt at an exclusively historical comparison, we chose to limit it to Nazism on the one hand (thereby excluding other forms of Fascism) and Stalinism on the other. This choice does not mean that the Leninist period is deliberately excluded from the field of comparison, if only by the fact that contributor Nicholas Werth is a historian who has demonstrated how much the Stalinist system, especially in the rationale of organized terror, owes to its predecessors.[23] It is one of the major differences, often emphasized, between Stalin and Hitler: the first inherited a system that survived him; the second founded a system that died with him. Yet this choice eliminates the post-Stalin USSR from the comparison for historical reasons.

Part 2 is placed in a rather different perspective because it compares the two political systems as they now exist in the public space of former popular democracies, and the comparisons take into account either both fascism and Communism in their most general terms, only Nazism and Stalinism, or any other variant of the equation. It is not a question here of defining the best possible level of the comparison but of analyzing what emerges in the public space as a fact of memory's history.

The second stumbling block for any attempt at comparison is the almost trivial question of knowing what are its interests and its aims, especially if there is a claim of eliminating all ideological considerations as far as possible. Without returning to the long list of arguments in favor of such a comparison a priori, and at the same time allowing the reader to decide the relevance of the outline offered here, two prior reasons that justify such an undertaking will suffice.

In the first place, on a heuristic level, the principle that demands that every historical event be reduced to its absolute singularity, thus making any comparison bound to fail, must be abandoned. Taken to its logical conclusion, this argument would insist that there is no way to imagine history and thus make the past intelligible. To affirm, for example, that Nazism and, even more, the extermination of the Jews are unique historical events means logically that these phenomena had formerly been, often in an implicit way, compared and measured using the same yardstick of other a priori similar happenings. "Totalitarian regimes deny human freedom in an extreme manner," writes Hannah Arendt, who makes their obliteration of all freedom the principle criteria of these regimes.[24] Following this, if we want to understand the nature of one of these regimes, and a fortiori if we want to prove its uniqueness, it would be better to compare it to other regimes that deny any freedom than to compare it to democratic regimes, even if this last also has its legitimacy, though for other reasons. This is almost a truism, which is worth being recalled since the question of Nazism's uniqueness—a demonstrable historical reality—has today become a dogma and not a concept that allows us to reflect on the event. Furthermore, to recognize this uniqueness in no way means that National Socialism would be radically incomparable to every other political system, if only for the reason that Nazism, like other political regimes, also borrowed from political systems contemporary to it, beginning with Italian Fascism. As Ian Kershaw and Moshe Lewin have so cogently asserted: "The terror of Stalinism does not need to be minimized to emphasize the uniqueness of the Holocaust—the only example offered up to now of the history of a deliberate policy aimed at the total physical destruction of each member of an ethnic group. There is no equivalent under Stalinism. Although the waves of terror were evidently massive, and the resulting toll in human lives enormous, no ethnic group was isolated in order to be totally annihilated physically. And among Stalin's victims, an especially heavy tribute was, we know, exacted from the government and from the party."[25]

In other words the uniqueness of genocide only shows its true dimensions when it is measured against another mass crime and another freedom-destroying system.

In the second place, comparing Nazism and Stalinism comes from an intellectual tradition—not simply ideological—that is difficult, even presumptuous, to dispose of in an offhand way. This is not the place in which to retrace the history of this debate, but we must remember that it was born at the same time as the systems themselves and has never ceased "haunting" the social sciences. [26] The concept of totalitarianism has been criticized ever since its appearance, and its principal theorists have clearly seen its limits from the beginning, knowing that it does not take into account the historical dynamics of the regimes under consideration, that it is more descriptive than analytical, and that it has resisted poorly historiographic evolution and the thorough empirical knowledge that is constantly accumulating on such systems. Finally, the concept has a tautological character since, if it is considered in its ideal-typical version, it is essentially constructed following the observation of two or three historical experiences (fascism, Nazism, Stalinism, or Communism) to be used later mainly as a frame for interpreting these same experiments. "Totalitarian societies are basically comparable and each one is historically unique; why they are the way they are, we do not know," Carl Friedrich, one of the principal theorists of totalitarianism, had already written in 1954. [27] Raymond Aron for his part, while developing a theoretical perspective based on reflections about totalitarianism, refused the kinship between Nazism and Stalinism by putting foremost, more than Arendt had done, the specificity of the extermination of the Jews. [28] It remains, however, even after all propositions are taken into account, that this theory, even with its limitations, is an almost necessary consideration in any attempt at comparison.

In addition, like all concepts, that of totalitarianism has its history, and it has evolved, depending on the authors, the places, and the period. We find in the second part of the present work an idea of its present timeliness in central and eastern Europe, where the comparison between Nazism and Stalinism (or Communism) is at once not only more systematic, more "natural," but also more fundamental in its stakes than it is in France.

In truth, the term "totalitarianism," like the spontaneous comparison of Nazism and Stalinism, is as deeply embedded in common understanding as in the language of the university, despite the reluctance or hostility it provokes. It is not possible to see this as a victory of "American Imperialism" in the semantic Cold War. If it was it would represent a very belated one. In *La Nature du totalitarisme* (The nature of totalitarianism), Arendt has already pointed out that the evermore popular use of the term, going back, according to her, to the days following World War II, meant that the general public was perfectly conscious of the appearance of radically new phenomena in the history of mankind, even if opinion registered a strong resistance to new things.[29] Following in her footsteps, Pomian remarks that "the appearance of a new term in the political lexicon and its propagation and installation in different languages, are not frequent occurrences [. . .], and they generally signal changes in the order of the facts themselves, and becoming conscious of them leads to the creation of neologisms."[30]

Once we admit that the comparison is a necessary step and once the principles that can be used to defend it are set forth, we must ask ourselves about its intrinsic relevance and the different uses to which it can be put.

If a quick typology is attempted, three objectives can be detected that are not heterogeneous but that coexist to variable degrees in most of the analyses.

The first use, and the most obvious one, arises from the attempt to analyze together two or more systems defined as totalitarian in order to show evidence that they are all types belonging to a single political type. This unavoidable step raises the most problems: What are the best terms for the comparison (a problem raised earlier)? What historical period and what durations should the comparison cover? To be truthful, and at the risk of oversimplifying, the primary product of this objective—and we have seen that historical works that are successful comparisons on this subject are relatively rare—gives the impression that the list of similarities and differences keeps growing at the same rate and that the procedure always stumbles over the same obstacles: the difference of the initial project and the respective intentions of Bolshevism and Nazism, the difference in the level of development of the societies investigated, their unequal life span, the uniqueness of the genocide of the Jews, and so on.

To avoid this difficulty, Kershaw and Lewin propose that our reasoning should not be based on tables of similarities and differences. Rather we should start from the idea that Nazism and Stalinism, to confine ourselves to these two alone, rest on common ground.[31] They were implanted in countries that both experienced authoritarian monarchies before World War I, that had made more-or-less important concessions to parliamentarianism; that both possessed a powerful bureaucracy, strong military traditions, a dominant class of large landowners; and that both, in an unequal way, were on the way to industrial modernization (this being very limited in Russia, however). Both finally had imperialist aims in central and eastern Europe and came out of World War I traumatized and in the grip of civil war, even if the upheaval in Germany was in no way as massive as it was in Russia.

At the end of their collective work, which analyzes differences and similarities in the role of dictators, in repression, in the conduct of the war, in the revolutionary nature of political action, and in the problem of "modernization," they nevertheless conclude that the differences are more important than the similarities. This is a conclusion hinted at in the complementary texts of Philippe Burrin and Nicolas Werth, which appear in the first part of this volume. In addition, Kershaw and Lewin do not subscribe to the commonly held idea—which constitutes one of the key arguments of François Furet—that World War I was the deciding matrix of totalitarian systems that emerged during or in the wake of the conflict. In any case, in the opinion of Kershaw: "The First World War certainly provoked a 'brutalization' [a concept developed by George Mosse], but on a very low level compared to what was happening at the same time in Russia. This part of the explanation [of the emergence of totalitarian systems] is not sufficient."[32]

The second function consists of searching, by comparison, for a better comprehension of each system. Seen from this angle, all the strategies can be uncovered. Thus for Claude LeFort, "The concept of totalitarianism has relevance [. . .] in its application to communism, more so than to Nazism or fascism, only if it designates a regime in which the center of power cannot be located; it is not thought to reside either in someone (a monarch, despot or tyrant), or in several individuals (aristocrats or oligarchies), or, strictly speaking, in the people, if we mean by that the group of individuals who are recognized, not by governments, but by the law, as citizens."[33]

Kershaw for his part thinks that the idea of totalitarianism is just a way to identify the uniqueness of Nazism: "In the framework of the concept of totalitarianism, National Socialism is the one and only example of a regime which appeared in a country endowed with an advanced industrial economy and with a system of political democracy (and an even older political pluralism). In all other cases—the Soviet Union, China, North Korea, and Cuba—the 'totalitarian phase' of the setting up of the authoritarian regime took place under backward economic and political conditions, in an agrarian economy, in a poor society without a tradition of political pluralism, not to mention democracy, and where diverse forms of tyranny had traditionally prevailed."[34]

Along these same lines we can assume that the debate that divided historians of the USSR into two schools of thought, one called "totalitarian" and the other "revisionist," had as an objective to find the best keys to interpreting the Soviet system. This did not divide the historians disagreeing on the resemblances or differences with Nazi Germany but rather those of the USSR who stressed the primacy of politics and ideology, as opposed to others for whom a social analysis of Soviet society took precedence.[35] It is also a characteristic of the debate on the history of Nazism, between "Intentionalists" and "Functionalists," that pits the partisans of the primacy of ideology against those who argue for the primacy of the historical dynamic of social forces at work in Nazism.

From this perspective the comparison has only a heuristic value—it is only of help in bringing out more clearly the singularities of each system. And from this perspective as well, the theory of totalitarianism, independently of the question of the comparison, was partially invalidated, if only by the fact that it neglected the evolution peculiar to each society caught in the stranglehold of totalitarianism and overestimated their "atomized" character, postulating that the ideological hold had caused the disappearance of any impulse toward inertia, toward dissidence, and indeed toward resistance. This essential point is developed too by Burrin and Werth in part 1.

There is finally a third usage that is the basis for a large part of the theory of totalitarianism, notably in political science and political philosophy and that, paradoxically, was not much taken into account by historians. This concerns the ways totalitarian systems constitute something new in regard to classical tyranny, authoritarian regimes, or other forms of ancient or modern dictatorships. This, we know, is the major contribution of the thought of Hannah Arendt and is, no doubt, the point where the concept of totalitarianism is strongest. At the risk of once again stating a truism or of paraphrasing Arendt, we can point out that, independent of their degree of resemblance or difference, nowhere else in history can one find two political systems so radically different in form from anything known up until then; emerging at the same time, on the same continent, and with a "common compost"; and that became rivals so quickly and then engaged in total war with each other. This issue does not come by definition within the context of contemporary history. It refers back to a long history of political systems, in no way exhausted by historians, and by itself justifies the necessity of pursuing a reflection on the comparison. On its own merits it invites a reading by historians of Arendt's work.

Of the three usages summarized here, only the second is actually considered in this work as part of what could properly be called a historical comparison.

In fact part I attempts rather to understand the respective uniqueness of the two systems by accepting the idea of an apparent strong resemblance rather than refining the reading grids that claim to identify only one type. Part I, therefore, is developed around a common inquiry, alternately argued by specialists of Stalinism and Nazism. It puts forward three distinct issues to be addressed from a long list of possibilities:

The nature and the place of the dictator. In each of the two systems discussed, the analysis seeks to go beyond the apparent similarities of absolute power exercised with equal intensity on both sides and seeks to understand the mechanisms belonging to each kind of domination.

Political violence. The forms, extent, and concrete methods of political violence need to be explored. The approach should not limit itself to superficial resemblance, for example, as in simply comparing the respective number of victims. Especially if such considerations insist on an equal respect for the suffering experienced by both sides, it does not help at all in understanding the nature of the political, social, and cultural processes set in motion.

The "social response" to ideological domination. The degree of adhesion, indifference, refusal, or resistance of Russian and German societies needs to be examined. This is an essential point, facilitated by the most decisive advances in the historiography of Nazism as much as in the more recent one in studying the USSR.

In and of itself, this grid is very incomplete. If it takes into account certain distinctive, habitual criteria of totalitarianism—the existence of supreme leaders, of an ideology with totalitarian aims, of a single party, of a mobilization of the masses through propaganda, of a systematic use of terror—it neglects others. This is in part a voluntary choice, which allows us to avoid classic grids of interpretation while taking into account historiographic criteria that make possible illuminating real differences behind apparent similarities. It is in part an obligatory choice, which makes it necessary to abandon other elements that are just as important, such as the question of the inheritance from the First World War or even questions concerning respective intentions and finalities of the two ideologies, that are treated here only incidentally. Once more, the central objective is to undertake an effective comparison, treating each of the systems considered with the same attention and an equal degree of knowledge and of the difficulties involved. This is an approach rather infrequent in French historiography.

The second part of this work, which concerns the current debate about a "double inheritance" in Central and Eastern Europe, also responds to another imperative, which seems to be part of the same inquiry, even though all of the contributors are not equally convinced of the relevance of taking up a historic comparison as well as a comparison of memory in the same book. This idea comes from the editor of this book and the author of this introduction, but it is also found in the collective work of Kershaw and Lewin.[36] In dealing with the past, it is important to point out the different levels of analysis in the debate over the validity of comparison.

To begin with, a *historic* level of comparison can be delineated, as in part I. This is the most frequent. Next, a *historiographic* level can also be delineated, which is not the history of Nazism and Stalinism per se but the manner, the tools, and the concepts used by historians and the social sciences to write these histories. We have seen several instances of astonishing similarities in the respective *historiographical* debates over Nazism and Stalinism, especially in weighing political as opposed to social factors. No doubt these debates result from a general state of historiography, notably the evolution of paradigms in social history. They are also without doubt the consequence of the fact that the majority of historians express themselves from the same "place," recognizing in common a belief in democratic values antinomic to the two systems studied. But they are perhaps too an obvious indication that the comparison is based on objective elements and, because of this, can create a rather important element of the historical comparison strictly speaking, even if we must be careful about accepting this last argument. We debated introducing this dimension in this way into the work (it was one of the objectives of the roundtable of the IHTP), but it seems to have appeared naturally, in the different areas that were studied, to the degree that each of the authors of the first part had developed his analysis in systematically taking into account recent developments in historiographic debates in his respective area. In this regard it should be pointed out that Philippe Burin and Nicolas Werth belong to the same generation of historians, and as consequence both seek to move beyond the quarrels that have stirred debate in their fields in recent years. Burrin, especially, has tried in the same way as Kershaw to go beyond the debate between Intentionalists and Functionalists;[37] Werth places himself in a perspective that tries to go beyond the quarrels between the "totalitarian" school and the "revisionist" school.[38] It is necessary to add, however, that the respective levels of the historiography of Nazism and Stalinism are not equivalent, that the first benefits from an advantage due to a rapid development that goes back three decades and to archives almost completely accessible since the end of World War II (thanks to the Allied occupation), while the second is still in the full process of development since the end of the Cold War. This is especially true in particular areas treated by Werth: for example, the question of knowing to what extent Russian society was able to join or participate in the Bolshevik project and in what ways. This issue still inspires many monographs, while studies dealing with German society and its relationship to Nazism have existed for a long time.

The comparison *of memories* requires a distinct approach since the comparison itself emphasizes the historical legacy of the systems as well as the managing of the past and its traumas. To study it makes one conscious of the dangers of confusing the objectives and the uses of a comparison already heavily weighted with ideological concerns. This can be a liberating experience for the historian, who does occasionally find himself held prisoner, so to speak, by the emotional stakes involved when dealing with memory.

In this sense, examining the former "other Europe" rather than France or Western Europe is justified by the fact that in these countries the comparison between Nazism and Stalinism comes not only from a discussion among academics or intellectuals but also concerns the entire society. The countries of the former Communist bloc were all confronted, before 1945 and Soviet domination, with the experience of Nazism, whether it was by occupation and partition by the Third Reich, as was the case in Poland or in part of Czechoslovakia, or they became allies of Nazi Germany, as was the case with Slovakia, Romania, Bulgaria, and Hungary. Some experienced both situations, as was especially true of the thorny case of the former GDR (German Democratic Republic, or East Germany).[39]

These choices seem all the more interesting since all of these countries have known for a decade the contradictions and the dilemmas of a painful administration in the recent past, of the uncertain politics of memory, of a truncated debate in most instances, of an eventual purge, and of the judgment of crimes committed by defunct Communist regimes. Even if this level of comparison is of a completely different type than a strictly historical comparison of the Nazi and Stalinist governments, it nevertheless seems necessary to take it into account. Beyond any similarities or differences between the two regimes, they have a point in common that no one would have been able to perceive even a decade ago: they have both bequeathed to posterity very difficult questions about how to write their history and how to insert it in a collective memory and a national heritage.[40]

Part 2 then is constructed around a common query to which each contributor responded in his own way. Alexandra Laignel-Lavastine minutely analyzes the different uses of the political stakes in comparing Nazism and Stalinism in Romania by insisting on the reappearance of revisionist tendencies. Paul Gradvohl ponders the evolution of the historiographic debate and historical institutions in Hungary, emphasizing the importance of the writing of history as a political weapon. François Frison-Roche examines the little-known case of Bulgaria, where debates of the "double experience" have brought up taboo questions such as the fate of Bulgarian Jews during the Second World War. Andrzej Paczkowski highlights the problems raised by the memory of the "double occupation" of Poland by the Nazis and Soviets, which never had, at least until the fall of the Communist system, the same stature in Polish social memory. Finally, Étienne François has the difficult task of taking up the East German question and the immense problem raised by the gulf that existed between the memory of Nazism in the FRG (Federal Republic of Germany, the former West Germany), based on the recognition of German culpability, and in the GDR, based on the fiction of the "anti-fascist state," a subject he examines from the angle of the opening of the Stasi archives.

By way of concluding, Pierre Hassner and Krzysztof Pomian provide their reactions to the texts presented here, applying to them their competence in the issues involved and their familiarity with the lengthy history of the concept of totalitarianism.

In concluding this rapid typology of levels of analyses and registers of discourse, we want to make clear that this work attempts to avoid two of them: the *ideological* level of analysis and the *"historical-judiciary"* stance. If it is obvious that the comparison of Nazism and Communism can spring from a desire to stigmatize the Communist heritage and its deliberate refusal to offer an explicit or implicit self-defense, we must resist the temptation to exempt it from scientific analysis on the pretext of undesirable uses of such work that can be made on an ideological level. This is one of the classic traps of the study of contemporary history, and it can have serious consequences if historians succumb to this form of self-censorship. In this sense the comparison is approached here with care, though without false modesty or second-guessing by authors who have expressed themselves with complete freedom and from a variety of viewpoints.

The "historical-judiciary" stance, however, is more difficult to avoid, for the historian cannot free himself entirely from a tendency to judge or pass moral judgment, especially when examining subjects like these. He must

refuse to don the robe of a judge in the court of History and must not think
of himself as the "avenger of the people," otherwise he conflates historical
concepts and criminal accusations, which are no doubt relevant in the case
of a trial, but not in the framework of a historical analysis. In this sense this
volume does not propose to "repair" the crimes of the past nor to "serve"
memory. It does not call for any kind of "Nuremberg of Communism." It
aspires only to be a modest contribution to the understanding of the two
greatest scourges of the twentieth century.

   Translated by Lucy B. Golsan and Richard J. Golsan

Notes

   1. François Furet, *Le Passé d'une illusion: Essai sur l'idée communiste au XXe siècle*,
Paris, Robert Laffont/Calmann–Lévy, 1995.
   2. On these questions see Pierre Grémoin, *Intelligence de l'anticommunisme: Le
Congrès pour la liberté de la culture à Paris (1950–1975)*, Paris, Fayard, 1995; and idem,
"Le Totalitarism: Marqueur dans l'espace politique et intellectuel français," in "La
Question du totalitarisme" issue, *Communisme*, nos. 47–48, 3d and 4th qtrs., 1996, pp.
47–56.
   3. See his most recent work, *Der europische Burgerkrieg, 1917–1945, Nationalsozialismus und Bolschewismus*, Munich, Herbig, 1987. One can also refer to his point of
view on *Le Passé d'une illusion* in "Sur la théorie du totalitarisme," *Le Débat*, no. 89,
March–April 1996, pp. 139–146. See also his dialogue with François Furet: Furet
and Ernst Nolte, *Fascisme et communisme*, Paris, *Commentaire*/Plon, 1998. Ernst Nolte
thinks that "the historical-genetic vision" of the theory of totalitarianism, which sees
in Nazism not only a regime of the same kind as Bolshevism but also a "reaction" to
this last—an idea that has contributed to releasing the famous "quarrel of historians"
in Germany—constitutes one of the "rare and indispensable paradigms" that will
finally be accepted, even if it takes "several decades.'""Sur la théorie du totalitarisme,"
p. 146.
   4. Karel Bartosek, *Les Aveux des archives: Prague-Paris-Prague, 1948–1968*, Archives
du communisme, Paris, Seuil, 1996.
   5. The day of the IHTP was divided into three parts. After a problematical introduction from François Bédarida (IHTP-CNRS [Centre National de la Recherche
Scientifique]) (of which a reworked version appeared in François Bédarida, *Histoire:
Critique et responsabilité*, Paris/Bruxelles, IHTP/Complexe, 2003), a first debate, presided
over by Pierre Ayçoberry (University of Strasbourg-II), reunited Jean Solchany (IEP
of Lyon) and Philippe Burrin (Institute des hautes études internationales de Genève),
who spoke on the present historiography of Nazism. A second debate, presided over

by Pierre Hassner (CERI-CNRS), brought together Nicolas Werth (IHTP-CNRS), Stéphane Courtois (University of Paris-X-CNRS), and Serge Wolikow (University of Dijon) to speak on the historiography of the USSR and the Communist international. Finally, a discussion chaired by Krzysztof Pomian (CNRS) included Andrzej Packowski (Institut d'études politiques de Varsovie), Karel Bartosek (IHTP-CNRS), Alexandra Laignel-Lavastine (LASP-CNRS), and Étienne François (director of the Marc-Bloch Center of Berlin), who spoke on the historiography of Nazism and Communism in the popular ex-democracies. The work presented here does not constitute an inventory of the acts of that day, even though in the second part the majority of the contributions of the last roundtable are addressed.

6. The scholarly dialogue between Furet and Nolte is not included in this critique. Among recent attempts by historians to take up the comparison on an empirical level, see "Sur les camps de concentration au XXe siècle," *Vingtième Siècle: Revue d'histoire*, no. 54, April–June 1997, which takes up part of the proceedings of the conference organized by Lucette Valensi at École des Hautes Études en Sciences Sociale in June 1995. The most recent important reference on the subject, always from the viewpoint of an empirical comparison, remains the collective work edited by Ian Kershaw and Moshe Lewin, who have brought together several specialists from both camps and directly confront an essential question: to what point can the theory of totalitarianism continue to "stand up against" the scholarly progress made on Nazi Germany and Stalin's USSR. Ian Kershaw and Moshe Lewin, eds., *Stalinism and Nazism: Dictatorships in Comparison*, Cambridge University Press, 1997. This work, which has greatly inspired us, is one of the best references on the subject. Yet it has not caused much discussion in France, even though there was an enormous reaction to Furet's comments and also *Le Livre noir du communisme*. Among the rare reviews, see especially Christian Ingrao, *Annales*, 53d year, no. 1, January–February 1998, pp. 172–176. Notwithstanding, the work of Kershaw, as a specialist on Nazism, and his positions on the theory of totalitarianism have since become well known in France (see note 32 below).

7. Stéphane Courtois, Nicolas Werth, Jean-Louis Panné, Andrzej Paczkowski, Karel Bartosek, and Jean-Louis Margolin, *Le Livre noir du communisme: Crimes, terreur, repression*, with the collaboration of Rémi Kauffer, Pierre Rigoulot, Pascal Fontaine, Yves Santamaria, and Sylvain Boulouque, Paris, Robert Laffont, 1997 (2d ed. 1998, Bouquins series). [For the English translation, see Stéphane Courtois, Nicolas Werth, Jean-Louis Panné, Andrzej Paczkowski, Karel Bartosek, and Jean-Louis Margolin, *The Black Book of Communism: Crimes, Terror, Repression*, trans. Jonathan Murphy and Mark Kramer; consulting ed. Mark Kramer, Cambridge, Harvard University Press, 1999. The references refer to the second French edition.]

8. Ibid., p. 14.

9. See especially Margarete Buber-Neumann, *Prisonnière de Staline et d'Hitler: Vol. 1, Déportée en Sibérie*, Paris, Seuil/La Baconniére, 1986 (1st ed., Stuttgart, 1949); and

Prisonniére de Staline et d'Hitler: Vol. 2, Déportée à Ravensbruck, Paris, Seuil, 1988 (1st ed., Stuttgart, 1949); and *Milena*, Paris, Seuil, 1986 (1st ed., 1977). [All three translated from the German into French by Alain Brossat.] See also Vassily Grossman, *Vie et destin*, Paris, Julliard, 1983.

10. On this point, see Daniel Lindenberg, "Remous autour du *Livre noir du communisme*," *Esprit*, January 1998, pp. 190–194, who revolts against the abusive use of the theme of the "competition between victims."

11. Courtois, "Introduction," *Le Livre du communisme*, p. 23.

12. Alain Besançon, *Le Malheur du siècle: Sur le communisme, le nazisme et l'unicité de la Shoah*, Paris, Fayard, 1998. On this same theme, see the numerous issues recently appearing in the review *Commentaire*: "Sur le fascisme, le communisme, et l'histoire du XXe siècle" (vol. 20, no. 79, autumn 1997); the issue that includes articles by Alain Besançon, Martin Malia, Pierre Chaunu, and the exchanges between François Furet and Ernst Nolte, op. cit. (vol. 20, no. 80, winter 1997–1998); "Communisme, fascisme, et histoire du XXe siècle" (vol. 21, no. 81, spring 1998, [anniversary number]); "Mémoire et oubli du communisme" (vol. 21, no. 82, summer 1998); and "Mémoire et oubli du communisme" (vol. 21, no. 83, autumn 1998).

13. If the "hypermnesia" of Nazism is easily verified, "amnesia" is a proposition that remains to be supported. For example, see Alain Besançon, "Mémoire et oubli du bolchevisme," (paper presented at the annual public session of the five academies, IHTP, October 21, 1997), reprinted in idem, *Le Malheur du siécle*, p. 157. The only concrete reference cited in support of the demonstration of an inequality of treatment between the memory of Nazism and that of Communism is in the comparison of the appearance of several key words taken from a base of givens on the Internet from the newspaper *Le Monde* between 1990 and 1997.

14. Jean-Jacques Becker, "*Le Livre noir du communisme*: De la polémique à la compréhension," *Vingtième Siècle: Revue d'histoire*, no. 59, July–September 1998, p. 179.

15. Regarding Communist memory in France, there are relatively few works given the recurrence of the theme in public debate and in the polemics. See the pioneering work of Marie-Claire Lavabre, *Le Fil rouge: Sociologie de la mémoire communiste*, Paris, Presses de la FNSP, 1994.

16. This is the title of chapter 6 of Furet's *Passé d'une illusion*, and the title of his work (posthumous) with Ernst Nolte that includes an inventory of their correspondence, Furet and Nolte, op. cit.

17. Furet, *Le Passé d'une illusion*, p. 238.

18. Ibid., p. 218.

19. Krzysztof Pomian, "Totalitarisme," *Vingtième Siècle: Revue d'histoire*, no. 47, July–September 1995, p. 4.

20. A review that appeared in *Holocaust and Genocide Studies*, vol. 13, no. 1, spring 1999, pp. 117–119. One can also refer for this to Richard Pipes, one of the great

American specialists of Russia and of the USSR, for his point of view on the work of François Furet. See "Permanence de l'illusion," in "Communisme et fascisme au XXe siècle," *Le Débat*, no. 89, March–April 1996, pp. 147–152.

21. It is partly the political orientation given to this work by the publisher [Robert LaHout] and one of the chief contributors, Stéphane Courtois, that provoked the public disagreement with two other contributors, Jean-Louis Margolin and Nicolas Werth. See Margolin and Werth, "Communisme: Le Retour à l'histoire," *Le Monde*, November 14, 1997; and Stéphane Courtois, "Comprendre la tragédie communiste," ibid., September 20, 1997.

22. Among the most recent, other than the works of Ernst Nolte, see Alain de Benoist, *Communisme et nazisme: 25 réflexions sur le totalitarisme au XXe siècle (1917–1989)*, Paris, Le Labyrinthe, 1998. Benoist's work is in the classic vein of radical totalitarianism, postulating an identity between the two political systems. [Alain de Benoist is a leading figure in the extreme-right intelligentsia.]

23. See, among others, the first part, which Werth devotes to the USSR: "Un Etat contre son peuple: Violences, répressions, terreurs en Union Soviétique," in *Le Livre noir du communisme*, pp. 39–312. This piece supplements and refines the texts he presents in part 1 below.

24. Hannah Arendt, *La Nature du totalitarisme*, trans. with a preface by Michelle-Irène Brudny de Launay, Paris, Payot, 1990, p. 77 [for the English edition, see *The Origins of Totalitarianism*, San Diego, Harcourt, Brace, Jovanovich, 1979; all references are to the French edition]. This text, which includes several studies dating from the late 1940s and the beginning of the 1950s, admirably clarifies her major work, *Le Système totalitaire*, Paris, Seuil, 1972 (1st ed., New York, 1951). More willing reference is made here to the former than to the latter.

25. Ian Kershaw and Moshe Lewin, "Introduction: The regimes and their dictators: perspectives of comparison," in Kershaw and Lewin, op. cit., p. 8.

26. An important literature exists on the history of this concept. Among the most penetrating or most recent analyses, see Pierre Ayçoberry, *La Question nazie. Les interprétations du national-socialisme (1922–1975)*, Paris, Seuil, 1979; Krzysztof Pomian, "Totalitarisme," in Jean-Pierre Azéma, François Bédarida, et al., ed., *1938–1948. Les anneés de tourmente: De Munich à Prague. Dictionnaire critique*, Paris, Flammarion, 1995, pp. 1073–1082 (a text that must be read along with Pomian's article of the same title in *Vingtième Siècle*); and Michelle-Irène Brudny, "Le totalitarisme: Histoire du terme et statut de concept," in "La question du totalitarisme" issue, *Communisme*, nos. 47–48, 3d and 4th qtrs., 1996, pp. 14–32. See also the works cited above and the essay by François Furet, which is devoted to long elaborations of this question. See also Madeleine Grawitz and Jean Leca, ed., *Traité de science politique*, vol. 2; *Les Régimes politiques contemporains*, chap. 3, "Le Totalitarisme," by Luc Ferry and Evelyne Pisier-Kouchner, pp. 115–159.

27. Carl J. Friedrich, ed., *Totalitarianism*, Cambridge, Harvard University Press, 1954, cited in Furet, *Le Passé d'une illusion*, p. 502.

28. On this point see the analysis in Michelle-Irène Brudny de Launay, preface to *La Nature du totalitarisme*, p. 19 and passim.

29. Arendt, *La Nature du totalitarisme*, pp. 88–81.

30. Pomian, "Totalitarisme," *Vingtième Siècle*, p. 6.

31. Kershaw and Lewin, "Introduction," in op. cit., p. 4.

32. Ian Kershaw, "Le Nazisme: Totalitarisme ou domination charismatique?" interview with Bruno Cabanes, Edouard Husson, and Christian Ingrao, *European History/Revue européene d'Histoire*, vol. 3, no. 2, 1996, pp. 266–267. From Kershaw, on the question of totalitarianism, one can refer to three of his most important works published in French: *Hitler: Essai sur le charisme en politique*, NRF/Essais, Paris, Gallimard, 1995; and *Qu'est-ce le nazisme? Problèmes et perspectives d'interprétation*, Paris, Gallimard, 1992 and 1997 (in Folio/Histoire series), and *Hitler, 1889–1936*, vol. 1, Paris, Flammarion, 1999, p. 1000 [for the English edition, see *Hitler, 1889–1936: Hubris*, New York, W. W. Norton, 1999; all references are to the French edition]. See also Ian Kershaw, "L'Introuvable Totalitarisme," interview with Jean Hurtin, in "Hannah Arendt" issue, *Le Magazine littéraire*, no. 337, November 1995, pp. 61–63; idem, "Retour sur le totalitarisme: Le Nazisme et stalinisme dans une perspective comparative," *Esprit*, January–February 1996, pp. 101–121; and idem, "Nazisme et stalinisme: Limites d'une comparaison," *Le Débat*, no. 89, March–April 1996, pp. 177–189.

33. Claude Lefort, *La Complication: Retour sur le communisme*, Paris, Fayard, 1999, p. 11.

34. Kershaw, "Retour sur le totalitarisme," p. 114.

35. On this point see Nicolas Werth, "L'Historiographie de l'URSS dans la période post-communiste," *Revue d'études comparatives Est-Ouest*, vol. 30, no. 1, 1999, pp. 81–104.

36. See especially George Steinmetz, "German Exceptionalism and the Origins of Nazism: The Career of a Concept," in Kershaw and Lewin, op. cit., pp. 251–284; and Mark von Hagen, "Stalinism and the Politics of Post-Soviet History," in ibid., pp. 285–310, Von Hagen very directly takes up the points of comparison in the area of historiography and the politics of memory.

37. See especially Philippe Burrin, *Hitler et les Juifs: Genèse d'un génocide*, Paris, Seuil, 1989. See also his clarification, "Hitler-Staline: La Comparaison est-elle justifiée?" *L'Histoire*, no. 205, December 1996, pp. 48–55.

38. See especially Werth, "L'Historiographie de l'URSS."

39. We have intentionally avoided an analysis of two other totalitarian experiments, those in Yugoslavia and Albania, because they arise from different historical situations. The expected text on Czechoslovakia has not been included.

40. On this point the present volume finds its place in the line of recent work done on memory and historiography in the countries of Central and Eastern Europe. See especially the studies conducted by the IHTP under the direction of Karel Bartosek: "Les Régimes post-communistes et la mémoire du temps present," *La Nouvelle Alternative*, no. 32, December 1993; and "Memoire des guerres et des résistances en

Tchéco-Slovaquie, en Europe centrale et en France" issue, *La Nouvelle Alternative*, nos. 37 and 38, March and June, 1995. See also Antoine Marès, ed., *Histoire et pouvoir en Europe médiane*, Paris, L'Harmattan, 1996; and the numerous articles by Timothy Garton Ash in the *New York Review of Books*, collected in *History of the Present: Essays, Sketches, and Dispatches from Europe in the 1990s*, London, Penguin, 1999. On the problem of the "épuration" and the role of the judiciary in the repression of crimes of Communist regimes, see the essential and almost exhaustive work, which treats all the experiences of democratic transitions in the twentieth century, Neil J. Kritz, ed., *Transitional Justice: How Emerging Democracies Reckon with Former Regimes*, 3 vols., Washington D.C., U.S. Institute of Peace Press, 1995 [preface by Nelson Mandela]. In particular see volume 2, *Country Studies*, which discusses the countries of the former Communist bloc.

1. A Historical Comparison

Presentation

In the landscape of contemporary history, Nazism and Stalinism are two massifs that continue to grow. Their respective sizes are not equal; the former is larger for multiple reasons, of course, the first of which is a somewhat greater linguistic and cultural proximity and an incomparably easier access to sources. The historiography of Nazism has flourished for decades thanks to the seizure by the Anglo-American allies of the archives of the defeated Third Reich, documents that were rapidly made available and that have been consulted at an ever increasing rate, notably because of a growing historical sensibility particularly attuned to the Holocaust.

By contrast, historians of Stalinism have for too long run up against the closure of the archives of a regime that considered the past a state secret. All that was available to Western historians, whose thin ranks already had to contend with the competition of Sovietologists, was limited documentation: the publications of the regime itself, the testimony of exiled former officials, and the "archives of Smolensk," seized by the Nazis during their attack on the USSR in 1941 before falling into the hands of the Western Allies.

Given these circumstances, it is easy to grasp the importance of the opening of the Soviet archives following the collapse of the USSR. Specialists of Nazism have benefited as well, first because they now have access to a large amount of German archives seized within the Reich by the Soviets and transported to their own country, and second because they have access to material preserved in the formerly occupied countries of Eastern Europe.

But for the historians of Stalinism, one must speak of a veritable revolution. It is easy to understand why these scholars immersed themselves in this windfall that permitted them to explore a regime that had been effectively a *terra incognita*. One could even speak of the Soviet Union as being an unknown continent, for what had to be discovered just to begin to understand it—and the dossier is far from closed—were factual considerations as elementary as the number of individuals held captive in the Gulag and the number of victims of Stalinism. This of course did not prevent a number of researchers from undertaking at the same time an in-depth study of Soviet society deriving from broader historical problematics.

This archival revolution should progressively reduce and finally eliminate the gap between the two historiographies. This in turn will allow for focused dialogue and cross fertilization, eliminating in the process an unfortunate reciprocal ignorance and indifference. This situation is all the more striking because parallels between the Nazi and Stalinist historiographies are not lacking. These parallels are partly a reflection of a change in focus of research in contemporary history in general—from political and ideological history to social and cultural history. They are also the reflection of similar questions addressing a similarity of objects of study, to whit, that of regimes characterized by an unprecedented will to control society and the deployment of an extraordinary mass violence. These similarities are undoubtedly at the origin of the concept of totalitarianism, an idea that figures prominently among the analytical tools of sociologists and political scientists. But among historians, totalitarianism has served more as a concept to react against by stressing that historical reality is very different, indeed quite opposite, from the kind of understanding allowed for by such absolutism. They have taken this position without having truly reflected on the heuristic value of totalitarianism for historical research.

What follows is a comparison by stages. It is not a question here of an exhaustive historical comparison but rather of a series of parallel investigations that share the same perspective and follow a common articulation. The approach adopted is that of exploring and illuminating the structures and interactions of two political regimes, including their violent manifestations within societies subject to their power. In order to do this, three areas are explored, each chosen to reveal what is most similar—not identical—in these two admittedly exceptional systems.

The first focuses on the nature and function of each regime type, with particular attention paid to the place and the role of the holder of absolute power. The second concerns mass violence in the diversity and specificity of its forms. The third area explored is the role and extent of power imposed on the societies themselves, the forms of autonomy that existed, and the forms of "inertia," even "resistance," within civil society.

In each of these focuses, the authors have tried to provide chapters that are informative and "reflexive" in the sense that they attempt, on the one hand, to refer to the respective historiographical debates that continue to enrich their fields while, on the other hand, to pave the way to a comparison based upon the historical realities of the regimes in question.

Translated by Lucy B. Golsan and Richard J. Golsan

THE DICTATOR AND THE SYSTEM

Nicolas Werth

Stalin's System during the 1930s

Like Adolf Hitler, Iosif Vissarionovich Stalin has been the subject of numerous impressive biographies. From Boris Suvarin to Dimitri Volkogonov, via Adam Ulam, Roy Medvedev, Robert Conquest, and Robert Tucker, a great number of sovietologists have written on "their" Stalin. The psychohistorical "Stalin-centered" approach that underlies these biographies is founded on the conviction that, as Conquest writes, "everything that happened during these years is ultimately derived from the peculiar mentality of Stalin."[1] From this perspective the disturbing episode of the Communist Party purge of 1937–38 can only be explained by the dictator's "paranoid" motivations. The Great Terror could have resulted only from a preestablished plan, long contemplated by Stalin, that began with the ordered assassination of Sergei Kirov on December 1, 1934, and subsequently developed step by step to the bloody purges. The American historian Merle Fainsod arrives at such a conclusion—placing the central role of the dictator at the forefront—in his classic study on the Smolensk region: "in the political domain, Stalinism signifies the burgeoning of a totalitarian regime under which all the lines of control ultimately converge in the hands of the supreme dictator."[2]

This Stalin-centered approach attempted to reconstruct the "intentions" of the dictator based on fragmentary and often secondhand documentation while omitting some of the fundamental questions regarding the functioning of institutions and the mode of government. In reaction to this, another developed during the 1980s, the "revisionist" approach. Relying principally on the regional archives of Smolensk, but with a reading much different to that of Fainsod, revisionist historians accentuated the dysfunctional nature of administrations in conflict with one another as being at the core of a poorly ordered state, the conflicts between the center and the periphery as well as the permanent disparity between the central authority's proclaimed objective and its realization. They stress the excesses, the deviations, and the general drift. These all represented aspects of the same phenomenon—a central element of Stalinist political culture, *pereguib* in Russian. Whether a matter of collectivization, the periodic purges, or the Great Terror, the development of events did not at all follow some plan "preestablished" by Stalin, according to the historian John Arch Getty, one of the leaders of American revisionists. On the contrary, after Moscow's announcement of a "campaign"—with often rather vague objectives—local functionaries interpreted the orders in their own fashion, obeying them or not, acting "zealously" or attempting to "sabotage" the initiative. The process developed without control, reflecting hidden social conflicts, latent social violence, the existence of local power structures, and clans and other cliques over which the center had no hold. Far from being an operation planned by a paranoid despot, the Great Terror was rather a blind drive forward into chaos. In the end Stalin was a weak dictator. Until the end of the 1930s, he had no apparatus capable of implementing his instructions: at the local and regional level, political actors possessed a great degree of autonomy. Moreover, at the central level, Stalin was constantly caught between two rival factions within the heart of his political bureaucracy: a "moderate" group led first by Kirov and, after his assassination, by André Zhdanov and Sergo Ordzhonikidze, and a "radical" group whose main leaders were Viacheslav Molotov, Lazar Kaganovich, and Nicolai Ezhov.[3] It is only in 1937 that Stalin, relying on the radicals, would settle exclusively in favor of the idea of a police state and assure his preeminence, however relative.[4]

Today scholars have access to a substantial portion of the documents from the Party's directing bodies (the Politburo, Orgburo, and Secretary of the Central Committee), to the ruling elite's correspondence, and to the majority of documents of high-level and intermediary Soviet administrative authorities. These have shed light on and have allowed us in large measure (at least in regard to the prewar years, which several important studies have examined) to move beyond the debate over the omnipotence or weakness of Stalin by resituating the dictator's actions within the functioning of a specific system, the burgeoning "administrative command system." The documents now available permit a better understanding of the mechanisms of high-level decision making and the implementation of adopted measures. Despite the difficulty of reconstructing the ensemble of decision-making processes, it has become possible to document and identify Stalin's personal stamp and follow its logic in this or that administration. It is also easier to gauge various political agents' margins of autonomy or their recommendations, to distinguish between the long-term political project and improvisatory measures, trial-and-error adjustments, and the breakdowns in a political system attempting to manage the immense socioeconomic changes brought about by the forced march of collectivization and industrialization. As Alain Blum and Catherine Gousseff have written: "the Soviet State itself has begun to be understood as an object of social history, through the study of its protagonists, the functioning of its administration, the forms of negotiations and conflicts that traversed it. . . . It is a matter of understanding all levels of State functioning and of definitively renouncing the use of the term 'State' as a simple and impersonal form, imposing its will. Rather, it must be reexamined as a place of tensions and contradictions, of conflicts and negotiations."[5] This approach surely allows a better evaluation of the place and role of the dictator in the Stalinist system.

The work of the Russian historian Oleg Khlevniuk has problematized the two principal versions of "top-level" political history of the 1930s.[6] One version is that of a long-term plan for liquidation of the Leninist old guard, implemented by Stalin at the beginning of the 1930s, and whose centerpiece was the assassination of Kirov, leader of the moderates. The opposing version is one in which Stalin, at least during 1937–38, merely played the role of arbitrator between rival factions. Through his studies on the workings of the Politburo, Khlevniuk has shown how Stalin progressively succeeded in transforming this collegial directive committee into a simple registration desk for Stalinist decisions. He has shown how Stalin successfully imposed (while contravening Party rules) his despotic, police-implemented "logic of the clan" against "the bureaucratic logic of the industrial State." It was around this principle that several of Stalin's close companions in arms rallied during the 1930s, especially the omnipotent director of the Commissariat of Heavy Industry, Sergo Ordzhonikidze.

At the same time, other historians have proposed a social and political approach using different observation points: economic administrations, the Gosplan, the People's Commissariat of Transportation, the Statistics Administration, the Department of Justice, and the Department of Foreign Affairs.[7] These scholars have also analyzed the tensions between, on the one hand, the professional strategies of "traditional" administrations concerned with maintaining their roles, personnel, autonomy, and place in the government—the logic of local political administrations that had learned to defend themselves against and resist the center's often confused impulses—and, on the other hand, the police-state approach, or the despotic strategy implemented by the political police and the Stalinist clan. These conflicts were radically resolved during the Great Terror purges.

All of these studies converge on the same observation: the 1930s, the formative stage of Stalinism as a political system, were years of considerable tension between two forms of organization and two power strategies.[8] One was the strategy of an "administrative system of command"—proliferating administrations under an increasingly complex, diverse, heterogeneous, and hypertrophied state apparatus—charged with controlling a growing sphere of activities and supervising a social body resistant to the changes the regime wanted to impose on it by force. The other was the perceived strategy of the business of the country being conducted in a crudely despotic way by Stalin and his small cadre of directors. There is undoubtedly a major incongruity between the logic of the clan—involving allegiance and the destruction of all political, personal, and professional relations of solidarity not based upon political adhesion to Stalin's politics or person—and the administrative approach of a modern industrial state founded on the principle of competence. This tension allows an understanding of what constitutes, for Moshe Lewin, the "essence of Stalinism"; namely, "institutional paranoia," defined as "a feeling of impotence developing in the close circle of high-level directors, then with the supreme leader. The more central power is reinforced, the more this feeling of impotence persists and grows."[9] Integrating into its analysis the key question of state construction and the institutional, economic, and social upheavals of the 1930s, this hypothesis is undoubtedly more fruitful than that of the mere "personal paranoia" of the dictator, long advanced as an explanation for the terror exercised against many Communist cadres at the end of the 1930s. It allows us to move past the rather unproductive debate over the omnipotence or weakness of the dictator.

From the moment they came to power, the Bolsheviks had a keen sense of just how precarious the instruments of state control at their disposition were. Given that in Leninist theory the state was eventually supposed to disappear, the Bolsheviks never developed an in-depth analysis of bureaucracy. For them the strike by the tsarist functionaries, the first active opposition to the regime, reinforced the idea that bureaucracy was a class issue and that the replacement of the old regime's *tchinovniki* by the proletariat would settle the question definitively. Having renounced their illusions regarding the disappearance of the state after a brief "leftist" phase, and for want of a blueprint from which to work, the Bolsheviks had to tinker with their army and their administration through emergency improvisations with some of the "specialists" won over from the tsarist regime, but who were nevertheless still suspect.

At the same time, the new gestating state was bestowed with a large number of plebeians who made up for their limited political experience and professional qualifications with their undeniable activism. This activism was a mixture of devotion to the Bolshevik cause and the "traditional" behavior of the old regime's small bureaucrat. Suspicion in regard to rather unreliable apparatuses—composed of a heterogeneous group of plebeians recently recruited to the Bolshevik Party, functionaries won over from the tsarist bureaucracy, and "bourgeois specialists"—partially explains what one might call a political culture of the clan, parallel to the culture of conspiracy of small revolutionary groups. During and after the civil war, Bolshevik leaders—

considering that they could only count on a small circle of collaborators for quickly and efficiently carrying out important directives—developed the practice of sending plenipotentiaries and other managers to take charge of regular administrations. These authorities were often poorly defined since they stemmed from a double legitimacy: that of the Party and more traditionally that of the state. Documents from the highest Party levels reveal the extent to which the culture of conspiracy was maintained, including during the "peaceful years" of the New Economic Policy (NEP): even Central Committee members (not to mention regional Party secretaries) were kept ignorant of many Politburo decisions.[10] Despite the official prohibition on "fractions" at the heart of the Party,[11] top-level private correspondence testifies that they existed.[12] For well-known reasons, Stalin—the great strategist of manipulating apparatuses—managed to form the most stable and efficient political clan (by far) from the network of militant Bolsheviks dating back to the civil war years (the "Tsaritsyne Group" and the "Caucusus Group," comprising Ordzhonikidze, Anastas Mikoyan, Kliment Voroshilov, Budienny, Kirov, Enukidze, Molotov, and others). This gave Stalin an advantage over other potential successors to Lenin during the second half of the 1920s.

One of the major problems the Bolshevik leadership faced throughout the 1920s and 1930s remained the question of training political and economic cadres of the regime. As Lenin observed at the Tenth Congress in 1922, were not the old regime's functionaries of "bourgeois origin" or Bolsheviks "bureaucratized" in the final hour responsible for the fact that "the car was not heading where the driver wanted it to go"? This is a theme Stalin would develop ad nauseum throughout the 1930s in order to explain that, having just traced the political lineage, "90% of the difficulty came from the absence of an organized system of control for executing decisions . . . poor choice of staff . . . bureaucracy, and the criminal nonchalance of local apparatuses."[13]

Toward the end of the 1920s, two different problems became evident. In 1928 this was illustrated by two highly publicized events: the "Smolensk scandal" and the "Chakhty affair." The first revealed the total degeneration of regional Party direction, with these local Bolsheviks corrupted by their relations with representatives of socialist groups stigmatized by the regime (*nepmen* and kulaks), entangled in sordid ethical affairs, and organized in mafia-alike cliques (including Party officials, soviets, unions, and political police) that impeded national laws from penetrating the provinces they controlled.[14] This emblematic case, undoubtedly only the tip of the iceberg, presents a challenge for historians of the nature of the Soviet state during the 1920s. There were several factors involved: the absence of clear demarcations of duties between the various administrative organs (the authority of Party secretaries was broad and poorly defined), the absence of specialized training for staff (thus, to take only one example, in 1930 only 4 percent of judges and 10 percent of prosecutors had legal training), and "local cliques" controlling the judicial, law-enforcement, and administrative offices while largely ignoring Central Committee directives. These all contributed to shaping the contours of a state one can barely call "modern."[15]

The second is the well-known Chakhty affair, in which the Stalinist leadership and the political police completely fabricated a vast act of "sabotage" organized by "bourgeois engineers" in the Donbass mines. This event served as a "reminder" that when the Bolshevik regime launched itself into the "construction of socialism," it should have immediately developed a new "red technical intelligentsia."

As Stalin would assert on several occasions throughout 1928–29, the top priority for Communists was education and "technical mastery." Certainly much was to be done in this area: in 1928 only 8,000 Party members (1 percent of the manpower) had degrees from higher institutions, and there were only 138 Communist engineers in all of Soviet industry.[16] The central Party apparatuses (including Gosplan, the Supreme Council of National Economy, the People's Commissariat of the Finances, and the Statistics Administration) were in charge of managing the country's grandiose planning and accelerated industrialization projects, in which relatively autonomous (with regard to the political sphere) administrative and professional strategies had been perpetuated. Within these apparatuses the vast majority of cadres were non-Communist, and nearly all of them were non-Stalinists.

In his "Notes from an Economist" (published in *Pravda* on September 30, 1928), one of the fundamental texts of the final opposition to the totalitarian current, Nikolai Bukharin predicted that the elimination of the market, forced collectivization, accelerated industrialization, and administrative management of the economy (which would take the place of planning) would inevitably lead to the creation of a bureaucratic monster engulfing the Party and allowing despotic forms of power to emerge. These were not, according to Bukharin, embryonic in Leninist Bolshevism.[17]

These predictions would be largely realized. The consequence of the immense changes wrought by the "second revolution"—the "revolution from above" deliberately set in motion by Stalin's group in order to establish its political preeminence and erect an "industrial state"—was a proliferation of bureaucratic apparatuses in charge of organizing an expanding sphere of activities. The most important point to underscore here is that, despite the appearance of reinforced centralization, this process generally escaped supervision and control from the center, and economic planning was transformed into a chaotic and short-term administrative management of resources and economic priorities. Several factors generated fierce tensions and incredible chaos: a permanent state of emergency, the promotion of unrealizable objectives, haste, the inclination to reorganize all existing administrative structures from top to bottom, passive resistance to reforms—indeed, to the entire political project of transformation—by existing apparatuses, and mobilization (through antibureaucratic rhetoric) of unskilled staff in order to short-circuit established administrative routes. During the span of a few months, the political-administrative system as it had functioned during the 1920s was profoundly destabilized.

In the vein of essays by Moshe Lewin and Sheila Fitzpatrick on these decisive years in the Stalinist system's formation,[18] recent work by American historian David Shearer provides an accurate portrayal of the permanent state of crisis, emergency, and mobilization through which Soviet industry administratively reorganized at the beginning of the 1930s.[19] The grand project of radically recasting industrial structures elaborated at the end of 1929 (proposing strict vertical centralization in place of the extant decentralized economic councils) in reality led to a chaotic proliferation of administrations by the end of the process, which vexed the country's highest directors.[20] The redundancy and complexity of training structures, multiple centers, a "deluge of red tape,"[21] and *neplanovost* (the absence of firmly established procedures for disseminating instructions) rendered the immense industrial bureaucracies inefficient. They were shown to be incapable of controlling basic aspects of the factories—labor flow, costs, and forms of work organization.

On the other great "front," the forced collectivization of the countryside, the problem was quite different. Nevertheless the dysfunction that resulted from setting up a vast and complex network of peasant supervision in some ways resembled that of the "administrative system of command" attempted in industry. Since the organizations existing in rural areas at the end of the 1920s were both incapable of and often resistant to implementing collectivization, it was carried out by "shock methods," by massive mobilizations (as with the movement of the "25,000"—workers and Komsomols sent to direct the "collectivization brigades," or "dekulakization") maintained by the political police, who bypassed normal administrative routes and destabilized existing institutions. Thus massive arrests and deportations of peasants resistant to collectivization were implemented by a diverse group of ad hoc committees composed of "activists" of indeterminate status supervised by the

State Political Directorate (GPU; Gosudarstvennoe politicheskoe upravlenie). These events seriously undermined the judiciary apparatus that had been so painfully reconstructed since the end of the civil war.[22] The excesses attained such serious proportions that the Party's highest command had to intervene, through a famous circular, in order to control the violence, reminding the activists that only representatives duly mandated by judiciary or police authority were invested with the power to arrest suspects.[23] The creation of tens of thousands of kolkhozes and sovkhozes gave birth to an administration as proliferate as it was inefficient, composed of a surfeit of minor functionaries (presidents of kolkhozes, brigadiers, accountants, and supervisors of all sorts). These functionaries were usually in solidarity with the people under their jurisdiction and therefore eminently suspect in the eyes of central authorities. The considerable growth in the spheres controlled by local and regional Communist organizations—notably economic—led to a blurring of the demarcation between the state and the Party, among other things. Meanwhile—as a number of Stalin's Bolshevik opponents had predicted in the 1920s—the Party was "economized" and transformed into a tentacled bureaucracy in charge of managing the daily problems of an "administrative system of command" born from the urgency of the "Great Retreat."

For Bolshevik political culture, the malfunctioning of the bureaucratic machinery could only be explained either in class terms, by the "bad" social origins of the cadres and functionaries in charge of implementing the Party line, or in terms of "backwardness" or a "lack of culture" among local workers. In 1929 the regime launched a massive effort to train a new generation of politically loyal specialists, expecting their "technical skill" to constitute the basis of the new state. The 1930s were marked by a twofold movement of elimination of the old non-Communist cadres and specialists and promotion of a "new Soviet technical intelligentsia."[24] Having started with the purges of "bourgeois" engineers during 1928–29, then moving to the central economic administration during 1929–30, and subsequently overhauling the entire administration during 1930 and 1932–33, the process would in reality continue, to varying degrees, throughout the decade.[25] The training of a new industrial and administrative elite would stretch across several years: the *vydvizhentsi* ("promoted") of the First Plan, Communists from "politically correct" social origins, were in place only after 1937–38.[26] Until then the administration had to accommodate *nolens volens* diverse administrations comprised of *praktiki* (officials devoted to the cause, though often incompetent, who were trained on the job) and skilled administrators with diverse political backgrounds. The level of training of political cadres remained very low: at the beginning of

1937, 70 percent of regional Party secretaries and 80 percent of the directors of *gorkomy* (city Communist committees) had not been educated beyond primary school.[27] "When one sees our military cadres, it is enough to make a person misanthropic," K. Voroshilov, people's commissariat of defense, wrote Stalin on July 26, 1932. "I no longer know what to do to make these people assume their responsibilities, to work differently, in our way, our socialist way. I cannot even say that these people do not work; on the contrary, they work until they are exhausted, but with no results."[28] Correspondence between directors is inexhaustible on this topic.[29] Faced with disorder, inefficiency, and a growing bureaucracy, central authorities had recourse to two devices. One was to reinforce at all levels the principle of *edinocalie* ("one sole leader") and send plenipotentiaries during the frequent moments of crisis to "beat some of them to a pulp as an example to the others."[30] The second was to apply strict "Bolshevik control" over the local administrations, but the Communist overseers had the reputation not only of not mastering the situation but also of not reporting the real state of things to superiors (if not engaging in passive resistance to the politics of the center).

Applied throughout the management of the economy, the principle of *edinocalie*—incarnated by directing "commandants of production" to manage their enterprises in military style—rapidly replaced the functional organization of which the planners had dreamed. During this same time, around the beginning of the 1930s, there was a great amount of political latitude given to the new regional directors in charge of implementing the politics of the Great Retreat. Invested with immense power, these local authorities did not delay in completely changing into virtual "little Stalins" (as Fainsod has shown especially through the example of I. P. Rumiantsev, first secretary of the Smolensk region). They were glorified as the "best Bolsheviks of the region," each having their "little family" constituted on the principle of personal devotion to the local "boss," and each making and unmaking the careers of one another.[31] In this regard the old traditions denounced at the end of the 1920s in the context of sensational affairs such as the Smolensk scandal proved to be firmly entrenched and particularly difficult to uproot.

In order to palliate the absence of reliable politico-administrative reins, the highest-ranking directors of the Party—apart from Stalin—were called upon to continuously crisscross the country, applying the most unpopular of measures even among local Communists. Most of them spent several months per year on these tours.[32] Constant duplication of normal administrative routes, the permanent delegitimization of local authorities by dispatching plenipotentiaries, instructors, and other "shock groups" (supported as always by the political police)—measures justified by an obsessive fear of the "sabotage" of governmental actions by apparatuses allegedly unfit for implementing the center's political line—reflected the principal tension within the mode of government during these formative years of Stalinism. The only real political cleavages at the heart of the Stalinist leadership (which are better known today) came from these measures and the necessity of perpetuating or even replacing them with a more regularly functioning bureaucratic machinery. The two main protagonists here were, during the end of 1936 and the beginning of 1937, Stalin and Ordzhonikidze.

Recently declassified documents of Party directives and correspondence between Bolshevik leaders have shed light on, at least for the 1930s, the functioning of power at the highest level and the manner in which Stalin imposed his will, the despotic logic of the "clan," and the police at this general level. This imposition gradually restricted the sphere of autonomy of regional authorities as well as central administrations (*vedomstva*), all immense bureaucratic machines, the most important of which (heavy industry, transportation, commerce, provisions, and defense) were directed by Stalin's colleagues in the Politburo. After the defeat of the so-called rightist opposition (Bukharin, Aleksey Rykov, Mikhail Tomsky) at the end of 1930, the *vedomstva* and their directors (members of the Supreme Court of the Party) represented, in effect, the main counterweight objectively limiting the power of the secretary general. Stalin's personal, omnipresent dictatorship—interventionist to the smallest of details in the battle with the "family circles" of regional "little Stalins"—was, from this point of view, very different from the Hitlerian dictatorship. As work on the Hitlerian state (most notably that of Martin Broszat) has shown, the Hitlerian dictatorship was founded on the Führer's "charismatic rule," on amorphism and the absence of structures, and on a "neo-feudal" style of command, allowing the Gauleiter Nazis a large amount of space for maneuvering within their regional fiefs.

In order to impose an order-taking bureaucracy, Stalin and his closest colleagues (whose power had been gradually diminished to the benefit of the man they called the "patron," the "godfather," or the "best friend") modified the functioning of the Party's collective bodies to his own advantage. This was done in the name of a centralization necessitated by the anarchic proliferation of the bureaucratic "administrative system of command."

At the end of 1930, the Stalinist group took control of the government (the Council of the People's Commissaries and the Council of Deputies), until then directed by Rykov. Molotov replaced Rykov, with the goal of "eliminating all gaps between State directorship and Party directorship." "With the arrangement I am proposing to you," Stalin wrote Molotov, "we will finally have a perfect unity between the top levels of the State and the Party, and this will reinforce our power."[33] The "unity" thus obtained would intensify centralization: coordination between the different people's commissariats was made thereafter in the Politburo and in limited commissions (permanent or provisional) set up in 1931–32, which joined Stalin and his closest collaborators.[34] Then, as the role of the Politburo as an organ of collective decision making gradually declined, this coordination was made in Stalin's own office. Of course the installation of compartmentalized and exclusively vertical links between the person in charge of each administration and the directing team promoted the development of interinstitutional conflicts and rivalries, ultimately leading to the weakening of the various ministers' autonomy.

Analysis of Politburo documents and those of its limited commissions reveal, among other things, an increasingly marked refusal of any delegation of power to local administrations.[35] This parallels an unprecedented development of the "conspiratorial" character of decisions taken.[36] The refusal to delegate power was motivated by Stalin's growing mistrust of "bureaucrats," an obsessive theme in correspondence between the secretary general and his collaborators during 1931–32.[37] Against a state threatened with breakdown by the "heroes of *vedomstvennost*,"[38] Stalin would privately develop his own vision of a state reduced to a limited group ("our group historically formed in the struggle against all opportunism," Kaganovich wrote in August 1931) of a few faithful collaborators.[39] They were to be freed from the "tutelage of bureaucrats" by "surrounding themselves with new people who believe in our cause and who can successfully replace the bureaucracy."[40]

There was another significant development: a drastic reduction in the number of Politburo plenary meetings from eighty-five in 1930 to thirty-two in 1933, twenty in 1935, nine in 1936, six in 1937, three in 1938, and finally two in 1939. These were progressively replaced by informal meetings in Stalin's office—the General Secretariat—of his closest collaborators and the few directors responsible for the adopted measures. Analysis of Politburo protocols gives rise to the conclusion that from 1934 on, most of the resolutions officially adopted as Politburo decisions were in fact decided by two or three directors. Most often these three were Stalin, Kaganovich, and Molotov, and the directives were countersigned by other less "active" members of the Politburo "through consultation."[41] The recent publication of the entry register at Stalin's office along with the list of visitors received and the durations of their conversations is also quite enlightening. It allows us to ascertain who Stalin's privileged interlocutors were at any given time and, by comparing this information with other sources (for example, correspondence between directors and decisions recorded in Politburo protocols), to reconstruct the mechanisms of decision making at the heart of an increasingly restricted circle in which Stalin played the most important role through his universal intervention. Significantly, Stalin passed an increasing amount of time with only a handful of privileged colleagues: Molotov throughout the 1930s; Kaganovich, most notably during 1932–37; Voroshilov during 1936–39; Ezhov during 1937–38; Zhdanov from 1935; and Ordzhonikidze during 1933–36.[42] During absences from Moscow (usually to Sochi for two or three months during the summer), Stalin governed through letters or telegrams—virtual plans of action executed immediately—sent regularly to his collaborators. "From the Boss," Kaganovich wrote to Ordzhonikidze on August 2, 1933, "we receive frequent and detailed instructions which do not allow us to miss anything; it is true that all this makes for more work, but we will never get there otherwise."[43]

Stalin's interventionism extended to even the most seemingly secondary affairs, nevertheless elevated to the rank of "exemplary" affairs by the secretary general. This was the case in the episode of faulty combine harvesters at the Zaporozhe Communard factory in September 1933, which served as a pretext for Stalin to demand a reinforcement of legal responsibility regarding industrial cadres and to condemn the "laxity" of Kaganovich and Ordzhonikidze.[44] Nevertheless this left open zones of autonomy—even at the highest levels of the State-Party—where skilled professionals of "traditional" administrations operated. Recent studies by Alain Blum on the Directorship of Accounting of the National Economy statisticians and by Sabine Dullin on the People's Commissariat of Foreign Affairs diplomats have shed light on this aspect. For instance, until 1937, statisticians produced data that contradicted figures presented by those in power and by Stalin in particular. The administrative and scientific strategy continued to function, even though the impossibility of interpreting some data (particularly following the famine of 1932–33) "was leading to distorted presentations."[45] Throughout the course of 1934–36, the Stalinist leadership let conflicts develop between the police-state approach to demography (represented by the People's Commissariat of Internal Affairs [NKVD; Narodnyi komissariat vnutrennikh del], which was in charge of civil records) and a scientific approach defended by the statisticians and demographers. The idea of the police state would only triumph after the annulment of the January 1937 census, whose results ran counter to the data that had long been furnished by Stalin.

In the area of foreign affairs, the People's Commissariat of Foreign Affairs was an institution of the highest professionalism as well as very politically heterodox. Its leadership positions counted a large number of diplomats who had belonged to non-Bolshevik socialist parties as well as members of various forms of opposition to the Stalinist current, especially Trotskyites. Directed by Maxim Litvinov, it would retain (until the end of 1936) not only a margin of autonomy but also a certain influence in its recommendations. Until Stalin and his close Politburo collaborators placed it under the tutelage of the People's Commissariat of Foreign Affairs, Litvinov knew how to have some of his choices confirmed by the Stalinist group. The latter usually demurred (through indecision) regarding long-term foreign policy, given the unstable international context.[46] These choices were characterized by a politics of collective security, circumspection, and prudence in regard to Nazism and the conviction that the USSR could not remain on the sidelines of an "inter-imperialist" conflict for long.

The autumn of 1936 marked a turning point for internal politics as much as it did for international politics. From this time on, exacerbated by Stalin's increasingly acute perception of the danger of war, the idea of the despotic police state would prevail. The Spanish Civil War played a major role in this. Stalin's "institutional paranoia" was accentuated by the prospect of a large international conflict that the USSR would not be able to avoid. He had not forgotten one of Lenin's most important political lessons: the profoundly destabilizing role of all war for political regimes, whatever they were.[47] In September and October 1936, after having named Ezhov to head the NKVD, Stalin engaged in a vast populist, anti-bureaucratic policing campaign against industrial cadres suspected of concealing the actual output of production. This occurred in conjunction with great economic difficulties due in part to the disorganization introduced into enterprises by the Stakhanovist movement. Even hardened Stalinists such as Ordzhonikidze (and to a lesser degree Kaganovich) objected to this new delegitimization of professional experts, the latest wave of *spetzphagie* (the common term used during those years). They had meanwhile become defenders of stability regarding the cadres and henceforth favored professional experts (who were still too rare in the country) over a purely Stalinist political route.[48]

At the end of 1936 and the beginning of 1937, an exemplary dispute developed between Stalin and Ordzhonikidze, people's commissariat of heavy industry, regarding the interpretation of the economic difficulties and, in particular, of the large number of industrial accidents that occurred during 1936, the so-called Stakhanovist year. While Stalin exclusively adopted the police-state version of affairs, supposing the cause to be large-scale sabotage and implicating many industrial cadres (including insufficiently "vigilant" Communist workers), Ordzhonikidze rejected this approach because it opened the doors to a vast purge of the industrial administrations of which he was in charge.[49] Over the years Ordzhonikidze had become an ardent defender of his commissariat's interests. It was a symbol of the power of the industrial state and the "administrative system of command," built with whatever human resources were at hand since the beginning of the 1930s. Yet for Stalin, to leave a sprawling administration encrusted in its old ways constituted a real limitation on his personal despotic power. The conflict between these two men and these two power strategies culminated in the tragic death of Ordzhonikidze, driven to suicide on February 18, 1937, only a few days before the opening of the Central Committee plenum. For this meeting he had prepared an explosive report denying the reality of the alleged sabotage of the Soviet economy.

After Ordzhonikidze's death, Stalin (supported by the "historical group constituted in the struggle against all opportunism" [Kaganovich, Voroshilov, Molotov, Mikoyan, and A. A. Andreiev] as well as by a certain number of newly promoted Stalinists [Zhdanov, Georgy Malenkov, Ezhov, and Lavrenti Beria]) developed his offensive against not only the ever suspect cadres of economic bureaucracies but also against a part of the military cadres and the regional directors of the Party, who often formed local power bases. Stalin organized a clever strategy founded on an approach to political action that was at the same time populist and police based. The populist strategy—the leader's singular strategy for communicating with the masses over the heads of the bureaucracy—was developed particularly along the lines of the model elaborated on the occasion of the Poschyev-Nikolaienko affair. This strategy allowed Stalin to place the "common people, the simple members of the Party . . . , otherwise closer to the truth than some gentlemen" at the forefront.[50] Against those "who wash their dirty laundry together, congratulate each other, and send stupid and nauseating reports of their success back to the Center," Stalin marshaled the "political vigilance of the common people, of simple Communists like Nikolaienko."[51] This affair was supposed to illustrate to the masses the leader's lasting concern with defending the "common people" against the arbitrariness of the "gentlemen" and "bureaucrats." The edifying story of Nikolaienko also contributed to the construction of the myth that the leader, placed above "affairs" that justified reinforced vigilance, was a stranger to mass terror.

The other decisive aspect of the Stalinist offensive was "the alliance of the sovereign with the political police."[52] More than any other Bolshevik director, Stalin viewed the political police as the absolute recourse of power, the only truly secure body for establishing his personal authority. Since the 1920s Stalin had maintained very tight relations with the political police in order to fabricate affairs that compromised his political opponents even at the Party directorship's very core.[53] This alliance, maintained especially by his personal secretary and directed by A. N. Poskrebyshev, was strengthened after several events had left their mark on the dictator, such as the suicide of his wife in November 1932 and Kirov's assassination in December 1934.[54] In the interinstitutional conflicts that developed during the 1930s, Stalin favored the police approach more often than his colleagues. Recent research on the Great Terror has led to a now well-documented view of a centralized process initiated at the highest level by Stalin and implemented by the massive machinery of Ezhov's NKVD (with more than 370,000 functionaries). During the two years the People's Commissary of the Interior was occupied with (from the end of September 1936 to November 1938) Stalin's initiative, Ezhov became the favored interlocutor of the secretary general. He was received in Stalin's office 306 times for a total of more than nine hundred hours of meetings.[55]

We now know that what is called the Great Terror combined two distinct levels of activity. One was a dozen large mass-terror operations, including arrest and execution quotas affecting more than a million people. These operations in fact represented the ultimate radical attempt at social purification in a prolonged series of repressive actions starting with "dekulakization" at the beginning of the 1930s. Their goal was to put an end to "social disorder" and finally rid the "new socialist society" of its "socially foreign elements."[56] The other level was repression more specifically targeted at part of the political, economic, and military elite, supposedly in order to destroy all political, professional, and administrative solidarity-generating links that did not derive from adhesion to Stalin's politics or person. It was also supposed to promote a new social stratum of directors who would owe their vertiginous careers to the leader, for which they would have total devotion. The replacement of cadres was spectacular: at the beginning of 1939, 293 of the 333 regional Party secretaries and around twenty-six thousand of the thirty-three thousand senior civil servants of the Central Committee's nomenklatura had held their positions for less than one year. At the beginning of 1937, 88 percent of the regional secretaries had belonged to the Party since 1923; two years later this portion had fallen to 18 percent—the great majority (65 percent) of those newly promoted to these key positions had belonged to the Party since the Great Retreat of 1929.[57] The replacement of politico-administrative personnel by the "First Plan promotions" of 1936–38 was accompanied by a strengthening of Moscow's tutelage over regions now rid of their "gentlemen [*grands seigneurs*]."[58] At the central level this was accompanied by a loss of autonomy for the commissariats of the people, replaced by limited commissions of Stalin's closest collaborators. In this respect the example of foreign affairs is especially enlightening. The People's Commissariat of Foreign Affairs not only was subjected to a vast purge but also, from the beginning of 1937, lost the autonomy it had safeguarded until then (due to the high professional skills of its diplomats). A permanent commission on foreign affairs (Stalin, Voroshilov, Molotov, Kaganovich, and Ezhov) effectively eliminated the role of Litvinov's commissariat, and Soviet ambassadors were called directly into Stalin's office to receive their orders.[59]

An analogous process developed in the spheres of economy and national defense, with the implementation of the Permanent Commission for Economic Affairs and the Defense Committee of the USSR. The creation of two permanent commissions (foreign affairs and economic affairs) to which were added various limited commissions (all composed of the same five or six collaborators in Stalin's primary circle) already existing, completed the marginalization of the Politburo. Its actual force had continued to dwindle over the span of several years (as earlier mentioned),[60] and half the members— all those who were not members of the primary circle—were arrested and shot in 1937–38.[61]

As the consummate expression of "institutional paranoia" (which is surely at least one of the keys to understanding Stalinism), the Great Terror led to a bolstering of Stalin's personal power (which in May 1941 included the positions of secretary general of the Party and president of the Council of People's Commissariats), the triumph of the "logic of the clan" and of a despotic conception of the mode of government, and a new evolution of the cult of personality.[62] As Ian Kershaw and Moshe Lewin have shown, this cult's function was quite different from the charismatic role that characterized National Socialism's cult of the leader.[63] A primary difference was the relationship Stalin was able to maintain with the "masses." He was so conscious of his unpopularity and had such fear of even the slightest physical contact with the population that, given the "imagined" risk of assassination attempts, he initiated the Politburo's decision (October 20, 1930) to formally prohibit the secretary general from putting a foot on the street. The numerous joyful reactions in public opinion following Kirov's assassination (gathered by informants for the political police) and the spread of popular verses to the effect of "they've killed Kirov; soon it will be Stalin's turn!" accentuated Stalin's obsession with an attempt against his life. After World War II this obsession would grow larger until the dictator's death. Moreover the cult of Stalin was indispensable to *his* power, not to the functioning of the Party. Whereas Hitler's "heroic mission" was central to Nazi ideology, the cult of Stalin was more a parasitic growth that the dictator's successors got rid of as soon as they came to power. Conscious of being remote from the original Leninist model, Stalin had not ceased to build a historical legitimacy by writing his own hagiography, rewriting the history of Bolshevism, and constructing his vision of a system centered on himself. He constantly tested each of his collaborator's degree of devotion, persecuting especially those who could have "unmasked" him, those who had retained the memory of Leninist Bolshevism's "heroic years" and could therefore reproach him for betraying the original doctrine, and those who in one way or another seemed to him superior in a given domain.[64] He "managed" his closest collaborators by using their least faults, examples including Kaganovich for his ties to a General Iaki, who was executed for an alleged "military plot"; Molotov for alleged embezzlement by his wife, Paulina Zhemchuzhina, people's commissary of the fishery industry, who was dismissed from her functions in November 1939 and then exiled; and Mikoyan because he had been the only one out of the twenty-six Bolshevik commissaries of Baku not executed by the British in 1920.[65] The places left vacant by purges at the Party's top levels were distributed by Stalin among a new generation of the "promoted," who all owed everything to the dictator and who had no memory of the Leninist past: Beria (named as people's commissary of the interior in November 1938 at the age of thirty-nine), Malenkov (at thirty-six named to head the all-important directorship of Central Committee cadres), Ivan Voznesensky (named as president of Gosplan at the age of thirty-six and first vice president of the People's Council of Commissaries at thirty-eight), and Chcherbakov (named as first secretary of Moscow's Party organization at the age of thirty-eight).

Did the reorganizations in the highest echelons of power and the upheavals in political personnel and administrative cadres during the great purges of 1937–38 result in a more normal functioning of the State-Party? Did they reflect an end to the tensions between the bureaucratic strategies and the despotic approach? Even if we now have a better understanding of the process and tensions at work in the building of the Stalinist state and the mode of government during the 1930s (thanks to some of the recent research based on the newly accessible archives), the events that took place during and after

World War II remain largely in the shadows. After the climactic phase of the Great Terror, how did the deeply overhauled administrations (directed by the *vydvizhentsi* [the "promoted"] of the First Five-Year Plan, this new elite to which, at the Eighteenth Party Congress in March 1939, Stalin had assured that there would no longer be a threat) function? What were the terms of agreement of the "Big Deal" (to borrow the now-classic expression of historian Vera Dunham) between a Stalinist state aspiring to stability and the new service elite, including the functions, privileges, and hierarchies codified in the new "rankings," not to mention the tsarist regime's *tchiny*?[66] After the great purges, was the transformation of those proliferating, stubborn, and inefficient administrations of the 1930s effectively realized into an order-following bureaucracy assuring proper transmittal of the central authority's decisions? These are some of the questions that no recent study based on the newly available documentation has been able to answer fully.

The tremors of the Great Terror, far from reducing the proliferating bureaucracies, paradoxically increased the number of administrative posts of all sorts. Thus between 1937 and 1939, while the population actively involved in industry increased by a mere 2 percent, administrative positions and political supervisory staff[67] increased by 26 percent (this figure grew past 50 percent in regard to key positions).[68] As Max Weber remarked, once planted, bureaucracy belongs to a species of social formation that is very difficult to uproot. Until the war the harm caused by the upheavals of the Great Terror was surely greater than the benefits the directors hoped to get from a completely renovated and better-educated staff who would have a "100 percent Stalinist" political background—a terrorized and thus order-following personnel. Witness, for example, the 1940–41 crisis that spanned military training (the newly promoted had a dramatic lack of experience),[69] justice, and diplomacy.[70] Among the economic cadres the situation appears to have been less unfavorable, given that the newly promoted generally had skills superior to the *praktiki* of the preceding generation, largely decimated by the purges. During these years, even the Gulag's daily management and economic role was profoundly disrupted by various internal reorganizations due to the abrupt growth in its numbers.[71] In some ways the tremors of 1937–38 reproduced mechanisms analogous to those that had induced *nolens volens* the turmoil of the Great Retreat. But to a large extent the system's adaptation to perturbations and shocks throughout the years was an integral part of its mode of functioning. As shown by the extraordinary capacity of the system to overcome the ordeal of the war, the "administrative system of command" established in the 1930s during a state of emergency, improvisation, continuous purges, and violence had learned how to function under "severe conditions."

As many historians have long emphasized, the contrast between the "revolutionary" Stalinism of the 1930s and the wartime and postwar "second" Stalinism is obviously great. The first is characterized by excess, "outrageousness," the refusal of any stabilization, an ongoing delegitimization of social positions, and (as discussed above) the severe tensions between the two strategies of power, which generated the confrontations that peaked in 1937–38. The second is conservative and nationalist, marked by the resurgence of "archaic," regressive, and reactionary elements such as xenophobia, "Great Russia" chauvinism, and anti-Semitism. It aspires to a greater stability. According to Moshe Lewin, this post-1930s Stalinism even reveals the existence of "forces concerned with stability and legality," those same forces that would enable the regime "to evolve into a tranquil bureaucratic system topped by an institutionalized oligarchy" after the death of Stalin.[72] The few studies on administrative functioning during the postwar years reveal the effective emergence of elements of continuous stability.[73] These elements secured less chaotic and steadier operations through more-predictable institutions. They confirmed the slow yet real progress of centralization. They also showed the way for setting up centralized means of controlling and directing local agents and of more effectively shattering "localism" through management generally regularized and supervised by the Career Center for Functionaries. Taking into account that this picture emerges from fragmentary research, it nevertheless remains contrastive: the stability of cadres and the professionalization of careers were certainly stronger than prior to the war in sectors such as justice. But in other sectors the practices of the 1930s were perpetuated: the supervision of kolkhozes, where the administration had to manage the strongest tensions between the regime and society; the purges; the arrests; the ill-timed mobilizations; and the sending of plenipotentiaries to take over for local functionaries whom the central authorities distrusted. Likewise the apparent "routinization" of postwar Stalinism, its capacity for stabilization reinforced by victory in the Second World War,[74] would not cause the tensions, maneuvers, and countermaneuvers at the Party's highest levels to disappear: witness some of the still poorly elucidated "affairs" (for example, the Leningrad and Mingrelie affairs) that developed in a context of final struggles between the various Stalinist "clans" in anticipation of the dictator's succession. This "second" Stalinism undoubtedly remains an extensive field of exploration for historians.

Translated by Thomas C. Hilde

Notes

1. Robert Conquest. *Inside Stalin's Secret Police*. Stanford, Stanford University Press, 1985, p. 3.

2. Merle Fainsod. *Smolensk à l'heure de Stalin*. Paris, Fayard, 1967, p. 27. This rather abrupt conclusion is largely inconsistent with Fainsod's remarkable field research emphasizing that "the impression one gets from the archives is that of chaotic disorder where the Communist Party appeared more as a defenseless victim than the master of a cataclysm it had triggered."

3. Among the most significant works developing this version of the facts, which nevertheless have differences of interpretation regarding the "factions" and "trends" at the Politburo, are John Arch Getty. *Origins of the Great Purges: The Soviet CP Reconsidered, 1933–1938*. Cambridge, Cambridge University Press, 1985; Gabor T. Ritterspoon. *Simplifications staliniennes et complications soviétiques, 1933–1953*. Paris, EAC, 1988; and John Arch Getty and R. T. Manning, eds. *Stalinist Terror: New Perspectives*. Cambridge, Cambridge University Press, 1993.

4. According to Gabor Ritterspoon, the Great Terror, far from consolidating Stalin's dictatorial power, had led to its relative weakening. "Staline en 1938: Apogée du verbe et défaite politique," chap. 4 of op. cit., pp. 211–260. For a similar point of view, see Getty and Manning, op. cit.

5. Alain Blum and Catherine Gousseff. "La Statistique démographique et sociale: Élément pour une analyse historique de l'état russe et soviétique." *Cahiers du monde russe*, vol. 38, no. 4, October–December 1997, p. 443.

6. See Oleg Khlevniuk. *1937—Stalin, NKVD I sovetskoie obscestvo* (1937: Stalin, the NKVD, and Soviet society). Moscow, 1992; idem. *Stalin I Ordjonikidze, konflikty v Politburo v 30-ye gody* (Stalin and Ordzhonikidze: Conflicts at the Politburo during the 1930s). Moscow, 1994; Oleg Khlevniuk and A. Kvachonkine, eds. *Stalinskoie Politburo v 1930-ye gody: Sbornik dokumentov* (The Stalinist Politburo during the 1930s: A collection of documents). Moscow, 1995; and Oleg Khlevniuk. *Le Cercle du Kremlin: Staline et le bureau politique dans les années 30. Les jeux du pouvoir*. Paris, Seuil, 1996.

7. David R. Shearer. *Industry, State, and Society in Stalin's Russia, 1926–1934*. Ithaca, Cornell University Press, 1996; R. W. Davies. *Crisis and Progress in 1932–1933 Soviet Economy*. London, Macmillan, 1996; D. Rees. *Stalinism and Soviet Rail Transport*. London, University of Birmingham Press; New York, St. Martin's, 1995; Alain Blum. "À l'origine des purges de 1937: L'Exemple de l'administration de la statistique démographique." *Cahiers du monde russe*, vol. 39, nos. 1–2, January–June 1998, pp. 169–196; Peter H. Solomon. *Soviet Criminal Justice under Stalin*. Cambridge, Cambridge University Press, 1996; Sabine Dullin. "Diplomates et diplomaties soviétiques en Europe (1930–1939)." Ph.D. diss., University of Paris-I, 1998.

8. This observation has been sketched from fragmentary data by Moshe Lewin, particularly in his articles "The Social Background of Stalinism" and "Grappling

with Stalinism," translated into French and collected with other essays by Lewin in *La Formation du sytème soviétique*. Paris, Gallimard, 1987.

9. Moshe Lewin. "Bureaucracy and the Stalinist State." In *Stalinism and Nazism: Dictatorships in Comparison*, ed. Ian Kershaw and Moshe Lewin. Cambridge, Cambridge University Press, 1997, p. 67.

10. As such, a Politburo circular dated May 5, 1927, makes clear the absolute necessity of secrecy in political affairs: "the old tried and tested conspiratorial principle means that only those people who need to know do know."

11. This prohibition constituted one of the key points of the Tenth Party Congress, which adopted the New Economic Politics in March 1921.

12. S. Kvachonkine, O. Khlevniuk, L. Rogovaia, and L. Kocheleva, eds. *Bolshevitskoie rukovodstvo: Perepiska, 1912–1927* (The Bolshevik leadership: Correspondence, 1912–1927). Moscow, 1996.

13. *XVII S'ezd VKP (b): Stenograficeskii otcet* (Seventeenth Congress of the RCP(b): Stenographic record). Moscow, 1934, pp. 34–35.

14. D. Brower. "The Smolensk Scandal and the End of the NEP." *Slavic Review*, vol. 45, no. 4, 1986, pp. 689–706; T. H. Rigby. "Early Provincial Cliques and the Rise of Stalin." *Soviet Studies*, vol. 33, no. 1, 1981, pp. 3–28.

15. John Arch Getty. "Les Bureaucrates bolcheviques et l'état stalinien." *Revue des études slaves*, vol. 64, no. 1, 1992, pp. 27–52.

16. Sheila Fitzpatrick. "Stalin and the Making of a New Elite." *Slavic Review*, vol. 38, September 1979, p. 378.

17. It is not without interest to note how certain themes developed here by Bukharin regarding the bureaucratization of the Politburo agree with certain theses advanced a few years earlier by Trotsky in *The New Course*. New York, New International, 1943.

18. Lewin, *La Formation*; idem. "The Disappearance of Planning in the Plan." *Slavic Review*, vol. 32, no. 2, 1973, pp. 271–287; Sheila Fitzpatrick. "Sergo Ordzhonikidze and the Takeover of the VSNKH." *Soviet Studies*, vol. 36, no. 2, 1985, pp. 153–172.

19. Shearer, op. cit.

20. Sergo Ordzhonikidze, people's commissar of workers' and peasants' inspection, then of heavy industry, was surprised by the fact that "every time reductions in personnel were decreed, the operation ended up increasing spending and personnel." *Stati i retchi*. Moscow, 1934, vol. 1, p. 228.

21. An expression fashionable in the 1930s for designating the increase in the number of official documents inundating the administrations. Lewin, *La Formation*, p. 31.

22. Peter Solomon qualifies the justice of these years as "campaign justice." Op. cit., pp. 81–110.

23. The famous circular was dated May 8, 1933, and secretly sent to all the organizations of the Party, the GPU, and the public prosecutor's office. It recognized that

arrests could be made by "anyone at all," according to the principle of "arrest first, ask questions later." The directive required that the number of people detained in prisons (with the exception of the forced-labor camps and colonies) decrease by half within a period of six months and not exceed 400,000 people.

24. On these well-known aspects, see the pioneering works of Sheila Fitzpatrick: *Education and Social Mobility in the Soviet Union, 1921–1934.* Cambridge, Cambridge University Press, 1979; and *The Cultural Front: Power and Culture in Revolutionary Russia.* Ithaca NY, Cornell University Press, 1992. See also K. F. Bailes, *Technology and Society under Lenin and Stalin: Origins of the Soviet Technical Intelligentsia.* Princeton: Princeton University Press, 1978; and N. Lampert, *The Technical Intelligentsia and the Soviet State.* New York, Oxford University Press, 1979.

25. Some numbers illustrate the magnitude of the phenomenon: 3,000 engineers arrested in 1928–1929 in the Donbass; 5,000 to 7,000 functionaries and cadres arrested in 1930 in the central economic administration; 4,500 railways functionaries arrested in 1930–1931 for "sabotage," including 1,300 engineers (around 25 percent of all cadres at this level); 140,000 functionaries dismissed during the purge of administrations in 1930; plus another 153,000 in 1932–1933. At the same time more than 140,000 workers were promoted "on the job" to administrative positions in 1929–1931. In 1933, 233,000 Communists, mainly adults, were involved full time in specialized secondary studies or higher, more than two-thirds of whom were in engineering. This was the generation of Brezhnev, Kosygin, and Ustinov; in short, of the Politburo of the CPSU during the 1960s and 1970s.

26. [*Trans.* The term "promoted" is from the Russian *vydvizhentsi.* The term has a rather negative connotation. It derives from the verb *vydvigat,* which literally means "to move out, pull out, push forward, bring forward, advance, promote." Formally, *vydvizhentsi* means "a worker promoted to an administrative post," however, in a Stalinist context this term refers to a worker (not necessarily bright or talented) who is given the opportunity to "move out" very quickly by joining the party. *Vydvizhentsi* were the "very quickly promoted" because somebody had to take the posts of arrested professionals and intellectuals. The whole system of worker promotion to positions of authority survived until the final days of the Soviet Union, so the term has a rich history. It still sounds negative to a Russian ear. Thanks to Evgenia Cherkasova for this explanation.]

27. Report by Malenkov to Stalin, February 14, 1937, cited in Khlevniuk, *1937,* p. 78.

28. CRCEDHC, 74/2/37/58.

29. For some enlightening examples, see the letters of Stalin and Kaganovich during 1931–33, CRCEDHC, 81/3/99 and 100; Voroshilov and Stalin, CRCEDHC, 74/2/37 and 38; and Ordzhonikidze and Molotov, CRCEDHC, 85/28/440 and following. Regarding the correspondence between Stalin and Kaganovich, see Yves Cohen, "Des Lettres comme action: Staline au début des années 1930 vu depuis le fonds Kaganovich." *Cahiers du monde russe,* vol. 38, no. 3, July–September 1997, pp. 307–346.

30. This is how Poschyev, a Politburo member sent to Kharkov to instill some order into local affairs, defined "the Bolshevik art of governing." Cited in Lewin, *La Formation*, p. 342.

31. For another example of these "local cliques" and their grip on local political life, see Stephen Kotkin, *Magnetic Mountain: Stalinism as Civilization*. Berkeley, University of California Press, 1995, esp. chap. 7 (pp. 280–354).

32. H. Kuromiya, "The Commander and the Rank and File: Managing the Soviet Coal-Mining Industry, 1928–1933." In *Social Dimensions of Soviet Industrialization*, eds. W. G. Rosenberg and L. H. Siegelbaum. Bloomington, Indiana University Press, 1993, pp. 146–165.

33. See Stalin to Molotov, September 22, 1930, in *Pisma I. V. Stalina V. M. Molotovu, 1925–1936* (Letters from Stalin to Molotov, 1925–1936). Moscow, 1995, pp. 222–223.

34. The Executive Committee for Decision Making, replacing the Council of Assistants, which was done away with in December 1930; the Defense Commission (including Stalin, Molotov, Voroshilov, Kouibychev, Ordzhonikidze), replacing the Council of Labor and Defense, composed of tens of members; and the Currency Commission. Throughout the 1930s other limited commissions would gradually replace the Politburo, which was reduced to a simple office of records for decisions taken by Stalin.

35. Each year between 3,000 and 4,000 topics were placed on the agenda of the Politburo; that is to say between 200 and 400 topics per meeting, taking into account the steadily decreasing number of meetings. A large number of these matters would have been treated by the appropriate administrations without reaching the higher authorities, if Stalin had been less interventionist.

36. For example, fewer and fewer people received Politburo protocols for their information. Thus the members of the Central Committee were only rarely informed about the decisions made. One example: of the 163 topics appearing formally (the decisions had been made privately by Stalin) in Protocol No. 65 of November 22, 1938, only four were passed on—as information—to the members of the Central Committee. On the "culture of conspiracy," see Gabor T. Ritterspoon, "The Omnipresent Conspiracy: On Soviet Imagery, Politics, and Social Relations in the 1930s." In *The Stalinist Dictatorship*, ed. C. Ward. Oxford, Arnold, 1998.

37. In this regard we can cite some key excerpts from Stalin's letters. "That the Politburo control systematically and especially the People's Commissariat of Transportation and the People's Commissariat of River Transportation and require them to work as Bolsheviks. These two commissariats are within the scope of the apparatchiks and, in particular, Rukhimovich's clique." Stalin to Kaganovich, August 30, 1931, CRCEDHC, 81/3/99/13–14. "Things are going very badly in the area of artillery. Mirsokhanov botched a magnificent factory. Pavlunovski destroyed the artillery. Ordzhonikidze must be given a scolding for having trusted two or three of his favorites. He was ready to give state benefits to these imbeciles. These bureaucrats, the Mirsokhanovs and Pavlunovskis, must all be driven out." Stalin to Kaganovich,

October 21, 1933, CRCEDHC, 81/3/100/38–39. "The People's Commissary of Foreign Affairs must be whipped for his blindness, his short-sightedness, his bureaucratism." Stalin to Kaganovich, August 8, 1934, CRCEDHC, 81/3/100/158. On Stalin's attitude toward "bureaucrats," see Cohen, op. cit.

38. The closest translation of *vedomstvennost* would be "bureaucratism."

39. Kaganovich cited in Oleg Khlevniuk, *Politburo: Mexanizmy politiceskoï vlasti v 1930-ye gody* (The Politburo: Mechanisms of political power during the 1930s). Moscow, Rosspen, 1996, p. 84.

40. Stalin to Kaganovich, September 19, 1931, cited in Cohen, op. cit., p. 336.

41. Khlevniuk, *Le Cercle du Kremlin*, p. 123.

42. In 1931 the members of the Politburo spent a total of around 650 hours during the year in Stalin's office (Kaganovich consulted with Stalin for 167 hours, Molotov for 126 hours, Tchoubar for thirty minutes, etc.). In 1935 the Politburo members were received for nearly 1,400 hours during the year (Molotov met with Stalin for 315 hours, Kaganovich for 261 hours, Ordzhonikidze for 218 hours, Voroshilov for 198 hours, etc.). In 1937 they were received in Stalin's office for more than 2,700 hours during the year (Molotov spent 602 hours, Ezhov 527 hours, Voroshilov 438 hours, and Kaganovich 406 hours, but M. Kalinin spent only 32 hours, etc.). For the complete tables of Stalin's visitors, see Khlevniuk, *Politburo*, p. 290 ff.

43. *Stalinskoie Politburo*, p. 126.

44. Regarding this episode, see Khlevniuk, *Le Cercle du Kremlin*, pp. 95–97. One could cite numerous other areas of a "technical" nature, such as the import plans for cast-iron pipes or the construction plans for this or that factory, which Stalin followed to even the most minute of details if he judged that they "shed light on" some crucial political question.

45. Blum, op. cit., p. 174.

46. Dullin, op. cit., chap. 10.

47. On this point see Stalin's telegrams, starting in October 1936, to the Soviet diplomatic representatives in Spain. What they show is a well-affirmed interpretation of the Spanish Republican losses as due to being victims of their own ineptitude at eliminating spies within their ranks. Oleg Khlevniuk, "The Influence of the Foreign Context on the Mechanisms of Terror" (paper from the colloquium "La Russia nell'eta delle guerre (1914–1945): Verso un nuovo paradigma," Cortona, October 24, 1997). This interpretation reveals the Stalinist obsession with a "fifth column," potentially present in the USSR itself. Its necessary elimination is at the heart of the Great Terror trials instituted after the nomination of N. Ezhov to the post of people's commissar of the interior at the end of September 1936. It was a matter of eliminating all potential representatives—both social and political—of a mythical fifth column.

48. Significantly, of the 823 directors enrolled in 1936 in the nomenklatura of the People's Commissariat of Heavy Industry (directed by Ordzhonikidze), 169 had belonged to non-Bolshevik political groups, 160 had never belonged to any political

party, 71 had served in the White Army and 287 in the tsarist army (before 1917), and 334 were of noble or bourgeois social origin. This is to say that a large majority of these directors were eminently suspect from the moment the police-based vision of politics triumphed.

49. There was a distinct contrast between the Ordzhonikidze of 1929–1930—people's commissary of workers' and peasants' inspection and sworn enemy of bureaucrats in the Supreme Council of the National Economy—and the Ordzhonikidze of 1934–1936—people's commissary of heavy industry, who exhorted business directors "to work calmly, without letting a frenetic rhythm develop" and who was firmly opposed to the "constant top to bottom reorganizations of industrial administrations." On the Stalin/Ordzhonikidze conflicts and their interpretation, see Shearer, op. cit., pp. 234–242; Khlevniuk, *Stalin I Ordjonikidze*; and Fitzpatrick, "Sergo Ordzhonikidze and the Takeover of VSNKH."

50. Nikolaienko, a simple Party militant, had denounced the "anti-Party machinations" of the wife of Pavel Poschyev, first secretary of the Communist organization in Kiev and a deputy member of the Politburo. For this reason she was excluded from the Party. On the Nikolaienko affair, see Robert Conquest, *La Grande Terreur.* Paris, Laffont, 1995, pp. 557–558; and Khlevniuk, *Le Cercle de Kremlin*, pp. 233–236. On Stalin's populist strategies, see Nicholas Werth, "L'Appel au petit peuple selon Staline." *Vingtième Siècle: Revue d'histoire*, no. 56, October–December 1997 (special issue, "Les Populismes"), pp. 132–142.

51. *Bolshevik*, 1937, no. 7, p. 24.

52. The expression is Moshe Lewin's. See *La Formation*, p. 401.

53. The political maneuvers involving Stalin and the GPU in the hunt for Trotskyist opposition members during the 1920s and 1930s are well enough known. Recent studies have shed light on other operations mounted by Stalin and the GPU not only against opposition from the "right" but also against Kalinin, Tukhachevski, and other directors faithful to the "Stalinist line."

54. After the suicide of N. Allilueva, Stalin confided entirely in the services of the GPU for taking care of his home. In her memoirs Stalin's daughter Svetlana Allilueva recalls that, after this episode, the political police played a steadily increasing role in Stalin's personal life. Svetlana Allilueva, *Twenty Letters to a Friend.* London, 1979, pp. 138–143.

55. This calculation is based on the entry register of Stalin's office. *Istoriceskii Arxiv*, no. 6, 1994; and nos. 2–6, 1995. During this period, only Molotov was received more often by Stalin.

56. On these matters, see Nicholas Werth's chapters in the present volume.

57. *XVIII Siezd VKP (b)*, pp. 675–676.

58. Fainsod, op. cit., and more recently Getty, op. cit., have mainly developed this aspect. On this question the example of the Smolensk region is particularly revealing: after the arrest of Rumiantsev, the regional "little Stalin," and his team (in July 1937), all newly named directors were Communist leaders from the Moscow

organization, young Party cadres educated in the Party's training colleges throughout the first half of the 1930s. An analogous process took place in nearly all regional and city committees of the Party.

59. Dullin, op. cit., pp. 592–596.

60. In 1937 the Politburo met six times; in 1938, three times; and in 1939, only two times.

61. This included Rudzutak, Eikhe, Poschyev, Kossior, Tchoubar, and Ezhov.

62. On the reorganizations of the Party's and state's most top-level authorities after the Great Terror, see Oleg Khlevniuk, *Le Cercle du Kremlin*, pp. 266–276.

63. Kershaw and Lewin, op. cit. See, in particular, Kershaw, "Working towards the Führer: Reflections on the Nature of the Hitler Dictatorship," pp. 88–106; and Lewin, "Stalin in the Mirror of the Other."

64. This last aspect was well evidenced by Nikolai Bukharin. During a meeting in Paris with the Menshevik director Fyodor Dan at the beginning of 1936 (this was the last trip abroad for Bukharin, who was arrested in February 1937, judged in March 1938 during the third trial in Moscow, and executed on March 14, 1938), Bukharin explained that "the greatest problem for Stalin is to be able to convince us all—and himself—that he is a greater man than all of us. This is maybe his only human trait. That which is no longer human in him, but truly diabolical, is that he cannot keep himself from avenging this 'problem' on anyone who is better off than him, more gifted. . . . If someone is a better orator than he is, this is the same as saying that this man is condemned, for he is a constant reminder to Stalin that he is not the best, that he is not first." Conversation between Nikolai Bukharin and Fyodor Dan, Archives of the Institute of Social History, Amsterdam, cited in *Osmyslit' Kult' Stalina* (Understanding the Stalinist cult). Moscow, Progress, 1989, p. 610.

65. One could multiply the examples of the pressures and humiliation to which Stalin's close collaborators were submitted toward the end of the 1930s. The spouse of Kalinin (president of the Supreme Soviet of the USSR) was arrested and sent to the camps; Molotov had to chastise himself at the Eighteenth Party Congress (March 1939). As Bukharin stated with the utmost clarity in 1936, Stalin had become the symbol of the Party to Communist leaders, the incarnation of the march of history. Nothing he did could be called into question. "You do not understand," Bukharin explained to the Menshevik leader Fyodor Dan, who had asked him why Stalin evoked such fascination, "our confidence is not in him, but in the man who has the confidence of the Party. It happened in this way. He became a sort of symbol of the Party, the poor people, the workers, and the people believe in him. It is our fault, no doubt. It is why we are all entering his gaping mouth, knowing full well that he will devour us all. He knows it well and awaits the right moment for devouring us all." Conversation between Bukharin and Fyodor Dan in G. M. Ivanova. *Gulag v sisteme totalitarnogo gosudarstva* (The Gulag in the totalitarian state system). Moscow, Ed. MONF, 1997.

66. Vera Dunham, *In Stalin's Time: Middleclass Values in Soviet Fiction.* Durham NC, Duke University Press, 1990.

67. Not including resulting relevant jobs in economic administration, education, or health care.

68. Lewin, "Bureaucracy and the Stalinist State," p. 64.

69. Recent research on the purges in the Red Army mention a less considerable ratio of purged officers (in 1937–1938) than generally believed, around 15 percent (and not 40–50 percent). A. Cristiani and V. Mixaleva. *Le Repressioni degli anni trenta nell'armata rossa.* Naples, IUO, 1996; *Izvestia TsK,* 1990, no. 1, pp. 188–189; Getty and Manning, op. cit., pp. 199–201. Moreover a significant part of expelled officers (around 30 percent) were reinstated in 1940–1941, most notably because of the lack of qualified cadres.

70. Solomon, op. cit., pp. 230–266; T. J. Uldricks, "The Impact of the Great Purges on the People's Commissariat of Foreign Affairs." *Slavic Review,* June 1977, pp. 187–203.

71. Ivanova, op. cit., pp. 100–108.

72. Lewin, *La Formation,* p. 406.

73. On the functioning of the justice administration, see Solomon, op. cit. (note 7); on rural administration, see some aspects of Vladimir F. Zima. *Golod v SSSR 1946–1947 godov: proizhozdenie i posledstvia.* Moscow, 1996. On the penitentiary administration, see Ivanova, op. cit.

74. Precisely what was lacking in Nazism in the obviously unique historical context of the war years. See Hans Mommsen, "Cumulative Radicalization and Progressive Self-Destruction as Structural Determinants of the Nazi Dictatorship," in Kershaw and Lewin, op. cit., pp. 75–87.

Philippe Burrin

Charisma and Radicalism in the Nazi Regime

The Nazi regime, from its inception, has evoked lively debate about its structure and nature. Although most contemporary observers have held it to be the dictatorship of one man, others, especially on the Left, have judged as fallacious the image that the Third Reich projected, above all through the annual congress of the Nazi Party in Nuremberg, that is, the image of a regime dominated solely by one man who inspires and directs it at will like some well-regulated machine. Some of these critics have pointed to stage managers in the wings: the Junkers, high finance, and the German elite. Others have spoken about conflicts between "hard liners" and "moderates" and of an eventual settling of scores between the army and the Party, with Hitler being led in every possible direction.[1]

The discussion has never truly ended since then, even if, for the public, the absolute power of Hitler has remained a basic truth, nurtured by so many biographies, documentaries, and films. Yet among historians, the question has enjoyed a formidable comeback since the 1970s, the starting point for the debate between the "Intentionalist" and "Functionalist" schools of thought. The debate has dealt with Hitler's role: did he decide about everything, was he even the principal actor? And regarding the running of the regime, did it follow a dynamic that was driven and controlled from above, or the dynamic that was uncontrollable and unpredictable? Although the debate is not presently as intense as it has been in the past, it has continued to nurture the approaches of historians and to restore complexity to the analysis of a regime that one should remember was slowly constructed and did evolve over time.[2]

The first part of this chapter thus examines the place and role of Hitler at the heart of the Nazi regime, with an analysis of his formal powers, the basis for his authority, and the manner in which he used it. It also discusses the running of the regime, with its enthusiastic supporters and administrative structure. It then deals with the question of the regime's dynamic and, necessarily, of its radicalization.

The centrality of Hitler is not just an artifice of Goebbels's propaganda, and rare are those historians who would question that he occupied an essential place in the regime. Thus this analysis deals less with his power than with its very limits. How can one in effect deny its reality? Although Hitler was not the founder of the National Socialist Party, he did take it over in the early

1920s and rather easily succeeded in getting rid of recurring opposition. It was he who crystallized the doctrine of the movement in *Mein Kampf*, with elements, of course, that were the bread and butter of the extreme Right in Germany ever since the end of the nineteenth century, but he brought them together within a synthesis that he intended to be ideological, political, and strategic. It was Hitler, finally, who led the Nazi Party to power by ably exploiting the crisis of the Weimar Republic.

After 1933 his authority became immense on both the formal and informal levels. The stages that marked the accumulation of formal powers are well known. Named chancellor in January 1933, Hitler seized the office of head of state the day following the death of Hindenburg in August 1934. And he had the armed forces publicly swear their support for him, an oath that was addressed to his person, as Führer, and not only as the bearer of constitutional authority. In 1938 he became de facto minister of war and then, at the end of 1941, commander in chief of the army. To these powers we should add the informal authority he derived from the popularity he enjoyed that, with time, became nothing short of amazing, reaching its peak in the summer of 1940 with the victory over France.

However one may see it, the person of Hitler is identified with the Nazi regime and the National Socialist Party. One can rightly state that Nazism cannot be dissociated from Hitlerism, something that is difficult to affirm for Bolshevism and Stalinism. Hitler never had to present himself as the dauphin and successor of some grand personage nor claim for himself a doctrine considered to be a tradition, with its own founding fathers and epigones. Rather he presented himself as someone sent by Providence, a Messiah whom the German people had been expecting for centuries, even for two thousand years, as Heinrich Himmler enjoyed saying.[3]

So here we have a man who holds immense power, but how does he use it? This is a legitimate question, and historians who are not satisfied with the interpretation of an all-powerful Hitler have explored it in two different directions, which do not exclude each other. One questions Hitler's aptitude for decision making and effective political power. The other looks at the constraints of a system that limited his sphere of control and even reduced it.

We begin with the limits of a power that came from the very nature of the regime. A first interpretation of a structural type was formulated by a contemporary of the time, the German Franz Neumann, who had sought refuge in England. This jurist and political analyst of Marxist inspiration set forth in his book *Behemoth*, finished in 1941 and published the following year, the strongest criticism of the unitary image projected by the Third Reich.[4] What he observed was the fundamental pluralism of a regime that was torn between forces that, behind a façade so polished through propaganda, ferociously struggled to take over the traditional prerogatives of the state. As a result of this, the classic state, Prussia, disappeared to the advantage of "four centralized and compact groups, each functioning according to the principle of authority and each enjoying its own administrative, judiciary and legislative powers."[5] Despite their rivalries, Neumann added, these groups of divergent interests and increasing powers—the Party, the army, the bureaucracy, and heavy industry—knew how to make peace and compromises, and Hitler limited himself to their recognition. That is what the concept of polyarchy refers to, though here with an ironic twist. Used by Carl Schmitt in the 1920s to denounce the evolution of the democratic regime toward a juxtaposition of institutions that would remove themselves from a single power that would control and decide,[6] it is used by Neumann against a dictatorship that claimed to have restored this unity of power, a government to which Schmitt brought, moreover, his zealous support. The biblical figure of Behemoth, borrowed from Thomas Hobbes, symbolizes the chaos engendered by the disappearance of the state and the total absence of laws, the opposite figure to the "Leviathan," which Hobbes preferred.

Neumann's interpretation, which was to influence decisively the entire functionalist school, is on target in underlining the plurality of the Nazi regime, which comes from the fact that the latter did not intend to bring about a social revolution, as did Bolshevism, but rather a political revolution through stages, and whose aim was power and expansion. To do this Hitler needed the cooperation of high-level administrators, industrialists, and the army. In fact it was the alliance with the conservative elites that allowed him to become the head of a government at the heart of which he was a minority. Then he was able to consolidate his power before gradually increasing it, thanks to his popularity and to his party of the masses, once he had eliminated the plurality that came from free association, labor unions, and political parties. This cooperation of the conservative elites marks the structuring of the regime in a manner that has no equivalent in dictatorships of the Bolshevik type.

Thus, different from Lenin and his comrades, Hitler came to power in a country that was provided with an experienced, developed, and structured administration and that enjoyed a strong esprit de corps. His problem was not that of reconstructing a state and of replacing an administration that was socially suspect and, in any case, quite inferior to the new tasks that the Bolshevik regime was to assign to it. His goal was to guarantee the cooperation of an effective bureaucracy, without becoming its hostage, by having it serve his politics. It was the same for the economic world, whose professional associations were politically aligned and administratively supervised but at the same time retained a degree of autonomy.

Neumann's analysis is nevertheless somewhat schematic (not to mention the excessive importance it gives to "big money" and to its own underestimation of Nazi anti-Semitism). On the one hand, Neumann endows the four forces that he favored with a cohesion and homogeneity that nothing proves they ever truly had. He transfers the unity that he deconstructs at the state level to a lower level, and he does so without any further analysis. Yet he does not take into account the different churches, the principal element of pluralism that continued to exist and that the Nazi regime had to tolerate, grudgingly, until the end. The other forces were far from having such cohesiveness. The unity of the industrialists suffered from dispersion, even from the contradiction of the interests of its members. The unity of the armed forces was weakened after the reestablishment of the universal military draft in 1935 by the influx of new leaders who were younger and more devoted to the regime. The bureaucracy, including the higher administration, no longer acted as a bloc, moving between zeal and reticence according to the policies that it had to implement. As for the Nazi Party, which had become the only legal political organization, its role remained limited, not only because of the few areas of influence that were handed over to it (Rudolf Hess, Hitler's replacement as head of the Party, was named minister without portfolio with a right of control over the naming of higher functionaries and legislative work) but also, and especially, on account of its structure. Quite different from the parties of the Bolshevik type, the Nazi Party was neither centralized nor even seriously coordinated. After 1933 its sections, beginning with the ss (*Schutzstaffel*, the Nazi special police), continued to jockey in order to get away from the control of the weak administration in Munich, and they easily succeeded with Hitler's support.[7]

On the other hand, this interpretation, if it is somewhat valid for the first years of the regime, when the alliance with the conservative forces established a semblance of polyarchy, hardly accounts for the displacement of the balance of power that only increased with time. Hitler rather easily succeeded in controlling his allies, thanks to the use he made of Nazi Party organizations: the Labor Front replaced labor unions and worked against employers; the sa (*Sturmabteilung*, the Nazi storm troopers) and then the ss competed against the army; and everywhere regional directors of the Party imposed themselves at administrative levels. Then there was a progressive alignment of the conservative forces, gradually disillusioned that the regime would ever respond to their desire for a tempered restoration of order and authority. It is true that German elitist groups suffered from a weakness that made them relatively unstable. The abolition of the monarchy, the imposition of a rump army by the Treaty of Versailles, and the leveling of the landed classes through hyperinflation and then through the depression of the 1930s all undermined the Weimar Republic and worked to weaken the conservative elites after 1933. Because they remained under his yoke, although not without some rebellion (thus was seen the attempt on the Führer's life in July 1944), Hitler used them all the more willingly as the war imposed its own priorities. But he never lost sight of the objective he had of forming new elites that would assure the continuity of his regime.

A second interpretation, presented particularly by Martin Broszat,[8] continues the line of thought outlined by Neumann, but as it takes some distance from an analysis in terms of social forces, it gets much closer to the administrative organization. Attentive to the evolution of the regime, Broszat places a break in 1938 that separates, broadly speaking, an authoritarian phase from a totalitarian one. Before 1938, mainly because of the importance of the conservatives, the regime opted for continuity: there was a collegial context for decisions and a coordinated operation of the administration. With the elimination of the last representatives of the conservative elites (the removal of Hjalmar Schacht in 1937 and the departure of Werner von Blomberg and Konstantin von Neurath from the government in 1938), the turning point was the suspension of cabinet meetings and the resulting disappearance of all governmental coordination (the ministerial Council for the Defense of the Reich created for this at the beginning of the war soon sunk into insignificance because of Hitler's lack of interest).

The end of governmental collegiality formed the logical end to an evolution whose main characteristic was a growing recourse to the delegation of powers that Hitler had practiced without regard for the administrative unity of the state. From this there resulted a situation characterized by the multiplication of special bodies, the hybridization of administrative machinery, the autonomization of policies, and the exacerbation of institutional and personal rivalries.

The delegation of powers ended up effectively multiplying some special administrative organizations, to which Hitler assigned the implementation of a particular mission by granting, with this end in view, all the necessary powers. Some of these arrangements were of a functional nature—the construction of highways, the Four Year Plan, the recruitment of a work force throughout occupied Europe, and others. Their appearance evidently meant an encroachment on the powers of public authority, but it often also took on the form of a predation or of an administrative hybridization. When the Gauleiter Fritz Sauckel was given the mission of finding workers throughout Europe essential to the war economy, he constructed his apparatus by taking the Department of Manual Labor away from the Ministry of the Economy. Hybridization was produced between state organisms and some organizations of the Party, as when Himmler amalgamated the security services of the ss with the state police, or it occurred between state organisms and professional associations, as in the Four Year Plan and Albert Speer's machinery.

Other special measures had a territorial framework. After the outbreak of war, Hitler confided the administration of conquered territories to some of his lieutenants, to Gauleiter like Arthur Greiser or to *Reichsleiter* such as Alfred Rosenberg, by granting them extended powers. In the annexed territories, particularly in the Polish "corridor," the result was a quasi-removal of the regional administration from the control of the central ministries.[9]

The multiplication of special organizations could only exacerbate institutional and personal quarrels. Free rein was given to the politics of "to each his own," even for the traditional ministries, for such was henceforth the rules of a game in which much was to be gained and much lost. To become a pure executive instrument of the Führer was the objective that the logic of the regime imposed, and Himmler strongly pursued it, freeing himself successfully both from the state—as head of the police he was formally placed under the authority of the Ministry of the Interior—and from the Party—as ss chief he had to report to Nazi authorities in Munich.

By the effect of such a dynamic, the structure of the regime became mobile, reconfiguring itself according to certain priorities. One only has to compare the situation in 1935 with that of 1943 in economic matters, for example, to appreciate the extent of this plasticity. In the mid-1930s the Ministry of Economy controlled the conduct of business; by the mid-1940s its role had become minor. Three centers of power had emerged whose relations mixed rivalry and cooperation, the former winning out over the latter: the Ministry of Armament and Munitions directed by Speer, which functioned closely with heavy industry; the office of Sauckel, which controlled the contribution of the foreign workforce that had become crucial to the economy of the Reich; and Himmler's police organization, which developed a small economical empire, notably by capitalizing on the miserable workforce of prisoners in concentration camps.[10]

With the multiplication of these special groups cutting into the power and organization of the state, the structure of the Third Reich resembled a patchwork quilt fashioned out of traditional administrations and hybrid agencies between the state, the Party and private interests. This evokes what another exile, Ernst Fraenkel, had called the duality of the Nazi state (remember that Neumann questioned whether one could talk of a state), which was more the entanglement than the juxtaposition of a state of law and a special regime, the first existing only through the tolerance of the second, which sought to expand as much as possible to the former's detriment.[11]

To this malleability of the administrative organization of the Third Reich, complicated by the fact that its organisms, which had become superfluous, had never been done away with (thus the Four Year Plan), one should add an element that has often been neglected, a growing juridical informality. The making of laws respected forms less and less. The boundary between decree, edict, and law became blurred, and jurists themselves came to accept that an oral declaration of Hitler had the force of law (as when he designated Hermann Göring and Hess as his successors in a speech at the beginning of the war).[12] Still more serious and rather significant, legislation was less and less submitted to the principle of publicity, an indispensable condition of an efficient administration. Out of 650 orders, decrees, and written directives by Hitler that have been recorded for the 1939–45 period, 494 were not published in the *Journal officiel*.[13] One can imagine the confusion and litigation that resulted from this. Thus, through an unpublished decree, Himmler was charged in 1939 with the "strengthening of the German race," which gave him the power to seize the lands of any nonnative peoples residing in the annexed territories. Opposition was then voiced in the courts, which did not know about (for good reason) the decree in question. "Euthanasia," the putting to death of the mentally ill, beginning in autumn of 1939, also gave way to judiciary cases that obliged the Ministry of Justice to inform the judges of the existence of the secret order by which Hitler had authorized the process.

There can be no doubt that, with the Nazi regime, one is dealing with a structure *sui generis*, and functionalist historians willingly speak of disorder, even chaos. But if one can admit that it became difficult for the leaders of the Third Reich to have a general view and that it was necessary for them to expend ever more energy to maintain some kind of coherence, the regime remained (as I understand it) perfectly manageable. Bodies of coordination continued to exist, such as the Chancellery of the Reich and the Chancellery of the Party, and the most complicated dossiers were regularly the object of interministerial meetings that brought secretaries of state together. This was the case in Wannsee in January 1942, when the extermination of European Jews was organized.

The coordination was also assured, especially so, by Hitler himself. The disintegration of administrative unity in no way interfered with the concentration of all the different strands of authority in Hitler's hands. Instead of and in place of some kind of collegial body for deliberation and decision making, a modus operandi was set up by which about one hundred people became responsible and individually accountable to him alone.[14] Some directed traditional organizations, ministries, or the three defense services; others were in charge of special functions such as the administration of occupied and annexed territories; others still were regional directors of the Party—the Gauleiter—who traditionally enjoyed, by right, to call upon Hitler directly. If the immediate relationship with the Führer was the source of all power, this bilateral framework reinforced in return the authority of Hitler, who was quite conscious of it, as demonstrated in his prohibition to let his ministers meet during the war, even if simply to have a beer together.[15]

One must emphasize that this personalized power—in the double meaning of the term, centered around the person of Hitler and founded upon direct person-to-person relationships[16]—did not mean the substitution of a Party logic for a bureaucratic one. The Nazi regime was not a party-state as in the USSR, where the primacy of the Party left no doubt. In its own case the duality of both the Party and the state kept up a permanent tension between two bureaucracies, with each having its own identity. Controlling both, Hitler followed but one logic, that of personal confidence. As proof he confided considerable powers, and even his succession, to a man like Göring, who had no position in the Party, and he promoted to the top of the regime unknown men such as Joachim von Ribbentrop and Albert Speer.

What we see here in the end was no surprise. Hitler had extended to the state the method of direction that he exercised in the Nazi Party before 1933: a refusal of all unitary structure that would result in a juxtaposition of services and organizations; a direct link with the functional or regional directors of the Party; and a delegation of powers as needed, without worrying about any form of reasonable control. After 1933 and as the regime evolved, this way of doing things produced its effects on the entire country.

Hitler therefore controlled the regime, but to what extent did he actually decide policy? Functionalist historians have given considerable importance to this question, although their answer has not attracted much adherence. Certainly Hitler had a style of direction that was much his own. We know about the disorderliness of his work schedule, his reluctance to organize his time in a structured manner, the little time he gave to preparing his dossiers, and his way of acting suddenly, of intervening abruptly, and in detail, often after his attention had been gotten by one close to him or by the press.[17]

Hans Mommsen judges, because of this, that Hitler was a "weak" dictator who ordinarily preferred not to make any decisions, preoccupied as he was with maintaining his prestige and his authority, or if he did take a position, he did so under the influence of those close to him.[18] This difficulty of controlling affairs in a sustained manner would have been reinforced by the vague character of his ideology, better equipped as it was to designate broad ambitions and directions than to trace practical paths.[19] In sum, what this approach insists upon is the declining influence of Hitler's intentions and calculations, even in major undertakings such as the extermination of the Jews, which is presented as the result of a process rather than a deliberate decision, the product of a combination of unforeseen circumstances, the local initiatives by zealous lieutenants, and of a kind of ideological ambience created by the tirades of the supreme commander.[20]

Regarding Hitler's ability to decide, it is important not to interpret every hesitation on his part as indecisiveness. And we should not underestimate his decisiveness in important areas. We have sufficient sources for us to have little doubt regarding his detailed, precise, and continuous action in areas such as external politics, military affairs (no other leader during the Second World War followed as closely and took such an important part in the conduct of the war), and the war economy (a historian of the former GDR has noted that the Nazi regime was characterized during the war by an "extremely concentrated" power).[21]

The dilatory behavior of Hitler can be seen above all in the area of civil affairs, particularly in administrative affairs. Again we should consider how far-reaching this was.[22] In his anti-Semitic politics, if it is true that Hitler demonstrated, particularly during the first years, a certain reserve and seemed to act intermittently rather than continuously in setting politics of the regime, he nevertheless maintained a certain direction. While his actions seemed to comprise periodic impulses and successive adjustments, there was never any going back or unexpected detours. Everything went in the direction of the removal of the Jews from Germany.[23]

Likewise, regarding the influence of his lieutenants, Hitler had a marked concern for his prestige, and he liked to persuade rather than impose. Hence long "discussions"—in reality monologues—were typical of the relationship that he had with his paladins. One should note that he willingly left subordinates on their own, indicating a long-term objective and letting them choose the methods. But of course this does not prove that they influenced him. If he granted some leeway for action, it was always under the condition of obedience and conformity to his policy. He never hesitated to separate himself from those who bore him umbrage or whose behavior might harm him. The very fact that he was assailed with requests for a decision, even on points of detail, by his closest associates, Goebbels or Himmler, proves the constant need they felt to lean on his authority and to sound out his thoughts.[24]

Certain historians have held that he decided even less easily because his ideology did not have the consistency that it is usually said to have. For Broszat this ideology was, so to speak, of a utopian nature. It pointed toward a future where everything would be changed. The German people, forming a racially purified *Volksgemeinschaft* ("popular community"), would dispose of a "living-space" from which the Jews would have disappeared. But the means for succeeding in this were by no means clearly indicated. Since the "positive" objective of the "popular community" showed itself to be in fact out of reach because it would have called into question what had been concretely gained, the "negative" elements of the ideology, especially the anti-Semitic persecution, would have been selected, so to speak, through default.[25] The disappearance of the Jews, which would have had a "metaphorical" value in the beginning, would have become a reality through the effect of an evolution that no one had foreseen or wanted.[26] But this is to make light, it seems, of the central role anti-Semitism had in the Hitlerian ideology. Inscribed within a logic of hate, the disappearance of the Jews represented a concrete objective, even if the choice of the method—emigration, expulsion, concentration within a "reservation," or extermination—remained open for a certain time.

If there were an example of the way by which ideology directed the politics of the regime and contributed to the institutional deformation discussed earlier, the administration of annexed territories would provide us with one. Here it can be seen that the space for maneuvering granted by Hitler made sense, and doubly so. On the one hand, the organization of an administration largely removed from the directives of the ministries in Berlin allowed one to implement a radical politics, especially regarding the expulsion of nonnative peoples, without the obstacles of what remained both legitimately and effectively in the juridical order of the Reich. On the other hand, it served as a test case for a more ample Nazification of society than what the balance of power authorized in the Reich—for example, vis-à-vis the different churches. Whereas Stalinism duplicated its structures in annexed territories, the Nazi regime made them the field of experimentation for policies that would later be adopted in the Reich itself. Expansion was the necessary condition for changing society.[27]

In the final analysis the evolution of the Nazi regime must be taken seriously. One would underestimate its importance by viewing it only as a result of Hitler's tactic *divide ut impera*, as though this evolution did not have some effects in return on the politics of the regime. And it is important to take just as seriously Hitler's ability to decide rather than merely to give occasional directions and a legitimacy post hoc,[28] even if all of his initiatives were apparently not calculated. The strict alternative between monocracy and polyarchy thus appears to have only a limited validity. Neither concept allows one to account for the evolution of structures and of Hitler's decisive role.

The concept of charism that Max Weber elaborated is, in this regard, more satisfactory. Charism is an extraordinary quality attributed by a group of the faithful to a person who presents himself as though invested with a mission.[29] This charismatic domination, taken in its ideal as well as typical form, thus distinguishes itself from both traditional domination, founded upon the principle of heredity and the prestige of the past, and a legal-rational domination based upon laws and exercised with the help of a bureaucracy. Charismatic domination distinguishes itself from these in that it is a mode of exceptional power and rests on the leader's giving individual commands, the legitimacy of which derives from the fact that such orders are invested with a part of his charism and that by their nature they dismiss traditional procedures, precedents, and economic logic.[30]

The Nazi regime provides numerous illustrations of each of these points.[31] This does not mean, however, that the two other types of domination do not shed some light on the Nazi phenomenon as well. Hitler's power was partly founded upon traditional motives. Named chancellor by President Hindenburg and invoking the great figures of Germany's past, the Nazi leader found support in an entire segment of the population that missed the monarchy and wanted a substitute for it. What the conservative forces that had put Hitler in power aimed at was precisely the "traditionalization" of Nazism.

As for legal-rational domination, it accounts for a large part of the regime's operation. The government and the population valued the maintenance of a system of norms, which Hitler realized, at least in the early years, as can be seen in the promulgation of the Nuremberg laws in 1935.

In sum, the Nazi regime can be seen as the coming together of these three types of domination, more precisely, as the imposition of a charismatic domination upon a legal-rational one. In institutional terms the latter is more visible in Himmler's operation and in the administrations of annexed territories. But it is important not to limit oneself to it. One of the constitutive characteristics of charismatic domination is a certain kind of attitude and disposition. Ian Kershaw has shown how emblematic was the formula of one high Nazi functionary who called for "working toward the Führer."[32] Obedience was not enough; one had to fully adopt, and even anticipate through action, the policies of Hitler. This attitude infiltrated most of the institutions, quite beyond the charismatic cenacle, and it contributed to the realization of objectives that were literally illegal and that were sometimes even presented as a simple "wish" of the Führer. Thus do we better understand the participation of so many state services in the criminal undertakings of the Nazis.

The concept of charism also allows one to understand the evolution of the regime. There is little doubt that the personalized structuring of power produced a dynamic effect, the best illustration of which is probably found in the astonishing increase of armament productions realized by Speer from 1942 on. But it also had a radicalizing effect. The existence of special bodies that depended directly on Hitler and the diffusion throughout the regime of an attitude of mind that was propitious to the realization of his orders made possible the explosion of violence fermenting in Nazi ideology.

Translated by Peter S. Rogers

Notes

1. See Gerhard Schreiber, *Hitler, Interpretationen, 1923–1983: Ergebnisse, Methoden, und Probleme der Forschung* (Hitler, interpretations, 1923–1983: Results, methods, and problems of research). Darmstadt, 1984; Günter Scholdt, *Autoren über Hitler: Deutschprachige Schrifsteller, 1919–1945, und ihr Bild vom "Führer"* (Authors on Hitler: German-speaking writers, 1919–1945, and their image of the "Führer"). Bonn: Bouvier, 1993.

2. See the work of Ian Kershaw, who has organized his study of the Nazi regime around this debate: *Qu'est-ce que le nazisme? Problèmes et perspectives d'interprétation* (*What is nazism? Problems and interpretive perspectives*). Paris: Gallimard, 1992.

3. Heinrich Himmler, *Discours secrets* (Secret speeches). Paris: Gallimard, 1978, p. 168.

4. Franz Neumann, *Béhémoth: Structure et pratique du national-socialisme, 1933–1944.* Paris: Payot, 1987. Originally published as *Behemoth: The Structure and Practice of National Socialism.* London: 1942.

5. Ibid., p. 437.

6. Ibid., pp. 57–58. Neumann refers to the work of Carl Schmitt, originally published in 1923 and translated into French under the title *Parlementarisme et démocratie* (Parliamentary government and demorcracy). Paris: Seuil, 1988.

7. See Dietrich Orlow, *The History of the Nazi Party 1933–1945*, 2 vols. Pittsburgh: University of Pittsburgh Press, 1969–1972.

8. See Martin Broszat, *L'État hitlérien: L' Origine et l'évolution des structures du Troisième Reich* (The Hitlerian state: The Origin and evolution of the structures of the Third Reich). Paris: Fayard, 1985 (1st ed., Munich: DTV, 1970).

9. See Dieter Rebentisch, *Führerstaat und Verwaltung im Zweiten Weltkrieg* (The Führer state and administration in the Second World War). Stuttgart, 1989.

10. See Walter Naasner, *Neue Machtzentren in der deutschen Kriegswirtschaft, 1942–1945* (New centers of power in the German war economy, 1942–1945). Boppard am Rhein, Boldt, 1994.

11. Ernst Fraenkel, *The Dual State.* Oxford: Oxford University Press, 1941.

12. Martin Moll, *"Führer-Erlasse," 1939–1945* ("Führer-decrees," 1939–1945). Stuttgart: Franz Steiner Verlag, 1997, p. 20.

13. See ibid.

14. In 1941 a jurist of the Crown, Ernst Rudolf Huber, recorded no less than forty-two state executive organisms immediately submitted to Hitler. Ernst Rudolf Huber, "Reichgetwalt und Reichsführung im Kriege" (Executive authority and governmental leadership in the war), *Zeitschrift für die gesamte Staatswissenschaft*, no. 101, 1941, p. 561.

15. Moll, *"Führer-Erlasse,"* pp. 31–32.

16. During the war, access to Hitler was placed more and more under the control of those close to him, especially Martin Bormann, to such an extent that Martin Broszat talks of a "despotism of the court." Broszat, *L'État hitlérien*, p. 461.

17. One may find numerous examples of this in Beatrice, Helmut Heiber, ed., *Die rückseite des Hakenkreuzes. Absonderliches aus den Akten des Dritten Reiches* (The reverse side of the swastika: Unusual facts from the documents of the Third Reich). Munich: DTV, 1933.

18. Hans Mommsen, "Nationalsozialismus," in *Soujetsystem und demokratische Gesellschaft. Eine vergleichende Enzyklopädie* (Soviet and democratic society. A com-

parative encyclopaedia), ed. C. D. Hernig. Fribourg en Brisgau, Herder, vol. 4, p. 702.

19. Hans Mommsen, "Hitlers Stellung im nationalsozialistischen Herrschaftssystem" (Hitler's position in the National Socialist leadership), in *Der Führestaat: Mythos und realität* (The Führer state: Myth and reality), ed. G. Rischfeld and L. Kettenacker. Stuttgart: Klett-Cotta, 1981, p. 70. (French translation in Hans Mommsen, *Le National-socialisme et la société allemande. Dix essais d'histoire sociale et politique* [National socialism and German society:Ten essays of political and social history]. Paris: Éditions de la MSH, 1997, pp. 67–99.)

20. See Christopher Browning, *The Path to Genocide: Essays on Launching the Final Solution*. Cambridge University Press, 1992.

21. Dietrich Eichholtz, "Daten und Fakten zur Kriegswirtschaft und Kriegstechnik, 1940–1945" (Dates and facts of the wartime economy and technology, 1940–1945), *Bulletin des Arbeitskreises "Zweiter Weltkrieg,"* nos. 1–4, 1984, p. 102.

22. We can easily document situations where Hitler's lack of action was founded on his refusal to follow up on directives that already had the approval of the appropriate ministers. But Hitler would have the bureaucracy look over a dossier again until it conformed to his own wishes.

23. See Saul Friedländer, *L'Allemagne nazie et les Juifs. 1. Les Années de persécution (1933–1939)*. Paris: Éditions du Seuil, 1997.

24. See Hermann Weiss, "Der 'schwache Diktator': Hitler und der Führerstaat" (The "weak dictator": Hitler and the Führer state), in *Der Nationalsozialismus: Studien zur Ideologie und Herrschaft* (National Socialism: Studies in ideology and mastery), ed. Wofgang Benz, Hans Buchheim, Hans Mommsen. Francfort: Fischer, 1993, pp. 64–77.

25. Martin Broszat, "Zur Struktur der NS-Sassenbewegung"(Concerning the structure of the National Socialist racist movement), *Vierteljahreshefte für Zeitgeschichte*, no. 1, 1983, pp. 52–76.

26. Martin Broszat, "Hitler und die Genesis der 'Endlösung': Aus Anlass der Thesen von David Irving"(Hitler and the genesis of the "final solution": On the basis of the thesis of David Irving), *Vierteljahreshefte für Zeitgeschichte*, no. 4, 1944, pp. 739–775. See also the similar interpretation of Hans Mommsen, "Die Realisierung des Utopischen: Die 'Endlösung der Judenfrage' im 'Dritten Reich'" (The realization of utopia: The "final solution of 'the Jewish question" in "the Third Reich"), *Geschichte und Gesellschaft*, no. 3, 1983, pp. 381–420 (French translation in Mommsen, *Le National-socialisme*, pp. 179–223).

27. See MacGregor Knox, "Conquest, Foreign and Domestic, in Fascist Italy and Nazi Germany," *Journal of Modern History*, no. 1, March 1984, pp. 1–57.

28. Ian Kershaw, for example, presents the role of Hitler in terms of functions that he fulfills (he unifies, he encourages, he permits): the words "decision" and "decider" are not used. "'Working towards the Führer' Reflections on the Nature of the Hitler

Dictatorship," in *Stalinism and Nazism. Dictatorships in Comparison*, ed. Ian Kershaw and Moshe Lewin. Cambridge, Cambridge University Press, 1997, p. 110.

29. Charism in Hitler's case is of a personal nature. In the case of Stalin, an analysis in terms of charismatic domination probably requires that one begin with the charism of the Communist Party, Stalin's charism being usurped and derived from it.

30. See Max Weber, *Economie et société* (Economy and society). Paris, Pocket, 1995, vol. 1, pp. 320ff.

31. See Ian Kershaw, *Hitler: Essai sur le charisme en politique*. Paris: Gallimard, 1995.

32. See Kershaw, "'Working towards the Führer.'"

THE LOGICS OF VIOLENCE

Nicolas Werth

Strategies of Violence in the Stalinist USSR

In the Stalinist USSR the massive violence exacted by the regime was directed at the interior of Soviet society itself. This violence was directed in the first place—the crucial episode being collectivization/dekulakization—against the vast majority of the nation: the peasantry, which was regarded by the regime as a hostile, "dismal," and reactionary mass. It was carried out in the name of a voluntary project of radical transformation of the country's social and economic structures. This project was to force history, to gain one hundred years in one decade, and to metamorphose the country into a great industrial power, the sine-qua-non condition for the victory of the Stalinist politics of "socialism in one country." The result of this offensive was an extraordinary brutalization of the relations between state and society. The "revolution from above" commenced by the Stalinist group at the end of 1929 included collectivization, dekulakization, the imposition of an administrative system of command over the economy, and accelerated industrialization. It gave rise to a surprising mixture of modernization (if this can be measured by the number of tons of steel produced) and political and social regression: the "military-feudal exploitation" of an expropriated peasantry subject to a new form of serfdom, the development of a system of forced labor, the deportation of thousands of families, famine, trials for political sorcery, and execution quotas approved region by region by the Political Bureau, to name a few. This sociopolitical regression would set forth a process that would affect a growing number of "domestic enemies."

Solidly documented numbers today provide a sense of the extent of this violence.[1] From the end of the 1920s to the beginning of the 1950s—the time span of one generation—one male adult in five passed through the Gulag camps. To these 15 million Soviets condemned to forced labor (of whom more than 1.5 million died in prison) are added more than 6 million people collectively deported (by family and indeed by entire ethnic group) to the most inhospitable regions of the country by a simple administrative act. They suffered the loss of civil rights, being placed under house arrest, and the imposition of work and life conditions carrying a high mortality rate (around 1.5 million died during deportation).[2]

In twenty-five years—from 1929 to 1953—around 3.6 million people were condemned by a special court dependent on the political police. Of these, 770,000 received the death penalty. And of these condemned, more than 680,000 (88 percent) were executed during the two years of the Great Terror (1937–38), most of them on the basis of "execution quotas" planned and approved by the Political Bureau.[3] The violent expropriation of 25 million peasant households must be added to these numbers.

To complete this brief inventory of mass crimes and violence, there remains the central question of the famine of 1932–33. This famine alone, with its 6 million deaths, exacted by far the heaviest toll of Stalinist repression and constitutes an extreme and previously unknown form of violence. After having been collectivized, the kolkhoz peasants of a number of the richest agricultural regions of the country (the Ukraine, North Caucasus, and Black Lands) were robbed of their entire harvests, then "punished" for having tried to resist—passively—this plundering. This punishment managed to transform the situation from one of scarcity to one of famine. Describing this state crime continues to rouse bitter discussions (as mentioned below).

The massive Stalinist repression was characterized under its various guises by volatility and unpredictability. It affected the most diverse categories of society, from top-level Party dignitaries and the political and economic cadres to the most modest elements of the kolkhoz peasantry and a "collectively punished" ethnic group. The types of political logic at work in this repression of "enemies" were also diverse by their very nature. We are able to discern at least four of these strategies, although they were frequently combined.

The first arose from the paranoia of a dictator constructing his own cult against "comrades in arms" who were a risk for exposing the "treason" of "Lenin's best disciple" (as discussed in an earlier chapter).[4]

The second—the terror directed at Party or economic cadres at the end of the 1930s—might appear as a primitive means for constructing a centralized and despotic state in the face of the local "little Stalins'" desire for independence. It might appear as the result of a confrontation between two strategies—that of administrations attempting to preserve their mode of operation, professionalism, autonomy, and place in the state against that of the "clan," founded on total allegiance to Stalin. Was this not also part of the populist strategy of the "good tsar" chastising the "bad bureaucrats" given to perpetrating acts of violence against the "common people"?

A third strategy of violence, whose victims were mainly the "common people," rested on a virtual criminalization of the daily behavior of "ordinary" citizens who refused, for example, the new forms of "state ownership" and struggled for their very survival, pinching a bit of wheat from the fields or tools from the factory (according to Stalin, the entire country was "a nation of thieves").

A fourth aspect of Stalinist repression was violence exercised against a number of non-Russian ethnic groups. This was rooted in the old traditions of "Great Russian chauvinism," xenophobia, and anti-Semitism. These prejudices were completely absent among the Bolsheviks of the preceding generation, but they underwent a resurgence along with other regressive aspects during the "second Stalinism" of the postwar years.

The application of these different repressive strategies—this multiform violence against various "enemies" whose definition shifted according to various criteria dependent as much on the domestic situation as on the international contingencies of the moment—rested on a balancing act between "extralegal" repression under the scope of the political police and "legal" repression under the scope of "ordinary" tribunals. This alternation, or sometimes confusion, between "massive transgressions of socialist law" and campaigns to correct "excesses" constituted a key aspect of the Stalinist system's political functioning, as the historian Moshe Lewin has remarked.[5] This complex legal/extralegal relationship may help in understanding a number of significant shifts in the long Stalinist period's repressive politics.

The implementation of these various policies raises the question of the sequence of, respectively, the "programmatic" ideological project, improvisation, the blind inability to come to terms with a problem, and terror as a response to the uncontrolled set of social crises put in motion by the voluntarist politics undertaken by the Stalinists during the 1930s. What was ultimately the role of the center—and of Stalin in particular—in implementing this repression? And what was the role of the often poorly controlled conflicts and the local settling of scores, the latent and methodical social violence, the dysfunctional nature of concurrent administrations, the "slip-ups," the "excessive zeal," and other "intoxicating successes"?

Throughout Stalin's dictatorship of a quarter century, repressive phenomena varied, evolved, and took on different forms and scope. They reflected transformations of the regime itself in a changing world. This adaptable violence was characterized by various levels of intensity, continual displacements, shifting targets, often unpredictable sequences, and excesses that blurred the line between the legal and extralegal. It evolved through three main series of events.

The first was the "Great Retreat" at the end of 1929, which was marked by dekulakization and forced collectivization of the countryside, a virtual war against peasants. This was the decisive step in modeling Stalinism as a repressive system. It culminated in the famine of 1932–33.

In some respects dekulakization constituted, as historian Andrea Graziosi has forcefully characterized it, the "second act" of the great conflict between the state and the peasantry.[6] This conflict began in 1919–22, when large factions of the peasantry rose up against forced requisitions, conscription into the Red Army, and attempts at collectivization of part of their lands. The regime's unpopular antipeasant practices were forged through these extraordinarily violent (on both sides) antipeasant wars, which reached their peak in 1920–22 after the defeat of the Whites at Tambov, in the Ukraine, in the northern Caucasus, and in western Siberia. Among many of the Bolshevik leaders during this time there developed a sense of extreme vulnerability in the face of a hostile "flood of peasants."[7]

Dekulakization marked the resurgence, against a pacified society, of infinitely larger-scale illegal, violent, and terrorist practices than those experienced some years earlier. Coming at the outset of collectivization, dekulakization was a matter of neutralizing the peasantry by destroying its elites, its most economically dynamic and politically dangerous elements. To see this assault through, the Stalinist leadership framed the offensive in terms of class war. They played on—not without initial success—a number of latent tensions at the heart of the peasantry (between poor peasants and the kulaks) and also between the cities and the countryside.

From its early stages, dekulakization resembled an immense pillaging and settling of scores.[8] The manner in which categorization of kulaks for deportation was conceived signifies the place devolving upon "the initiative of the masses" or "local activists"—the Komsomols, members of the rural soviets, poor peasants. They were gathered together and organized in hastily improvised "dekulakization brigades." Only those lists of "first category kulaks" and other "anti-soviet elements" targeted by the Unified State Political Directorate (OGPU; Ob'edinënnoe gosudarstvennoe politicheskoe upravlenie) were under the exclusive jurisdiction of the political police. The lists of "second and third category kulaks" were established at a local level by a commission composed of diverse representatives and functionaries as well as "local activists," all operating with quotas determined at the regional or national level.

To what extent were these quotas (a device one finds running throughout the Stalinist years) a sign of truly repressive planning, that is, of a project conceived, mastered, and programmed into the long term? Deportation quotas fixed region by region revived the same numbers culture that had invaded the most diverse domains of political, economic, and social life during the First Five-Year Plan. They also revived the same "social engineering," producing a jumble of quotas for dekulakization, for eradicating malaria, and for eliminating illiteracy, for example. But in reality the now possible reconstitution of the whole process of dekulakization, the development of operations, and the chain of command and manner in which orders were applied reveals above all the extent of improvisation and the reign of chaos. One of the most remarkable examples, given this insight, is the 1930–31 deportation without destination of a number of kulak convoys.

As a resurgence of the culture of civil war, dekulakization abruptly produced an immense flux of manpower into the forced-labor system, which remained embryonic by the end of the NEP. There were only around forty thousand convicts in the entirety of the "special camps of Solovki" under the OGPU. The influx was so significant at the time that the forced-labor camps were in a position to absorb only a few tens of thousands of "heads of de-kulakized families." The others—nearly five hundred thousand families of men, women, and children; or more than 2.2 million people—were deported between 1930 and 1933 by a simple administrative act to "special population zones" in the most inhospitable regions of the country (the far north, the Urals, Kazakhstan, and Siberia). These regions were to be "colonized" under the framework of the First Five-Year Plan. This first wave of deportation established a set of practices that would continue until the end of the 1950s. Starting in 1933, the kulaks were succeeded by "socially dangerous" or "socially foreign" elements who were expelled from the towns during police raids. Then, from 1935, several hundred thousand people were deported from border zones under the framework of "border ethnic cleansing." Finally, from 1941, entire peoples were "punished for collaboration with the occupying Nazis." The total of all of these is more than 6 million people.[9]

During 1930 and 1931, complete disorganization and a total lack of co-ordination between the deportation project directed by the OGPU and the resettling of deportees by overwhelmed local authorities would transform dekulakization into a historically unprecedented process of banishment and subsequent abandonment. At the highest level of the Party, the Politburo set up a "kulak settlement commission" only a few months after the beginning of dekulakization. As V. P. Danilov has written: "this reaction belatedly but perfectly reflected the general situation in the politico-administrative milieu of the period. The highest ranking directors, like their regional and local level subordinates, had not acquired the ability to foresee the consequences of their decisions."[10] After weeks, indeed months, of wandering, many of the convoys dumped the exiles in the middle of the taiga, often with neither tools nor provisions. During the first two years (1930–31), a half million of the more than 1.8 million deportees died or fled the country.[11] The scattered data on this or that group of deportees testifies to an annual mortality rate of 15 percent for adults and 50 percent for young children. In terms of "enhancing colonized regions," deportation/abandonment was a resounding failure: by autumn of 1931 less than 10 percent of the deportees were engaged in "productive" work. [12]

From the end of 1931, the OGPU—which had received the entire job of managing the "special populations"—tried hard to make the operation profitable. The "special displaced persons" were registered, assigned housing, and contracted out to agricultural, forestry, and industrial enterprises, all usually dependent on large "combines" in charge of exploiting the natural resources of the country's northern and eastern regions. Thus was improvised a specific status on the scale of expulsions halfway between that of a forced-labor-camp detainee and that of a private citizen deprived of his civil rights but not deported. Throughout the 1930s the legal and administrative status of the special displaced person (also called "work colonist") was gradually constructed according to the questions that were asked: Is there a right to return? Will deported children remain banished once they reach adult age? Would they be able to continue their "normal" studies? What status would a free person who marries a deportee have? On all these matters the authority's attitudes were changing, incoherent, and contradictory. But how could a situation initially based on utter illegality be legalized? Moreover, how could clear boundaries be drawn, given that the special displaced persons worked in the same places and lived in the same precarious conditions as free persons in the grand job sites of the five-year plans? Perceived by the authorities as being a reservoir of deviancy and pollution, the purgatory of deportation, a universe of porous boundaries particular to the Stalinist system of repression, continued to fuel the exercise of violence.

Contrary to the expectations of the Stalinist group, the "liquidation of the kulaks as a class" could not manage to neutralize the peasant resistance to collectivization, an expropriation experienced as an immense violence, as the destruction of a secular culture, and as the imposition of a "second serfdom." For the state the role of the kolkhoz was strategic. It was supposed to assure delivery of agricultural products through the extraction of an increasingly large amount of the collective harvest. An entire apparatus was mobilized to force the kolkhozes to fill their obligatory collection-plan quotas as well as to break resistance—whether active or passive—by not only the peasantry but also the new training staff, who were often in solidarity with their administrators. This apparatus was composed of a crowd of "plenipotentiaries" with uncertain mandates, *troiki* (extrajudicial colleges) of the OGPU, and "brigades of judges and prosecutors" sent to the countryside to administer an expeditious justice. In the cycle of seizure-resistance-repression set in motion by forced collectivization, the functioning of justice quickly became disorganized. There was hardly a line any more between the legal and the extralegal. From 1930 to 1932 more than half a million people, mainly peasants, were condemned to forced labor by GPU organs alone based on one of the fourteen paragraphs of Article 58 of the penal code, which suppressed a vast range of "counterrevolutionary activities."[13] This augmentation of tyranny likewise increased the disorganization: massive arrests of hundreds of thousands of people whom there was not time to judge were followed by "prison clearing" campaigns and then mass amnesties for unduly arrested kolkhozniks.

This breakdown was in keeping with the "excess," "rashness," and "inability to come to terms with problems" all so characteristic of these formative years of Stalinism. Forced collectivization, accelerated industrialization, and the destruction of the market precipitated a cascade of crises: immense social trauma, a massive and anarchic rural exodus, an unprecedented degradation of working conditions, and a profound loss of cultural identity. Social insubordination, delinquency, theft, and "speculation" proliferated in this chaos and extreme destitution. When the stores were empty, the factory once again—as during wartime Communism—became a natural source of supplies, a place of trafficking, and a black market for the workers. For the peasant forced onto the kolkhoz whose harvest was taken in nearly its entirety by the state, "theft of a few grains" quite often became the only means of survival.

In the eyes of the regime, the society began to appear entirely ungovernable, unfathomable, and hostile. The summer of 1932 was a turning point: economic and social difficulties exploded not only on the "collection fronts" but also in the increasingly poorly supplied cities. The perception of the enemy evolved: the struggle was not fought on the "class front" but between *gosoudarstvennost* (the principle of the state) and *stikhiinost* (social chaos), between the socialist order and, as Stalin wrote in July 1932, "habits of individual rapacity, and practices and traditions (serving as the basis for theft) which weaken the grounds of the new socialist society."[14] As such, thieves were no longer to be viewed "as ordinary thieves. . . . This manner of treating these gentlemen . . . only encourages their essentially counter-revolutionary 'work.'"[15]

This was the logic underlying the "heinous law" of August 7, 1932, which allowed penalties for conviction ranging from ten years in camp to death for any theft of "social property." It opened the way to a criminalization-politicization of an increasing number of minor offenses, a tendency that would develop throughout the 1930s and 1940s, feeding the Gulag with prisoners. It also sheds light on the regime's responsibility for the terrible famine of 1932–33.

The origins of this last great European famine are to be found in the practice of massive requisitioning in place since 1929–30. In 1931 "state collections" of cereals reached 45–46 percent of the entire harvest in the great wheat-growing regions of the northern Caucasus and the Ukraine. Such a removal naturally disturbed the production cycle, already disrupted by forced collectivization during which the peasants had butchered most of their livestock.[16] In June 1932 the collection quotas for the coming harvest were announced: they were even greater than those of the previous year, while the harvest promised to be mediocre. A vast front of passive resistance organized, including the local Communist directors (in the Ukraine at the beginning of August, some of the district Party committees declared the collection plan unrealistic) and the kolkhozniks, as well as the kolkhoz brigadiers and presidents. Plenipotentiaries, supported by OGPU detachments, went out to "take the cereals" by force. Under the most diverse pressures, even going as far as torture, the kolkhozniks were compelled to give up their reserves, including seeds for future crops. Districts that did not fulfill the plan were "blacklisted": all stores were closed and the importing of food or manufactured products was suspended, and all arrears and other debts became due immediately. From January 1933, in order to keep the starving from fleeing to the cities, sales of train tickets were suspended in the "punished" regions. OGPU detachments were deployed in order to limit the exodus of those who, according to Stalin, "go on strike and engage in sabotage . . . , lead a war of attrition . . . , [and] a fight to the death against soviet power."[17]

The responsibility of the Stalinist directors is unquestionable within the process that led to the famine of 1932–33. In similar reports by various political, administrative, and police sources at various levels, they were warned time and again, from the summer of 1932 on, of first the risk, then the reality, of famine. One might even say that it was a deliberately planned step toward genocide of the Ukrainian nation, although this interpretation is arguable.[18] Even if the "imperialist Moscovite" dimension was present—and felt as such by the victims—a geographical study of the famine shows that the Ukrainian (the brunt of the famine), Cossack, Russian, and Kazakhstani regions were hit at the same time. The map of the famine cuts largely across the richest cereal-production zones and, as a result, those most subject to the state's predatorial seizures. The exception is Kazakhstan, a specific case marked by a politics of denomadization, which generated a relatively higher death rate than that of the Ukraine. These zones also appeared as the most resistant not only to collectivization but also to the politics of requisition during wartime Communism.

As the outcome of a strategy of extreme violence and repression implemented with collectivization, the famine of 1932–33 is also a pivotal event in opening the doorway to that other paroxysm of Stalinism, the Great Terror of 1937–38. Denied by the regime, the famine was a major milestone on the route to the fictionalization of political discourse, which triumphed in 1934 at the Seventeenth Party Congress (the "Congress of Victors," in Kirov's words). As an expression of extreme violence and regression, it pushed aside limits to what was "possible," assuring a sort of "natural selection" of political and police personnel, those who would be the agents in the climactic radicalization of the Great Terror. The processes that led to the Great Terror have been and remain among the most fervently argued questions for historians of Stalinism.

Focus on the debates about the process of the political purges alone has resulted in neglect of the role of continuous struggle between the *gosoudarstvennost* and the *stikhiinost*, the daily violence exercised against all forms of (criminalized and politicized) social insubordination by a society considered to be a hostile "enemy of the state," independent of any class criteria. It is unquestionably the backdrop on which a second repressive strategy developed: that of the political purges directed at the administration and the Party. For a state desirous of controlling society, the form of its administration is essential. But then one of the lessons that influenced the Stalinist management of the 1932–33 events is the unreliability of this form, as much in regard to management of the kolkhozes and various administrations as in regard to many Party committees. The problems are of several orders, ranging from passive or active resistance against the center's politics to disorganization and disorder resulting from the same mode of intervention based on "mobilization" and the arbitrary short-circuiting of normal administrative functions. But how does one reconcile the repressive police-state approach and normal management (founded on a strong state in sole position to master social chaos)? How does one surmount the considerable tension between the despotic approach and the bureaucratic approach? Resolution of these conflicts is at the heart of the Great Terror, but the purge of political and administrative elites is only one of its aspects.

Between 1932 and 1937, that is to say before the Great Terror, the number of prisoners in the colonies and labor camps of the Gulag multiplied sixfold.[19] This influx of prisoners was largely the result of a politics of criminalization of misdemeanors, of innumerable petty thefts of "social property," of petty juvenile delinquency, hooliganism, "speculation," and insignificant infractions of "passport legislation" instituted in an attempt to "purge" the cities of "socially dangerous elements." This reflected the new perception of "the social enemy," a dispersed adversary since the "victory of socialism" and the destruction of the "hostile classes." Scattered, hidden, and carrying on the work of "undermining" the regime, this opponent was difficult to distinguish, especially in a society where the social upheavals at the beginning of the 1930s had confused everything, reducing social mobility and complicating individual lives. In reality, beginning in 1932–33, in the definition of and search for "the enemy," the criterion of class that had been dominant to that point now lost much of its pertinence. In the "socialist society" to be constructed henceforth, the enemy was no longer the kulak, who had been "eliminated as a class." At most it was the ex-kulak who had escaped deportation and internment. But most often it was the kolkhoznik (that is, the worker) who would not submit to the new rules of socialist life. Significantly, the definition of "socially dangerous elements" elaborated in 1935 included very different categories. These ranged from vagabonds, individuals having or having had "ties to the criminal world," people settled in cities without registration (*propiska*), and young homeless people (*bezprizornye*) to the droves of ex-kulaks who had fled their places of house arrest—more than 600,000 people now living on the margins of society without papers or legal status. Many of them also joined the world of crime peculiar to the 1930s, halfway between political banditry and common banditry.[20] There was a fine boundary between "socially dangerous elements" and the "downgraded elements" of the old, yet still present, "hostile" classes (the ex-kulaks, members of the clergy, "owner classes" under the old regime, "bourgeois specialists," and so on). "Destroying a class," Nikolai Krylenko explained in front of an assembly of judges in March 1934, "does not mean that the anti-Soviet class consciousness of its members has been eliminated. . . . The enemy of class survives in the person of representatives of these past classes."[21]

Against these arbitrarily defined yet omnipresent enemies, no clear partitioning of judicial and police spheres was possible. Numerous debates took place during these years about the legal definition of crimes and misdemeanors punishable (or not) under Article 58 of the penal code and about the necessity of replacing "class justice" with a new "socialist law" intended to "reinforce the State."[22] But despite these debates, no institutional stabilization took shape in a context paradoxically marked by a strong sense of the authorities' vulnerability in the face of a hostile, classless, unclassifiable society. Given a justice apparatus that was overwhelmed, destabilized, and delegitimized by contradictory policies alternating between mass amnesties for the kolkhozniks and the new institution of crimes of uncertain status (such as "disorganization" or "denigration" of the Stakhanovist movement), the extralegal logic of the NKVD amplified. By 1937 the NKVD counted nearly 370,000 functionaries, not including informers, who have been estimated to have numbered several hundred thousand, having increased as the network of work camps and colonies developed (1.2 million prisoners at the beginning of 1937). After the "lull" of 1934, the annual number of condemnations pronounced by the NKVD picked up again, rising in 1935 to a level higher than that of 1933.[23] Deportation raids on "socially dangerous elements" or the "socially foreign" multiplied in a context marked by a virtual obsession with numbers, filing, and the social identification of those moving from the cities (illustrating the "passportization" implemented in 1933).[24]

It is on these grounds of struggle against a society viewed as hostile, elusive, and ungovernable that one must place the political purges culminating in 1937–38 (of which the various stages—from the Party purges of 1933 to the great Moscow trials—have been abundantly analyzed and debated).[25] The rhetoric of the "masked enemy" or "two-faced man" progressively infiltrated the now immense Party—a social microcosm now counting several million members—and took hold at the center of the process. "An enemy with a Party card is more dangerous than a counter-revolutionary who operates out in the open," *Pravda* wrote in November 1932 just before the onset of the Party purges. The route from the great purges of 1933 (during which one-third of the Communists were driven out of the Party or left on their own accord)[26] to the massive arrests of members in 1937 was certainly not a rectilinear route. And until 1936, the Party purges essentially remained internal- and bureaucratic-control operations involving a limited number of arrests.[27] They nevertheless created an immense source of potential suspects. As a report by Malenkov dated February 15, 1937, underlined, the number of "ex-Communists"—1.5 million people—was almost as high as that of the Communists. In some of the most important Party organizations (at Leningrad, Moscow, Kharkov, and Kuzbass), the number of expulsions far surpassed the number of members who had passed all the steps of inspection, exchange, and verification of member cards without mishap.[28] Until the beginning of 1937, the local Communist bureaucrats had managed to retain their "family circles," their autonomy, and their many privileges acquired during the years in which the regime had not yet clearly defined the role of these proliferating apparatuses (which, in charge of supervising and controlling the social body, were indispensable yet inefficient). A similar process can be observed in certain central administrations. Faced with increasing pressure from the NKVD, they attempted to safeguard their professionalism, their modes of operation, and their non-Communist or non-Stalinist cadres (who were often in the majority until 1937). Each was swept away in the turmoil of the Great Terror after the summer of 1937.[29]

Long centered on Stalin's "paranoia" and his "thirst for power," on the great public trials of the "old Bolsheviks," the repression of Communist cadres, and the "public face" of the Terror, studies devoted to the cataclysmic years of 1937 and 1938 are now oriented toward the mechanisms of repression, the sociology of group victims, and the "conspiratorial face" of the Terror. Recent research shows that the massive repression carried out in 1937–38 (1.5 million arrests and condemnations by the NKVD, of which 680,000 resulted in executions) was essentially the result of large, centralized, secret terrorist operations (about a dozen) organized at the highest levels by Stalin and Ezhov, the people's commissar of the interior.[30] These repressive operations were directed against a heterogeneous group of "enemies" "defined on the basis of criteria such as ethnogeographical (non-Russian border populations), political ("ex-Communists," "ex-socialist revolutionaries," "ex-Mensheviks," and such), and pseudo-social ("ex-kulaks," "ex-nobles," "ex-landowners," and former clergy), in other words, certain social deviancies (being aimed in particular at "bandits" and other recidivist criminals judged "beyond redemption"). The most important of these operations indiscriminately targeted "socially dangerous elements" (recidivists), "socially and politically foreign elements" ("ex-kulaks," "ex-nobles," "former clergy members," "ex-Mensheviks," and such), and estimated regional quotas of those individuals to be shot and those to be interned in camps. Upon the request of local NKVD authorities concerned about "overdoing" it, the initial quotas were revised upward several times (rising from 260,000 to 400,000 people).[31] This operation might be considered the radical outcome of repressive measures taken against the "social enemy" throughout the preceding years, such as the eradication effort waged for several years against marginal and marginalized social groups.

Moreover, in the context of high international tensions, the threat of war, the rise of Russian nationalism, and the sacred value of borders, a large number of repressive operations took "the foreign enemy" as their pretext and "espionage" as their theme ("liquidation operation of Polish diversionist spy groups," Germans, Finns, Latvians, Kharbin Estonians, and such). Specifically targeted were those individuals having foreign ties, however tenuous, due to their nationality, their past, or simply their residence. Thus inhabitants of border zones were particularly affected.[32] At the same time, vast deportation operations were carried out against ethnic groups settled in the most endangered border zones. The largest case was the 1937 deportation to Uzbekistan or Kazakhstan of nearly 180,000 Koreans from the Vladivostok area.[33] This was a development of the two previous years' actions taken against other ethnic groups (Finns, Poles, and Germans), with the objective of "clearing the borders" for an eventual "theater of war." In many ways the large campaigns of mass repression during 1937–38 were in the tradition of (and constituted the outcome of) the deportation operations inaugurated with dekulakization. The difference was that many of these were even more violent, having as their goal the conclusive eradication (that is, the physical elimination of more than 680,000 people) of all elements judged "foreign" to the "new society" under construction and considered as potential candidates for a mythical "fifth column" in times of elevated international tensions.

Contrary to a still widely held opinion, recently available documentation on the sociology of the victims of the Great Terror shows that Party and economic cadres, military personnel, diplomats, members of the intelligentsia, and administrators and functionaries of all ranks only represent a small minority of the 680,000 people executed in 1937–38. As spectacular and politically significant as it was, the often high percentage of arrests of the Communist nomenklatura (from 50 percent to 95 percent) of a given region represented only a small fraction of the entire number of arrests.[34] Moreover, recent data on purges in the military show that about eleven thousand of the thirty-five thousand officers arrested were reintegrated into the ranks of the Red Army after 1939.[35] In this case the superior interests of national defense managed to contain to a point the devastating effects of the paranoiac and terroristic police-state approach.

The Great Terror had a better-known public dimension parallel to its secret terrorist aspect: that of the large and small public trials, those "formidable mechanisms of social prophylaxis."[36] This made it possible simultaneously to designate scapegoats responsible for the difficulties encountered in "constructing socialism"; to justify through the myth of "sabotage" the endemic dysfunction of a chaotic industrialization ("Every accident should have its name and nationality!"); to promote a new elite of younger, better-educated, and more-obedient director cadres; and to develop a populist strategy that, by exploiting the discontent of the "common people" against the arbitrariness of the "little leaders" and "bad bureaucrats," contributed to building the myth of the "good tsar" Stalin, stranger to mass terror and defender of the people. Nevertheless, the populist appeal to the "militant base" to denounce the "abuses" of local apparatuses—the manipulation of tensions between the kolkhozniks and their supervision and between the workers and their directing cadres—was not an easy weapon to wield: witness the "slip-ups" of the public trials of rural district directors organized during the summer of 1937 and the increasing disorganization of enterprises following the "vigilance campaigns"[37]—in reality denunciations—instigated by the central authorities.[38] In general, since the regime mistrusted its people anyway, the implementation of repression did not rest on any significant recourse to denunciations coming from society. The "spontaneous" denunciations, it appears, did not constitute the starting point for the files reviewed by the NKVD.[39] Most of the victims of the Great Terror were individuals placed on file by the political-police services. When the quotas were higher than the number of suspects, the NKVD either used depositions extorted during interrogations or resorted to police raids in public places, a common practice throughout the 1930s.[40]

Despite these excesses and slip-ups, the Great Terror was not an uncontrollable process. Witness how it stopped at the moment its effects for the regime—notably the liquidation of military and economic cadres—risked outweighing the objectives sought in the context of rising international tensions. The system was able to show a great capacity for stabilization, which later strengthened the victory in the "Great Patriotic War."

The Great Terror was a virtual knot of "cumulative radicalization" in which were enmeshed several repressive processes directed at both the society and the administrative apparatuses. The extreme violence of the former eased the way to the latter. After this paroxysmal phase, a "second Stalinism" was progressively put in place during the years after the war. This second Stalinism was nationalistic, conservative, and stabilized, marked as it was by the bid to institute a clearer compartmentalization between the legal and the extralegal and to outline the boundaries between police, judicial, and administrative strategies. The goal of this effort to found a "bureaucratic law" was to permit a "routinization" of the system and to assure an accommodating framework in which the state's institutions and administrations could function normally. Without this framework these institutions and administrations would have been able to act in absolute arbitrariness—as during the 1930s—thus undermining the authority of the state instead of serving it.

But the transition to second Stalinism had to pass through the "years of agony" marked by the sovietization of the country and conquered societies following the German-Soviet pact, then after June 1941 by the war against the Nazi occupiers, and finally after 1944 by the second sovietization of territories annexed prior to the war. A remarkable fact is that repression against the sovietized societies (the Baltic countries; western Byelorussia and western Ukraine, attached since 1920 to Poland; and Moldavia) duplicated the methods employed against Russian society with neither more nor less violence: social expropriation and deportation primarily of kulaks and other "socially foreign elements" and subsequently of "nationalist elements." The Polish and Baltic peoples deported to the Urals, Kazakhstan, and Siberia in 1940–41 (about 400,000 individuals) had the same status as the kulaks deported ten years previously or the Soviet Koreans deported in 1937: special displaced persons deported by a simple administrative measure, placed under house arrest, and generally assigned under contract to an agricultural, forestry, or industrial enterprise.

The practice of deporting national minorities widened during the war. These groups were favored targets in the context of Russian nationalism's powerful resurgence, the latter being an indispensable element for reuniting the social body in the face of the hereditary enemy. These deportations affected around 2.6 million people from 1940 to 1945.[41] The majority of them were members of a "suspect" nationality (the German communities settled in Russia since the eighteenth century) or were accused of collaboration with the occupying Nazis (Crimean Tatars, Chechens, Inguches, Karachays, Balkars, and Kalmuks) without even the slightest of grounds. Since the kulak deportation and abandonment of 1930–31, the technology of expulsion had gained in efficiency. Given the context of war (or rather in 1941, a context of near defeat), the implementation of the "total" deportation of entire minority groups practically resembled an elaborate machine of repression, requiring the mobilization of thousands of NKVD agents, whose numbers exploded, reaching over 1 million by the end of the war (850,000 civilians and 650,000 military personnel).[42] The large deportation raids on "punished peoples" organized at the end of 1943 and the beginning of 1944 were meticulously prepared: over six days, 194 convoys of sixty-five trucks removed more than 520,000 Chechens and Inguches to Kazakhstan and Kyrghyzstan. Special NKVD troops numbering 119,000 men were deployed for this operation. Those arrested and deported were not only the minority members living in their own region or autonomous republic but also all those dispersed across the USSR as well as those serving in the armed forces. In the context of a severe shortage of labor, the "economic allocations" of deportees seem to have been better organized than at the beginning of the 1930s. Nevertheless the conditions of the "special displaced persons" were such that the death rate of these groups remained very high. Thus of the 600,000 people deported to the Caucasus in 1943–44, 150,000 (25 percent) were deceased by the beginning of 1948, while less than 30,000 were born in the meantime.[43]

A long process of pacification/sovietization of the western territories annexed during 1939–41 followed the deportations of "punished people" after the summer of 1944. In the face of strong resistance by nationalist guerillas in the western Ukraine, Moldavia, and the Baltic countries, the pacification and border-cleaning operations stretched out until the end of the 1940s. Several hundreds of thousands of nationalists were arrested and sent to the gulag, where they would henceforth constitute the hard core of "political" prisoners isolated after 1948 in "special system" camps. Moreover, between 1944 and 1949 more than half a million people were deported individually or in families from the Baltic countries, the western Ukraine, and Moldavia as "family members of nationalist elements."

All told, during the decade (1939–49) of territorial expansion, war, and sovietization of conquered or reconquered areas, around 3.2 million people were deported, the great majority of them on the basis of ethnicity rather than class, as was the case during dekulakization. During the 1940s the influx of large national contingents into the Gulag profoundly transformed the general character of the concentration-camp universe, where representatives of the "punished peoples" and national resistance fighters occupied a prominent place from then on. At the beginning of 1950, more than 90 percent of the "special displaced persons" were representatives of national minorities.[44] The enemy had undeniably changed in the context of the second Stalinism, marked by the resurgence of obscurantist, retrograde, and regressive elements such as anti-Semitism (which was entirely absent among the Bolshevik directors of the first generation) or xenophobia combined with the exaltation of "Great Russia." Thereafter the enemy was targeted and delimited ethnically.

A second change was a clearer distinction between the legal and the extralegal. A normal functioning of justice was presented as one of the main conditions for the "reinforcement of the State." Numerous postwar campaigns were launched to control, centralize, and master the administration of justice, which had been deeply disorganized during the 1930s by the absence of a clear jurisdiction and the purges' decimation of judiciary personnel.[45]

After the wave of unlawfulness during 1937–38, the number of people condemned by the NKVD diminished considerably: for the postwar years (1947–53), there were about 50,000–80,000 convictions per year as opposed to the 200,000–250,000 annually during 1930–36. During the postwar years, the number of people executed after irregular procedures did not exceed a few thousand per year.[46]

But the repression implemented by the regular courts did not cease to grow heavier through an increasing criminalization of misdemeanors and the slightest forms of social insubordination and through the application of penal sanctions out of proportion with the crimes committed. In this regard one may draw out two highlights in the development of the process. The first, during the summer of 1940, penalized "work discipline" infractions (punishable for the first time by imprisonment) or the production of "rejects." These were inevitable given the conditions under which Soviet industry functioned, the petty theft in the factories, and general "hooliganism," whose vague characterization by the authorities allowed all sorts of abuse. As a culminating point of the confrontation between the regime and the working world (in one year more than 2 million workers were condemned according to the decrees of June 26, 1940), the set of repressive measures of the summer of 1940 aimed at putting order back into enterprises shaken by the wave of "indiscipline." This was largely a result of the populist campaigns of the preceding years, founded on a delegitimization of supervision, authority, skills, and social positions. This example reveals the whole catalog of effects that fed a spiral of repression and violence of different intensities with an undeniably cumulative effect.

The second highlight strengthening the criminalization of social relations was in 1947, a year marked by the promulgation of the June 4 law that, by Stalin's own initiative, considerably aggravated the sanctions affecting all forms of theft (not only of private property but especially of "social property"), thereafter punishable by seven to twenty-five years in the camps. In many respects this severe hardening of penal legislation recalls the context in which the other "heinous law" (of August 7, 1932) had been promulgated but which had progressively fallen into disuse. In both cases it was a matter of a brutal reaction by the regime to various forms of the struggle for survival, particularly by rural populations, which had been reduced to theft in a situation of extreme misery, scarcity, and actual famine (that which hit certain regions of the Ukraine, Volga, and Moldavia in 1941 caused a comparatively high death rate of 500,000 people).[47] This reaction was in keeping with a vast offensive led by the authorities (beginning in 1946) to regain control of a society that, profiting from a relative relaxation of controls during the war, had taken some liberties. Among the most notable measures decided upon in 1946–47 to put an end to this social "disorder"—still felt to be a threat to the socialist order—was the kolkhoz administration's retaking of small individual patches of land exceeding the authorized acreage, the strengthening of penal sanctions against those who changed their place of work or residence on their own initiative, and the law of June 4, 1947. In eight years 1.3 million people (including nearly 400,000 women and adolescents) were condemned according to this law, three-quarters of them to a sentence of five or more years in the camps. In 1951 this category represented 40 percent of all prisoners in the Gulag (1 million out of 2.5 million). The massive influx of "female thieves" into the Gulag—generally war widows with young children who belonged to the most underprivileged rural and urban social strata—provoked "disturbances" identical to those that had followed the application of the law of August 7, 1932. Campaigns of "struggle against the waste of social property" were succeeded by amnesties—kept secret—of tens of thousands of women and adolescents unfairly condemned to punishments out of all proportion to the infractions committed.

Recent studies on the Gulag (it may be more precise to speak of two Gulags, that of the camps and that of "special populating") reveal the features of this vast and multiform penal universe, where waste, sloppiness, randomness, and improvisation seem to have played a more important role than that of a systematic will to exterminate. These studies include the analysis of the number and composition of prisoners and Gulag death rates, which were substantially revised downward (around 5 percent per year during the period of 1934–53, with a minimum of 1 percent at the beginning of the 1950s and a maximum of nearly 21 percent in 1942) in relation to long accepted "estimates";[48] the study of condemnations, which suggests a repression founded at least as much on extreme penalization of types of social behavior as on political-ideological standards for rooting out deviant language and "bad" class origins; and the analysis of prisoner profiles, which makes it difficult to define clearly a specifically targeted social or national group.[49] All of this research stresses the striking uniqueness of the Stalinist concentration camps, especially in relation to those of the Nazis.

There are many elements that make clear that the Gulag had reached its apogee at the beginning of the 1950s: the repression of minorities, the extreme penalization of minor forms of delinquency, the systematic prolongation of ten-year "political" sentences by simple administrative measures pronounced by special courts (which reached their end in 1947–48), and the solid drop in prisoner death rates. There were thus a little more than 5 million outlaws: around 2.7 million "special displaced persons" and 2.5 million prisoners (of which one-quarter were political prisoners and three-quarters were common-law prisoners).

This hypertrophied Gulag had become in reality an increasingly unmanageable machine. To the problems of profitability in a chaotic forced-labor system were added those posed by management, with a corrupt and costly supervisory staff (nearly 200,000 people) of immense penitentiary groups, each handling tens of thousands of prisoners with different statuses, from political prisoners belonging to national minorities, who were not only isolated but also well established in their "special regime" camps, to the mass of ordinary citizens who had become victims of the penalization of an increasing number of social behaviors.[50]

Even more fundamental in a society where one out of five adult males passed through the Gulag is the question of the "culture of the camps" contaminating various aspects of social life. This contamination produced a series of perverse effects that typified the central notion of *toufta*, a term implying at the same time false balance sheets, slap-dash jobs, unproductive waste, disorder, and corruption. All of these elements were characteristic of the Soviet economy under Stalin and after.[51]

In 1951–52, before the death of Stalin, the minister of the interior, Sergei Kruglov, as well as a number of Gulag authorities, had proceeded toward the anticipated release of the "less socially dangerous." This was done in order to place them under house arrest, where they could still work in enterprises and construction sites—still lacking free manual labor—in the inhospitable regions of the country. These measures attest to a growing awareness of the crisis in a hypertrophied and increasingly unproductive concentration-camp system. Other measures (such as the decree issued on July 14, 1951, abolishing a number of penal measures that sanctioned unexcused delays in work or the unauthorized change of workplace) also revealed that authorities were conscious of the necessity of relaxing the pressure on society somewhat.[52] Nevertheless no radical measure could be taken while the dictator was still alive. Scarcely three weeks after his death, a large amnesty, on Lavrenti Beria's initiative, allowed the release of around 1.2 million prisoners, or nearly half the number in the Gulag.[53] In order to justify this measure, Beria had explained in a note sent on March 24, 1953, to the Presidium of the Central Committee that out of the 2,526,402 prisoners in the Gulag, only 221,435 were "particularly dangerous criminals of the State." The great majority of them, he recognized, were not individuals liable to cause harm to the interests of the state.[54] This remarkable and surprising acknowledgement opened the way to a gradual dismantling of the forced-labor system, the "special populatings," and a depenalization of social behavior as well as to restrictions on the omnipotence of the political police. From 1954 to the beginning of the 1960s, this gradual evolution would allow the society, little by little, to emerge from Stalinism. But this was a conditional emergence, without rights to examine or inventory what had happened during the preceding quarter century, without reparations for or rehabilitation of the vast majority of victims (except for a few of the Stalinist directors, victims of the "cult of personality"), and without judgment or condemnation of the executioners.

Translated by Thomas C. Hilde

Notes

1. Since 1990, several studies on Gulag statistics, deportees, condemnations, and executions during the Stalinist period have appeared in Russia. In 1990–92 the historian V. N. Zemskov published the first precise statistical data on the Gulag based on Gulag archives (conserved at GARF—Archives of the State of Federated Russia). For a presentation of this research, see Nicolas Werth, "Goulag, les vrais chiffres," *L'Histoire*, no. 169, September 1993, pp. 35–52. The most complete article on penal statistics during the 1930s is John Arch Getty, Gabor T. Ritterspoon, and V. N. Zemskov, "Victims of the Soviet Penal System in the Prewar Years: A First Approach on the Basis of Archival Evidence," *The American Historical Review*, vol. 98, no. 4, October 1993, pp. 1033–1084.

2. On the deportations see the articles by V. N. Zemskov in the journal *Sotsiologiceskie Issledovania*, nos. 1, 6, 10, 11, 1991; and nos. 2, 8, 1992; Nikolai Bougai, *L. Beria—I. Stalin: Soglasno Vasemu Ukazaniu.* Moscow, AIRO-XX, 1995; O. L. Milova, ed. *Deportatsii narodov SSSR, 1921–1950-ye gody.* 2 vols., Moscow, RAN, 1992–93; and Pavel Polian, *Prinuditel'nye migratsii v SSSR, 1921–1954.* Moscow, 1997. A useful synthesis on this question in French is Jean-Jacques Marie, *Les Peuples déportés d'Union soviétique*, Questions au XXe siècle. Bruxelles, Complexe, 1996.

3. V. P. Popov, "Gosudarstvennyi Terror v Sovetsoï Rossii," *Otecestvennye Arxivy*, no. 2, 1992, pp. 28–30.

4. Regarding this well-known facet, one may refer to the best biographies of Stalin, all of which analyze it to varying degrees: see Adam Bruno Ulam, *Staline: L'Homme et son temps*, 2 vols. Paris, Calmann-Lévy, 1977; Robert Tucker, *Stalin in Power.* New York, Norton, 1990; D. Volkogonov, *Triumf i Tragedia: Politiceskii Portret I. V. Stalina.* Moscow, 1989. See also Moshe Lewin, "Stalin in the Mirror of the Other," in *Stalinism and Nazism: Dictatorships in Comparison*, ed. Ian Kershaw and Moshe Lewin. Cambridge, Cambridge University Press, 1997, pp. 107–134.

5. Moshe Lewin, *La Formation du système soviétique*. Paris, Gallimard, 1987, pp. 402ff.

6. Andrea Graziosi, *The Great Soviet Peasant War: Bolsheviks and Peasants, 1917–1933*. Cambridge, Harvard University Press, 1996.

7. This crucial facet is developed in Nicholas Werth, "Un État contre son peuple," in *Le Livre noir du communisme*, ed. Stéphane Courtois, Nicolas Werth, et al. Paris, Laffont, 1997.

8. This has been emphasized particularly in Moshe Lewin, *La Paysannerie et le pouvoir soviétique*. Paris, Mouton, 1966, pp. 482–513.

9. Nicolas Werth, "'Déplacés spéciaux' et 'colons de travail' dans la société stalinienne," *Vingtième Siècle: Revue d'histoire*, no. 54, April–June 1997, pp. 34–50.

10. Viktor P. Danilov and S. A. Krasilnikov, *Spetzpereselentsy v Zapadnoï Sibiri, 1930-vesna 1931 g.* Novossibirsk, 1992, pp. 14–15.

11. N. A. Ivnitski, *Kollektivizatsia i raskulacivanie*. Moscow, 1994, pp. 257ff.

12. Nicolas Werth and Gael Moullec, *Rapports secrets soviétiques: La Société russe dans les documents confidentiels, 1921–1991*. Paris, Gallimard, 1995, pp. 358–361.

13. Popov, op. cit., pp. 27–28.

14. Stalin to Kaganovich, July 20, 1932, cited in Yves Cohen, "Des lettres comme action: Staline au début des années 1930 vu depuis le fonds Kaganovich," *Cahiers du monde russe*, vol. 38, no. 3, July–September 1997, p. 322.

15. Ibid.

16. Moshe Lewin, "Prendre les céréales: La Politique Soviétique des collectes agricoles avant la guerre," in *La Formation du système soviétique*. Paris, Gallimard, 1985, pp. 204–257.

17. Stalin to M. Cholokov, May 6, 1933, cited in Werth, "Un État contre son peuple," p. 187.

18. Interpreting the famine of 1932–33 has given rise to bitter polemics these past years regarding the degree of the Soviet government's responsibility and about how to characterize this tragedy (e.g., a crime against humanity, or genocide). Among the essays developing opposing points of view, see R. W. Davies, M. Tauger, and S. Wheatcroft, "Stalin, Grain Stocks, and the Famine of 1932–1933," *Slavic Review*, no. 3, 1995, pp. 642–657 (the authors minimize the responsibility of the Soviet government); and L. Woisard, "Le Génocide ukrainien," *L'Intranquille*, nos. 2–3, 1994 (supporting the thesis of genocide by famine).

19. Increasing from around 200,000 to 1,200,000 in January 1937. For penal statistics see the articles cited in note 1.

20. David Shearer, "Crime and Social Disorder in Stalin's Russia: A Reassessment of the Great Retreat and the Origins of Mass Repression," *Cahiers du monde russe*, vol. 39, nos. 1–2, January–June 1998, pp. 119–148.

21. *Sovetskaia Iustitsia*, no. 9, 1934, p. 3.

22. On these debates see Peter Solomon, *Soviet Criminal Justice under Stalin*. Cambridge, Cambridge University Press, 1996, pp. 153–195.

23. Popov, op. cit., pp. 28–29.

24. N. Moine, "Passeportisation, statistique des migrations et contrôle de l'identité sociale," *Cahiers du monde russe*, vol. 38, no. 4, 1997, pp. 587–600.

25. For divergent interpretations of this process, see Robert Conquest, *La Grande Terreur.* Paris, Laffont, 1995; and John Arch Getty, *Origins of the Great Purges: The Soviet Communist Party Reconsidered, 1933–1938.* Cambridge, Cambridge University Press, 1985.

26. Nicolas Werth, *Être communiste en URSS sous Staline.* Paris, Gallimard, 1981, pp. 207–229.

27. At the end of December 1935, drawing up a balance sheet of the "verification of Party cards" campaign, Ezhov declared that during that year, 15,218 "enemies" expelled from the Party had been arrested. This number represented less than 4 percent of the total of those expelled. Later, however, a large number of Communists expelled during one of the many purges of the 1930s were arrested.

28. Oleg Khlevniuk, "The Objectives of the Great Terror, 1937–1938," in *Essays in Honor of R. W. Davies.* Birmingham, 1997, pp. 159–160.

29. On these questions see the chapter "Stalin's System during the 1930s" above.

30. Oleg Khlevniuk, "Les Mécanismes de la 'Grande Terreur' des années 1937–1938 au Turkmenistan," *Cahiers du monde russe*, vol. 39, nos. 1–2, January–June 1998, pp. 197–208; Werth, "Un État contre son peuple"; A. E. Gurianov, ed., *Represii protiv Poliakov i polskix grazdan.* Moscow, Zvenia, 1997.

31. Oleg Khlevniuk, *Le Cercle du Kremlin, Staline et le Bureau politique dans les années 30: Les jeux du pouvoir.* Paris, Seuil, 1996, pp. 208–210.

32. N. V. Petrov and A. B. Roginskii, "'Pol'skaia operatsia' NKVD 1937–1938 gg," in Gurianov, op. cit., pp. 22–43.

33. Marie, *Les Peuples déportés d'Union Soviétique*, pp. 25–34.

34. For a regional example, see Werth and Moullec, op. cit., pp. 569–575.

35. John Arch Getty and R. Manning, eds. *Stalinist Terror: New Perspectives.* Cambridge, Cambridge University Press, 1993, pp. 199–202.

36. Annie Kriegel, *Les Grands Procès dans les systèmes communistes.* Paris, Gallimard, 1972, p. 160.

37. Sheila Fitzpatrick, *Stalin's Peasants: Resistance and Survival in the Russian Village after Collectivization.* Oxford University Press, 1994, pp. 296–312.

38. Gabor T. Ritterspoon, "From Working Class to Urban Laboring Mass," in *Making Workers Soviet*, ed. L. Siegelbaum and R. Suny. London, 1994, pp. 288–305.

39. For a discussion of the denunciation practices in the USSR of the 1930s, see Sheila Fitzpatrick, "Signals from Below: Soviet Letters of Denunciation of the 1930s," in *Accusatory Practices*, ed. Sheila Fitzpatrick and R. Gellately. Chicago University Press, 1997, pp. 85–120.

40. Werth, "Un État contre son peuple," pp. 213–214; Khlevniuk, "Les Mécanismes de la 'Grande Terreur,'" p. 203.

41. *Istoria SSSR*, no. 6, 1989, pp. 135ff; *Voprosy Istorii*, no. 7, 1990, p. 44.

42. Report on the civil and military personnel of the NKVD, December 30, 1945, in *Loubianka, 1917–1960: Spravocnik*, ed. A. I. Kokurin and N. V. Petrov. Moscow, Demokratia, 1997, p. 47.

43. V. N. Zemskov, "Spetzposelentsy," *Sotsiologiceskie Issledovanija*, no. 11, 1990, p. 9.

44. Of the 2,753,000 "special displaced people" and "worker colonists" counted in a census at the beginning of 1953, the "ex-kulaks" numbered no more than around 25,000 (i.e., less than the 27,000 or so deported according to the law of June 2, 1948, punishing the "noncompletion of a minimal number of workdays in the kolkhozes"). A large proportion of the 2,200,000 kulaks deported at the beginning of the 1930s were deceased. But an estimated 800,000 kulaks (principally the children of deported kulaks) were freed from their status as pariahs after 1939 and especially during the war, when they were mobilized into the army.

45. Solomon, op. cit., pp. 366–403.

46. Popov, op. cit., pp. 28–29.

47. On the famine of 1946–47, see the work of V. F. Zima, *Golod v SSR, 1946–1947 g: proizxozdenie i posledstvia*. Moscow, RAN, 1996.

48. V. N. Zemskov, "Gulag," cited above. The death rates in the Gulag varied considerably, depending on the camp (the harshest were those of the Kolyma) and the year. Here are some death rates: 1934–4.3 percent; 1937–2.8 percent; 1938–7.8 percent; 1941–6.9 percent; 1943–20.3 percent; 1945–6.7 percent; 1947–3.7 percent; 1949–1.2 percent; and 1952–0.6 percent.

49. The exception being deportees, among whom 90 percent (at the beginning of the 1950s) were representatives of national minorities.

50. On these difficulties and the crisis of the Gulag at the beginning of the 1950s, see G. M. Ivanova, *Goulag v sisteme totalitarnogo gosudarstva*. Moscow, 1997, pp. 156–185; Werth, "Un État contre son peuple," pp. 201–204.

51. See the article *"Toufta,"* in Jacques Rossi, *Le Manuel du Goulag*. Paris, Le Cherche-Midi, 1997, p. 267.

52. Significantly, this text of the Presidium of the Supreme Soviet of the USSR—which abolished Article 5 of the decree of June 26, 1940—was not published in the press at the time of its promulgation so as not to suddenly disrupt "labor discipline" in the factories, maintained in large part by the repressive arsenal of decrees from the summer of 1940. Responsible during a little more than a decade for the condemnation of more than 11 million people (in general to corrective labor punishments at the worksite), these decrees were only abolished by a text of April 25, 1956, decriminalizing labor laws.

53. Nicolas Werth, "L'Amnistie du 27 mars 1953: La Première grande sortie du Goulag," *Communisme*, nos. 42–44, 1995, pp. 211–224.

54. V. F. Nekrassov, *Beria: Konets kariery*. Moscow, Politizdat, 1991, pp. 184ff.

Philippe Burrin

The Congenital Violence of Nazism

The extreme manifestations of Nazi violence, particularly the extermination of European Jews, has today received sustained attention among researchers as with the general public. Their monstrosity justifies this attention, but it should not have us separate them from the global criminality of the Nazi regime.[1]

Violence is at the heart of Nazism. This marks a difference from Bolshevism, where doctrine and reality found themselves in an antinomical relationship. Instead of the disintegration of the state and the advent of the Leviathan—and in the perversion of fraternity in the Gulag—in Nazism, doctrine and reality were fused from the start. The cult of heroic virility, the affirmation of the rights of the strongest, and the discourse on salutary toughness indicate that violence was not only a means but also constituted a value in itself. It was worth a "law of nature" and was even the only one apt to guarantee both survival and victory in the struggle of the races, which has been the thread of the history of the living world in the Nazi vision.

Established as a doctrine and exalted in speech, Nazi violence passed all the more forcefully into action since it was required by the fundamental project of the regime: the transformation of German society into a warring tribe, the domination of the European continent, and the racial reshaping of the "living space" that the Nazis claimed in Eastern and Central Europe. Leaning toward war, the Third Reich carried violence in its womb. And war, once it came, only increased a violence that turned against the conquered peoples and especially against any nonnative peoples who had the misfortune to reside within the "living space."

From 1933 to 1945 the curve of Nazi violence showed a constant process of spreading and of radicalization, an increase in the circle of victims and in the very forms that violence took. This should not be viewed as the effect of some determinism. There was an apprenticeship of violence, but this would have taken place with a less disconcerting ease had the political ideology, culture, and mentality of the Nazis not predisposed them to it. In order to understand the specificity of this violence, one must first look at the different political and ideological motivations that encouraged it, the actors who implemented it, and the form that it assumed.

One can distinguish three motivations to Nazi violence, all of which have become confused in historical memory but that are useful to separate for analytical purposes: political repression, exclusion and social repression, and racial politics. As for political repression, it was a question of neutralizing the enemies of the regime in the Reich as well as in the occupied territories. This form of repression corresponded to the desire for control and change that motivated Nazi leaders. It took the form not only of a struggle against active opponents but also of criminalizing numerous forms of behavior and attitudes that belong, in a liberal regime, to the private sphere and form part of an individual's rights. In the occupied countries it also took on the form of terrorist practices that targeted civilian populations in order to have Nazi order reign there.

In the period before the war, this politically motivated violence had a relatively limited importance, except for the first month of 1933, when a wave of terror struck the enemies of the Nazi Party. About fifty thousand people were imprisoned in makeshift camps where the SA, in particular, brutally settled scores against those interned. Political repression decreased after the consolidation of the regime and the increased isolation of those that opposed it. The population of the concentration camps, henceforth unified under the control of the SS, even reached a low level in the middle of the 1930s (seventy-five hundred prisoners in 1936–37).[2] But the camps had become an institution ready to serve as soon as the need was felt. During the entire duration of the regime, repression struck above all the members of parties on the Left, though foremost against those of the Communist Party. From about the first half of the 1930s, it no longer spared the members of the clergy. It then took on the conservative opposition, particularly after the attempt to assassinate Hitler in July 1944.

Along with politically motivated repression there was the criminalization of deviant opinions. Thus the Jehovah's Witnesses brought upon themselves the fury of the regime by their refusal of the military draft. Seditious remarks of any kind were pursued with the same vigor, particularly criticism of Hitler or his racial politics. If in this area repression remained relatively foreseeable, a sword of Damocles was held over the population, especially over those who did not conform, at least externally, to the expectations of those in power. Rumors about the concentration camps produced some effect, as did the action of the traditional repressive organisms of the state, which, under constant pressure from Hitler, punished with increasing severity. Civil courts handed out 16,560 death sentences between 1933 and 1945, nearly all carried out.[3] As for the military courts, they condemned about 50,000 people to death[4] and had executed 13,000–15,000 soldiers of the Wehrmacht (for the sake of comparison, during the First World War, 48 German soldiers were condemned to death and executed).[5] Yet the Nazi Party suffered nothing that was comparable to Stalin's purges. The episode that comes closest to these, the Night of the Long Knives in June 1934, when the leaders of the SA were executed, produced about 80 victims.

The outbreak of World War II spurred on these forms of violence, especially in the occupied territories. There was very much an unleashing of repression, which could be called terroristic in the USSR, Poland, and the Balkans before the murderous wave spread into the West from 1943 on. In the case of war against partisans, the number of civilians, victims of political and military reprisals throughout Nazi Europe, are difficult to estimate; it certainly goes beyond the figure of one million. The number that is usually quoted, 15 million civilians (including 12 million from the USSR), includes an unusually high mortality rate and deaths connected to conditions of life under the Occupation. Economic exploitation, in particular, was pitiless since Hitler wanted to preserve the level of alimentation for the German population, the price of which was borne by those living in the occupied countries. Add to this the deportation of workers carried out by force in Eastern Europe. As a total, some 8 million foreigners were forced into labor to make the German economy work, many among them in conditions close to slavery.[6]

Concentration camps reflected this evolution as well. They became virtual Towers of Babel in which men and women of every nationality coexisted, whereas German prisoners now formed only a small minority, a privileged one at that. At the beginning of the war, the population of the concentration camps approached 25,000 people. This figure had been multiplied by four in 1942, and in January 1945, there were 714,211 prisoners, of whom 202,674 were women.[7] In all at least 1.5 million people had experienced the hell of the camps. Two-thirds lost their lives as a result of physical cruelty, exhaustion, or sickness.

The second form of oppression derived from social reform and aimed at the homogenization of the *Volksgemeinschaft* ("popular community"), that is to say, of the population defined as German.[8] The regime did not limit itself, in effect, to the indoctrination or surveillance of a population whom it wanted to be in conformity with its expectations. It had recourse to repression and to exclusion, taking as its target all those who did not seem capable or desirous of belonging to the "popular community." It mainly targeted two kinds of groups. On the one hand, there were the "asocial," among whom were counted Gypsies, tramps, beggars, prostitutes, alcoholics, the jobless who refused any employment, and those who left their work frequently or for no reason.[9] On the other hand, there were homosexuals, whose behavior conspired against the imperative to reproduce and who were the target of a ferocious repression. The courts condemned about 50,000 individuals for homosexuality, half of whom were sentenced between 1937 and 1939. Many among them were sent to camps, where most of them died, after they had served their regular sentence.[10]

As to the motivation of the violence that targeted these categories of people—and which was intensified in the second half of the 1930s—one can certainly note the concern to put unproductive individuals to work at the very time when preparations for war would bring about a smaller workforce. Basically it was a question of getting rid of any kind of behavior that did not meet the social norms of the regime. These standards were moreover the object of a large consensus of the population, be it the virtues of work and discipline or of sexual conformity. This policing of morality was susceptible to an indefinite extension against every form of social deviance, as is shown by the small war waged by urban authorities against bands of youngsters (*Edelweissipiraten*) who dressed provocatively or met to listen to jazz and who at times came to blows with members of the Hitler Youth.[11]

A third motivation to violence, and by far the most important, derived from Nazi racism. This manifested itself in two initiatives: the decontamination of the German people and the cleansing of territories that belonged in the "living space." Regarding the first initiative, one often misunderstands that racism, before it is ever directed against nonnative populations, first turns itself, logically so, against its own society in order to get rid of any germs of decadence. Such was the objective of one of the first laws of the Nazi regime, which imposed sterilization on persons suffering from physical handicaps or from neurological and psychiatric troubles that doctors of the period thought to be hereditary. About 400,000 people underwent this treatment; there were deaths and countless traumatisms. In 1937 Hitler extended the law to several hundred young Germans born of black fathers who had belonged to French occupying forces stationed in the Rhineland between 1919 and 1930.[12]

According to the same logic, there was the operation called "euthanasia," which was in reality the ongoing serial extermination of the mentally ill who were classified as both incurable and unproductive.[13] Begun in the autumn of 1939, this program created more than 17,000 victims in two years among the patients of psychiatric establishments. It was at this time that the procedure for killing with camouflaged showers was invented as well as the incineration of bodies and the recuperation of gold teeth, methods that were all used again later in the extermination of the Jews. At the same time about 5,000 children born with deformities were killed by lethal injection.

The operation was interrupted in the summer of 1941 by Hitler after members of the clergy protested. Nevertheless it would be pursued sporadically, although the target populations changed. About 20,000 sick prisoners were gassed in concentration camps as were about 30,000 Polish workers and captured Soviets sick from tuberculosis or struck with mental illness. [14]

Performed secretly and administered by doctors, the so-called euthanasia affected people whose physical state reduced them to total impotency, even sexually. They of course represented no danger to Nazi power, and there was therefore no question of repression or of terror, which supposes some form of publicity. Their elimination was founded upon premises that were strictly racist. To kill these people declared "unworthy to live," utilitarian motives sufficed. Himmler's men thus killed, through gassing in trucks or by firing squads, thousands of patients from psychiatric establishments situated in annexed Poland and in the occupied USSR, with the aim of freeing up lodgings for the troops. [15]

The second part of racial purification concerned nonnative elements in the heart of the Reich as well as in the conquered territories of the "living space": annexed regions, by right or by fact (such as Alsace-Lorraine), occupied Poland, and occupied areas of the Soviet Union. In the Reich a politics of apartheid was established to separate Jews from the "Aryan" population, even on the sexual level (the Nuremberg laws of 1935). This policy was then extended to foreign workers, whom the war economy required importing by the millions, all the while stiffening sanctions, particularly for the Poles. Sexual relations with a German woman would bring about the death penalty. The violation of any one of numerous prohibitions imposed upon workers from the East (for example, frequenting cafes or attending German religious services) was punishable by being sent to a concentration camp. [16]

In the territories belonging to the "living space," purification began with the liquidation of different elite groups. In the annexed part of Poland as in occupied Poland, the policy claimed several tens of thousands of victims before being interrupted after protests from leaders of the Wehrmacht. In the occupied Soviet Union, the liquidation of elites was relentless, anti-Communism and anti-Semitism making military protests fade away. Soviet prisoners of war were submitted to a triage in order to isolate, in addition to the Jews, all those who held positions of responsibility in the Communist Party and the Soviet state or who belonged to the intelligentsia. Several hundreds of thousands of prisoners thus selected were shot (the most current estimate for those executed places the number at 600,000). [17]

By massacring Polish and Soviet elites, the Nazis wanted to do away with not only the administrative pillars of states condemned to disappear but also the bearers of any political or national identity that no longer had a right to existence. A series of measures was supposed to weaken the conscience of populations—for example, the closing of cultural and educational institutions, with the exception of primary schools and certain technical establishments—and to reduce them to the status of an unqualified labor force, subject to the tallage of the conquerors, until the time when they could completely Germanize their "living space."

The final objective was expulsion. No time was lost to begin deportations in the annexed Polish territories. Out of 12 million Polish Jews and non-Jews who resided there, about 1 million were deported, without property or food, to the General Government (the unannexed part of Poland under German military command),[18] where they were left on their own. The needs of the army for transportation obliged Himmler to suspend these deportations as early as 1940. This also happened in Alsace-Lorraine after tens of thousands of people had been sent to Vichy France. But the objective remained, as demonstrated by the famous East Plan, which was elaborated the day after the attack against the USSR in June 1941 and provided for the deportation of 31 million Slavs toward Siberia and their replacement with 4 million German settlers.[19]

In undertaking ethnic cleansing, the Nazis came up against a major problem: the demographic preponderance of Slavic populations. Hence the desire, expressed by Himmler, to reduce their birth rate by every means, even mass sterilization; it remained only a wish. This demographic anxiety probably had its role in the manner in which the Wehrmacht treated the majority of Soviet prisoners of war. Along with the hundreds of thousands who were shot, nearly 2 million more died from hunger, cold, and sickness in the space of a few months after their captivity during the summer and autumn of 1941. The German army was not prepared to care for such a mass of people, but this lack of preparation cannot be understood without recalling factors such as political suspicions, racial and cultural disdain, and Hitler's prohibition to bring such men into the Reich to work (the military crisis at the turn of 1941–42 made him reverse this decision and offered a chance at survival to Soviet soldiers already taken prisoner).

Another method for reducing the demographic imbalance consisted in recuperating "German blood" present in the Slavic populations. The East Plan foresaw that 10–15 percent of Poles would be Germanized (and would thus not be deported to Siberia)—likewise 50 percent of Czechs, 35 percent of Ukranians, and 25 percent of Ruthenians.[20] Germanization touched people who, for the most part, had no language or cultural link to Germany but who possessed some physical trait that could connect them to the "German race." It remained necessary to acculturate and to make Nazis out of them, thus requiring forceful means for those who resisted. The evolution of the war placed narrow limits on this undertaking, but thousands of Slovenians, whom Himmler had decided would be Germanized, for example, were nevertheless deported into the Reich. Likewise thousands of Polish orphans were placed by adoption into German families.

For some populations terminal expulsion did not seem to be the acceptable solution, whereas their Germanization, immediate or delayed, was in principle excluded. So for Gypsies and Jews, the purification of the "living space" ultimately meant extermination after the abandonment of other solutions like emigration, deportation, and confinement on reservations.[21] Different from other victims of Nazi violence, entire families of Jews and Gypsies were here targeted—genocide brooks no exemption of any individual. This is an essential distinction that nevertheless leaves intact the specificities of extermination aimed at Jews.[22] On the one hand, they represented a key adversary in Nazi ideology, which animalized them (calling them vermin, microbes, and such) and demonized them (the "Jews" in charge in Moscow, in London, and in Washington). On the other hand, their extermination was planned as an operation that was both global, including all the Jews of Europe under Nazi influence; systematic, given that it was subject to a centralized management; and urgent, to the extent that it was important to accomplish it before the end of the war.

These three motivations to violence (political, social, and racial) were, we should repeat, conflated in historical reality. But it is evident that the racist logic penetrated and overdetermined the first two. It conditioned political repression since the treatment of all opposition was much crueler in the East, where, not coincidentally, the populations were judged to be racially inferior. Racial thinking flowed over into "social reform" as well since the Nazis were inclined to racialize social deviances more and more by attributing them to genetic factors. As a result those targeted included not only the concerned individuals but their families as well. All now fell into the category of those who were forced to undergo sterilization.

Who were the main actors of this violence overdetermined by the racist ideology? It is useless to expatiate on the institutions mainly responsible—the police and the ss, the Wehrmacht, occasional proxies such as the Chancellery of the Führer, to which Hitler confided the murder of the mentally ill—or even those who carried out the executions—the guards at the concentration and extermination camps and the police responsible for the massive shootings of Jews in the USSR and in Poland. This represents as a total some 100,000–200,000 Germans, who were helped by thousands more from other nationalities. These people went through an apprenticeship of mass murder, and it is not easy to weigh the part played by ideological motivation, particularly anti-Semitic hate, or that of situational factors.[23]

Beyond these organizations and teams, there is the contribution made by the militants of the Nazi Party. With them a culture of violence, nurtured by the experience of the First World War, had combined with the experience of confrontations during the Weimar Republic era—putsch attempts at the beginning of the 1920s through the smoldering civil war of 1930–33, which claimed several hundred lives. These militants were on the first line in pogromlike activities, as on "Crystal Night"; or during the days that followed the Anschluss, when unmentionable humiliations were inflicted upon the Jews of Vienna; or in punitive actions during the war, actions that were aimed at their compatriots or foreign workers who violated the rules of apartheid.

It is true that the perpetrators benefited from the support of a substantial part of the population. At times the support was active: without the help of denunciations, for example, the efficiency of the Gestapo would have been reduced.[24] Often there was only simple approval: noisy in the case of the execution of the directors of the SA in 1934 and during the campaign against the "asocial"; ambiguous for the "euthanasia" of the mentally ill. In addition, to the extent that Nazism exploited traditional militarism and nationalism, it had to implicate in its initiative a large part of society, beginning with the male population called into military service. The violence of the Nazi regime found a part of its propulsive force by spreading the spirit of national violence, with a fearful efficiency, to areas where its ideology could find support on rooted prejudices, such as those against Poles, Russians, or Jews.

All in all, the contributions of another group, the scientists, were important in a different way.[25] We should not lose sight of the crucial role that categorization played in Nazi violence, as in Stalinist violence. The definition of target populations used by jurists or experts of all kinds was the necessary condition for discrimination and persecution. One only has to think of the role played by criminal biology in the racialization of social deviances, by medicine in the experiments on prisoners and in the procedures of extermination of the mentally ill and of Jews, or by specialists of the social sciences (geographers, town planners, economists, and such) in planning for the social and racial remolding of the territories in the East, with its implicit threat of death, actual or potential, for the indigenous populations.[26] This was a vast array of scientific expertise without which Nazi violence would not have had the face we know it by.

In conclusion, we should briefly evoke the differentiated character of this violence along a public/secret cleavage. There is first of all a form of public violence that can be qualified as popular, even if it was usually implemented or orchestrated by the Nazi Party. This violence aimed at stigmatizing in public, with popular support, deviant behavior that did not merit prison or the concentration camp. It borrowed its methods from the traditional repository of community violence: being placed in the pillory or being led about through the city as an alcoholic with a sign around one's neck, the shaving in public of the hair of women who had sexual relations with foreigners, and other such punishments. Toward the end of the war, this kind of violence was waged against foreign workers who had become restive and were made to pay for the Allied bombings. Another form of public violence was metered out by the military and the police to set an example. This was essentially used in the occupied countries, especially in the East and in the Balkans. This included, for example, the burning of villages and public hangings, with the bodies being exposed for several days.[27]

But secrecy enveloped the violence of the camps.[28] This violence was physical, that of corporal punishment, the usual method for whipping someone into shape, or that of clinical experimentation, which made thousands of adults and children die. This was violence also to the psyche, for the mark of the Nazi camps was, more than the higher mortality rate than existed on the average in the Gulag, the perversity that impregnated the relations of guards and prisoners and was marked by an effort to break the latter, to degrade them, and to have them lose their dignity as human beings. The most emblematic illustration of the consequence of this perversity was the figure of the "Muslim," a term that designated, in the language of the camps, the prisoner who had come to the last stage of psychological and somatic degeneration. Hannah Arendt rightly judged that, between Stalin's camps and those of the Nazis, there existed something of the difference between purgatory and hell.[29]

The mass murders were also secret. These were carried out either by firing squad (Soviet prisoners, Polish elites, and especially Jews and Gypsies) or in the gas chamber (mental patients, sick prisoners, Gypsies, and Jews).[30] Both methods attested to the rationalization of an industrial type of massacre accompanied by a dehumanized representation of the victims. But the gas chamber represented a most advanced stage of rationalization, especially of dehumanization, doing so in the way it suppressed its victims during their last moments.

Whereas death by a firing squad gives martyrs the possibility to give one another some comfort and to experience some kind of solidarity in their suffering, there is no such connection in the gas chamber camouflaged as a shower. The sudden darkness provoked madness, suffocation increased, and panic reigned; families pressed together broke apart in a savage rush toward the door. Then each one tried to breathe the oxygen near the ceiling. The strong crushed the weak; there were neither parents, nor relatives, nor friends. The human being found himself reduced to the most elementary drive, the will to survive, which dissolves, along with the social bond, every feeling of solidarity and dignity.

Translated by Peter S. Rogers

Notes

1. Few works account for the different forms of Nazi violence. On mass murder see François Bédarida, ed., *La Politique nazie d'extermination* (The Nazi policy of extermination). Paris: Albin Michel, 1989; and Michael Berenbaum, ed., *A Mosaic of Victims: Non-Jews Persecuted and Murdered by the Nazis*. New York University Press, ca. 1990.

2. See Marin Broszat, "Nationalsozialistische Konzentrationslager, 1933–1945" (National Socialist concentration camps, 1933–1945), in *Anatomie des SS-Staates* (Anatomy of the SS state). Munich, DTV, 1984, vol. 2, pp. 11–133.

3. Eberhard Kolb, "Die Maschinerie des Terrors" (The Machinery of terror), in *Nationalsozialistische Diktatur, 1933–1945: Eine Bilanz* (National Socialist dictatorship, 1935–1945: An Evaluation), ed. Karl Dietrich Bracher, Manfred Funke, and Hans-Adolf Jacobsen. Dusseldorf, Droste Verlag, 1983, p. 281.

4. Manfred Messerschmidt and Fritz Wüllner, *Die Werhmachtjustiz im Dienste des Nationalsozialismus* (Military justice in service of National Socialism). Baden-Baden, Nomos Verlagsgesellschaft, 1987, p. 87.

5. Omer Bartov, *L'Armée d'Hitler: La Wehrmacht, les nazis, et la guerre* Paris: Hachette, 1999, pp. 143–144. (1st ed., *Hitler's Army: Soldiers, Nazis, and War in the Third Reich*, Oxford University Press, 1990, pp. 95–96).

6. See Ulrich Herbert, *Fremdarbeiter: Politik und Praxis des "Ausländer-Einsatzes" im der Kriegswirtschaft des Dritten Reiches* (Foreign workers: Politics and practice of "Foreign units" in the war economy of the Third Reich). Bonn, Verlag Dietz, 1985.

7. Broszat, op. cit.

8. See Michael Burleigh and Wolfgang Wippermann, *The Racial State: Germany, 1933–1945*. Cambridge, Cambridge University Press, 1991.

9. See W. Ayas, *"Asoziale" im Nationalsozialismus* ("Antisocials" in National Socialism). Stuttgart, Klett-Cotta, 1995.

10. Burleigh and Wippermann, op. cit., p. 197.

11. See Arno Klönne, "Jugendprotest und Jugendopposition: Von der JH-Erziehung zum Cliquenwesen der Kriegszeit" (Youth protest and youth opposition: From the Hitler youth training to the small group formations of the war period), in *Bayern in der NS-Zeit* (Bavaria in the National Socialist period), ed. Martin Broszat. Munich, Oldenbourg, 1981, vol. 4, pp. 527–620.

12. See Gisela Bock, *Zwangssterilisation im Dritten Reich* (Forced sterilization in the Third Reich). Opladen, 1986.

13. See Michael Burleigh, *Death and Deliverance: "Euthanasia" in Germany, ca. 1900–1945*. Cambridge, Cambridge University Press, 1994.

14. Hans-Walter Schmuhl, *Rassenhygiene, Nationalsozialismus: Euthanasie* (Racial cleansing, National Socialism: Euthanasia). Göttingen, 1987, pp. 361–364.

15. See Götz Aly, ed., *Aktion T-4: 1939–1945* (Action T-4: 1939–1945). Berlin, Hentrich, 1987.

16. See Diemut Majer, *"Fremdvölkische" im Dritten Reich* ("Folk outsiders" in the Third Reich). Boppard am Rhein, Boldt, 1981.

17. Bartov, op. cit., p. 126. See Christian Streit, *Keine Kameraden: Die Wehrmacht und die sowjetischen Kriegsgefangenen, 1941–1945* (Not comrades: The German army and Soviet prisoners of war, 1941–1945). Stuttgart, DVA, 1978.

18. See Jan Gross, *Polish Society under German Occupation: The Generalgovernment, 1939–1944*. Princeton, Princeton University Press, 1979.

19. See Mechtild Rössler and Sabine Schleiermacher, eds., *Der "Generalplan Ost"* (The "General Plan for the east front"). Berlin, Akademie Verlag, 1993.

20. Helmut Heiber, "Der Generalplan Ost" (The General Plan for the east front), *Vierteljahrshefte für Zeitgeschichte*, 1958, pp. 281–325.

21. See Raul Hilberg, *La Destruction des Juifs d'Europe* (The destruction of the Jews of Europe). Paris, Fayard, 1988; Michael Zimmermann, *Verfolgt, vertrieben, vernichtet: Die nationalsozialistische Vernichtungspolitik gegen Sinti und Roma* (The National Socialist extermination Politics against Sinti und Rome). Essen, 1989.

22. See Ulrich Herbert, ed., *Nationalsozialistische Vernichtungspolitik, 1939–1945: Neue Forschungen und Kontroversen* (National Socialist extermination policies, 1939–1945: New researches and controversies). Frankfort, Fischer, 1998.

23. One can consider the divergent interpretations of Daniel J. Goldhagen, *Les Bourreaux volontaires de Hitler: Les Allemands ordinaires et l'Holocauste* (Hitler's Willing Executioners: Ordinary Germans and the Holocaust). Paris, Éditions du Seuil, 1997; and Christopher Browning, *Des hommes ordinaires: Le 101e bataillon de réserve de la police et la Solution finale en Pologne* (Ordinary Men: Reserve Police Battalion 101 and the

Final Solution in Poland). Paris, Les Belles lettres, 1994. Browning seems to me more convincing on this point.

24. See Robert Gellately, *The Gestapo and German Society: Enforcing Racial Policy, 1933–1945*. Oxford, Clarendon, 1990.

25. See Benno Müller-Hill, *Science nazie, science de mort: L'extermination des Juifs, des Tziganes et des malades mentaux* (Murderous Science: Elimination by Scientific Selection of Jews, Gypsies, and others, Germany, 1933–1945). Paris, Odile Jacob, 1989; and Robert Proctor, *Racial Hygiene: Medicine under the Nazis*. Cambridge, Harvard University Press, 1988.

26. See Götz Aly and Susanne Heim, *Vordenker der Vernichtung: Auschwitz und dei deutschen Pläne für eine eurpäische Neuordnung* (Precursors of extermination: Auschwitz and the German plans for a new European order). Hamburg, Hoffmann und Campe Verlag, 1991.

27. See the exhibit catalogue *Vernichtungskrieg: Verbrechen der Wehrmacht 1941 bis 1944* (Extermination war: Crimes of the German army, 1941–1944). Hamburger Edition, 1996.

28. Wolfgang Sofsky, *Die ordnung des Terrors: Das Konzentrationslager* (Order of terror: The Concentration Camp). Frankfort, Fischer, 1997; Klaus Drobisch and Günther Wieland, *System der NS-Konzentrationslager, 1933–1939* (System of the National Socialist concentration camps, 1933–1939). Berlin, Akademie Verlag, 1993.

29. Hannah Arendt, *Le Système totalitaire* (The Origins of totalitarianism). Paris: Éditions du Seuil, 1972, p. 183. For some elements of comparison, see Gerhard Armani, "Das Lager (KZ und GULag) als Stigma der Moderne" (The Camps (concentration camps and gulags) as the stigma of modern times"), in *Terroristische Diktaturen im 20. Jahrhundert* (Terrorist dictatorships in the twentieth century), ed. Matthias Vetter. Opladen, Westdeutscher Verlag, 1996, pp. 157–171.

30. Eugen Kogon, Hermann Langbein, and Alalbert Rückerl, *Les Chambres à gaz: Secret d'État*. Points-Histoire. Paris, Éditions du Seuil, 1987.

POWER AND SOCIETY

Nicolas Werth

Forms of Autonomy in "Socialist Society"

Resistance! Where then was our resistance? . . . . If during the times of the mass arrests, as in Leningrad when they arrested a quarter of the city, the people did not remain in their holes, deathly afraid each time the front door was opened . . . , if they had understood that they had nothing left to lose, if they had bravely made barricades with their axes, hammers, pokers, with whatever was at hand? . . . If . . . If. . . . We quite deserved everything that was to happen. – Alexander Solzhenitsyn, *The Gulag Archipelago*

This moralizing and "fundamentalist" reflection by Alexander Solzhenitsyn on the absence of resistance to the Stalinist regime echoes the long-dominant position of a Sovietology for which the matter of resistance has had little relevance. In a state that controlled all aspects of social life and an atomized society that had become docile following a massive indoctrination set up by the "propaganda state," what place could there be for dissenting opinions, for forms of insubordination or discontent, not to mention acts of resistance?[1] The shift from a Sovietology founded on "categories" of totalitarianism to historical studies based on a large amount of factual documentation have nonetheless led historians such as Merle Fainsod and Leonard Schapiro (erstwhile pillars of totalitarianism historiography) to admit the existence of several zones of autonomy, if not resistance, in the economic domain as much as in the social or political, an elusion of the diverse forms of control and constraint implemented by the Bolshevik regime. Fainsod, author of a pioneering study on the Smolensk region during the 1920s and 1930s, has recognized that the Stalinist system was largely an "inefficient totalitarianism."[2] This is a rather ambiguous characterization: against what value may this "inefficiency" be effectively measured, an ideal and utopian standard of "total control," or in regard to a totalitarian model defined by a number of static "categories"? Does this claim of "inefficiency" not imply a permanent tension between an ongoing, endless politics of control and repression as well as diverse levels of social resistance?

Over the past twenty years, the increasing interest in social history, in "history viewed from below," has given rise to research on the spaces of impermeability in the regime, the zones of autonomy of sociodemographic behavior, strategies of circumvention and survival, deviancy, and the forms of social insubordination, opposition, and passive or active resistance. It has also given rise to studies on the modalities of integration and adaptation to the new "socialist society," strategies of social promotion, and the forms of adherence to certain values put forward by the regime.

In many ways the questions raised by historians studying the forms and modalities of Soviet society's opposition and "resistance" to the grip of the Stalinist regime refer to a debate central to the historiography of Nazism. This revolves around the notions of *widerstand* (radical and determined resistance to the regime) and *resistenz* (all behavior revealing a limit to the total grip of the regime).[3] In the historiography of Stalinism—less advanced than that of Nazism in this regard—this debate has certainly remained an underlying one, more often implicit than explicit, and also less marked by the weight of "collective guilt."[4] The vast majority of historians of Stalinist Soviet society have implicitly adopted the functionalist, behavioral, and societal concept of *resistenz*, introduced—for National Socialism—by Martin Broszat. This approach has enabled them to integrate a vast palette of collective and individual social behavior into their analyses, moving from partial refusal (which could coexist perfectly well with a partial adherence to certain of the regime's values) to the most active forms of resistance, passing along the way through various degrees of protest. As with the historiography of Nazism, this "societal" approach has overflowed the study of resistance alone into a much larger field: the zones of conflict—but also the zones of reciprocal avoidance and ignorance—between the governed and the governing, the spaces of autonomy for public opinion, daily behavior in a police state, and the impermeability of "shadow cultures" (to use the expression of T. H. Rigby) to Stalinist and Bolshevik ideology.

Moreover the broadening of research on everything that seemed to present obstacles to the regime's control and penetration of society has often shed light on the complex dialectic between adherence and refusal, consent and discontent, compromise and passive resistance, and resignation and deviance.

This new research has had to face a number of methodological difficulties. The first is the temptation to define "resistance" through the prism of confidential reports by the political-police or Party apparatuses, given that this is the point of view of power itself. More generally the historian has to guard against interpreting all social behavior in exclusively political terms: to impute political motives to any attitude distant from that of the regime or, conversely, to infer some "consensus" from the apparent absence of opposition. One must never forget the fact that resistance is the counterpart of power and that the nature of the power determines the nature of the resistance. The more domination aspires to totality, the larger the will to control the most diverse spheres of social and economic life, the more there is resistance. In effect it is the power itself that circumscribes an increasing amount of social behavior as acts of resistance, opposition, or deviance, which therefore might not exist under a different regime. Many types of behavior or language—those carefully noted by the political police as "hostile" or "deviant"—might naturally pass unnoticed or be deemed harmless in a different political context.[5] In this particular context it is often difficult to separate the evaluation of an action from its motivation, to distinguish clearly where the dividing line exists between individual intentions—the consciousness of committing deviant acts—and the politicization of behavior by the regime.

The second difficulty is in establishing a typology of deviant behavior, taking care to question the meaning of these acts (or their absence) according to a given context while excluding actions that would not raise even the slightest bit of interest for the regime and not setting up watertight barriers between the different "levels," given that the boundaries between them are permeable and mobile. Passive discord may turn into protest, but between this and a global rejection of the regime—including significant risk taking—there is generally a "qualitative leap" that few individuals are ready to make.

The third challenge is in establishing a quantitative balance sheet. In regard to several forms of resistance, such as the riots and mass demonstrations that followed collectivization and dekulakization, the statistics of the GPU yield fairly reliable weekly information. Data from the People's Commissariat of Justice or of Prosecution regarding the number of condemnations for "anti-Soviet propaganda and agitation" are even more difficult to interpret: do significant fluctuations in the number of condemnations reflect the level of discontent or rather the level of repression of politicized and criminalized beliefs? The political police's *svodki* (secret reports) are a precious source but particularly tricky to use.[6] Without critical analysis, these documents cannot be considered as even a primitive barometer of "popular opinion." For example, does the sudden surge of reports noting hostile comments in the work environment after the promulgation of the laws of June 1940 (which harshly punished absenteeism, production of defective goods, and abandonment of work posts) simply reflect a sudden increase in worker protests? Does it not also answer to a desire to be able to understand the daily reactions of the working world to these laws?

A fourth difficulty particularly concerns the analysis of forms of integration into, support of, and adherence to the regime. Regarding these questions, the historian is disadvantaged in a way by the immense amount of propaganda literature produced by the regime. By placing emphasis on "the unshakeable union between the Leader/Guide (or the Party) and the people," it often masks the real points of convergence—most often not admitted—between the regime and part of the population (possibilities of individual promotion, instrumentalization of latent tensions in the social body, populism, exploitation of nationalist strains, and such). Moreover the historian is handicapped by the fact that the newly accessible documentation on the state of opinion and the society issues from police and political apparatuses of control. Taking as a given the support of the immense majority of the population to the politics and values of the regime, these documents focus their attention on deviancy, opposition, and resistance. They allow little grasp of the ensemble of attitudes situated on a scale from resignation to adherence via indifference, consent, and partial or fickle support.

Well before the opening of the ex-USSR archives, Anglo-Saxon "revisionist" historians had sought to ground the Stalinist regime within a specific social consensus, whether active or passive. This was in reaction to a dominant historiography founded on the postulates of totalitarianism, which disclaimed any relevance to social history and denied the existence of any sort of "civil society." But in the already "classic" works of Sheila Fitzpatrick on the process of ascending social mobility during the 1930s, as well as in the recent work of David Shearer on the engineers' and industrial cadres' support of the "Great Retreat" of 1928–30, the accent has been placed more on research of a social base backing the regime's initiatives than on a deepened analysis of attitudes of support and adherence.[7] To understand these sorts of behavior, study of the various channels of social promotion and political strategies proves insufficient. Without a doubt, one must (as Stephen Kotkin has recently done in his book on Magnitogorsk during the 1930s) attempt to reconstitute the daily framework of "Stalinism as civilization," tracking within the period's "Bolshevik speak" elements that reflect a certain appropriation of the official discourse and "socialist values" by the population.[8] Broadly speaking, these values were generally limited to a few common places, meaning that despite the harshness of the times and the absence of alternatives, the country emerged little by little from its secular backwardness and oriented itself toward a "radiant future," or at least toward an as-yet-blurred form of "progress" and "modernity."

In this largely unexplored area, one must keep guard against hasty conclusions: recent research has led to a downward reevaluation of the population's adherence to the cult of Stalin.[9] Moreover, during the past few years, a trend can be detected particularly regarding the especially complex subject of the attitudes of the "masses" toward the Great Terror, a "reasonable" terror, or as some historians have suggested, a terror that was popular among the "common people."[10]

Handled with vigilance and a critical spirit, however, the newly accessible sources—reports by the political police on the country's situation and on "popular opinion"; criminal police documents; archives of the Ministries of Justice, of the Interior, of Prosecution, and of Inspection of Workers and Peasants; and of the local organizations of the Party; and others—prove invaluable for undertaking studies on the forms of autonomy and social resistance. They underline the permanence of major tensions throughout the Stalinist period between, on the one hand, a regime attempting to extend its control to an increasing number of spheres of social life and, on the other, a society that opposed this control through an infinite range of diverse forms of resistance, generally passive in nature, and that experimented with diverse forms of survival while implementing various strategies of circumvention and avoidance. The regime's difficulties in reining in a restive society in turn nourished the violence of the state. This dynamic provides a certain corrective to the static view of a society submitting to totalitarian order, of a triumphant regime having succeeded in its enterprise of control and domination.

Several recent studies have underscored the extent to which recognition of the need to confront a refractory society (*stikhiinaia*) shaped the political practices of Stalinism (and Leninist Bolshevism), beginning with the Great Retreat of 1929. In his last work historian Vladimir Brovkin appropriately recalls the widening distance between the society and the regime under the NEP, the frustrations of an urban proletariat who saw the Party as having betrayed the ideals of socialist emancipation, the muted hostility of peasant society toward the regime, and the "degeneration" of local Party organizations drowning in a "sea of peasants."[11] Among the reasons driving the Stalinist group to launch its great offensive of brutal economic and social transformation, a major role was played by the wish to make a preemptive strike against social and political processes that risked definitively escaping state-Party control.

Taking into account the permanent tensions generated by these series of events—social resistance to the regime's grip, a political offensive seeking to retake control and modify economic and social parameters, the reaction of social resistance, and repression by generalized criminalization of social behavior judged deviant or nonconformist—surely allows a better grasp of the internal dynamic of Stalinism. In this dynamic the leaders' perception of the system's vulnerability in the face of a fractious society was undoubtedly a more important element than has been generally thought.

One of the main difficulties that an open, functionalist, and societal definition of "resistance" presents is to grasp its often blurred contours and therefore to elaborate even an approximate typology of it. In the case of National Socialism, where historiography regarding the question of resistance is fairly advanced, several classifications have been proposed besides those of Philippe Burin in the present volume.[12] These classifications generally distinguish between public and private behavior, instinctual reactions and organized action, defensive actions and more "offensive" actions, and behavior reflecting a fundamental rejection of the regime and attitudes revealing partial discord. Among the most developed typologies is, for example, Detlev Peukert's "pyramidal model," which starts from a base of "nonconformism," followed by the "refusal to cooperate," then "protest," and ends with the narrow tip of actual "resistance," limited to behavior reflecting a global rejection of the system. One may also mention the classification by Gerhard Botz founded on three large categories: "deviant behavior," "social protest," and "political resistance."[13]

Noting the problems of definition that all overly rigid classifications pose, historian Ian Kershaw has proposed a "minimal" typology that, according to him, is more likely to take into account the blurring of outlines and the overlap between the various sorts of behavior analyzed. He thus distinguishes between "resistance," a term that "should only be applied to effective participation in *organized* action having as its declared objective the weakening of the regime and its eventual overthrow"; "opposition," which includes "all *actions* relevant to absolute resistance, but also others with partial and limited goals . . . which were sometimes individual or group actions partially in agreement with the regime and its ideology"; and finally "discord," a general term apt to take into account "the *passivity* of oppositional sentiments that were not necessarily translated into actions, and the often spontaneous expression of criticism towards this or that aspect of Nazism."[14] To the ascending scale proposed by Peukert, Kershaw therefore prefers a "series of concentric circles whose boundaries melt into each other: a 'soft belly' of 'discord'; a narrow band of 'opposition'; and a small core of fundamental 'resistance' at the center."[15]

To date, no large research project comparable to the "Bavarian project" in the historiography of Nazism has allowed for a deepening of our global understanding of the forms of resistance and adherence, whether passive or active, of Soviet society under Stalinism.[16] No overall typology has been developed. Only a few paths of research have been explored in a rather fragmentary way on subjects as diverse and precise as resistance to collectivization during 1929–30, resistance to Sovietization in the western margins of the USSR in 1940–41 and after 1945, and the riots and revolts within the Gulag.

We will attempt here to give a preliminary typological sketch of "societal resistance" to Stalinism, taking partial inspiration from the broad and open categories proposed by Kershaw for the case of Nazi Germany, which allow for an account of the overlap between different levels.

Active Resistance (*Soprotivlenie*)

A first and very small group of actions may be considered actual resistance, designated in Russian by the term *soprotivlenie*. One may define this type of resistance as participation in more or less organized *collective* action expressing a global rejection of the system or, at least, of a central component of the regime's politics. In different contexts and on different scales, the peasant revolts and demonstrations against collectivization, certain worker riots at the beginning of the 1930s, resistance to Sovietization in the western Ukraine or in the Baltic countries in 1945–48, and the revolts organized by national groups in the camps during the postwar years may be considered *soprotivlenie*.

Active and organized resistance to collectivization, which reached its apogee during the first half of 1930, has been the subject of several recent studies based on largely unedited documentation.[17] These types of resistance are remarkable for many reasons. Their magnitude (nearly fourteen thousand riots and "mass demonstrations" registered by the political police during 1930, of which more than sixty-five hundred were in the month of March alone) forced the leadership in power to back off—a unique fact during the entire Stalinist period—and announce a pause in the frantic pace of collectivization decreed at the end of 1929. Study of the strongest resistance zones leads to the question of the relation between these riots and the great peasant revolts of 1920–21. One notes in effect a remarkable permanence in the regions most defiant to the regime: the Ukraine (especially in the west), the Cossack regions of Don and Kuban, the central region of the Black Lands, and western Siberia. This permanence invites historians "to study the beginning of the 1930s in light of the period from 1917–1922" (Andrea Graziosi) and to examine certain regions (especially the Ukraine) with an eye to assessing the link between the peasant movement and the national question. In some districts of the western Ukraine—which managed to escape Soviet control for a few weeks—the peasant resistance to collectivization took on an openly anti-Soviet and nationalist color. Insurgent peasants demanded not only a halt to collectivization and dekulakization but also "the abolition of the Soviet regime" and the proclamation of an "independent Ukraine." In the Cossack regions, where the memory of the "de-cossackization" of 1919–20 remained vivid, the peasant revolts, with their monarchist slogans, also reflected a radical rejection of the regime.

Unlike what had happened during the civil war, however, the peasant revolts and riots did not lead to broader insurrectional movements such as those that had made peasant bastions of entire provinces in 1920–21 (Tambov, Tyumen, Tobolsk, and others) from which all Soviet power had been banned.[18] Unlike the insurgents of 1920–21, heavily armed (the majority of them were deserters from the Red Army) and trained by political leaders close to the socialist-revolutionary milieu, the rioters of 1930 had only knives and lacked experienced leaders. A detailed study of GPU reports reveals that the actual "revolts"—that is, armed demonstrations directed by an "operational collective" calling for the forcible overthrow of the local Soviet power and seeking to enlarge territory gained by the rebels—remained relatively small in number (176 during 1930) and limited in time (a few weeks) and scope (on the scale of districts rather than of entire provinces). The human losses recognized by the authorities (around 1,500 Soviet functionaries and "activists" killed, 7,000 wounded or beaten up—but what was the number of victims on the side of the insurgents?) throughout a thousand confrontations "quelled by armed force" suggest violent but nevertheless limited engagements.[19]

Most of the resistance was actually reflected by the thousands of riots, demonstrations, protest marches, and other brief assemblies that each time mobilized from hundreds to thousands of people in front of (often ransacked) public buildings. The apparently limited aspect of these actions, where the female peasants often played the main roles (in part because the men thought the repression would be less brutal if women and children were on the front line), could not disguise the extent of the social trauma. For most of the rural population, this trauma was embodied in a frontal assault led by the regime and its representatives against an entire culture—a way of life and of secular behavior. As Lynne Viola has shown in her recent work, the forced collectivization of the countryside was much more than the expropriation of the peasants and their forced service in the kolkhozes.[20] It was a war waged against an entire traditional peasant culture: much of the peasant turmoil was provoked by the administration closing churches and confiscating their bells, by antireligious vandalism conducted by young Communist "activists," by the propagation of apocalyptic rumors, and by the specter of a "second serfdom." The demands made by the peasants reflected their sense of having had their entire identity and values violated. They demanded the dissolution of the kolkhozes, restitution for everything that had been confiscated, and the return from deportation of the "dekulakized" as well as free elections in the rural soviets, legislation of "peasant unions," restitution of its goods to the Church, freedom of worship and commerce, and the punishment of "impious komsomols." Save for protests directly related to collectivization, "dekulakization," and the antireligious offensive, other demands were in line with demands formulated by the peasantry since the first years of the Soviet regime.[21]

Obliged to withdraw, the Stalinist leadership managed to neutralize the peasant resistance, although not without skillfully throwing responsibility for the "excesses" of collectivization on functionaries and local activists "drunk on success." The flood subsided only gradually at the cost of a hurriedly (and often only on paper) organized dismantling of two-thirds of the kolkhozes. The leadership resigned itself to putting the brakes on the pace of collectivization, though without renouncing their long-term objectives. The number of riots and mass demonstrations fell from sixty-five hundred in March to around two thousand in April, about thirteen hundred in May, six hundred in July, and a few hundred per month throughout the autumn.[22] The arrest and deportation of the most enterprising peasants and "agitators," the resumption of field work, the increased weight of fiscal pressures on peasant "individuals" who remained outside the kolkhozes, and the absence of organization and means ended up winning out against the peasant resistance, at least under the forms that it had assumed during the winter of 1929–30. But this opposition did not cease. It presented itself differently afterward under the most diverse guises. Issuing from that moment on was more a social disobedience and a refusal to cooperate than organized resistance.

The revolts and riots linked to collectivization represent for the 1930s the most prominent form of collective and organized resistance to one key aspect of the regime's politics. It was not, however, the only form.

In the urban environment documentation available today confirms the existence (briefly evoked at the time by the newspaper of the Menshevik emigration, *Sotsialisticeskii Vestnik*) of significant worker riots during the difficult spring of 1932, which was marked by food shortages, precursors of the great famine of 1932–33. Detailed reports on this unrest underline its extent, notably in certain mines of the Donbass and in the region of Ivanovo-Voznessensk (several tens of thousands of strikers in the textile industry) as well as its partially political dimension.[23] Unleashed in the middle of a period of scarcity by a brutal reduction in rations, the protest movement revealed all the workers' accumulated frustrations and hatred against a regime that—having broken up all independent union movements and worsened laborers' conditions during the great antiworker offensive of 1929–30—had betrayed the socialist ideal of the emancipated proletariat. In the window of a special shop for Party and GPU officials in Ivanovo-Voznessensk, one found undeniably political tracts:"Even while the starving workers of Vichuga and Teikovo were fired upon because they clamored for bread, here, behind the store's drawn curtains, the communist officials and red cops of the GPU were getting fat."[24] The strikes resulted in heavily politicized meetings, demonstrations, and hunger marches, including men, women, and children in long processions. The demonstrations degenerated into riots: the symbolic edifices of power—the Party committee's building as well as that of the political police—were ransacked, their occupants set upon and beaten. These limited riots, which were more like small peasant efforts than a tightly structured action taken by the worker militants, were easily suppressed by armed force. Once the alert had passed, the authorities directed a parody of public justice; since it was unthinkable to pass judgment on "authentic" workers, the accused were all presented as "socially foreign elements" and their actions as so many "acts of political banditry." The regime reacted to these worker riots, these extreme manifestations of discontent, by measures alternating between limited economic concessions (a temporary augmentation of investments in light industry), the stiffening of antiworker legislation, and the reinforcement of police control in the enterprises.

It seems that, at least at the level of present research, the worker riots (of which there are other examples in October 1941, during the winter of 1946–47 [marked by shortages in the city and by famine in some areas of the countryside], and much later in Novocherkassk in June 1962) nevertheless remained an exceptional form of resistance in the labor world.[25] The latter was completely shattered by, simultaneously, an intense renewal of the labor force (in one decade the number of workers quadrupled, and the hard core of the working class during the 1920s was dissolved into the mass of new arrivals into the countryside) and a very specific stratification set up by the new industrial state. In the framework of a complex system in which about fifteen categories of rationing coexisted (particularly during 1930–34 and then also between 1941 and 1947), the workers laboring in large factories or industrial centers with state priority were privileged at the expense of workers in light industry and inhabitants of "nonpriority" cities.[26] This stratification—

factory by factory and city by city—obviously did not create conditions for even minimal worker solidarity.

The examples we have elicited all are regular episodes of collective but poorly organized resistance. Once each confrontation had passed, they did not lead to any long-term social restructuring of the individuals who had participated.

These episodes contrasted with other forms of resistance that were structured more around a firm objective: driving out the occupier. It is not surprising that the strongest active resistance the Stalinist regime had to face was that which accompanied the Sovietization of the western Ukraine, Moldavia, and the Baltic countries in 1939–41 and especially after 1945. The process of Sovietization extended over nearly six years (1945–50) and provoked a series of armed resistance and large-scale repression that resulted in tens of thousands of victims and the deportation or consignment to the Gulag of hundreds of thousands of people (800,000 to 1 million people, according to various sources).[27] The power of the resistance movement in these annexed regions arose naturally from the fact that the new regime was considered by the majority of the population to be one of foreign occupation that moreover imposed profoundly unpopular structural reforms such as collectivization.

The strongest armed resistance to Sovietization took place in the western Ukraine, where a fairly powerful clandestine armed organization, the ONU (Organization of Nationalist Ukrainians), had existed since the first Soviet occupation (September 1939 to June 1941). It recruited its members from a peasantry profoundly hostile to collectivization. An interesting study of these frontier regions along the borders of Poland, Romania, and the Ukraine, which had been centers of active resistance to Soviet power during 1920–21 and 1930, would be the continuity of forms of opposition, the complex relations between the peasant movement and the national Ukrainian movement, the phenomenon of "contamination" on both sides of the border before 1939, and the local permanence of people, that is, of networks engaged in resistance.

Under a Nazi occupation that was rather welcomed (at least at the beginning) in the countryside of the western Ukraine, the leadership of the ONU attempted unsuccessfully to form an independent Ukrainian government in Lviv. In July 1944, when the Red Army reentered the region, the ONU formed the Supreme Council for the Liberation of the Ukraine and organized an actual army, the UPA (Insurgent Ukrainian Army), which included in autumn 1944 more than 20,000 men. From July 1944 to December 1949, Soviet authorities on seven occasions called on the insurgents to lay down their arms in return for a promise of amnesty, but without tangible results. According to a report by the Soviet Ministry of the Interior, the Ukrainian "bandits" carried out more than 14,400 "terrorist raids" from July 1944 to March 1953. These were basically attacks against local representatives of Soviet authority, the burning or ransacking of public buildings, and armed attacks on trains or convoys.[28] Up until the beginning of 1947, UPA guerillas, supported by a peasantry that refused collectivization, managed to control a part of the "deep country" in a few mainly border districts of the Ukraine and even of western Byelorussia. UPA forces also operated within Poland and Czechoslovakia, passing from one country to another to elude the special forces of the NKVD. In order to deprive the rebellion of its bases in Poland, in 1947 the government there displaced all of the Ukrainian population living in Poland to the northwest of the country at the request of the Soviet government. Rural Ukraine was pacified only by 1950 at the expense of punitive operations creating tens of thousands of victims, displacement of entire villages, and massive deportations of the population to Siberia and Kazakhstan (between 300,000 and 400,000 people). Judging from the last amnesty proposal signed by the Ukrainian minister of the interior on December 30, 1949, "insurgent bands" were not recruited exclusively from the peasantry. Among the various categories of "bandits" the text also mentions "young people who have fled the factories, the Donetz mines, and the technical training schools."[29] At this point, however, no study other than hagiography has allowed for the establishment of even a cursory sociology of this major form of resistance to the Soviet regime.

In the Baltic states resistance was not structured as strongly as in the Ukraine. There was no organization similar to the ONU capable of forming a lasting federation out of the numerous small groups resisting the occupiers, which were more active in Catholic and rural Lithuania than in the more urbanized and majority Protestant countries of Latvia or Estonia. According to the sources of the Soviet Ministry of the Interior, from the summer of 1944 to the end of 1946, several hundred "bandit" groups in the three Baltic countries committed more than eight thousand "terrorist acts," during which around 13,000 civil and military functionaries were killed.[30] Another partial summary refers to 25,000 people killed in clashes between the Soviet forces of order and Lithuanian guerillas in 1947–48.[31] In order to eradicate these groups, which, thanks to support from among the local population, controlled a part of the " deep country" (especially in Lithuania), the Soviet government organized two large centralized deportations of "kulak families, nationalists, and bandits" (around 50,000 deported in May 1948 and 95,000 in February–March 1949). From 1944 to 1953 a total of between 200,000 and 250,000 Baltic peoples were deported—not counting the 150,000 Baltic peoples who were sent to the Gulag—mainly for "counter-revolutionary activities" or "treason against the Fatherland."[32]

One of the continuities of the Ukrainian and Baltic resistance to Sovietization was action by clandestine networks of detainees founded mainly by "nationalist" Ukrainian and Baltic resistors sent to the Gulag. After the war they composed a large part of the approximately 600,000 "political" prisoners serving heavy sentences of ten to twenty-five years in the camps. The 1948 creation of "special regime camps" for political detainees considered "particularly dangerous" separated "resistants" from "common law" detainees, thus eliminating the principal obstacle to the growth of solidarity among prisoners. Many "special camps" detainees, ex-members of the ONU, the UPA, or other "partisan" groups, reconstituted structures of solidarity that had only needed a catalyst for reactivation. Judging from the inspection reports ordered by gulag directors at the beginning of the 1950s, the network of clandestine nationalist organizations had managed up to a point to transform the special camps into centers of insubordination from which informers had been eliminated and where production plans were never fulfilled. The penitentiary authorities tried to react by organizing massive displacements of detainees from one camp to another, with the idea of breaking up the networks. But they usually only ended up disseminating "leaders" who often managed to reconstitute groups on a broad scale with different core groups in different gulags.

Between 1948 and 1953, according to fragmentary data available today, dozens of hunger strikes, group escapes, general "disorder," and riots broke out in the Gulag.[33] Most of these were organized by "resistance collectives," the vast majority of whose members were nationalist militants. The most significant revolts took place just after the death of Stalin and the amnesty that followed (which did not include the "politicals"). Large strikes followed by revolts in Gorlag (May 1953, 14,000 participants), Rechlag (July 1953, 12,000 participants), and Steplag (May–June 1954, 5,000 participants) revealed the power and authority of the clandestine organizations, structured on a national basis mainly by Baltic peoples or Ukrainians. The demands made by the mutineers—reduction of the workday to eight hours, amelioration of living conditions, review of condemnations, and granting of a statute privileging "political prisoners"—which had been rejected earlier, were partially satisfied during the reforms of the camp system introduced in 1954–55.

Insubordination and Deviancy (*Stikhiinost*)

In its efforts to control society, the Stalinist regime had to confront a wide range of forms of social insubordination (*stikhiinost*)[34] more often than organized collective resistance (*soprotivlenie*). A complex and shifting notion, *stikhiinost* includes a vast palette of actions and behavior reflecting a form of insubordination, disobedience, or social deviance committed generally by individuals and more rarely by limited groups of individuals. For the authorities, *stikhiinost*—an expression referring to a restive, ungovernable, and even hostile society—represented something different than a simple summation of individual acts of social and criminal defiance. It reflected, if not overt political opposition, at least an often intangible (which rendered it even more pernicious) form of collective "anti-Soviet" or "petite bourgeoise" consciousness.

In reality the motivations for these acts varied. They could sometimes reflect a steadfast rejection of the system, as in the extreme case of "banditism" during the 1930s. This is a specific example of deviance involving both resistance against the new social and economic order of the collectivized countryside and traditional common-law criminality. More often, however, the deviant behavior one may classify under the term *stikhiinost* does not necessarily imply a global rejection of the political system and social order. Rather it included strategies for bypassing the controls, limitations, and prohibitions implemented by the regime in the most diverse spheres of economic and social life. And these give testimony to the numerous types of deviance (small-time trafficking, "false cooperatives," "false kolkhozes," black market activity, and such) induced by the "parallel economy" and "deficit economy" and classified by the authorities under the generic term "speculation."

Insubordination and social deviance often appeared—even more mundanely—in the framework of a struggle for survival under conditions of severe poverty, scarcity, and even famine. The innumerable minor forms of "waste of social property," illegal appropriation of plots of land, minor theft, and embezzlement systematically and strictly criminalized by those in power represented the primary cause of condemnations to the toil of forced labor.

The refusal to cooperate (the "strategy of the weak," according to James Scott's apt characterization), in its various modalities, constituted another aspect of *stikhiinost* at the limits of social disobedience and "disagreement." In the factories this encompassed massive absenteeism, production of rejects, sloppiness, and *tekucka* (frequent change of workplace), while in the kolkhozes and sovkhozes it encompassed the refusal to go to work, plant the fields, or maintain agricultural machinery; the noncompletion of obligatory delivery plans; and other disruptive behavior.

Among the most significant cases of the refusal to cooperate—and the most difficult to interpret—was the still individual but often widespread reluctance, even refusal, of some Soviet functionaries (kolkhoz directors, directors of enterprises, judges, and procurers) to apply directives or laws. What motivated this "abstinence from efficiency" (to use Moshe Lewin's phrase), incompetence, lack of discipline, ignorance of what was expected of them from higher places, or a deliberate refusal to implement measures of which they disapproved?

The most violent form of social insubordination, one that had dramatically worsened during the 1930s, was what the authorities termed "banditism." This phenomenon reached its apogee during the civil war and had never been totally eradicated during the 1920s. It reflected the tremendous regression and extreme violence that had accompanied the great social upheavals at the beginning of the 1930s, especially in the countryside, which had been subjugated to forced collectivization and dekulakization. Most of the "brigands" were recruited from the "dekulakized" who had succeeded in either escaping deportation or fleeing from the "special populatings" (more than 600,000 "special displaced persons" left their place of deportation illegally, at least during the period between 1932 and 1940, for which there are more-or-less reliable statistics).[35] Living on the margins of society, these new pariahs often joined a world of crime halfway between political and common-law banditism. Operating in small-armed bands, these "avengers" (as they called themselves) mainly attacked local representatives of Soviet power—kolkhoz presidents, functionaries, Communists, and other "activists"—and set fire to kolkhoz buildings, "collective" grain silos, and machinery and tractor warehouses. In 1931, 40 percent of the kolkhozes in western Siberia, one of the regions where banditism was particularly developed (along with the Ukraine, the Caucasus, the Urals, Byelorussia, Kazakhstan, and Central Asia), suffered a "bandit attack" or "terrorist act." Throughout the country, 17 percent of all kolkhozes were attacked by armed groups in the spring of the same year.[36] During the entire 1930s, as the recently declassified archives of the "worker and peasant militia" (the criminal police) show, banditism continued endemically in a large number of regions. The small and overwhelmed local police forces appear to have been powerless to curb "terrorist acts" directed at representatives of power. This was the case especially in 1932–34, when there was an aggravation of criminality in rural areas following a general decline generated by shortages, famine, and a new turn of the repression-resistance-repression cycle. For the authorities, banditism was a "degenerate" form of the final battle waged by the "debris of moribund classes." The activities and functioning of these small, armed groups in fact bring to mind the model (proposed by Eric Hobsbawm) of "primitive rebels" engaged in an already lost struggle against the modern state. The eradication of these fringe groups constituted one of the primary objectives of the most significant repression operations launched after the summer of 1937. In this regard we should recall that the Great Terror was not only the extreme outcome of the political purges, it was also the culminating point of a struggle waged throughout the 1930s against "social disorder" generated by the great upheavals at the beginning of the decade.

Sheila Fitzpatrick ranks "hooliganism," especially in rural areas, among the other forms of social insubordination reflecting a diffuse form of opposition to the regime. In contrast to traditional hooliganism—"adolescent, overtly iconoclastic, directed against patriarchal authority" (and moreover often associated with the actions of the young Communists under the NEP)—the hooliganism of the 1930s often expressed a steadfast rejection of the new kolkhoz order.[37] Hooligans, including peasants of all ages, prevented kolkhoz meetings intended to demonstrate the reality of "kolkhoz democracy"; loudly opposed the execution of "collection plans," or the vote in favor of obligatory loans to the state; pillaged public buildings; and verbally and physically assaulted local functionaries, kolkhoz political officials, and "rural correspondents" (*selkory*, part journalists and part informers who were to notify the regional authorities of "diverse facts of an oppositional character"). Also prevalent in the cities, hooliganism—a form of social protest in which it is still difficult to evaluate that part that was a rejection of the established order—was perceived by the authorities as the sign of a social disorder that could only be contained by an ever growing repression.[38]

As the foundation of *stikhiinost*, social insubordination was also expressed by an extraordinary inventiveness for skirting the numerous limitations, prohibitions, and controls implemented by the region, especially in the economic sphere. Under conditions of endemic destitution and the inconsistencies of coexistent provisioning, rationing, and pricing systems, as well as in spite of the promulgation of very repressive legislation, the authorities failed to eradicate the often large-scale "speculation" (that is, the resale of defective products) and theft that nourished the shadow economy. In March 1932 an inquiry carried out by the services of the People's Commissariat of Commerce, for example, found that 270 tons of bread—nearly 20 percent of the bread distributed in

Moscow under the framework of a centralized rationing system—were stolen daily and exported from the city by an army of *mecocniki* ("sack carriers") who had been believed to have disappeared after the civil war. During this same month, 30 percent of the production of the largest shoe factory in the country was redirected.[39] In August 1934 the highest Party authority, the Politburo, established a special commission to fight against "speculation." The general mobilization against "deviance" resulted in massive raids on "speculators" in the markets, who were often deported as "socially foreign elements," as well as in the condemnations of more than 105,000 people—in 1935 alone— for "speculation," a misdemeanor that had become strictly criminalized.[40] Ingenious schemes flourished parallel to these "elementary" forms of a black market: for example, "false artisanal cooperatives," which hid actual private enterprises employing hundreds of artisans at home working on raw materials misappropriated on a large scale; "fictional kolkhozes," where supplies, agricultural goods, and livestock continued to be privately and individually owned thanks to the complicity of an entire chain of shady functionaries; and clandestine "entrepreneur syndicates," which included hundreds of members, such as those liquidated by the NKVD's economic department in the Odessa region in 1936.[41]

Basically, however, these "circumvention strategies" remained relatively marginal phenomena in relation to the "survival stratagems" experienced daily, and at their own risk, by millions of citizens in a situation of absolute economic distress. Among these, the most frequent in rural areas were the attempted "nibbling" away of not-so-legal individual plots (one-quarter to one-half hectares) of "collective" lands. Periodically the government would launch vast "recovery of social property" operations. In the autumn of 1939, two million hectares (a quarter of the total legal surface area of the plots) were "recovered." Another large operation at the end of 1946 and beginning of 1947 yielded even more impressive results, naturally at the price of an aggravation of the peasantry's condition, already confronted that year with shortages and even famine in some regions.[42]

Theft of "social property" was the most common and massive response to the conditions of severe destitution created by the regime, especially in rural areas. Whether committed individually or collectively, and often with the complicity of local staff—brigadiers, kolkhoz directors, directors of stores and cooperatives, and officials at the silos—theft was viewed by the regime as one of the principal forms of social insubordination. It was fought without respite by ultra-repressive legislation, although the strict application of this legislation was often contested by some of the magistrates. Those condemned for the theft of "social property" represented by far (between 200,000 and 250,000 people per year) the main contingent of detainees in the Gulag (around 30 percent, compared with 20–25 percent for "political" prisoners).[43]

During the entire Stalinist period, the authorities had to face behavior reflecting what might be called a "refusal to cooperate." One can understand certain demonstrations in light of the penal legislation adopted by the government to suppress these "ordinary" acts (characterized from one day to the next as felonious and criminal acts). Disciplinary action was taken against the seemingly frequent refusal to work in the collective fields (kolkhozniks received practically nothing for their labor) by a 1948 decree (a difficult one to implement in practice, given the extent of the phenomenon) stipulating the deportation of kolkhozniks who had not performed a minimal number of "work days" during the year and thus "led a parasitic life."[44] The rejection of the kolkhoz system was equally reflected in the regular flux of generally temporary departures to the cities, notwithstanding the prohibition on leaving the kolkhoz. During the most difficult years of shortages (1936 and 1946–47) and famine (1932–33 and 1946–47), the flow of departures went as far as closing down entire kolkhozes, which continued to exist only on paper. Not all peasants left for the cities. Individual operations developed illegally next to deserted collective farms. Despite all the attempts to attain a collectivization rate of 100 percent, the percentage of individual operations remained between 3 percent and 8 percent total depending on the year.

In the factory environment the discontent could no longer be adequately expressed by organized forms of protest, and it generally resulted in all sorts of "negative" behavior—absenteeism, weak work discipline, the breaking of machinery, negligence, and sloppiness—that were all reflected in a significant increase in the production of defective goods. But what part did rebelliousness—as opposed to a lack of an ability to adapt to existent working conditions in the factories by newly arriving workers—play in these phenomena? It is difficult to say, and the official sources (which had a tendency to present every incident and every defective product as so many acts of sabotage) hardly shed light on this point. Equally difficult to interpret unequivocally was the extensive mobility of workers, who changed enterprises several times per year despite the growing weight of constraints and obstacles placed in their way. The permanent shortage of skilled labor was the last card available to workers in defending their interests, their final bargaining chip. The regime never succeeded in bringing the *tekucka* under control, even while engaging in an unprecedented repression of "work deserters."[45]

Recent studies have shown that among the types of "refusal to cooperate" was opposition by functionaries and administrative cadres (judges and directors of enterprises and kolkhozes especially) to the application of repressive measures disproportionate to their purported acts. In his study on the functioning of the criminal justice system under Stalin, Peter Solomon has revealed the reluctance by a number of magistrates to punish—with all the severity of the laws of August 7, 1932, and June 4, 1947—minor theft, often judged in terms of a more lenient article of the penal code.[46] Decrees in December 1938 and the summer of 1940 criminalizing tardiness to work, absenteeism, "abandoning one's work station," and minor "hooliganism" in the factory also met with opposition by judges and company managers, the latter frequently refusing to report their workers' tardiness to work or absence. Applying the decree to the deportation of those kolkhozniks leading a "parasitic life" was rendered difficult by lack of cooperation from directors. Kolkhoz cadres were close to the people under their jurisdiction, were often from the same rural area, and were certainly the most resistant body of a globally incompetent and largely inefficient bureaucracy. When pressure on the collective farms from the center reached a certain threshold, the directors' refusal to cooperate increased. The years 1931–33 and 1946–48 saw a brutal intensification of "state collections," condemning vast numbers of the peasantry to suffer scarcity, and even famine, in conjunction with an already severely degraded economy. During these years many rural functionaries displayed their solidarity with their charges. In 1932 more than one-third of the kolkhoz directors were dismissed (and often condemned) mainly for "allowing the anti-State activities of sabotage of the collectives."[47] A similar process on a smaller but still significant scale occurred immediately after the war, nearly twenty years after the introduction of collectivization. From 1946 to 1948 more than 21,000 kolkhoz presidents (around 10 percent of all directors at this level) were sentenced to the camps for "waste of kolkhoz property," a formulation punishing the distribution—minimal as it was—of an advance to the peasants prior to the collective being released from its obligations to the state.[48] One could multiply the examples illustrating the various forms of refusal to cooperate by basic functionaries.

The malfunctioning of the Soviet bureaucracy and permanent frustration among the country's leaders provoked by the inefficiency of proliferate and incompetent apparatuses constitute a field of study in its own right, which has been taken up elsewhere.[49] Nevertheless note here that these now well-documented refusals to cooperate generally are not easy to interpret: what was the role of lack of discipline, of incompetence, of ignorance of precisely what was expected of the "base" by the hierarchy, of effective solidarity with the "common people," and of opposition to measures ordered by the center? One thing is certain: beyond a certain level, repression based on the criminalization of "ordinary" behavior and on the obvious disproportion between minor crimes committed in situations of distress and the heaviness of the penalty came up against a refusal to cooperate by even some of those who had been placed in charge of supervising the restive social body.

Forms of Autonomy of Popular Opinion

Following Ian Kershaw, we define discord (or dissent, the third circle of our typology) as any form of nonconformist and "oppositional" sentiment expressing spontaneous criticism of this or that aspect of the regime and its politics. Discord reveals the limits of the official ideological and propagandist grip on public consciousness as well as the persistence of alternative routes of information. Nevertheless this implies neither a global rejection of the system nor even a gateway to acts of insubordination or deviance. Discord or discontent, as strong as they may be, may also coexist quite well with political conformism in the same individual and under other circumstances. Today historians of Stalinism may grasp the forms of discord through a number of recently declassified sources. These include reports on "popular opinion" compiled by local Party organizations and the political police, accounts of postal or military censorship, signed or anonymous letters sent to various bureaucratic authorities, and private journals, the most developed form of "inner emigration which allowed one to carry on despite totalitarian pressure, against it and with it."[50]

The manner in which these sorts of discord were sometimes tolerated and sometimes repressed, depending on the political situation of the moment, sheds an instructive light on the "threshold of tolerance" for the expression of opinions not in conformity with the Stalinist regime's official ideology.

In her work on the peasantry during the 1930s, Sheila Fitzpatrick recounts the words of a Finnish Communist militant, Arvo Tuominen, who in 1934 accompanied a "collection brigade" making the rounds in the countryside: "My first impression—and it would prove to be a lasting one—was that every peasant was a counter-revolutionary, and that the entire peasantry was in revolt against Moscow and against Stalin."[51] Throughout the 1930s the vast majority of police and administrative reports, where attention was particularly given to the rumors that fed conversations among the peasants, openly confirm Tuominen's "first impression": a massive and global hostility in the kolkhoz system toward the entire regime and Stalin in particular. Still, the accounts reported by the scattered network of informers undoubtedly constituted "only the tip of the iceberg," as Kershaw has emphasized in comparison to similar documents produced by the Nazi regime.[52] Naturally this global hostility to the "new serfdom" imposed by force at the beginning of the 1930s coexisted with "passive and active strategies of adaptation." It is nevertheless striking to observe that the main theme of these accounts, of *castuki* (popular couplets) and rumors reported during the 1930s, was the imminent fall of the regime. The trauma caused by collectivization and dekulakization had undoubtedly been so strong that one wanted to believe that the situation could not last forever. It seems that rumors—the traditional vehicle for information in the countryside—increased dramatically. Beyond what they revealed about peasant discontent, they reflected the general disarray of a world in upheaval from top to bottom, where anything could happen. The famine of 1932–33 (reports of which reached all the way to the most remote provinces, which had not had to suffer) and especially the fact that the authorities had not spoken of it, was interpreted as an auspicious sign that the regime was collapsing.[53] Kirov's assassination was sometimes welcomed with joy and gave rise to numerous *castuki* with the theme, "They've killed Kirov, soon they'll kill Stalin!" In the months following Kirov's death, "symbolic attacks" on public portraits of the leaders were reported in abundance as well as harshly punished according to Article 58-10 of the penal code (unrest and anti-Soviet propaganda).[54] "Defeatist" rumors of a coming war that would put an end to the Soviet regime occurred throughout the 1930s and with increased frequency after 1937–38. In rural areas the populist offensive led by Stalin against local directors accused of all the abuses that the "common people" faced daily did not reinforce the prestige of the leader/guide: no "naïve monarchism" would rally a peasantry that viewed Stalin as the main instigator of collectivization and the principal enemy of the peasant.[55]

In the work environment of the great urban centers, discord and discontent were more diffuse and more inextricably mixed with "elements of consensus," as several recent studies have shown. Unlike the kolkhozniks, who had been forgotten by the system, the workers had to construct their social identity. They were caught in a complex and contradictory network of hard daily realities, encouragement "to progress socially," and official values glorifying the proletariat.[56]

Disaffection felt by the workers toward the regime appears to have intensified between the beginning and the end of the 1930s, culminating in the second half of 1940 (after the adoption of antiworker legislation that summer). The proportion of workers in the Party fell significantly from 8 percent in 1933 to less than 3 percent by 1941.[57] Among the recurrent themes abundantly developed in reports on "popular opinion" in the factories (prepared at the same time by the information department of the Party cell and by the special department of the NKVD present in all large enterprises) was, above all, worker discontent in regard to the general degradation of life and work conditions, especially at the beginning and end of the 1930s.

One should remember that real incomes fell globally by about 45 percent between 1928 and 1940. The workers did not pass up an occasion to recall this degradation, even while Stalin was pronouncing with impunity that "life has become better, life has become happier." Criticism was particularly virulent against the increase in industry standards, the Stakhanovists who were often responsible for them, the requirement to subscribe to obligatory loans (one month's salary), and the December 1938 and June 1940 antiworker laws. These particularly unpopular laws gave rise to vague rumors about massive suicides of workers who had been fired for arriving late. Regarding this, the NKVD noted the appearance of a number of anonymous tracts and graffiti harshly criticizing "worker exploitation," an exploitation "worse than Hitler's."[58]

This discontent in regard to concrete realities often revealed a strong sense of alienation: the workers were a "common people," indeed slaves, exploited by the "newly privileged" or "Communist directors" in a system dominated by "Bolsheviks, Jews, and thieves." The existence of strong anti-Semitism in the work environment is attested to in the reports on "popular opinion." Jews were associated with the directing elites. This anti-Semitism led some to praise Hitler, the only leader capable of "ridding the earth of Jews and Bolsheviks." The sense of alienation rested on a staunch polarization between "Them" (the leadership, the newly affluent, Jews, as well as Party cadres) and "Us" (the common working people tricked and betrayed by the official discourse, which all the while prattled on about the proletariat). The "special" stores for the nomenklatura and privileges for the "new red bourgeoisie" were particularly despised. In the work environment the populist Stalinist discourse denouncing bureaucrats and corrupt cadres and praising the wisdom and political perceptiveness of the "common people" allowed for a certain assuaging of their hatred for both low-level and high-level "managers." The most frequent reaction to the great trials and political purges nevertheless seems to have been indifference: leaders settling their accounts among each other would not yield much for the common people anyway.[59]

Reactions reported by the network of informers during the years of the

Great Terror are, of course, particularly difficult to interpret. In the general climate of fear, one kept quiet or one outsmarted the "Bolshevik discourse" that one had more-or-less shrewdly absorbed: informers noted that the workers "interpreted" the decrees cracking down on absenteeism as being the work of "enemies of the people." Research on the main themes of discord and dissent are even less developed for the war and postwar years than for the 1930s. The war—and victory—was undeniably "consensus producing," and the cult of Stalin—"Father Victory"—spread even to rural areas where hatred of the kolkhoz system remained alive. Nevertheless, immediately after the war, a period marked by immense economic and social difficulties and by a reinforcing of controls, the great themes of dissent from the 1930s made their appearance again. This included the idea—transmitted by rumors in many regions during 1946–47—that the kolkhozes would soon disappear.[60]

A recent study (limited, unfortunately, to the 1930s) has shown very large fluctuations in the number of people condemned for their beliefs (Article 58-10 of the penal code): more than 100,000 in 1931, around 17,000 in 1934, more than 230,000 in 1937, and 18,000 in 1940.[61] The politics that would follow from the definition and repression of "counterrevolutionary language," punishable by five years in camp, gave rise to intense clashes in 1935–36 between the public prosecutor's office (A. I. Akulov and Andrei Vychinski), the People's Commissariat of Justice (Krylenko), the political police (Genrikh Yagoda) and the country's highest authorities (Stalin and Molotov). What language could cause such pursuit and condemnation? Criticism of the kolkhoz system and the decline in the conditions of existence, as well as couplets or anecdotes deriding the regime's politics or its principal leaders, including Stalin, were generally recognized as so common that repressing them could only lead to excesses similar to those that occurred in the countryside in 1930–32, when tens of thousands of kolkhozniks were condemned for "antikolkhoz attitudes." The language to be punished in particular was "pro-fascist," "trotskyite," "defeatist," and included "calls for action against the leaders." As in other domains, application of Article 58-10 gave rise to abuse or reticence. In 1935 the systematic pursuit demanded by the procurer general of the USSR (Akulov) of language expressing satisfaction with the assassination of Kirov came up against the reluctance of many judges under the pretext that such declarations (especially those coming from the "common people") reflected more a "political backwardness" than "counterrevolutionary" intentions. Apart from 1937–38, during which 300,000 people were arrested under the pretext of "counterrevolutionary propaganda and agitation," a minimal "threshold of tolerance" for dissident opinions had to be allowed *nolens volens* by the regime in the face of an evidently widely shared discontent. At the dawning of the war, in 1940, the number of condemnations according to Article 58-10 fell to its lowest level in seven years despite the fact that all reports on "popular opinion" signaled an aggravation of "unhealthy attitudes" in the population. It is true that during this year the struggle against *stikhiinost* turned to another front—that of "abandonment of work."

The Impermeability of Cultures

Lastly, a fourth circle of "societal resistance" (in the broadest sense of the term) would comprise everything relevant to the impermeability of cultures, traditions, ways of life, and of social and long-term demographic behavior profoundly antagonistic to the regime's values and ideology. We have a matter here of resistance expressed more in terms of avoidance and reciprocal ignorance than in terms of rejection or conflict. It could be a question of phenomena as diverse as the persistence of religious holidays in an overtly atheistic state, the upholding of the practice of *samosoud* (summary justice applied by the peasant community) in some rural areas, the local deeprootedness of schismatic religious groups, or the permanence of different and heterogeneous demographic models resistant to all attempts at homogenization, which was supposed to give rise to the formation of a new man, "*homo sovieticus.*"

Two examples may be used here to illustrate this form of impermeability: the vitality of religious practices in an overtly atheistic state, and the strength of demographic models that, as Alain Blum has shown, contributed to the failure of "Soviet integration."[62] In the middle of the 1930s, 70 percent of the churches or mosques in service prior to the Bolshevik Revolution had been closed. This proportion reached 95 percent in 1940 and leveled out at around 85 percent during the postwar years.[63] The decrease in the number of servants of the faith followed a parallel curve. Despite this vigorous antireligious offensive relayed by a significant amount of atheist propaganda, the population "was adapted to the circumstances and continued to believe," as an inquiry report by the Commission on Cults in the Voronej Province recognized in 1936. The "administrative battle against religion" even yielded reports contrary to those sought by the regime. Where the churches had closed, the influence of sects grew, "the most fanatic and mystical religious rites" appeared, and wandering priests who "illegally celebrated masses in homes" prospered, while "religiosity on the part of the population, reduced administratively to leading a clandestine life, took on the most secret forms." The report concluded that, far from turning away from religion, the population "had manifested an increasing interest in religious questions." This served to develop "a terrain favorable to all sorts of anti-Soviet propaganda, rumors, and gossip."[64]

An observation clarifying this document is that, during the 1930s, Voronej Province, one of the bastions of the "desert Church," was also the province that had had the largest number of sects under tsarism. In other regions the picture was quite different, especially in the industrial centers, where de-Christianization of some of the working world was already well advanced by 1917. What is remarkable is the long-term continuity of tendencies that the regime's antireligious politics was powerless to reverse.

Particularly striking in regard to the impermeability of religious beliefs to the regime's atheistic propaganda was the extremely high percentage of the adult population (57 percent) who responded affirmatively to a question posed during the January 1937 census: "Are you a believer?"[65] This result was even more significant given that it followed innumerable discussions and rumors regarding the risk that everyone took in affirming—individually and in writing—that they believed in God.

A large number of official documents and testimonies on the collectivized countryside in the 1930s take into account the vigor of traditional religious holidays, even after the church had been closed. Significantly the number of these holidays seems to have been never as important as since collectivization. It is not surprising that the authorities had viewed this as a form of protest against the collective-farm system. In some of the kolkhozes, more than one hundred days per year were taken off because of holidays (not only religious holidays for the most part but also pagan holidays, which had mostly fallen into disuse but were revived after the establishment of the kolkhoz system). During the month of July alone—a period of intense agricultural work—the kolkhozniks took an average of seven days off due to the holidays of Saint Alena on the third, Ivan Kupala (a pre-Christian holiday) on the seventh, Saint Peter on the twelfth, Saints Peter and Paul on the seventeenth, and on the twentieth one of the twelve occasions during the year to celebrate the day of Saint Paraskeva. Respect for traditional holidays and adages regarding propitiatory days for such and such agricultural work also served as a pretext for justifying the refusal to obey injunctions by authorities attempting to impose their own agricultural calendar based on "sowing plans" or "harvest plans."[66]

The loosening of antireligious pressure during the war led immediately to a potent return to religious rituals. One example of this is that in the city of Kuibyshev, the number of religious marriages increased tenfold between 1941 and 1946.[67] All the same, even during the years of the Great Terror, the number of people observing orthodox religious holidays remained high (an act that, as the NKVD remarked, could serve as a pretext for arrest and condemnation): according to informants of the Leningrad Party, nearly 133,000 people attended Easter mass in 1934, and more than 180,000 in 1937, even though many churches had closed in the meantime.[68] Still, in 1937 the proportion of newly born infants baptized even in an average-sized city such as Pskov was 59 percent, only a slightly lower number than ten years previously.

Attending Easter mass in Leningrad, a city under high surveillance by the NKVD, on May 1, 1937; formally responding in the affirmative to the question "Do you believe in God?" during the January 1937 census; baptizing one's child in Pskov; or getting drunk with one's kolkhoz colleagues in celebration of a traditional holiday dating from the origin of time or not going to work in the fields because of it were among the many individual and collective acts representing different forms of "risk-taking" and dressed in undoubtedly different meanings. These few examples (which one could multiply) once again illustrate the porosity of the boundaries between the refusal to cooperate, discord, and the insoluble attachment to fundamental practices or values.

On an entirely different plane, demographer Alain Blum has elicited the fact that the multiple societies that comprised the Soviet Union "continued to evolve; not to the rhythm that Moscow wanted to impose on them, but rather to that of the cultural space to which they were linked by tradition."[69] This autonomy in the dynamics of demography hardly implies that the regime's politics did not have dramatic ruptures at times, resulting in the deaths of millions of people, as with the famine of 1932–33. But traditional demographic models do not conform to the homogenization desired by the political power. As such, in the republics of Central Asia, the gap between Soviet legislation of the family and traditional practices, which were nonetheless prohibited throughout the 1920s (*kalym*, or buying one's fiancée, levirate, and polygamy), remained considerable during the entire Stalinist period. As the 1937 and 1939 censuses show, the traditional model of very premature and often arranged marriages persisted. This only began to change after the war, but the older marriage age, the beginning of a demographic transition, is explained mainly by the substantial imbalance between the sexes following the Second World War. Studies on births out of wedlock or on divorce confirm the uniqueness of the demographic models and familial structures, whether one takes the case of Catholic Lithuania, Protestant Latvia, Islamic Turkmenistan, or Christian Georgia. In other words they confirm a remarkable stability. This stability, largely impermeable to political demands and pressures, would reflect strong anthropological characteristics proper to each society, if one accepts analyses by Peter Laslett, Hervé Le Bras, or Emmanuel Todd.

"In the world created by the October Revolution," writes Martin Malia, "a world where the ideological and the political constituted the infrastructure and not the superstructure . . . , we have never dealt with a society, but always with a regime, and an ideocratic one."[70] In my view this overly abrupt observation illustrates the strictures of a Sovietology that, at the end of the 1990s, still only recognizes one pole of interpretation of Stalinism: the political pole in the strict sense of the term, centered on the dictator, privileging solely the project of an omnipotent power and its relentless achievement by the well-oiled machinery of the regime. Conversely, attempting to explain Stalinism, as some have done, solely by the "rural backwardness" of the USSR, seeking a "social base" for Stalin's initiatives in any way, making "management of chaos" the regime's modus operandi, and pretending that the terror was "popular"— is this not all tantamount to looking in vain for active historical forces where they did not exist?

Between these excessive poles of reactive historiography marked by stakes that do not arise from historical study, there is surely a place for an approach that explores spaces of autonomy left to society by contingent circumstances, the lack of coordination between the regime's components, and initiatives at the local and regional levels as much as it explores the behaviors of inertia, avoidance, nonconformity, and resistance (in the broadest sense of the term) that the social body displayed under severe pressure.

Translated by Thomas C. Hilde

Notes

1. The expression "propaganda state" is from Peter Kenez, *The Birth of the Propaganda State: Soviet Methods of Mass Mobilization.* Cambridge University Press, 1985.

2. *Smolensk à l'heure de Staline.* Paris, Fayard, 1968.

3. For a discussion of these notions of *widerstand* and *resistenz*, see Pierre Ayçoberry,

La Question nazie: Essai sur les interprétations du national-socialisme, 1922–1975. Paris, Seuil, 1979; and Ian Kershaw, *Qu'est-ce que le nazisme? Problèmes et perspectives d'interprétation.* Paris, Gallimard, 1997, esp. pp. 284–333.

4. With the notable exception of the Slavophile current, in the moralistic and "fundamentalist" vein of Solzhenitsyn. But can one include this current in actual historiography?

5. Nicolas Werth and Gaël Moullec, *Rapports secrets soviétiques: La Société russe dans les rapports confidentiels, 1921–1991.* Paris, Gallimard, 1995, pp. 16–19.

6. Nicolas Werth, "Une Source inédite: Les Svodki de la Tcheka-OGPU," *Revue des études slaves,* vol. 66, no. 1, 1994, pp. 17–27; Viktor P. Danilov and Alex Berelowitch, "Les Documents de la VCK-OGPU-NKVD sur la campagne soviétique, 1918–1937," *Cahiers du monde russe,* vol. 35, no. 3, July–September 1994, pp. 633–682; Vladen S. Izmozik, *Glaza i usi rezima: Gosudarstvennyj politiceskij kontrol' za naseleniem Sovetskoj Rossii v 1918–1928 godakh.* Saint Petersburg, Phoenix, 1995.

7. Sheila Fitzpatrick, *Education and Social Mobility in the Soviet Union, 1921–1934.* Cambridge University Press, 1979; idem, *Cultural Revolution in Russia, 1928–1931.* Bloomington, Indiana University Press, 1978; idem, "Stalin and the Making of a New Elite," *Slavic Review,* no. 38, September 1979, pp. 377–402; Nicholas Lampert, *The Technical Intelligentsia and the Soviet State.* London, Macmillan, 1979; David Shearer, *Industry, State, and Society in Stalin's Russia, 1926–1934.* Ithaca NY, Cornell University Press, 1996.

8. Stephen Kotkin, *Magnetic Mountain: Stalinism and Civilization.* Berkeley/Los Angeles, University of California Press, 1995. The questions posed in this work regarding the forms of adherence to the regime and integration of a society in full disruption are also discussed in two other recent studies on the social history of the 1930s: David Hoffman, *Peasant Metropolis: Social Identities in Moscow, 1929–1941.* Ithaca NY, Cornell University Press, 1994; and Kenneth Straus, *Factory and Community in Stalin's Russia: The Making of an Industrial Working Class, 1928–1933.* Pittsburgh University Press, 1998.

9. Elena Zubkova, *Russia after the War: Hopes, Illusions, and Disappointments, 1945–1957.* New York, Sharpe, 1998; Sarah Davies, *Popular Opinion in Stalin's Russia: Terror, Propaganda, and Dissent, 1934–1941.* Cambridge University Press, 1997.

10. On these questions the most debated recent work, given its often peremptory affirmations of the adherence by the "masses" to the politics of terror, is that of Robert W. Thurston, *Life and Terror in Stalin's Russia, 1934–1941.* New Haven, Yale University Press, 1996.

11. Vladimir Brovkin, *Russia after Lenin: Politics, Culture, and Society, 1921–1929.* London, Routledge, 1998.

12. For a quick presentation of these classifications, see Kershaw, op. cit., pp. 286–304.

13. Ibid., p. 315.

14. Ibid., p. 318 (italics are mine).

15. Ibid., p. 319.

16. Martin Broszat, ed. *Bayern in der NS-Zeit*, 6 vols. Munich/Vienna, 1977–83.

17. Andrea Graziosi, "Collectivisation, révoltes paysannes, et politiques gouverne-mentales," *Cahiers du monde russe*, vol. 35, no. 3, July–September 1994, pp. 437–632; Sheila Fitzpatrick, *Stalin's Peasants: Resistance and Survival in the Russian Village after Collectivization*. Oxford University Press, 1994.

18. Viktor P. Danilov, *Kretianskoe vosstanie v Tambovskoj gubernii v 1919–1921 gg (Antonovscina): Dokumenty i materialy*. Tambov, 1994.

19. Danilov and Berelowitch, op. cit., pp. 671–676.

20. Lynne Viola, *Peasant Rebels under Stalin: Collectivization and the Culture of Peasant Resistance*. Oxford University Press, 1996.

21. Andrea Graziosi, *The Great Soviet Peasant War: Bolsheviks and Peasants, 1917–1933*. Harvard University Press, 1996.

22. Danilov and Berelowitch, op. cit., pp. 674–675.

23. Werth and Moullec, op. cit., pp. 209–216; Jeffrey Rossman, "The Teikovo Cotton Workers' Strike of April 1932: Class, Gender, and Identity Politics in Stalin's Russia," *The Russian Review*, no. 56, January 1997, pp. 44–69.

24. Werth and Moullec, op. cit., p. 215.

25. Ibid., pp. 228–238 (for the riots of October 1941), 244–257 (for the worker riots of June 1962).

26. Elena Osokina, *Ierarkhija potreblenija: O zizni ljudej v uslovijakh Stalinskogo snabzenija, 1928–1935*. Moscow, MGU, 1993; idem, "A Hierarchy of Poverty: State Provisioning and Social Stratification in the USSR during the Period of Rationing, 1931–1935," *Cahiers du monde russe*, vol. 39, nos. 1–2, January–June 1998, pp. 81–98.

27. Nikolai Bougai, *L. Beria–I. Stalina: "Soglasno Vasemu Ukazaniju."* Moscow, AIRO-XX, 1995, pp. 221–250; Alexei Gurianov, ed., *Represii protiv Poljakov i polskikh grazdan*. Moscow, Zvenia, 1997, pp. 137–175, 215–225; Keith Sword, *Deportation and Exile: Poles in the Soviet Union, 1939–1948*. London, Macmillan, 1996, pp. 143–173.

28. Bougai, op. cit., pp. 208–210.

29. Ilya Bilinsky, *The Second Soviet Republic: The Ukraine after World War II*. New Brunswick NJ, Rutgers University Press, 1955, p. 132.

30. Bougai, op. cit., p. 225.

31. Ibid., p. 229.

32. Ibid., p. 232. Thus one may estimate that around 5 percent of the adult population of the Baltic countries were deported or imprisoned in the Gulag.

33. G. M. Ivanova, *Gulag v sisteme totalitarnogo gosudarstva*. Moscow, MONF, 1997; Marta Craveri and Nikolai Formozov, "La Résistance au Goulag: Grèves et révoltes dans les camps de travail soviétiques de 1920 à 1956," *Communisme*, nos. 42–43–44, 1995, pp. 197–210.

34. Difficult to translate [into French or English], this expression designates the disorder engendered by uncontrollable natural—or social—forces.

35. Nicolas Werth, "Déplacés spéciaux et colons de travail dans la société stalinienne," *Vingtième siècle: Revue d'histoire*, no. 54, 1997, pp. 40–41.

36. David Shearer, "Crime and Social Disorder in Stalin's Russia: A Reassessment of the Great Retreat and the Origins of Mass Repression," *Cahiers du monde russe*, vol. 39, nos. 1–2, January–June 1998, pp. 126–128.

37. Fitzpatrick, *Stalin's Peasants*, pp. 234–235.

38. Shearer, "Crime and Social Disorder in Stalin's Russia," pp. 129–130.

39. Elena Osokina, *Za fasadom Stalinskogo izobilija*. Moscow, Rosspen, 1998, pp. 144–145.

40. Ibid., p. 147.

41. Ibid., p. 223.

42. Vladimir F. Zima, *Golod v SSR 1946–1947 godov: Proizkhozdenie i posledstvija*. Moscow, RAN, 1996, pp. 18–29.

43. John Arch Getty, Gabor T. Ritterspoon, and Viktor N. Zemskov, "Les Victimes de la répression pénales dans l'URSS d'avant-guerre," *Revue des études slaves*, vol. 64, no. 4, pp. 651ff.

44. Zima, op. cit., pp. 180ff.

45. Regarding the struggle against the *tekucka* during the postwar years, see the clarifying examples in Elena Zubkova, *Obscestvo i reformy, 1945–1964*. Moscow, Rossia Molodaja, 1993, pp. 65–67.

46. Peter Solomon, *Soviet Criminal Justice under Stalin*. Cambridge University Press, 1996. Oleg Khlevniuk has also uncovered a number of examples of the "refusal to cooperate" on the part of judges, procurers, and company managers during 1935–38 in his work *1937: Stalin, NKVD, I sovetskoïe obscestvo*. Moscow, 1992.

47. Nikolai A. Ivnitski, *Kollektivizatsia i raskulacivanije*. Moscow, Interprax, 1994, pp. 199–200.

48. Zima, op. cit., pp. 104–105.

49. See the first chapter by Nicolas Werth in the present volume.

50. Kershaw, op. cit., p. 215.

51. Fitzpatrick, *Stalin's Peasants*, p. 288.

52. Ian Kershaw, *Popular Opinion and Political Dissent in the Third Reich*. Oxford University Press, 1983, p. 6.

53. Fitzpatrick, op. cit., pp. 289–290; Davies, *Popular Opinion in Stalin's Russia*, pp. 55–56.

54. Fitzpatrick, op. cit., pp. 291–292.

55. Ibid., p. 312ff.

56. Kotkin, *Magnetic Mountain*, pp. 215–230, 235–237.

57. Gabor T. Ritterspoon, "From Working Class to Urban Laboring Mass," in *Making Soviet Workers: Power, Class and Identity*, ed. Lewis H. Siegelbaum and Ronald G. Suny. Ithaca NY, Cornell University Press, 1994, p. 187.

58. Werth and Moullec, op. cit., pp. 224–228; Davies, *Popular Opinion in Stalin's Russia*, pp. 43–47.

59. Davies, *Popular Opinion in Stalin's Russia*, pp. 122–144.

60. Elena Zubkova, "Mir mnenii sovetskogo celoveka, 1945–1948 gg," *Otecestvennaja Istorija*, no. 3, 1998, pp. 41–43.

61. Sarah Davies, "The Crime of 'Anti-Soviet Agitation' in the Soviet Union in the 1930s," *Cahiers du monde russe*, vol. 39, nos. 1–2, January–June 1998, pp. 149–168.

62. Alain Blum, *Naître, vivre, et mourir en URSS*. Paris, Plon, 1995.

63. Nicolas Werth, "Le Pouvoir soviétique et l'Église orthodoxe de la collectivisation à la Constitution de 1936," *Revue d'Études comparatives Est-Ouest*, vol. 24, nos. 3–4, September–December 1993, pp. 41–106.

64. Ibid., p. 61.

65. Yuri Poliakov, V. Zhiromskaja, and I. Kiselev, "Polveka molcanija: Vsesoiouznaïa perepis naselenija 1937 goda," *Sotsiologiceskie Issledovanija*, nos. 6–8, 1990.

66. Fitzpatrick, op. cit., pp. 205–207.

67. Zubkova, "Mir mnenii sovetskogo celoveka," p. 58.

68. Davies, op. cit., p. 76.

69. Blum, op. cit., p. 141.

70. Martin Malia, *La Tragédie soviétique*. Paris, Seuil, 1995, p. 19.

Philippe Burrin

Nazi Regime and German Society

The Prisms of Acceptance

Since 1945 the word "totalitarianism" has evoked in many minds the image of a society engulfed by an absolute power, as though George Orwell's *1984* had become a reality. With the development of social history, particularly the history of everyday life, the perspective on Nazism has changed. Historians have been led to emphasize the niches, the private spaces, and the strategies of detour and avoidance—in short the areas of autonomy in society. The idea of a monolithic regime was rejected along with that of total control of every aspect of existence, even at the risk that the insistence on forms of normalcy and the lines of continuity might end up minimizing, if not occulting, the rupture represented by violence and the crimes of the regime.[1]

Nevertheless history "from below" has enriched our understanding of German society under the Nazis. It has imposed a differentiated image and has invited us to formulate more-complex interpretations. The question of the relationship between the regime and society can certainly continue to be formulated, with a profitable increase of knowledge. Up to what point was the effort of total control over society crowned with success? Conversely, what form of autonomy did society preserve? But in order not to be bound by a power-society dichotomy, it would also be good to reason in terms of interaction. The Nazi regime, like every type of totalitarian regime, sought to bring about adherence and cohesion. But it was not able to build these by force alone and certainly not by having recourse only to force. Would not society have brought its own contribution to the totalitarian remolding that the authorities were trying to realize? In fact the regime did not simply impose itself; it had to work with a civil society whose vigor had not been suppressed, even after it had to toe the line. In other words the paradox may be that support for the Nazi government by German society was also due to, and perhaps especially due to, the limited character of the control that the regime exercised over it.

Nowhere more than in the social arena have historians attempted to emphasize the composite nature of Nazi ideology, its confused character, and its subordination to opportunistic considerations.[2] Things become a bit clearer if one is precise as to the level at which one places oneself: change in the long term or the short term, level of structures or of perceptions? To make things

easier we will distinguish among the objectives of the regime two complementary facets, one concerning the structure and the other the cohesiveness
of society.

As for structural change, we should begin by taking seriously the extent of
Nazi ambitions. In its aims National Socialism was less ambitious, probably,
than in a revolution of the Bolshevik type since the principle of private property was not challenged. But Nazism was noteworthy nevertheless because, in
a country whose population was growing rapidly, it sought to strengthen the
position of country folk and reduce the size of big cities while decentralizing
the concentration of industry. In other words, recognizing that a return to
the past was impossible, Nazism sought nevertheless to find a middle path
between a modernization necessary to ensure its power and an anachronistic
social structure considered to be healthy and salutary.

It is easy to emphasize the distance, if not antinomy, between this ambition and any real changes. In agriculture the preparation for and then the
economic conduct of the war reinforced the rural exodus, quite the opposite
of the regime's objective. Feminine employment, which was to be reduced
in order to allow for a return of the wife to the home and to procreation,
again began to rise when full employment had barely returned. And it was
the same for industrial concentration, the expansion of technology at work,
the growth of the bureaucracy, and the increase in number of white-collar
workers. The natal politics of the regime, thanks to the importance of the
means used, was certainly an immediate success, celebrated as it should have
been. But, according to the opinion of demographers, this was only a question
of catching up with a lag that had become increasingly noticeable since the
end of the First World War. The Germans, especially German women, wanted
to decide on the size of their family, and there is no doubt that it was going to
remain well below what was desired in order to make possible the settlement
of the vast spaces of Eastern Europe.[3] In sum, it was the triumph of long-term
trends that prevailed during the same period in industrial societies.

Let us emphasize, however, that this perspective only has meaning relative to the course events actually followed. Through its expansion of the
war, Nazism brought about its own defeat, and it is true that this produced
changes that were more considerable, in terms of their effect on society, than
all of Nazism's efforts combined. Yet defeat deprived the Party of the time
and means necessary for the realization of its objectives, because military
expansion, racial cleansing, and social transformation joined forces. Everything indicates that in any case Nazism intended to use the conquered "living
space" to reshape German society. The settlement of eastern territories was

intended to strengthen the importance of country folk and of the middle classes and to reduce, at least in relative terms, industrial and urban concentration. Despite the limits imposed by the war, the policy carried out in the occupied territories—and especially in the annexed territories—allows one to distinguish the premises of a social transformation. These included, as an intermediary solution (while awaiting the expulsion of the majority of the nonnative peoples and the Germanization of the others), the creation of a form of colonial society, though one whose major characteristics were the domination by the Party, the engineering of a new social structure, and an increase in possibilities for social advancement.[4]

What about the other facet? This one concerned the formation of a *Volksgemeinschaft* ("popular community"), racially purified and demographically expansive, especially one that had become unified through a reduction in the cleavages (regional, social, and confessional) that divided German society. Pertinent criteria that can be considered here are the Nazi Party's replacement of the traditional institutions of socialization—the school, the family, and the various religious callings—as well as the reduction of social differences.

From the outset there was a considerable number of handicaps. The compromise set up with the traditional elite groups and the plebiscitary character of the regime made it necessary to hedge in order not to confront substantial parts of society head on. Despite the displacement of the balance of power, in general terms the status quo prevailed, and continuity won out. The traditional elites maintained their position, especially because of a system of education that remained selective and that was never questioned by the formation of new elites in Nazi educational institutions. Upward mobility, in other words, continued to be determined by one's origins, choice of schools, and family network. There is one exception to this: the advancement achieved through political activity in the Nazi Party. But this phenomenon remained limited and was soon eliminated by a tendency toward the interpenetration of new and old elites. The clearest example of this is provided by the ss, in which the children of the upper classes, even those of the nobility, were overrepresented after 1933.[5]

There was also the continuity of confessional cleavages, an element at least as important as the preceding one, given the place the Church enjoyed in German life. The regime tried to align the different denominations and loosen their hold on the faithful, especially on youth. In 1934 it even intervened in the institutional organization and theological debates of the Protestant church, but it was forced to step back since government interference risked reinforcing the antiestablishment current that had formed. From then on the regime practiced a policy of pressure and chipping away at authority, with little success, if we judge by the small number of Germans who chose to leave their church. We should also remember that the government had to keep its distance several times when it faced the risk of confrontation with the Catholic Church (over questions about the use of crucifixes, convents, and the creation of community schools through the fusion of Protestant and Catholic schools).[6] As proof of the extreme difficulty the Nazis faced with regard to religious policy, the definitive solution for which was put off until the end of the glorious war, it is only necessary to recall that Hitler continued, at least administratively, to declare himself a Catholic until his death.

One could hold that, for lack of an objective change in social differences and in the social structure, a modification came about on the subjective level in the perception of contemporaries, who would have seen the realization of a greater equality regarding conditions and opportunities in their society.[7] To judge by regional studies, it seems that this was not at all the case. On the contrary discontent and criticism of existing inequalities remained widespread.[8] But one should note that this did not exclude the existence of reasons to be satisfied with one's own fate. The study of different social categories in effect indicates that the amelioration of conditions was a reality, assuredly differentiated according to the ability of each group to articulate its interests, especially through professional organizations, the evolution of the economic priorities of power and the ideological importance that the regime attributed to different social sectors.[9]

Workers were the least favored group, if only because they lost every means of independent defense. Their standard of living increased modestly, however, because of the small pool of workers and the opportunity to work overtime, as the hourly salary was fixed. In addition to this there were a certain number of real benefits, such as canteens, dressing rooms, showers, and daycare centers in the factories. The regime's propaganda also exalted the nobility of manual labor through certain measures, such as the celebration of May 1 as National Work Day, through which it showed an interest that produced some results. All this of course did not turn workers into pillars of the regime, as is shown by demonstrations of discontent in the period just before the war.[10] At least they were not marginalized as a group from the regime. What probably contributed to this was the disintegration of traditional bonds, especially due to the influence of salary scales according to one's performance.[11]

At the other end of the scale, we do find a group that was favored, the employers, especially those in large firms. They were not interfered with in the choice of directors for their businesses beyond the cleansing of Jews, and they knew how to minimize the influence of the Labor Front on life within their firms.[12] Employers especially profited not only from the economy getting off to a new start and from the boom that came from rearmament but also from the discipline of the workers, the freezing of salaries, and their own cooptation in the organisms that directed the economy. They were probably neither sufficiently structured nor united enough to influence the regime and especially to direct its policies. But they did not hesitate to take every possible advantage of their position, even by giving their approval to the politics of expansion.[13] Some firms even did it with much resolve, such as IG Farben, which implicated itself not only in the predatory politics of the regime throughout Europe but also in its crimes through the unscrupulous use of forced labor and of workers from concentration camps.[14]

The same observation can be made for all the German elites, in whose behavior one could find a mixture of hedging, accommodation, and frank participation, which was also characterized by some questioning of conscience and efforts at breaking away.[15] Certain sectors distinguished themselves by their support of the regime. Foremost among these were the doctors, who exceeded in adherence. One out of two doctors belonged to the Nazi Party, and one out of ten to the SS, which was to have some effect on their participation in Nazi violence.[16]

Between elites and workers, the middle classes experienced a mixed fate. White-collar workers profited from the expansion of work in the private sector, public administration, and the parapublic sector (the Party machinery) as well as from the politics of leisure in the Third Reich. Artisans and shopkeepers enjoyed favorable measures but were more and more affected during the war by the priority given to the goods of production and restrictions on the labor force. Finally, the peasantry lived in conditions that belied its place of honor in the discourse of the regime and the growing control that the state exercised over its economic activity, not to mention the increased difficulties it encountered regarding labor.[17]

Vis-à-vis this German society, which had irreversibly become since the end of the nineteenth century a complex society, the task of dedifferentiation undertaken by the Nazis and characteristic of every kind of totalitarian regime encountered failure, one that was perhaps inevitable to the extent that, among others, a large range of special interests continued to exist. Professional associations, rather than playing the role of some substitute for the regime and of Nazifying their base, made themselves the spokesman of their clientele and made every effort to obtain satisfaction, usually to the detriment of other interests.

All in all there was under Nazism a certain material contentment, if one does not forget that people at the time judged things in relation to their recent experience of the economic crisis. But what do we then say about the war period, with its restrictions, separation of families, and bombings? Because it is a fact that the regime succeeded in maintaining its base of support practically to the end, this in spite of a war that, as was clearly evident from 1942–43 on, would end badly. In order to explain this, one may formulate the hypothesis that the attention given to social inequalities has overlooked another reality— that of the partial reconstruction of the individual's identity—due to several factors that made these inequalities appear, in the eyes of Germans, to be just one aspect of their situation.

The first of these factors was the work of training and propaganda taken up by the Nazi Party, with the aim of creating some form of allegiance, at the very least mass conformity. The Nazi Party had sought as early as the 1920s to project the image of a national party, the accomplishment in miniature of the "popular community" that it wanted to create on the national level. This presentation in itself seems to have found some credit and contributed to its electoral success. After 1933 the Party became a big machine whose supporters approached 2.5 million in 1933 before climbing to more than 8 million in 1945, one-third of whom were women (with time the proportion of people belonging to the upper classes who were among the new supporters eroded, whereas that of workers increased continuously).[18] To the supporters we should add the many tens of millions of its auxiliary organizations (specialized by profession, age group, and sex) whose involvement, it is true, was not usually the result of a free choice.

This enormous machine was animated by about 2 million little Führers too.[19] A vast circle of people had thus taken on importance and acquired a power that could compete with any bestowed by money, status, or birth. The Nazi Party quickly became the object of a lack of consideration, which only increased with time. But one should not therefore underestimate the role it played in social life. For example, its presence could be felt in the political evaluations that an increasing number of administrative formalities required, or in the interconnectedness of its organisms of assistance, not to mention the internalized pressure that the Hitlerian salute presented. Added to this was the invasion of public space by the celebrations that the Party organized, true political liturgies, some of which—such as the annual congress in Nuremberg—made quite an impression throughout the country, especially through news reports.[20]

The Nazi Party exercised a decisive influence on one group at least—

the youth. Through this the Party could reinforce its influence on family life, where its intrusion was unsettling. Obstacles to its formal hold were rather quickly eliminated. Even the associations of Catholic youth, protected for a long time by the Concordat of 1933, were dissolved on the eve of the war, making membership in the Hitler Youth organization henceforth obligatory for all young Germans. During the war the Party benefited by sending numerous children from the city to camps in the countryside in order to reinforce its hold on them, for these camps were placed under the authority of the Hitler Youth, now free of all competition from family or school.

But nothing would be more misguided than to impute the influence of the Party on youth exclusively to conditions that were favorable for indoctrination. Adolescent boys also had their own reasons for letting themselves be seduced. The regime flattered them by treating them as the future of the country. The competition between the Hitler Youth organization and schools gave them the opportunity to play one off against the other. They found the opportunity, and this was also true for a certain number of young girls, to liberate themselves from family authority. In sum, what showed itself here were the beginnings of a youth culture that could moreover assume other expressions and in turn revealed the limits of the Party's influence. For example, bands of youth wandering through the large cities appeared during the war and demonstrated, even violently at times, their hostility to being recruited.[21]

The second factor contributing to Nazism's success in society was the convergence of certain aspects of the regime's politics with aspirations that were already present in a diffused manner within German society. These include the desire for a society founded on merit and open to social climbing and for a consumer society.[22] The first of these aspirations can explain the sharpness of the criticism directed toward inequalities that have already been mentioned. Yet the second merits some attention. The Nazi policy on leisure, its support of a car for the people—the "vw" remained only a dream even in the war's aftermath—the increased use of radio and film, the appearance of television, and the development of advertising all proved seductive since it suggested that real steps were being taken toward the creation of a consumer society. By encouraging Germans to react as clients and consumers rather than as mobilized citizens, the regime was not helping preparations for war, but it did garner credit for the regime among the populace that the war did not erode one day to the next.

The third factor was nationalism. The feeling of injustice brought about by the Treaty of Versailles and by the loss of status as a great power—resentment toward the conquerors, particularly Poland, whose right to annex German lands had been recognized at Versailles but that had become the object of an almost unanimous rejection—had deep roots, and the Nazi regime knew how to exploit as well as reinforce them. Hitler's successes between 1933 and 1938—rearmament, remilitarization of the Rhineland, and the unification with Austria and with the Sudetenland—was greeted with enthusiasm. These accomplishments were all the more impressive since they had been obtained without firing a single gunshot. The Germans experienced a certain sullenness, though, at the outbreak of the war in the autumn of 1939. But the rapid defeats of Poland and France, then the attack against the USSR, explained as a preventive measure, were perceived not as so many aggressions but as actions of legitimate self-defense in the face of neighbors or powers who refused to grant Germany, in the concert of nations, the place that would be in conformity with its newly reestablished power.[23]

Finally—and this is the last factor, but one that cuts across those preceding —there was the cult of Hitler himself. A strong connection obviously existed, it seems, between the structuring of the regime in the form of a charismatic dictatorship on the one hand and the attitude of society on the other, for it was society that made charismatic domination possible by assuring Hitler the popularity that established his preeminence at the top of the regime. By projecting onto him expectations and representations that vary greatly in kind and encompassed all sorts of aspirations, the German population played a crucial part in the construction of the myth of the Führer and thereby contributed greatly to the uncontrollable dynamics of his regime. This personalization of power corresponded to an archaic conception of politics that satisfied a desire for emotional attachment of the monarchic type. It also signaled the fact that the confidence granted Hitler served to establish distance between him, the Party, and the government in the eyes of the German people. Hence the myth of the good king who is poorly advised could prosper right up to the end of the regime. This served as a kind of safety net for the Führer.

As to the reality of this cult, much evidence exists, including recent studies on the attitude of Germans who were in the military.[24] The person of Hitler incorporated national unity and the community of destiny of all Germans. His person symbolized a future of grandeur to which promises of a better life were attached. Plans for the period following the war, revealed with great fanfare from 1940 on, called for the construction of housing on a vast scale for the poor and the preparation of a program of social security.[25] The cult of Hitler also crystallized the resentment of a population that remembered the humiliation of Versailles and that willingly imagined itself to be surrounded and threatened, a chord Hitler knew quite well how to play in his war speeches.[26] With the help of the conflict's evolution and the help of fear of police repression, the Germans continued to support their leader. But all other factors were probably less effective than fear of the "Bolshevik hordes." Nevertheless the belief in the genius of Hitler had to accommodate itself with an increasing skepticism.

Viewed in relation to the duration of the regime and situated between the ideal poles of rejection or acceptance, the population's attitude settled early on the side of acceptance. The notion of acceptance should be contextualized in relation to deviance, dissidence, and opposition. Outright opposition was limited to small groups, which increased as the war evolved. Apart from the Communists and to a lesser extent the Socialists, the most active and belligerent enemies of the regime were disparate groups of students, high-level officials, officers, and property owners.[27] But a not insignificant part of the population wavered between deviance and dissidence, particularly in those segments where, because of a minority identity, historic experiences, or strong convictions, individuals were partly immunized against any effort the regime made to penetrate their resistance. This was the case of workers either attached to Socialist traditions or won over to Communism; of a good part of the Catholic world, with its reactions as a minority and its memory of Bismarck's Kulturkampf; and of various elements of the liberal middle class.

Acceptance included resignation, support, and adherence, all kinds of attitudes that are not necessary to illustrate here. It is also useless to emphasize that in reality these different attitudes were intricately woven together, with acceptance being the dominant feature. Thus the Catholic Church, which expressed its dissent on precise matters when its interests were directly touched upon, praised Hitler strongly and supported the regime publicly during the war.

What needs to be emphasized, beyond the make up of these different attitudes, is the varied forms that acceptance took, established as it was upon many perceptions, often approximate or ambiguous, as to the nature and ultimate objectives of the regime. Rather than see it as radically new and the bearer of a violence that knew no precedent, the Germans privileged in it what comforted their need for continuity or what answered their own aspirations—aspirations they considered legitimate. And as for Hitler, far from seeing him as the suicidal and bloody dictator that he was, they imagined him as one who listened to their deep desires for pacification and harmony, and not without some justification, for Hitler showed on several occasions that he knew how to take their pulse and account for their reactions. Thus he suspended the extermination of the mentally ill after members of the clergy protested in order not to compromise the support of the population in a war that was going to be long. The absence of protests, public or unofficial, of this very same clergy at the time of the deportation of the Jews dispensed it from showing the extent of his flexibility.

This is not to say that the Germans, living off of illusions, had no part in what was taking place. No one could ignore the fact that the "good Reich" of Hitler was overflowing with people who were excluded and persecuted. If the "popular community" was not an empty word for many, that community was nevertheless realized in solidarity with the regime's politics of repression and exclusion. This was especially true when it was a question of traditional prejudices, such as having Gypsies, "asocials," and homosexuals toe the line or when it was a question of persecuting Jews. [28] When for this last group the time for deportation and extermination did come, many of their compatriots turned their heads and closed their eyes. Emotion was not shown until violence had spread into their own streets, under their own windows, during "Crystal Night" in November 1938. The regime drew its own conclusions from this, and it took every measure necessary to cloak its later actions in secrecy. [29] Here also it satisfied a population that wanted to be concerned only with itself.

Acceptance therefore had its price. As Martin Broszat has written, the attitude of the German population during the war was a "mixture of panic and fidelity, of pity towards oneself and of lying, which made one morally blind in regards to the excesses that the regime committed against the Jews, the Poles, and the workers who had come from the East." [30]

Translated by Peter S. Rogers

Notes

1. See the exchange of correspondence between Marin Broszat and Saul Friedländer in "De l'historisation du national-socialisme" (On the historical making of national-socialism), *Bulletin trimestriel de la Fondation Auschwitz*, April–September 1990, pp. 43–90 (first published in *Viertelijahreschrift für Zeitgeschichte*, 1988, pp. 339–372).

2. For a general view, see Ian Kershaw, *Qu'est-ce que le nazisme?: Problèmes et perspectives d'interprétation* (What is nazism?: Problems and perspectives of interpretation). Paris: Gallimard, 1992, chap. 7.

3. See Jill Stephenson, *Women in Nazi Society*. London: Croom Helm, 1975; and Claudia Koonz, *Les Mères-patrie du IIIe Reich: Les femmes et le nazisme* (The Mothersland of the Third Reich: Women and nazism). Paris: Lieu Commun, 1989.

4. See Rolf-Dieter Müller, *Hitlers Ostkrieg und die deutsche Siedlungspolitik* (Hitler's war in the east and German settlement politics). Frankfort: Fischer, 1991.

5. H. F. Ziegler, *Nazi German's New Aristocracy: The SS Leadership, 1925–1939*. Princeton: Princeton University Press, 1989.

6. See K. Scholder, *Die Kirchen und das Dritte Reich* (The Churches and the Third Reich). 2 vols. to date, Frankfort, 1977–85; H. Hürten, *Deutsche Katholiken, 1918 bis 1945* (German Catholics, 1918–1945) Paderborn, 1992.

7. David Schoenbaum, *La Révolution brune: La Société allemande sous le IIIe Reich* (The brown revolution: German society under the Third Reich). Paris: Robert Laffont, 1979.

8. Ian Kershaw, *Popular Opinion and Political Dissent in the Third Reich: Bavaria 1933–1945*. Oxford, 1983. (French translation, *l'Opinion allemande sous le nazisme: Bavière 1933–1945*. Paris: Éditions du CNRS, 1995.)

9. See Norbert Frei, *L'État hitlérien et la société allemande, 1933–1945* (The Hitlerian state and German society, 1933–1945). Paris: Éditions du Seuil, 1994; and Pierre Ayçoberry, *La Société allemande sous le IIIe Reich, 1933–1945* (German society under the Third Reich, 1933–1945). Paris: Éditions du Seuil, 1998.

10. Tim Mason, *Sozialpolitik im Dritten Reich: Arbeiterklasse und Volksgemeinschaft* (Social politics in the Third Reich: Worker class and folk community). Opladen, 1977; Carola Sachse, ed., *Angst, Belohnung, Zucht, und Ordnung: Herrschaftsmechanismen im Nationalsozialismus* (Anxiety, pay, discipline, and order: Control mechanisms in National Socialism). Opladen, 1982.

11. Pierre Ayçoberry thinks that there was more disintegration than integration into the regime. See op. cit., p. 192.

12. Hervé Joly, *Patrons d'Allemagne: Sociologie d'une élite industrielle, 1933–1989* (Bosses of Germany: Sociology of an industrial elite, 1933–1989). Paris: Presses de la FNSP, 1996.

13. See Lothar Gall and Manfred Phohl, eds., *Unternehmen im Nationalsozialismus* (Business in National Socialism). Munich: Beck, 1998.

14. See Peter Hayes, *Industry and Ideology: I. G. Farben in the Nazi Era*. Cambridge: Cambridge University Press, 1987.

15. See Martin Broszat and Klaus Schwabe, eds., *Die deutschen Eliten und der Weg in den Zweiten Weltkrieg* (German elites and the way into the Second World War). Munich: Beck, 1989.

16. See Michael Kater, *Doctors under Hitler*. Chapel Hill: University of North Carolina Press, 1989.

17. See especially Michael Prinz, *Vom neuen Mittelstand zum Volksgenossen* (From the new middle class to blood brothers). Munich: Oldenbourg, 1986; and Gustavo Corni, *Hitler and the Peasants: The Agrarian Policy of the Third Reich, 1930–1939*. New York: Berg, 1990.

18. See Michael Kater. *The Nazi Party: A Social Profile of Members and Leaders, 1919–1945*. London: Basil Blackwell, 1983.

19. Frei, op. cit., p. 153.

20. See Klaus Vondung, *Magie und Manipulation: Ideologischer Kult und politische religion des Nationalsozialismus* (Magic and manipulation: Ideological cult and political religion in National Socialism). Göttingen, 1971; and Peter Reichel, *La Fascination du nazisme* (The Fascination of nazism). Paris: Odile Jacob, 1993.

21. See Arno Klönne, *Jugend im Dritten Reich* (Youth in the Third Reich). Cologne: Diederichs, 1982.

22. See Hans Dieter Schäfer, *Das gespaltene Bewusstein* (The divided consciousness). Munich, 1981.

23. On German morale during the war, see Marlise Steinert, *Hitlers Krieg und die Deutschen* (Hitler's war and the Germans). Düseldorf, 1970.

24. See Omer Bartov, *L'Armée d'Hitler* (Hitler's army). Paris: Hachette, 1999; and Klaus Latzel, *Deutsche Soldaten—nationalsozialistixcher Krieg? Kriegserlebnis–Kriegserfarung, 1939–1945* (German soldiers—National Socialist war? War experiences–war lessons, 1939–1945). Paderborn: Schöningh, 1998.

25. See Marie-Luise Recker, *Nationalsozialistische Sozialpolitik im Zweiten Weltkrieg* (National Socialist social politics in the Second World War). Munich: Oldenbourg, 1985.

26. Hitler, *Der grossdeutsche Freihitskampf* (Great Germany's struggle for freedom). 3 vols., Munich: Eher Verlag. 1941–44.

27. See. J. Schmädeke and P. Steinbach, eds., *Der Widerstand gegen den Nationalsozialismus: Die deutsche Gesellschaft und der Widerstand gegen Hitler* (The Struggle against National Socialism: German society and the opposition to Hitler). Munich/Zurich, 1985.

28. See Detlev Peukert, *Volksgenossen und Gemeinschaftsfremden* (Blood brothers and society outsiders). Cologne: Bund-Verlag, 1982.

29. See David Bankier, *The Germans and the Final Solution*. Oxford: Blackwell, 1992.

30. Martin Broszat, *L'État hitlérien*. Paris: Fayard, 1985, p. 454.

2. The Wages of Memory in Formerly Communist Eastern Europe

Alexandra Laignel-Lavastine

Fascism and Communism in Romania

The Comparative Stakes and Uses

The opening of the East's archives has raised the delicate question of an internal comparison of Nazism and Stalinism, which in the West has returned to the forefront of historiographical debates. The purpose here will be to question, from one parallelism to another, the rationale and the logic at work in the success encountered since 1989 by this comparative approach in the countries of Central and Eastern Europe. In Romania, especially, historians and philosophers close to politically liberal groups have loudly proclaimed that a comparison of Stalinism to Nazism is legitimate, and furthermore they have compared Communism to fascism *in general*, to the point that the idea of a "Red Holocaust" and a "Communist Genocide" have become part of today's vocabulary.

What do this reception and these practices indicate? Does this rush to adopt the "comparative" viewpoint by so many East European historians now appear more fraught with ambiguities than it first seemed?[1] There is not only a history to be written in the East about Communism and its archives but also a history to be accepted, a history made up of very different periods, of a variety of collective compromises, of many adjustments in prewar nationalist traditions. An important part of the population was not insensitive to this reappropriation, especially in the Romania of Nicolae Ceausescu. In short we are dealing with a region where it is hard to see how we could be satisfied with an approach consisting of *comparing with each other* the two great historical catastrophes of the century. Indeed, how can we approach the Communist period without raising the question of endogenous factors that made possible a long cohesion of the apparatus, or without coming back to an antidemocratic swing that was ratified in 1946–47 but that goes back to the 1930s, a period that raises the inevitable and highly sensitive question of the responsibility of the political elite and the intellectuals of the years between the two world wars? There are many aspects here that should not be missed in evaluating the operative value of a totalitarian conceptualization as it was practiced in the East. Far from addressing these worrisome questions, would such a procedure not allow the opposite, an opportune way of limiting them? To put it bluntly, it is a question of creating a limited area of *relevance* to the discourse.

It could be that the motives for a comparison between Communism and fascism would diverge greatly according to one's place on one side or the other of the former Iron Curtain. Therefore it is important to question the ends and to ask with Ian Kershaw, "What are they trying to show by this comparison? . . . What aim explains this?"[2] Kershaw insists furthermore on the plurality of possible uses of the concept of totalitarianism and on the necessity of not confusing them, a remark especially adapted to the East European situation: "In a strict sense," he observes, "it [totalitarianism] serves to compare the regimes of Stalin and Hitler, in a broad sense to compare Communism, as a state form of government, to Nazism (or to fascism). The broader use, which is naturally a way of taking on Communism rather than Nazism, is the equivalent of an evasion."[3]

How does this affect Romania? The question is worth raising because it is hard to imagine a worse misunderstanding in the East-West debate than that of considering it helpful in advancing critical thought in the East to approach Communism by favoring a historiography built less on proof from archives than on national interest—in Romania's case, on proof of a reconstruction of identity marked by the lost quest for a viable "Romanianism" in a country where the Communist regime has drawn a substantial part of its legitimacy from renouncing immediately any rhetoric of international proletarianism to be included in its discourse and has borrowed its symbolic themes directly from fascism.[4] The uneasiness stems from this, for to invoke under these conditions a "Red Holocaust" is perhaps a way of taking the shortest route and avoiding having to think about what the "Red" in question must have assimilated from the "Brown" (the ethno-nationalism of the 1960s) to assure the installation of a system that, for four generations, had not been based on terrorism alone.

Looked at more closely, one sees the same cause put forward in both East and West—that of knowledge or the scientific establishment of the facts—but in the West certain historians insist that from now on, in light of unsealed documents, it is time to match the condemnation of Nazism with an equally firm one of Communism;[5] while in the East one likewise deplores the notion that the same criteria for judging the two regimes might be applied in such a way that, in the words of a popular Bucharest publicist who commented a short time ago, "ten victims of the left [inferring here the sixty million victims of Communism] were not worth one victim of the right [here, the six million victims of Nazism]."[6] This is a statement that has now been taken as a creed in Romania. Taking everything into account, is it really the same country that both sides are talking about? For the East, particularly Romania, can there be a historiography whose statements from now on could be understood without any reference to power or to the role of memory?

The Archive and the Historian's Sleeve

In the case of Romania, this examination leads back directly to the question of the archives and, at the same time, to that of how much the categories of interpretation preferred by the community of historians since 1989 would depend on them. Not being the "mouth of truth," the archives are helpful only according to how they are used and according to the disposition— intellectual, methodological, and ideological—of the group using them—in this case the historians.[7]

The Romanian context would therefore demand from the beginning a distinction between the question of the accessibility *of* the archives and that of accessibility *to* them, this second being possibly as central as the first. If it is impossible to imagine the reconstruction of historiography in the absence of any archive caused by insurmountable institutional or political blockage, it is also necessary in hypothesizing an access to the document that the modes of examination be flexible enough and the problem open ended enough to be able, if necessary, to bend mentally to include anything from the material. If the facts are not given in the documents but nevertheless are each time chosen as a hypothesis, it remains that the argumentative availability alone confers on the archive its restraining epistemological character. As Arlette Farge has stated so well: "The archive always catches anyone by the sleeve who would escape too easily into a study of abstract formulas or a *discourse on*. This is one of the places from which symbolic and intellectual constructions of the past can be rearranged."[8]

As for Romania post-1989, it does not seem that the accessibility or lack of it for any given set of documents or archives, whether it be those of the Communist Party or about the Second World War, for example, has weighed in any determining way on the orientations adapted by the writing or the rewriting of the history of the twentieth century.[9] The important points of focus in the historical debate, the way in which historians define their objectives, construct their arguments, or favor certain aspects, in fact, appear to depend much less on the supply of available documents than on a predetermined number of imperatives (or at least considered as such) of a political and national order and one of identity, arising from reasons other than those of experts and documents.

Certainly many sources remain relatively closed in Romania, a situation due in large part to the policy of obstruction practiced from 1990 to the end of 1996 by a ruling class that was, by a crushing majority, from the old Communist apparatus. The process of demilitarizing the National Archives met with much unwillingness since its direction was given to a former general of the Securitate (ex–political police). Most of the sources, which were from the archives of the Central Committee of the Communist Party, are henceforth subject to the thirty-year rule (forty years or more for those items from the political police) and, in principle, available to historians.[10] Actually, legal restrictions concerning documents likely to endanger "state security," the definition of which remains rather vague, greatly reduce the practical access of the researchers. Furthermore the storage places are dispersed, inventories are incomplete, and authorizations are a long time in coming. And with the material, corruption and "clientelism" encourage bureaucratic inertia in an arbitrary way that does not facilitate the task of historians not in special favor with authorities. In the case of the PCR archives, for example, certain documents less than thirty years old are made available by special permission. Until very recently it was up to the Minister of the Interior to rule on such requests, and this created a worrisome tendency to favor former Communist Party historians. Finally, obtaining approval from these authorities often proved fruitless anyway, for it still remained to work through all of the staff levels in between and to overcome the unwillingness of the archivists themselves, badly paid and often made up of former political-police recruits who had been declared incapable and reassigned to the archives. Political ill will, disorganized material, and a permanent "secreto-maniac" mentality, all were elements that united to transform any research in the archives into a real warrior's training ground.[11] But however real these difficulties remain, there are certain comments widespread among historians on the inaccessibility of the archives that need to be adjusted (made less categorical) on many points.

In the first place it is hard to affirm that between 1990 and the autumn of 1996—which marked a clear softening due to the electoral victory of democratic opposition parties—historians were so jostled in tight rows in the archives that, thanks to the overcrowding, certain retention reflexes finally gave ground. In fact research teams were far from being organized in a way that they could systematically explore entire areas of the recent past.[12] If the study of the Communist period is slower here than in most countries—the first volume of the history of Romania from 1944 to 1989 was published in . . . Budapest—it would seem impossible to be satisfied with explanations attributing this to the simple fact that Romania is "the only country in the former Soviet block where access to Communist Party archives has been forbidden under various pretexts," as certain commentators insist.[13]

The Historiography of Communism: Documentary Contribution and Declaration of Identity

In addition, we observe that the archives have proved to be largely available where the demand was most insistent. Up until the present there has been especially a demand for the years 1940 and 1950, on the repression, the camps, and the collectivization of the countryside—in short, not only on the victims but also on the "heroes," especially those groups of armed partisans, some of whom stayed in the Maquis until the end of the 1950s.[14] On these questions the tenacity of the historians has paid off; a considerable mass of documents and testimonials were obtained by teams of researchers connected with certain journals, with the making of TV programs, or with the publication of document collections.[15]

These sources no doubt provide important clarifications, especially on the violent acts linked to collectivization. Elsewhere the publication of many stories of prison allows us to have a more precise idea of the conditions under which a considerable part of the Romanian elite was decimated during the Stalin period.[16] But although we find ourselves faced here with an undeniable mass of documents, dissatisfaction comes, especially from the way in which these items are organized and presented with a focus almost exclusively on the unveiling of the tragedy of the concentration camps and on a myth-like resistance, so much so that new entities come to be created and each life story is fitted into a vast "national anti-Communist movement," to use the now sacrosanct expression. Commentaries are rare that do not resonate with the care taken in removing anything that could be interpreted as a co-participation of Romanian society with the former regime. Thus the archive is used to create a collective "martyrology" in which history is outlined in black and white, pitting a criminal mafia against a society uniformly hostile to Communism. From the insistence on the unassimilated character of the regime to the accent put on the ethnically "foreign" origin (Jewish, Gypsy, Hungarian, and others) of its governing personnel, we are almost tempted to conclude that the Romanians must have lived through the history of the last half century without ever coming in contact with it. The Communist period is often described in terms of invasion, occupation, or colonization, acts perpetrated through so many "murders of the nation."[17]

This reassuring argument goes together with a symptomatic tendency to favor outside factors. The fact that more attention is paid to the years in which the Communist Party took power can be explained by the fact that it was a period in which the victim-executioner dichotomy can more easily be constructed, the Red Army used to explain the essential, and the theme of Western abandonment to conclude the demonstration. Compared to these external factors, the internal purges of the Party, the trials,[18] decision making, or the social dimension are much less interesting, to say nothing of the significant silence that surrounds, for example, the massive rally to the new regime of former members of the Iron Guard, the most popular extreme Right group of the 1930s, very "Romanian." The reminder of the weakness of the Left in Romania, coupled with the fact that the Communist Party counted hardly more than one thousand members after the war, also occupies a choice place in the repertory of arguments advanced to support the absence of native roots in Communism.[19] We could, however, reverse the direction of this argument: if the Left in Romania had been traditionally stronger, the takeover by the Communist Party at the end of the 1940s would not have found a terrain so well prepared by the two former dictatorships, that of King Carol II (installed in 1938) followed by that of Marshal Ion Antonescu (in the autumn of 1940). In matters of the liquidation of multiparty politics, of the suppression of freedoms, and of political imprisonment and forced labor (imposed on the Jewish population under Antonescu), the Communists had no need to invent, far from it. Let us note in passing that the relative weakness of left-wing thought in Romania helps explain that no reformist movement surfaced later within the PCR as it did in Poland, Hungary, and Czechoslovakia.

Curiously the archives also lack anything that could begin to answer the question of knowing in what measure—in the name of what hopes, what "illusions," or the result of what traumatic experiences—in the days after a crushing war fought at the side of the Reich until August 1944, Communism was able to appear to a part of the population as a possible solution for the future. In any case we can be sure of being denied any enlightenment, for the examination of the documents of the years 1945–46 is possible through a grid of teleological reading that would resolve that those years marked "the beginning of the end."[20] How was this [the Communist drama] possible? This question, which precedes, with a certain emotion, many of the analyses of Communism, risks remaining on a rhetorical level without an investigation of the legitimate sources of power, their movements, and their evolutions, systematically omitted in favor of an interpretation content to put the accent on the pure and simple brutality of police methods. To wonder about "the state of social and ideological areas having assured the longevity of the regime," to quote Catherine Durandin,[21] turns out here to be more a matter of documentary abundance than critical demands and interpretive design.

In a word one is struck by the absence of any documents that might discredit an account on Romanianism arranged around a mythical "we" eternally opposed to the Communist ideal. Suggestions in the direction of a more refined categorization, such as that suggested by Imre Toth, remains without echo, or almost so. A Communist from the very first, joining the party at sixteen, then excluded in 1959 for his position in favor of the Hungarian revolution in 1956, Toth suggested, in an interview he gave in 1988, substituting the distinction "collaborators and non-collaborators" for Communists and anti-Communists, which to him seemed more useful and more accurately reflected the situation of the country at that time. "I lived in Bucharest for a long time in the circles of the former aristocracy or of the Romanian upper middle classes, among people structurally anti-Communist, who were sincere and capable of convincing the Communists. It was among these that I met the most useful collaborators of the regime," he said. "I later knew committed members of the Communist Party who were not collaborators, who detested the politics of pompousness and elitism of the top leaders of the party and of the Securitat."[22] To admit such a distinction would be to include the most telling failures of the Great Romania of 1920 in creating the history of Communism. This would be to allow asking how, for certain ones even if they were a minority, Communism could appear at the beginning to be a way of ending the nationalism and the governmental anti-Semitism that, in Romania, was put into force beginning in 1937,[23] or further as a promise of social justice and a trend toward modernity. We are far from this; the majority of historians prefer to see Communism as a tragedy with which the "true" nation, the one before 1940, the European Romania, would never have associated itself.[24] A selection of archives according to the problematical, and not the reverse, seems to be the tendency that appears in Romanian historiography of the 1950s.

The national Communist phase (beginning with the 1960s) also presents formidable difficulties. Even though the archives during the Ceausescu period fall within the thirty-year restriction, this is not the only reason historians seem to show little interest in this period. Other sources could be exploited, especially oral ones (which has already been done for former political detainees of the 1950s)—this, however, on the condition that a global history be abandoned in favor of an inventiveness enhanced by a choice of approaches or the scale of the observation.[25] In the material on social history or the histories of representations or of elites, numerous working groups could have already been engaged.[26] The delays in creating this group are surely explained by the lack of means, the methodological delays accumulated during the last decades, and the fact that the very idea of present-day history still upsets the historical habits in a country where most institutions are still organized into two departments—national history on one side, universal history on the other. And certain blocking mechanisms of a psychosociological nature are also in full force. A double reminder is in order here to outline the logic.

The first, which heads the list, is the relationship of intellectuals to the national question. Throughout the major debate that took place between the two world wars, and that was already focusing less on the question of social reform than on the nation and its "specificity," the tendency of Romanian intellectuals to put the nation and its "values" at the center of their thought remains fundamental in understanding, under Ceausescu, their attitude toward the Party as much as toward society. It is useful here not to forget the *negotiated* aspect of the dynamic put into action beginning in the 1960s and concluding with this spectacular assertion of national values in the politics of a nation of the Soviet bloc. This already underlies "the spirit of the 1960s," which culminated in 1968 with Ceausescu's refusal to intervene in Czechoslovakia. Called upon once more to assume their traditional role of defenders of the "country in danger," many intellectuals rallied to the Communists. For the first time since the Party's foundation, it could establish a relationship with the intellectuals at least partly founded on shared values.[27] Thus one chooses to favor national unity and solidarity over social and political conflicts. It would be too late when, during the 1970s, National Communism was shown to be not a more liberal alternative to Bolshevism because more national, but an ideology at the service of a system highly centralized, associated with increasingly repressive politics. The Party had finally, permanently, and efficiently succeeded in short-circuiting any intention of opposition or reform at the center of an intelligentsia caught in the trap of its anti-Russianism and its anti-Marxism. In this way, beginning with the second half of the 1970s, it was also *independent of Party injunctions* that the national problem, strengthened by its precedence and its prestige, took on an authentic autonomy in the cultural sphere. It opposed the protochronist[28] sphere of influence over those in power and any promotion of native values, and its intellectuals were favorable to ideas more open to Western influences. But both sides accepted being placed on a common ground, that of a nation and a more or less metaphysical characterization of "Romanianess."[29] If the secondary groups intended to thus thwart the Party in its attempt to gain for itself an exclusive monopoly on the national discourse, it nevertheless remains that the result of these strategies, led by different camps, was to contribute to the self-perpetuation of the official ideology and from this of the regime itself.[30] In short, intellectuals and historians were not just content to fall in behind a state nationalism, but they also helped push the regime along this path. The enthusiasm of the Party for reviving an ethno-national metaphysic, whose model was borrowed from the theoreticians of the period between the two wars, is surely explained by the desire to impose its policy of autonomy vis-à-vis Moscow.

But this explanation "from on high" would not suffice, and this is exactly what complicates the historiography of that period. The nationalist phenomena could not have reached the proportions we see without the support in this direction supplied by a large fraction of the intelligentsia, which found it to its advantage thanks to the symbolic benefits they received in the social and cultural field. This diversion was necessary here in order to measure everything that today obscures an ultratotalitarian act of historiography, one that never ceases to invoke "the sinister parenthesis of the Soviet-Communist domination," understood as "an immense prison in which the Romanian people were incarcerated."[31] We note also that this type of reminder allows, in its wake, the erasing of a characteristic that sociologist Bernard Paqueteau calls the "corrupting social compromise." This compromise between society and the reigning power, beginning in the 1960s, supports a close historical association with the patriotic compromise mentioned earlier. This sociologist has given us a detailed analysis of the structuring of this "black society," described as a civil society turned against itself.[32] This goes back to all kinds of formulas of adaptation and coexistence with the system and to multiple networks of relations between individuals (family, work, and such) based on the exchange of services and the trading of possessions. These networks became associated in large measure with the existing power and its various organisms in a way that was, he notes, "both violent and muffled," an implicit contract became joined "in the form of a complicity to hijack the legacy."[33] What was put in place in this way is better described as a mafia-like system, made up of relationships of force or allegiance, than as a totalitarian system, imbedded in a system otherwise less divided and compartmentalized and in which the majority of participants accepted the rules of the game. Roughly from the 1960s, this process, he continues, made it difficult to point out a group of guilty ones since "there was no longer a political system led by Marxists who faced a non-Communist society, conforming to the theme of 'them and us.'"[34]

To return to the question of the archives, we are not surprised that, under these conditions, an undeniable "penury" of documents today prevents revisiting anything before the last three decades of the regime. Nevertheless, if all the documents of this period were available, it is not easy to see by what miracle an absolute and definitive truth about the "essence" of the Romanian people that conforms to a landscape of shared expectations could be revealed. The archives "should respond to the question: 'Who are we?'" claims Ana Blandiana, for example, one of the principal persons responsible for the International Center for Studies on Communism, which is linked to the new Museum of the Romanian Gulag being created on the sight of the prison at Sighet. In a disturbing and rather contradictory fashion, the most insistent demands for the opening are also made by those who seem to already know almost everything of what they have to tell us. Why "descend into the catacombs of our history?" the editor and philosopher Gabriel Liiceanu recently asked regarding the subject of free access to the files of the former political police. "Because it would permit everyone to reestablish, once and for all, the idea of good and evil and to do away with the thesis of a generalized complicity (we all would have collaborated)," he answered, adding that the responsibility certainly does not lie with the entire "people" but with "a handful of professionals of terrorism in the service of a regime that had succeeded in disfiguring Romania in the space of a few decades," who could be defined by "an uninterrupted series of crimes."[35] In this case, if we are already armed with clearly unimpeachable certainties, why exhaust ourselves searching through kilometers of archives?

In the case of Romania, we are therefore far from having the archives play a role in encouraging this indispensable cognitive dissociation between history and memory—the one being presented to construct a truth, the other to create a collective identity. It is much more the reduction of the one to the other that is striking in an arrangement of form and meaning of a Communist past that seems to conform especially to a demand for justification. Even so, Romanian historians willingly admit to lending themselves to this demand for justice, which a number of them consider as part of both a moral and professional obligation in a political situation dominated for a long time by the effort to keep ex-Communists in power. Andréi Pippidi was able to declare [in 1996]: "What remains to be done after justice has been done to men in the shadows [the victims of Communism] will be a problematical and conceptual history."[36] It is just this manner of arranging priorities—do justice first, then write the history—that is both necessary and problematic. In reality these two levels of discourse will always be confused in order to open the way for reconstructions of myth or identity, subordinated to the production of a positive and assumable national identity, which threatens to take precedence over a critical reappropriation without us ever being told when we move from one register to the other.

Antonescu and the Romanian Chapter of the Holocaust: Selected Sources

While instituting this myth of an innocent Romania, free of any possible opposition, as preceding the Communist period in historical writing since 1989, two major themes have dominated the Romanian historiography of World War II. One consists of vehemently denying the dimensions of the Holocaust in Romania and rejecting all historical responsibility of the Romanians in the extermination of the Jews.[37] Yet in Romania this policy produced more than two hundred thousand victims. Besides the pogroms of Dorohoi, Bucharest (1940), and the terrifying rampage at Iasi (which left twelve thousand dead within a few days), let us remember that the quasi-totality of the Jewish population of Bessarabia and North Bucovina (two territories reclaimed by the USSR in June 1941) was either massacred on the spot by Romanian and German troops or deported east to Transnistria, where under Romanian administration, between September 1941 and October 1942 there took place a kind of preview of what would later be the "Final Solution."[38] The other theme portrays Marshal Antonescu (who installed the State National Legionnaire in the autumn of 1940) as the savior of the nation, a great patriot, a hero of the anti-Bolshevik struggle, and indeed a visionary politician.[39] There are many indications of the popularity of this cult; statues were erected to the glory of the marshal in streets renamed for him, and the members of Parliament joined ranks in 1991 to observe a minute of silence to honor his memory.

An editorial in the most prestigious daily in the country, published in April 1993 on the eve of the inauguration of the Holocaust Museum in Washington, D.C., set the tone that also predominated in the community of historians: "As everyone knows, we read, many Jews claim that Romania figured among the countries responsible for the tragedy of the Holocaust. This attempt to blame the Romanian people ran into very strong objections, not only on the part of our historians but also of the entire Romanian people."[40] The statement is even more important since it came on the eve of the declassification of documents proving that the entirety of the destructive measures undertaken in Romania in 1941 and 1942 was certainly approved by Marshal Antonescu and carried out under the orders of the general headquarters of the Romanian army and of the minister of the interior. We now know of the responsibility of the marshal, among others, for the pogrom of Iasi and also of the assassination en masse of the Odessa Jews (between twenty-five thousand and thirty thousand dead), carried out under his direct orders on October 23 and 24, 1941.[41]

The decision not to accept this chapter of the national history by the majority of Romanian historians lies at the heart of our subject, for it shows a consummate art of manipulation of the archives, and this attitude is central to the identification of everything that, in this context, the use of ideas, such as that of the Red Holocaust, carries along with it of equivocation and cover up.

Yet we might also wonder how much of this revisionism results from ignorance after so many decades of falsified history. Since 1989, considerable files of documents have become accessible to historians,[42] and this leaves even less room for excuses since the Kafkaesque atmosphere that permeated the archives is no longer an important obstacle in obtaining material, for most of the archives for 1940–44 can now be found assembled at the Holocaust Museum in Washington. Since 1993, the museum has actually managed to obtain from Bucharest considerable amounts of material (microfilms from the political police, military archives, archives of the state, and others), totaling more than six hundred thousand pages. Their use would be essential if and when the grave question of the degree of collaboration between the Romanians (army, police, gendarmerie, and civilians) and the Germans in the planning and carrying out of the process of genocide in Romania is finally taken up.[43] On this subject Raul Hilberg has pointed out, "no country with the exception of Germany, participated so massively in the massacre of the Jews. The group behavior and that of individuals do not always show the same characteristics but in the case of Romania we find a pronounced analogy."[44] This finding is worthy of reexamination today in light of the new documentation available. It remains, however, that this archival minirevolution—the allocation of study grants, catalogs available on the internet, and American-type conditions for working—seems not to have convinced Romanian historians, judging from the almost total absence of interest.

The argument behind which certain specialists of the contemporary period hide, one claiming that all documentation relative to the years 1940–44 is alleged to have been hidden from the time of the war's end—which has caused the tremendous delay in catching up—does not hold up under closer scrutiny either. Before 1948, that is, before the regime had finished dismantling the group of historical institutions surviving from the previous period,[45] a complete catalog of documents relating to the role of Antonescu and his collaborators in the destruction of the Romanian Jews was available. For the preparation of trials aimed at war criminals and their assistants, hundreds of files were gathered together through depositions (from those directly responsible for the massacres—those who executed the victims, eyewitnesses, survivors, and others)—facsimiles of orders given by Antonescu and his staff headquarters for armed forces on the eastern front, chronologies, census, and photographs, among other items. A part of this extraordinary documentation, as well as other sources coming from the archives of the Federation of Jewish Communities, were meticulously assembled and edited by Matatias Carp in *Le Livre noir*, in three volumes, published beginning in 1946.[46] A remarkably incisive work for the period, it would have permitted a solid reconstruction of the amplitude of the unfolding tragedy. But no historians undertook this work.

These several findings encourage a more circumspect consideration of the hypothesis that the revisionist wave following 1989 was actually a pendulum phenomenon.[47] This resulted in the case of Romania seeming less a case of one revisionism succeeding another than a revisionism prolonging the one already strong before 1989.[48] The first attempts aimed at a positive reevaluation of Marshal Antonescu as a defender of "national integrity" go back to the 1970s. The rest of the official historiography on the question hardly varies throughout the Communist period, tending to attribute responsibility for the politics of anti-Semitism carried on between 1940 and 1944 to the Germans alone,[49] although this is just mentioned in the widespread, almost systematic disappearance of the Jews in the general category of "population masses" who were victims of Nazism. The school texts of the post-1989 era perpetuate, point by point, this same outline, a situation that reflects the questionable positions of the majority of current historians.[50] In fact this revisionist approach is today especially well represented among former Party historians and those of the Institute of Military History. Setting the tone is the fact that both are often close to the extreme Right.[51] It is also to be noted that access to Romanian archives is facilitated for them by the fact that numerous files of the old Institute of History of the PCR were acquired, after 1989, by the Ministry of Defense and of the Interior, two institutions that support their claims. In other words, working revisionists claim to rely heavily on sources, as shown by the impressive number of collections and documents published in the last seven years on the policies of Antonescu. All of this enters into the selection and the skill of an editorial perspective whose partiality—difficult to accept in the West coming from a scholarly group—in Romania enjoys a high level of acceptance, given both the lack of information of the reading public and the limits of a field of historiography whose practices are loosely codified and still unstable.

Thus the posture of victim, associated with the recurring theme of a nation isolated and surrounded by enemies, dominates the organization of a very serious collection of several volumes, edited by a team of National Archives historians and entitled, significantly, *La Roumanie: La Grande Sacrifiée de la Seconde Guerre mondiale.*[52] Nowhere in this work is there a critical reexamination of the Romanian alliance with Germany, an alliance that is, to the contrary, justified by a great number of politically strategic arguments. The possibility in a certain context to force archives to say just about anything is shown by yet another collection—*L'Emigration de la population juive de Roumanie au cours des années 1940–1944*—published under the auspices of the Ministry of Foreign Affairs. This time the central thesis is to attribute the responsibility for the massacres committed at Dorohoi, Iasi, in Bessarabia, and in North Bucovine not only to the Germans but also to the Soviets. "It appears," we read in this collection, "that the Bessarabian Jews, a province occupied by the Soviets in June 1940 would have known a very different fate in the years 1941–1944 if this famous June 1940 had not taken place."[53] The systematic massacre of the Jewish community in Bessarabia and Bucovine, massively deported to the camps of Transnistria—a measure decided on by Antonescu and carried out by his troops on territory under Romanian administration at the time—is assigned to the Soviet regime. The underlying reasoning seems to be the following: Jews and Communists being synonyms, so to speak, and a number of Romanians having been hissed at or molested during the retreat of the Romanian army from the eastern provinces following a Soviet ultimatum in June 1940, their massacre would come from a kind of historical fatality, in whose genealogy the USSR would have played an important role in starting, and so the Romanian government would be cleared of any responsibility. An undeniable compatibility in outlook in the context links Communism and revisionism, as if the latter must necessarily implicate the former, and in this way the idea of "Communism as an exclusive creation of Moscow" goes hand in hand with "The Holocaust as an exclusively German creation."

This reading, however, is far from being the only action of the nationalist historians. In their case, historical reconstruction goes hand in hand with a biographical recomposition. In absolving the Romanian government of its collaboration with Hitler's Germany, these former servants of the national-Communist regime also plead their own cause, careful to clear themselves of their own collaboration of the final decades. It is especially this consensual dimension of the phenomena that in the case of Romania takes on a disturbing air.[54] The least that can be said is that the reply to the revisionist offensive turned out to be very restrained in the camp of the historians of democratic orientation. Positions explicitly disagreeing remain exceptional.[55] The small place occupied by this subject in the arguments of historical journals specializing in these last years shows a strategy of avoidance, and it is a fact that no Romanian specialist of the period, up until now in Romania, has had the audacity to undertake a work actually based on documents for the years 1940–44, leaving this task to study centers, Jewish historians, or publishers affiliated with them.[56] From this comes the perverted effect of a "ghettoization" of research in this field nowhere more developed in the East than in Romania. It is not rare to hear important directors of contemporary research at posts in the country's most prestigious institutions allege the impossibility of establishing the historical truth about the Antonescu regime, taking into account the freeze resulting from the "simplistic outlook" that would predominate the subject in the West, particularly in "Jewish circles [*sic*]."[57]

It is a disturbing phenomenon of convergence that, in content, the tone hardly differs in the pages of the best Romanian journals from that of those in which the most critical analyses toward today's nationalist currents are usually found. The issue entitled "For a Non-Falsified History" and devoted to the "Antonescu Case" by the journal *22*—the weekly of liberal intellectuals most firmly engaged in favor of the process of democratization and an opening up to Europe—is revealing in this regard.

Here, for example, we read that, following the model of Marshal Pétain, who "refused to deliver to Hitler Jews of French nationality," Antonescu also was good enough to "resist the pressures of Berlin." Because of this fact, the author is astonished at the upsurge of repeated attacks on Antonescu from the foreign press, and he states that these reactions coincide with "a similar campaign against Marshal Pétain in France," which came out of "a hateful film produced by two former Trotskyites, presenting Pétain as a criminal."[58] In the same issue Florin Constantiniu, one of the most highly regarded historians of the contemporary period in Romania, in his turn develops an argument that follows step by step the same one put forward by his most questionable colleagues: that Marshal Antonescu should never be regarded as a war criminal since Romania was the victim of aggression by the USSR, and the retaking of territory lost in 1940 was a legitimate act since it was a matter of restoring the territorial integrity of the country. Pursuit of the war beyond this objective answered a dual necessity of a military kind (pursuing it to have total surrender from the enemy) and of a geopolitical kind (to obtain from the Allies a revision of the Vienna arbitration, by which the Romanians had been forced to cede back Northern Transylvania to Hungary).[59]

From these tendencies it is clear that we must look not just at the question of the archives and their access specifically speaking but also elsewhere in order to clarify the choice of paradigms and their current applications in Romania to the writings on fascism as much as on Communism. In fact we discover here a certain tendency to engage in a trial of Communism much more than in that of Nazism in general or of the fascist regime installed by Antonescu in particular, and along with him, currents of prewar nationalist thought that contributed to making it possible.

To formally record the catastrophe of Communism is no doubt a require-ment for the emergence of a European awareness, but each historian should also agree to relate his own European identity in the same problematical way, to work for a transition from a "totemic history" to a "critical history" (to use Pierre Nora's terms). In other words it would still be necessary, if this lucidity is to "create a bridge between Western Europe and the 'other Europe,'" as François Furet wanted,[60] that an equal effort take place on the other side of the former Iron Curtain, that the rewriting of this reading of Communism as a catastrophe not be a way of shirking a reflection aimed at assuming, even if only partially, Communism and fascism as chapters having their part in the nation's history. It is important to keep in mind the effects of this side-stepping, for in Bucharest François Furet's authority is invoked each time there is a question of deploring the fact that an "anti-Communist culture" of the same importance as the "antifascist culture" is still slow in being recognized at the century's end.[61] If we reject antifascism as a political dumping ground, having too often been used as an alibi for every blindness, should we not observe the same caution about anti-Communism? And it would be suitable not to lose sight of how much the use, in any context, of terms most often associated with the Shoah to suggest a certain equality in evil (for example, negation, genocide, and crimes against humanity) could also encourage in the East a political and ideological practice of comparison to banalize the genocide of the Jews, too happy to be thus involuntarily, but no less scientifically, supported.

If it is the historian's habit to compare in order to understand without relativizing one totalitarianism by another, it is also a way of comparing in order to minimize Auschwitz to the advantage of the gulags—"these countless Auschwitzes without crematoriums,"[62] according to a recurring expression in the East—and by doing this, to save themselves from both at the same time. Several operations are imbedded here whose commonly held logic is worth a straightforward explanation.

Fascism and Communism: Or How to Compare Them in Order to Be Rid of Them

It would be suitable in fact to wonder about the meaning of a defense that underlies the use of a word as connotative as "Holocaust (Red)," overused in Romania to qualify Communism, if only in that it signals an attempt to capture a legacy and adapt symbols to its own use. What causes the problem here, once again, is not that the dominant tendencies of historiography are driven by an important desire to reestablish that tragic and criminal face of Stalinism, but that one "genocide" is advanced systematically to overshadow another by those very people who elsewhere have never ceased to blame the West for practicing a double standard, two different sets of rules. The uneasiness comes from the *extent* of the procedure, which seems to be to create a thesis of a pure Romanian, European, and heroic identity and to inscribe it on the *internal level*, in the length and continuity of a positive patriotism, while rooting it and legitimizing it *externally* in an idea of Communism that, in the twentieth century, takes precedence in matters of terrorism and genocide. The pathos, indeed the intentionally provocative tone, of the militant parallelism must be understood in the light of what is at stake here.

This approach can also make use of the notion of a Red Holocaust in that it allows for a dual accentuation. In "Red Holocaust" in fact there is first *Holocaust*. The word allows the reality it describes to immediately attain, in the Western mind, a status equal to that of the extermination of the Jews by the Nazi regime. The spirit of the wording is one of a claim of victimization careful to legitimize itself in a sort of mimetic rivalry with Jewish memory.[63] This is indeed hostile to that memory in that it claims an exclusive monopoly on the status of victim. An article entitled "L'Autre Holocaust" stated very well, in this regard, a position largely shared among historians. "M. Moses Rosen [Chief Rabbi of Romania at the time of the publication of this article in 1993] did not understand that there was no need to blame the Romanian people for a mistake which was not theirs.

The very fact that the queen mother, Elena, was called The Just because she saved the Jews during the war contradicts these accusations. Nazism was a criminal system against humanity, denounced worldwide. But Communism also was and still remains a criminal regime against humanity. If the entire world today condemns Nazism to the point of continuing the search for those who served it, it is impossible to explain why the same thing is not being undertaken in regard to Communism. . . . Nevertheless, the survivors of Hitler's camps who were later thrown into Communist prisons," the author continues, "claim that these were much harsher. In spite of all this, it has not been judged suitable to build a Communist Holocaust museum beside the [Nazi] Holocaust museum,"[64] complains the journalist, who writes for the number-two daily newspaper of the country.

There was no distinction made here between the Nazi genocide and the mass murders under Communism. What is affirmed by the idea of a Communist genocide is also what it denies or relativizes. To speak of the Red Holocaust in this context is to, in a single movement, deny all singularity to the Shoah, both to its historical uniqueness and its irreducible moral. The conviction that the two events can legitimately be put on the same level in Romania is very evident. Even more, any position tending to differentiate between Hitler and Stalin immediately appears suspect in the eyes of the best historians. This dominant orthodoxy presides especially over the recent creation of the Memorial of Sighet, divided into the Museum of the Romanian Gulag and the International Institute of Communist Research. The idea for this project, now co-financed by the European Union and the Civic Academy of Bucharest and supported by the best-known intellectuals, was born in 1993. Ana Blandina relates its genesis in the following way: "It was after a visit to Poland. At Auschwitz, a center for research on Nazism was being constructed, sponsored by the Council of Europe. Why not think about undertaking a twin center of research on Communism? we asked ourselves. Why not suggest a larger and more complex outlook on the two types of suffering endured by the Europeans in this century? Why not accept a parallel between the two types of totalitarianism?"[65]

The passing from an equivalency—the extermination of a race and the extermination of a class would historically be equal—to the affirming of a hierarchy of evil brings with it the idea that the supreme horror would be that of Communism since it extended over a longer period, a nuance that Romanian intellectuals do not hesitate to accept.[66] From this point the shift was rapid, due to the mix, toward a kind of *reductio ad hitlerium* in reverse. Nothing in anti-Communism was unworthy of being rehabilitated. We see this type of procedure throughout an important television series entitled *A Memorial to Suffering*, of which several dozen episodes have already been shown in prime time. This documentary, which mobilized a team of specialists and was a great success with the public, illustrates in exemplary fashion on the visual level certain characteristic amalgams of this rehabilitated anti-Communism. The proposition being to reestablish the truth about the Communist "genocide," there follows one episode after the other numerous—and precious—testimonies from former political detainees, whose story is accompanied by the presentation of many documents from the archives. In a counterpoint, however, these images are always punctuated by a double reference: on the one hand, to Antonescu and the heroism of the Romanian army (they insist on the fact that to have turned the guns against the Germans on August 23, 1944, would amount to delivering the country to the Russians), for which both received enormous praise—omnipresent on the screen is a quote from the marshal, "Above all, country and the eternity of the people"—on the other hand, there is reference to orthodoxy. If a prison is shown, there will also appear superimposed upon it images of Christ on the cross and of icons. Let us note that, until now, there has not been a single historian publicly criticize the ambiguities fostered in this series. Instead it has been well received by those in charge of the Sighet Memorial. No quarrel among historians has arisen from it.

Western criticism of this type of amalgam has drawn, in a striking way, a lively bidding up by those responsible the theme of a Romania once more victimized by the West and the Left generally. Romulus Rusan, one of the founders of the Sighet Memorial, denounced a kind of conspiracy of silence: "It appeared to us, at a certain time, that the West did not want to learn the truth about Communism," he revealed in July 1996. Our critics, he complained, make an effort to "dissociate the two types of totalitarianism pleading, in reality, for a minimization of Communism and an amnesty for its crimes."[67] And certain intellectuals, like Horia Patapievici, one of the most brilliant essayists writing in Bucharest, denounced in this context the blindness of a West European public opinion completely intoxicated by Soviet propaganda services and, before that, by the ideology inherited from the French Revolution: "Crimes of the Left are tolerated but those of the Right are considered intolerable."[68] Several decades of historiographical debates and ideas on the meaning and the extent of the comparison of Stalinism and Nazism are here dismissed as a pure and simple war of ideological positions, the Left naturally directing the game, not to mention the plot. Also notable here is the surprising ignorance surrounding these undertakings by the historians involved.

Besides a certain provincialism on the part of the elite of an intelligentsia that never ceases to emphasize its European credentials, this type of proposal allows a glimpse into a more twisted logic that guides the insistence on the genocidal dimension of Communism each time it is considered in its global dimensions. In the first instance this insistence allows for an indisputable banalization of the Nazi Holocaust *in general* absolutely required by the concern to overshadow the implication of the Romanians *in particular* in this country's involvement in the genocide of the Jews (therefore as an event comparable to many others and on which there is no need to linger). In the second instance is the nonimplication of "Eternal Romania" in this process of destruction, which leads to the possibility of pleading a symmetrical nonparticipation of Romanian society in Communism. In this way a complete account of forty-five years of Party domination can be couched exclusively in terms of an imported Bolshevism, and the theme of a Red Army, which had only been a force of occupation and in no way one of liberation, can be introduced. It is this adjustment that makes the idea of a Red Holocaust not only completely coherent but also twice muted, the second accent falling exactly on a Communism presented as red and nothing but red. This was a way to avoid any connection with the years before 1945, to cover up everything the regime, in its Romanian version, had cleverly been able to reintegrate of the "brown"—for example, ethnocentrism, nationalist rhetoric, triumphant support of ancestral values and of the soul of the people, and an antiminority xenophobia—in order to maintain for several decades a relative cohesion and to assure itself of a true legitimacy in large sectors of the population.

In successive shifts it is finally the myth of "judéo-bolchevism," a category central to the nationalist and anti-Semitic propaganda of the 1920s and 1930s, that subtly reactivates the idea of a Red Holocaust; the circle is thus closed. "We are finally even," seem to say the most ardent users of the expression. Since you (the Jews) have had to suffer some harm from us (the Romanians), this is largely compensated by your responsibilities in the installation of a Communist regime after 1945—and the "genocide" that followed—a logical consequence of your long connivance with the Communist movement since the October Revolution. No matter if the PCR (forbidden in 1924) had counted some eight hundred members in the period between the two wars, which included a mix of ethnic origins, including native Romanians, with a Jewish population of nearly eight hundred thousand, the stereotype of the Jewish-Bolshevik symbiosis has obviously had a long life.[69] This fiction, however, carries with it its own series of massacres, beginning with the twelve thousand victims of the Iasi pogrom, "judéo-bolshevik provocations" having served, of course, as the official pretext for the triggering of the atrocities.[70] Serge Moscovici, in an autobiographical account of his youthful years in Romania, where he was born and that he left forever in 1947, reminds us of the strength and the omnipresence of this myth. "All of our threats came from there [from the Bolshevik Revolution]. It was a widespread belief. . . . Communism, enemy of the nation, was ceaselessly denounced. This was taught in the schools, written about in the newspapers, preached in the churches. No doubt this was the reason Romanian fascism was born but it also explains why it was the largest fascist movement in Eastern Europe. All of these myths were based on the struggle against Communism."[71] He still remembered that the same propaganda never ceased to associate Jews and Communists. "It was infuriating, intolerable, to hear it said, from morning till night, the Jews are Communists, as if it were their religion or in their genes. People forgot to ask themselves, at that time, why others weren't also, or so few of them."[72]

This last remark helps us understand the subsequent evolution of the situation, the weakness of the left in Romania having played its part in the fact that, from the years 1945–46, the social revolution could rapidly develop into a national one, as Moscovici once more observes with great analytical acumen: "Everything unfolded according to a perfectly logical design. In the 1930s, the Iron Guard had chosen the Jews as a cornerstone and the Judeo-Communism for a slogan for every act. At the time, the Jews had the role of enemies of a modern God—the nation. Then that of the gods of the modern enemy, Bolshevism. In the 1940s, they were seen as a birth stain that needed to be hidden, or an anomaly that should be normalized. The Iron Guard wanted to eliminate the Jews and therefore the Communists since they were all Jews. The example came from above, the Party was Romanized by first changing the names with Jewish consonants into names with Romanian ones."[73] And one must remember something too often passed over in silence today, how alive anti-Semitism still was, a fact that helped arrange things for the political forces in ascendance. The observation, corroborated by documents recently exhumed from Romanian archives,[74] is worth citing since it allows us to recreate the social construction of the mythic "judeo-bolshevik" in a historical, psychological, and ethical context that permits an inclusion of all it signifies. "It was whispered that the Jews were hand in glove with the Russians since they had had them come to Romania. All of that was old, worn out. . . . Of all the popular passions, it was the only one to remain intact. The liberal parties permitted a secret blossoming. The Communist Party avoided fighting it so as not to irritate the people. . . . The struggle against fascism, which had been launched with a hand over the heart, degenerated without transition into a struggle to have the fascists become red and thus to recuperate them."[75]

If it is perfectly predictable that Jews equal Communists constitutes, since 1989, one of the themes of the ultranationalist group and of the many historians of the twentieth century counted among their fellow travelers, it is something of an enigma that this myth should reappear in the writings of the most brilliant intellectuals of the century, minds that one would never suspect of being anti-Semitic or of having hidden sympathies for the extreme Right. Symptomatic in this regard is the text recently dedicated by the philosopher Gabriel Liiceanu to Mihail Sebastian, a Romanian writer of Jewish origin, whose journal covering the years 1935–44—an exceptional document for the period—was published in Bucharest by *Humanitas*, edited by Liiceanu himself. Here we see Liiceanu take up in his turn the stereotype of Judeo-Communism as if it were self-evident.

He begins by paying homage to Sebastian's political clairvoyance during the 1930s. With a remarkable lucidity for the period, Sebastian defined himself as a "dissident," showing an equal distrust toward fascism and Communism, both of them arising, in his eyes, from a "terrifying negation of the individual," and he untiringly denounced their common "mystic of the man in uniform," the man of the masses, their common aspiration for the "importance of the collective over the individual." "The critical mind," he wrote magnificently, "is always a civilian."[76] Departing from this anticonformist spirit, which characterizes Sebastian, Liiceanu attempts to extrapolate what the writer would have said if he had witnessed the takeover of power by the Communists after the war. The extrapolation presents this, attributed to Sebastian: "How is it possible that the very ones who, at a given moment of history, were made to put on the uniform of the victim and afterward (after 1945) put on that of the executioner? Wouldn't the one who suffered the most become a guarantee for the fact that henceforth suffering would no longer be possible? When a group of former victims found itself in the unusual position of making possible another calamity of history [Communism], or at least profiting from its installation, wouldn't they, in doing this, have missed the opportunity to finally put an end to suffering by the very fact of the extreme suffering they had recently endured? How could those who knew everything about human pain yet take part in this new scenario of suffering? Sebastian," Liiceanu continues, "died before he was able to write this, but his Journal, which we still have, leads us to believe that is what he would have believed and stood for."[77]

The procedure makes us even more ill at ease because the author, in a way, hides behind Mihail Sebastian in order to implicitly validate, as if it were a question of a proven historical truth that did not need reviewing, the fantasy that the installing in power of the Communist regime was the work essentially of Jews ("Those who . . . ," "a group of former victims," "their own"), a distinction that already poses a problem: Were these not people, Romanian citizens, just as non-Jews were? Additionally, if the author took care to explicitly underline the reality of the harm suffered by the Jewish community of Romania during the war, this strong statement also allows him to forget to mention by *whom* these persecutions were conducted and, incidentally, to wonder about the eventual *why* of those universal hopes that some immediately following the war could invest in the Communist movement, considering the nationalist drift of Romanian politics since 1920. The fact that some Communists, of all ethnic origins and who were converted in the early days, were later compromised in the politics of repression presents another problem, and it would be well to identify just what we are talking about. Certainly these questionable statements and omissions permit the reader to, as a last resort, get from this passage the following message: that the Jews, or rather the "Jew," must have been both victim and executioner at the same time. At least the philosopher, who has published Tocqueville, Hannah Arendt, and Martin Buber, says nothing that would contradict such a conclusion. If the statements coming from Liiceanu do not intentionally aim at banalizing the Holocaust but only enlarge the idea of a crime against humanity to include Communism, which is something he argues for elsewhere in other articles, the ambiguity of the passage quoted earlier and its symbolic usefulness are no less complete.

The principle source of our discomfort when faced with this position of parallel or comparable—which includes the idea of Communist genocide—comes finally from the fact that it gathers to it all the advantages of an operation that avoids studying the years 1941–44 and at the same time wards off Communism in its national aspects, which are the most difficult to assume. One sees it as two separate sections: as an externalized Communism requiring, most of the time, as its corollary a revised fascism. This detour was necessary in order to incorporate the ins and outs of the efforts made by many Romanian historians to credit at any price the idea of a Red Holocaust, the "red" in question revealing the tone of a historiography, arising much more from a *culture of shame* (with its own criteria; my image, my respectability, my innocence, and so on) than from an ethic of responsibility.

The Capture of Historiography by Ideology: In What Way?

In what sense do these orientations show an ideological seizure of the historian's work? If accurate, how does one characterize the forms and the levels of this dependence? Romania no doubt confronts us with a field of historiography that yet again has important difficulties in achieving autonomy, as much in relation to politics as in its relation to social demand. There are several reasons for this. The principal one, often spoken of and common to most post-Communist countries, understandably reverts back to the failure to fulfill needs in a discipline that for several decades was under the strict surveillance of the Party.[78] The secondary reasons are due to a specific climate in which it remains difficult for the historian to conceive of being able to withdraw into his discipline and exercise the necessary thoroughness and rigorous methodologies, but the history of the twentieth century and its principle protagonists are constantly put in the spotlight by the public and the media. The political actors for their part show themselves singularly inclined to return to a past that, in this region, will loom as a battleground, an essential instrument of legitimization, and an inexhaustible reservoir of symbols in a situation marked by almost structural deficits of legitimacy in which, as a consequence, there are very few arguments concerning rights that do not hark back to historical rights.[79] Furthermore, this area is characterized by a forceful effort in this sense, for the uncertainty of the state hierarchy together with the dissimilar ethic and political borders has traditionally conferred a major political function on history, and on historians a principal place in the construction and the consolidation of national identities. In a word we are concerned with countries where history has never ceased, for almost two centuries, to remain at the heart of all the competitions for the definition of nation, even to constituting "the essential axis of a survival strategy."[80] It is important, therefore, to keep in mind this specificity in order to understand, several years after the fall of Communism, the problematic character of an emancipation of historiography from ideology. It is probably better, when using this last expression, to think of it in two ways.

In the first instance, historiography can be said to be crisscrossed with ideological contests and thus is caught up in a militant urgency. It finds itself in the middle of partisan struggles reflecting the game played by opposing players for control of a political project. The effect of this is a politicizing of history that comes from a constant historicization of current politics in Eastern Europe,[81] whose expression is perhaps even clearer because the political field, as in Romania, remains extremely polarized between the new and the old elites, all caught in the game of trying to disqualify each other. It is impossible, for example, to explain the excesses associated with the contrasting line between Nazism and Stalinism if one entirely disregards a political situation during the first seven years of the transition, which was marked by a total absence of purification, whether it be symbolic or not, at the center of the state apparatus. The fact that the repeated calls for a "national reconciliation" had come from the groups emerging from the former regime, and who were anxious above all to maintain their clientele, had something scandalous about it for many historians close to democratic groups. From this came a reaction that was partly in answer to this that chose to emphasize only the criminal dimension of Communism to the detriment of a more complex assessment.

Even so, if these efforts of trying to outdo each other and these procedures of legitimizing/deligitimizing play a central role, in the type of historiographical elaboration both Manichean and reductive that has resulted, one still feels that the mechanisms at work are not completely explicable by arguments coming from purely rational and tactical calculations. Here we need to recognize two kinds of factors that are often assimilated in speaking of the deliberate utilization of history for pedagogical politics but that would actually blend two relatively distinct mechanisms. There would be present two spheres of interest having in common being rooted in the demands of the present, to present history, while going beyond it but that would at the same time operate on two different levels.

In other words it would be suitable—in a second relation—to speak of idealizing historiography in a more subtle sense by a group of *arrangements*, thus differentiating it from a pure and simple voluntary utilization, a system of constraints confined to a more obscure reasoning derived primarily from social imperatives linked to the reconstruction of a national identity traumatized by dictatorship, with all this reconstruction's demands of myths, of cover-ups, and of repression. Here we are not dealing altogether with a logic of the weight of the past (of an archeological kind) or a logic of choosing the past (of a teleological type),[82] but rather we are faced with a process in which the producers of the historical discourse seem to make up their minds *in relation* to a finality (furnish a normative basis for national identity) without this finality being necessarily *aimed at* expressly or consciously.[83]

In this regard the comparison of the countries of Eastern Europe seem to show that the degree to which the historiography, while claiming its neutrality, integrates identity claims is largely proportional to the amount of discomfort felt about a Communist past and also the importance of a collective denial. The hypothesis could be put forward that the more nationalism became part of Communism during the last decades, the more the specialist is asked to create compensatory material responding to the need to reintegrate a positive image of self, and the demand is stronger and more readily adopted by the community of historians. It would be a question of beginning here in order to define this second form of ideological dependence, a form that, in the case of Romania, appears especially active for several reasons that multiply and become more serious: because of the singularly destructive nature for the country of Communism, which is therefore shameful; because this disaster cannot be separated from the ultranationalist turn taken by the regime beginning in the 1960s; because the intellectuals themselves made a major contribution to the re-elaboration of the myth of a national character; and finally because of the absence of organized opposition to those in power comparable to Solidarity in Poland or the Charter 77 in Czechoslovakia, which was useful in reducing the crushing charge of the Communist period in the collective consciousness. To all of this must be added a "revolution," which was quickly spoken of as a plot and that for this reason could not carry out its role of catharsis.

In short, one must look at the trauma created by the trajectory as well as the intrinsically national specificity of Communism in order to understand the difficulties the historians encounter in detaching the Communist period from the myth that it was a "rape" or an aberration. Only when this is accomplished can the nationalist disaster of the interwar period, and then the Antonescu regime, be integrated into an investigation as to why the society itself proved so fragile when confronted with the totalitarian temptation. To quote the words of a Romanian historian that sum up the situation well: "What is hard to hear is always difficult to say."[84] This is difficult, archives or not, because of the fact that Communism had been a national phenomenon that, with its fall, brought about more than the collapse of a centralized regime linked to an internationalist ideology. Under the eyes of a Europe to which one longed to belong, it also meant that everything one could cling to in terms of pre-Communist myths became virtually forbidden as well, and from this comes the overriding need to *save* the latter in order to preserve and give credit to the principle of a "good Romanianism," of a Romanianism that would have no part either in the misdeeds of Communism or in those of fascism. And this is where the shoe pinches. It certainly seems essential to recall, as François Furet did, that the rebirth of a European conscience will depend on the aptitude of Westerners to examine with clarity the pro-Stalinist errors of a large part of their own political Left.

But this can only be on the condition that we not believe too naively that the fever of comparativism and totalitarianism would necessarily mean, in the East, a major advance in the direction of such a Europe. It is also by way of a redoubled attention to the *historicity* of the conceptual tools used that we can hope to avoid missing historical rendezvous in the future. And we must be careful not to be drawn into a historiographical interpretation limited, in a pretext of parallelism, to a national apologetic: Romania, or "innocence lost in a crowd of those permanently guilty."[85] This practice would risk compromising the chances of a real collective therapy that would finally return the present to its own problems and, in this way, restore history to its rightful distance.

Translated by Lucy B. Golsan

Notes

1. Anthony Todorov, for his part, notes that in the case of Bulgaria: "It is very popular to assimilate Communism to fascism or Nazism. Even though the two kinds of political regimes had many points in common (totalitarian similarities), this generalization refrains from reflecting on the obvious evolution of Communist power and on the important differences between the regime in the 1950s and that of the 1970s, for example.""Bulgaria: The Emergence of a New Official History," in "Les Régimes post-communistes et la mémoire du temps présent" issue, *La Nouvelle Alternative*, no. 32, December 1993, p. 10.

2. Ian Kershaw,"Nazisme et stalinisme: Limites d'une comparaison," *Le Débat*, no. 89, March–April, 1996, p. 180.

3. Ibid., p. 182.

4. On this point see Vladimir Tismaneanu,"The Ambiguity of Romanian National Communism," *Télos*, no. 60, 1984, pp. 65–79. On the reemergence of anti-Semitic themes at the center of the official ideology of the Ceausescu regime in the years 1970–80, see Michael Shafir;"From Eminescu to Goga via Corneliu Vadim Tudor: A New Round of Anti-Semitism in Romanian Cultural Life," *Soviet Jewish Affairs*, no. 3, 1984.

5. Noting that Communism and fascism are far from suffering the same discrediting, François Furet deplored that, a short while ago, "The populations who were victims of Communism" are "still far from enjoying the same compassion in Western

opinion that they deserve after this long period of misery." Interview, "Pourquoi les intellectuels ont admiré Hitler et Staline," in "Révélations des archives soviétiques" special issue, *Historia*, op. cit., p. 13. "The Soviet Union," he observes elsewhere, "although it has lost forever the extravagant privilege of being a universal model, remains protected by what still exists of its original promise. The failure of the ambitions of October, recognized by everyone, has not completely snuffed out the idea of Communism." *Le Passé d'une illusion: Essai sur l'ideé communiste au XXe siècle*, Paris, Laffont/Calmann-Lévy, 1995, p. 800.

6. Horia Patapievici, "Deux mesures et une montagne de cadavres," in *Politice*, Bucharest, Editura Humanitas, 1996, p. 212. Concerning the sources published in Romania, the articles or works cited are only available in Romanian except when otherwise indicated. To facilitate the reading and to lighten the notes, we have chosen to translate the titles into French.

7. As Étienne François points out in connection with the GDR archives, reminding us of several elementary preconditions to the work too easily forgotten, particularly to know that the archives "should undergo a serious and demanding critique of the sources and that their handling must be undertaken only by respecting ethical precautions and basic methods of research, and that, even when they are used well and according to what is pertinent, they do not relieve the historian of his habitual work of reconstruction and interpretation and will not have an answer for everything." "Les 'Trésors' de la Stasi ou le mirage des archives," in *Passés recomposés: Champs et chantiers de l'histoire*, Mutations no. 150/151, Paris, Autrement, 1995, p. 147.

8. Arlette Farge, *Le Goût de l'archive*, La Librairie du XXe siècle, Paris, Seuil, 1989, p. 117.

9. For a glimpse of these tendencies from 1990 to 1993, see Alexandra Laignel-Lavastine, "Roumanie: Lieux et domaines de la recherche en histoire du temps présent," *Bulletin de l' IHTP*, no. 54, December 1993, pp. 42–54. Concerning the first two years of the transition, see Catherine Durandin, "Roumanie: Retour à l'histoire et révisions," *Relations internationales*, no. 67, autumn 1991, pp. 295–298.

10. This according to the law adopted in April 1993. Note that in Hungary this delay was reduced to fifteen years for the period dominated by the Communist Party (1949–90), according to terms of a law passed on June 27, 1995. For more details on the situation of Hungarian archives, see Paul Gradvohl, "Histoires communes," in *Quels repères pour l'Europe?* ed. Joanna Nowicki, Paris, L'Harmattan, 1996, pp. 215–244. See also his report reviewing research led by the Centre Interuniversitaire d'Études Hongroises, with the help of the French Ministry of Education, of l'Enseignment Supérieur et de la Recherche: idem, *Construction de la mémoire du XXe siècle en Hongrie: Sortir de l'image du peuple victime de l'injustice des grandes nations*, April 1997.

11. These practical obstacles were unanimously denounced by the participants in a roundtable devoted to the archives, organized in Bucharest on March 8, 1996, by the Group for Social Dialogue and led by Sorin Antohi. One of its initiators, Stelian Tanase, who is working on a book about the Gheorghiu-Dej period, said

of his experience: "To undertake research today in Romanian archives means an enormous loss of time and many efforts at negotiating. Furthermore, the reading rooms are often closed and the personnel absent. You request one of the files, they give you another, or perhaps it is necessary to wait two months for them to grant your request. Whoever decides to jump into this adventure must be armed with tremendous patience and have contacts in high places they won't hesitate to use."

12. Andréi Pippidi, professor at the University of Bucharest and a renowned Romanian historian, recognized this himself in a recent study. See "Une Histoire en reconstruction: La Culture historique romaine de 1989 à 1992," in *Histoire et Pouvoir en Europe médiane*, ed. Antoine Marès, Paris, L'Harmattan, 1996, p. 251.

13. Marius Oprea, "Les Archives nationales ou l'histoire comme secret," *22* (Bucharest), February 4–10, 1997, p. 5.

14. These questions are the main preoccupation of most of the reviews like *Memoria* (more than fifteen issues), published in Bucharest under the aegis of the foundation of the same name, and of the Union of Writers and the *Archives du totalitarisme*, the publication of the National Institute for the Study of Totalitarianism, founded in 1993.

15. In the spring of 1996, the Romanian Information Service—the institution that today houses the archives of the former political police—furnished several statistics on this subject, issued by its spokesman, Nicolae Ulieru. Concerning the armed resistance of the 1950s and the peasant revolts of June 1956–57, the documentation delivered was probably more than two thousand pages, and for abuses committed during collectivization, 122 dossiers. Concerning the deportations for political reasons in the Baragan region, there were probably more than five thousand pages put at the disposal of various researchers and institutions.

16. See, for example, the collected volume *L'Instauration du communisme, Entre Résistance et répression* (in Romanian), Bucharest, Analele Sighet, 2, Fundatia Academia Civica, 1995.

17. This term comes from Serban Papacostea (present director of the prestigious Nicolae Iorga Institute of History), "Les Laudateurs de l'époque Ceausescu tentent de renouer le fil de la falsification de l'histoire," *Cotidianul*, October 12, 1992.

18. Certain works have been undertaken in this direction, but almost always by Romanian historians living outside the country. For example, we owe to Vladimir Tismaneanu, a professor in the United States, an important study on the life and the political itinerary of Vasile Luca (1898–1963), who was tried in 1952 for "deviation to the Right," then condemned to death.

19. Pierre Kende points out the same tendency elsewhere, noting that today "all the nations of Central and Eastern Europe try to retell these decades as being those of desecration, both physical and moral, as the distant reign of a personnel totally foreign to the nation. . . . This presentation is obviously far from reality even though it includes some truthful elements. . . . As a complex system with 'total' ambitions, the Communist system could not function during the long decades except for the active

collaboration of vast segments of the population." "Un Retour a quelle tradition?" *Vingtième Siècle: Revue d'histoire*, no. 36, October–December 1992, p. 86.

20. From the name of a recent conference, whose proceedings were published under the same title, *L'Année 1946: Le début de la fin*, Bucharest, Analele Sighet, 3, Fundatia Academia Civica, 1996. On the pitfalls of "the teleological illusion," see Pierre Bourdieu, "Le Mort saisit le vif," *Actes de la recherche en sciences sociales*, nos. 32–33, April–May 1980.

21. Catherine Durandin, *Histoire de la nation roumaine*, Brussels, Complexe, 1994, p. 128.

22. "Interview with Professor Imre Toth," conducted by Emil Hurezeanu, "Roumanie, pays de l'Est: Pour une histoire au présent," *Sources, Travaux historiques*, no. 20, 1989, p. 36. Historian and political scientist Michael Shafir remembers also that a number of artists, writers, and right-wing philosophers known for their nationalist leanings before the war were "Parodoxically seen as more 'functional' by the new leaders of the country than the rare true intellectuals of the Left, such as the poet Miron Radu Paraschivescu." Shafir, *Romania: Politics, Economics, and Society*, London, Frances Pinter, 1985, p. 146.

23. The first anti-Semitic legislation was put in place very early in Romania (at the end of 1937), under the Goga-Cuza government (120,000 Jews lost their citizenship). A second series of measures came about in August 1940 (removing Jews from the army and public functions and forbidding mixed marriages, among other things). On this point see especially Lya Benjamin, *Les Juifs de Roumanie entre 1940 et 1944*, vol. 1, *La Législation anti-juive*, Bucharest, Ed. Hasefer, 1993.

24. On the distinction between the two Romanias, see Alexandru Paléologu, "Eloge de la mémoire" ("éditorial"), *Memoria*, no. 10, April 1994, p. 12

25. On this point see Jacques Revel, ed., *Jeux d'échelles: La Micro-analyze à l'experience*, Hautes études series, Paris, Gallimard/Seuil, 1996.

26. We must, however, applaud in this climate the initiative taken by a group of researchers in founding the Center for the History of the Imaginary (directed by Lucian Boia), connected with the history faculty at the University of Bucharest. Even though the activity of this center remains marginal, we note that it has already devoted two interesting volumes bearing on the myths of Romanian Communism.

27. On this matter refer to the enlightening analysis in Michael Shafir, "Political Culture, Intellectual Defense, and Intellectual Consent: The Case of Romania," *Orbis*, vol. 27, no. 2, summer 1983, p. 410ff. On the ties formed between the Party and the intellectuals during the 1960s and of the "myth of rediscoveries," see Sorin Alexandrescu, "Une Culture de l'interstice: La Littérature roumaine d'après-guerre," *Les Temps modernes*, January 1990, pp. 136–158.

28. Of *protochronos*, first in time. The protochronism—a term forged in 1974 by the academician Edgar Papu—designates the current ultranationalist situation in Bucharest as a veritable ideology of the state, beginning in the middle 1970s, as a replacement, or almost, of Marxism-Leninism. This sphere of influence, which

prolonged the emphasis on the native in the period between the two world wars, systematized the claim of a Romanian participation in many schools of Western thought, hoping in this way to abolish any inferiority complex of Romanians in regard to Europe.

29. The Heideggerian philosopher Constantin Noïca, intellectual leader in the 1970s and 1980s and one of the most brilliant of the Romanian intellectuals, author of, among others, a work entitled *Le Sentiment roumain de l'être* (1978), is emblematic of this tendency.

30. Katherine Verdery insists on this aspect in her excellent work *National Ideology under Socialism: Identity and Cultural Politics in Ceausescu's Romania*, Berkeley and Los Angeles, University of California Press, 1991. As one of the central claims of the book, the nationalist discourse in Romania ended by becoming a sort of hegemonic idiom of all the symbolic competitions to the point of saturating the public discourse, the collective imagination, and the belief systems. It is not strange that this book received little attention in Romania, where a translation was published, since its structure of analysis would not lend itself to a reading of Communism based on the one dichotomy, victim-executioner.

31. Serban Papacostea, "Ion Iliescu, le troisième geölier de la Roumanie," *22*, November 6–12, 1996, pp. 67.

32. Bernard Paqueteau, "La Societé contre elle-même: Choses vues in Roumanie," *Commentaire*, no. 59, autumn 1992, p. 626.

33. Ibid., p. 624.

34. Ibid., p. 626.

35. Gabriel Liiceanu, "La Démocractie et le secret ne peuvent marcher main dans la main," *22*, February 16–24, 1997, pp. 8–9.

36. Pippidi, "Une Histoire en reconstruction," p. 261.

37. On this subject we rely on a very complete study by Victor Eskenasy, "The Holocaust and Romanian Historiography: Communist and Neo-Communist Revisionism," in *The Tragedy of Romanian Jewry*, ed. Randolph L. Braham, New York, Columbia University Press, 1994, pp. 173–236.

38. This does not take into account the massacre of more than one hundred thousand local Jews in Transnistria and in the Odessa region. In 1942 Antonescu, under Western pressure, decided to delay the plan of deportation of Romanian Jews. Since the Jewish community had become a bargaining point for the Romanian government, which was beginning to fear that Germany would lose the war, beginning in 1943, several thousand people who had been deported to Transnistria were finally authorized to reenter Romania and then to emigrate to Palestine during 1944. See the indispensable work, based on abundant archives material, of Radu Ioanid, "L'Holocauste en Roumanie: La Destraction et la survie des Juifs roumains pendant la Deuxième Guerre mondiale," 2 vols., Ph.D. diss., EHESS, Paris, 1993 (publication forthcoming).

39. See Dan Ionescu, "Marshal Ion Antonescu Honored by Old and New Admir-

ers," *RFE/RL Research Report*, August 24, 1990, pp. 35–40; and Michael Shafir, "Marshal Ion Antonescu: The Politics of Rehabilitation," *RFE/RL Research Report*, February 11, 1994.

40. *Evenimentul Zilei*, April 16, 1993.

41. Let us review the circumstances of the massacre of the Odessa Jews. On October 22, 1941, the partisans dynamited the general headquarters of the Romanian army. Marshal Antonescu ordered that, for each officer killed in the explosion, two hundred Communists would be executed (plus one hundred for each soldier) and that many others would be taken as hostages. (Order no. 562, 12 hours 50, signed by the chief of the military cabinet, Colonel Davidescu.) During the night and the following day, the twenty-third, around nineteen thousand Jews were executed. On October 24 Antonescu ordered new executions on the same day as the burial of the soldiers who died in the partisan attack. The complete text of this order, handwritten, whose original was recently found in the Romanian archives, is the following: "For General Macici: Regarding the reprisals, Marshal Antonescu orders: 1. The execution of all the Bessarabian Jews who are refugees in Odessa. 2. That all the individuals who are part of the order no. 302858/3161 of October 23, 1941, not yet executed, and others who could be added, be assembled in previously mined buildings and that these be blown up. This measure must be taken the day our dead are buried. 3. This order, once it is read, is to be destroyed." (AG 125004 M, M. St. M., roll 870, p. 702, U.S. Holocaust Memorial Museum, Washington, D.C.). A facsimile of this can be found in the article of Radu Florian, himself an escapee from the Iasi pogrom, "Le Régime Antonescu: Histoire et mystification," *Societate & Cultura* (Bucharest), no. 1, 1994, p. 13.

42. Not only in Romania itself, but also in the United States and Israel. For example, on this last point see Raphael Vago, "The Holocaust in Romania in the Light of Israeli Historiography," *Studia Judaica* (Cluj), vol. 4, 1995, pp. 30–43. And this is not counting the monumental total of Jean Ancel, *Documents Concerning the Fate of Romanian Jewry during the Holocaust*, 12 vols., New York, Beate Klarsfeld Foundation, 1985–86.

43. This new documentary data has allowed Radu Ioanid, fellow at the Research Institute of the Holocaust Museum, to undertake a precise reconstruction of the June 1941 Iasi pogrom, which counted from 8,000 to 12,000 victims. This work, based on a minute use of the archives, gives evidence of the Romanian responsibility in the organization and planning of the massacre—in this case of the direction of the Special Information Service in close collaboration with the Office of Staff Headquarters—the Germans having played only a minor role. Ioanid, "The Holocaust in Romania: The Iasi Pogrom of June 1941," *Contemporary European History*, vol. 2, no. 2, 1993, pp. 139–148.

44. Raul Hilberg, *La Destruction des juifs d'Europe*, Paris, Fayard, 1988, p. 656.

45. On the different stages that marked the ideological realignment of Romanian history, see Vlad Georgescu, *Histoire et Politique: Le Cas des communists roumains (1944–*

1977) (in Romanian), Munich, Ion DumitruVerlag, 1983. For an English perspective on this, see Keith Hutchins, "Historiography of the Countries of Eastern Europe: Romania," *The American Historical Review*, vol. 97, no. 4, October 1992, pp. 1064–1083.

46. This work was reissued in Romania by Diogène Publishers in 1996. Matatias differentiates the principal sequences of the procedure of destroying the Jews under Antonescu's regime into the following segments: the assassinations committed between September 1940 and January 24, 1941, the period during which the Iron Guard governed the country at Antonescu's side and that culminated in the pogrom of Bucharest (January 21–24, 1941) at the time of the legion rebellion; the Iasi pogrom (June 29–30, 1941); the extermination of the Jews during the joint offensive of Romanian and German troops in Bucovine and Bessarabia (summer of 1941); and the deportations to the camps of Transnistria under Romanian occupation (mid-September 1941–October 1942). Other material recounts a whole array of persecutions, from expropriations to pillaging, including forced labor.

47. See Antoine Marès,"L'Histographie de L'Europe Médiane comme miroir des identités nationales," in *Histoire et pouvoir en Europe médiane*, p. 24.

48. On this point see Ysrael Gutman and Gideon Greif, "The Destruction of Romanian Jewry in Romanian Historiography," *The Historiography of the Holocaust Period*, Jerusalem,YadVashem, 1988.

49. This is essentially the idea, accompanied by obvious attempts to minimize the number of victims, of the only work published between 1948 and 1989 on the Holocaust in Romania, focusing on the Iasi pogrom of June 1941: Aurel Karetki and Maria Covaci, *Jours ensanglantés à Iasi*, Bucharest, Editura politica, 1978.

50. According to a very recent outline, the text for Class 6, edited in 1993, speaks only, for example, on the Bucharest pogrom of January 1941 and of assassinations committed by legionnaires against the "democratic and antifascist forces." Concerning northern Transylvania under the Horthy administration, they mention, however, "hundreds of thousands of Roumains [*sic*] and Jews deported to the Hitler concentration camps" by the Hungarians. There is nothing that could involve the Romanian authorities and not a word on the Iasi pogroms, which implicated the police, the gendarmerie, both military and civilian Romanians. As for the collaboration with the Third Reich, we learn only that Romania was supposedly "dragged into the war" and that the "Romanian soldiers struggled courageously to retake the Eastern territories [Bessarabia, Northern Bucovine] annexed by the USSR in 1940." D. Almas, I. Nicoara, and A. Vianu, *Histoire universelle moderne et contemporaine*, Ed. Didactica si Pedagogica, ministère de l'Enseignement, Bucharest, 1993.

51. Among other examples of openly revisionist articles, see C. Botoran,"1940–1944: L'Holocauste des juifs en Roumanie?!" *Revista de istorie militara*, vol. 4, nos. 20–22, 1991; and Gheorghe Buzatu, "Le Maréchale Antonescu et le problème juif," ibid., vol. 7, no. 6, Bucharest, 1994.

52. Documents collected under the direction of Marin Radu Monacu, Bucharest,

1994. In the same spirit, see I. Scurtu and C. Hlihor, *Complot contre la Roumanie, 1939–1947*, Bucharest, Ed. Academiei de Inalte studii militare, 1994.

53. Editions Silex, Bucharest, 1993, p. 6.

54. For a comparative analysis see Leon Volovici, *Anti-Semitism in Post-Communist Eastern Europe: A Marginal or Central Issue?* The Hebrew University of Jerusalem (The Vidal Sassoon International Center for the Study of Antisemitism, Acta, no. 6), 1994.

55. See Victor Eskenazy, "Historiographers against the Antonescu Myth" (paper given at the conference on the Image of Antonescu in Romanian Historiography, Washington, July 1996). On several occasions historian Andréi Pippidi, distinguished himself by his very pointed remarks on this subject, reminded the audience that Romanian Jews were very submissive between 1941 and 1944 to the policy of "organized extermination" under Antonescu's leadership. "Le Jeu de la mémoire et de l'oubli," *22*, January 7–13, 1993. See also Pippidi, "Antonescu: Le Vocabulaire d'un dictateur," *Dilema* (Bucharest), March 8–14, 1996.

56. Among the works already published, see Benjamin, op. cit.; and idem, "Le 'problème juif' throughout the stenograms of the Conseils des ministres," Bucharest, Hasefer, 1996. See also the collection, J. Alexandru, ed., *Le Martyr des juifs de Roumanie: Documents et temoignages*, Bucharest, Ed. Hasefer, 1991. Also note works carried on in the framework of the Center of Hebrew Studies and the Jewish history of Cluj.

57. "Le Miroir de l'historien: Entretien avec le professeur Ion Chiper, chef de section à l'Institut d'histoire Nicolae Iorga," *Curierul national*, February 11, 1994. Under the title "Cohabitation et tragédie—les juifs dans l'histoire des Roumains" (*Revista Istoria*, vol. 3, nos. 3–4, 1992), the journal of this same institution published a strangely uneven issue, though symptomatic for this very reason of the hesitations and ambiguities prevailing at the core of many research institutions in Romania. For example, we find a first contribution entirely devoted to showing that "if Jews slowed the economic development of nonnative populations," they did not have to suffer from any kind of "intolerance under Antonescu" (pp. 345–356). To the contrary, the two other studies contained in this group were a critical examination of discriminatory legislative measures adopted successively against the Jews beginning in 1937 while revealing evidence of the racial character of the constitution voted into law in 1938 (pp. 57–69, 329–343).

58. Mihai Dim Sturdza, "Le Cas Antonescu après un demi-siècle," *22*, February 16–22, 1994; reprinted in *Romania versus Romania*, Bucharest, Ed Clavis, 1996, pp. 125–126.

59. Florin Constantiniu, "L'Honneur militaire au-dessus de l'intérêt national," ibid., pp. 131–132.

60. Furet, "Pourquoi les intellectuels ont admiré Hitler et Staline," p. 9.

61. For example, Alexandru Zub, "Les Archives comme problème national," *22*, March 18–24, 1997, p. 7.

62. The Romanian philosopher Gabriel Liiceanu especially uses the expression,

after the Bulgarian Gheorghi Demidov, in "Des Sociétés complices d'une histoire criminelle," *La Croix*, February 24, 1990.

63. Essayist and historian of ideas Horia Patapievici wrote openly about this in 1996: "Inasmuch as our fate and our dignity is important to us, we should take an example from the Jews, we should, for example set up an international institute on Communist extermination. . . . We should also have the power to make the civilized world accept this elementary truth, knowing that *the Communist idea implies a necessary devalorization of man and his extermination.* . . . Just as the Jews, by the symbol of the Holocaust, have covered with shame the very idea of racial discrimination, we should ourselves, sons of those who were subjected to Communist extermination, cast the same terrible shame on the ideas that formed the hard seed of Marxist-Leninist ideology." Patapievici, "Le refus de la mémoire," in *Politice*, pp. 203–204.

64. Roxana Iordache, "L'Autre Holocauste," *Romania Libera*, April 27, 1993.

65. Text of the paper given by Ana Blandiana at a roundtable discussion organized at INALCO on March 29, 1996, first published in the journal *Lupta* (Paris), then in the supplement of the Romanian daily *Romania Libera* on May 17, 1996.

66. Among French historians, Alain Besançon seems to be one of the authors most often cited by Romanian historians who support the idea of equivalency between Stalinism and Nazism. They very willingly take up for their own use the arguments of Besançon, in disagreement with Raymond Aron about the idea that the two totalitarianisms need to be distinguished from each other by their original aims. See particularly the transcription of the meeting and debate organized around Besançon's work at Bucharest in November 1993, published under the title "Le Communisme comme gnose moderne anticosmique," *22*, November 3–9, 1993. Historian Zoé Petre made known on this occasion her astonishment when faced with "the difficulty of Westerners in accepting the fact that Communism went much further than Nazism." Ibid., p. 13.

67. "L'Académie civique—une fondation pour l'histoire," interview with R. Rusan, *22*, supplement *22 plus*, July 10, 1996, pp. 2–3.

68. Are the *Aufklärung* and revolutionary ideology responsible for Communist crimes? This is exactly what Horia Patapievici would seem to suggest by attributing to the modern imagination, after 1789, the conception of the Left being "good" while the Right would automatically be "reactionary." "Deux mesures et une montagne de cadavres," p. 212. See also Patapievici, "L'Argument révisioniste" (revisionist in the same sense as Stephen Courtois understands it, a Communist revisionism). Patapievici defines it, from his perspective, as the discourse that "either intends a clear separation of Marxist-Leninist ideology from the practices of the parties that claim it as their own, or that rehabilitates even the policies of these parties," in *ICS: Periodic Studentesc de cultura si atitudine sociala*, vol. 2. no. 2, 1996, p. 12.

69. As a comparison on the Judaization of political splits and the social construction of the myth of Judeo-Communism in contemporary Poland, see Paul Zawadzki,

"Transition, nationalisme, et anti-sémitisme: L'Exemple polonais," in *Sociologie des nationalismes*, ed. Pierre Birnbaum, Paris PUF, 1997, pp. 103–119.

70. In his journal entry of June 30, 1941, Mihail Sebastian, a Romanian writer of Jewish origin, was dismayed to see the terms of the official communiqué published in the press on the day following the pogrom. "At Iasi, 500 Judeo-Masons were executed. The government communiqué added that they were accomplices of Soviet parachutists" (p. 353). Under the date of July 2, during the Romanian-German offensive in Bessarabia and Bucovine, Sebastian records the text of another communiqué: "During these last days, a certain number of units foreign to the people and hostile to our interests fired on Romanian and German soldiers. . . . Henceforth, for each German or Romanian military, 50 Judeo-Communists will be executed" (p. 354). In Sebastian, *Journal, 1935–1944*, ed. with preface by Leon Volovici, Bucharest, Humanitas, 1996; French edition, trans. Alain Paruit, Stock, 1998.

71. Serge Muscovici, *Chronique des années égarées*, Paris, Stock, 1997, p. 129.

72. Ibid., p. 177.

73. Ibid., p. 360.

74. As proof that anti-Semitism very soon made a reappearance inside the Party apparatus, see a document from 1952—the minutes of a meeting of the Central Committee—in which two primary objectives stand out: the struggle against legionnaire units (former members of the Iron Guard) and the struggle against Jewish elements—these two "enemies" placed on the same Party level. It was made clear by testimony from leaders at the Third Congress (1924) that the Jewish community of Romania was far from identifying itself with the Communist Party between the two wars, for these leaders went so far as to call for a struggle against "Jewish capital." On this question see the analysis of Bela Vago, "The Attitude toward Jews as a Criterion of the 'Left-Right' Concept," in *Jews and Non-Jews in Eastern Europe*, ed. Bela Vago and George Mosse, New York, John Wiley and Sons, 1974.

75. Serge Moscovici, *Chronique des années égarées*, op. cit., pp. 358–359.

76. Citations are taken from Gabriel Liiceanu, "De l'art d'être à la fois réactionnaire et bolchevique," reprinted in the dossier "Comment je suis devenu hooligan," which is a collection of the texts from the violent polemic that followed the 1934 publication of Sebastian's novel *Depuis deux mille ans*. This dossier, with replies from Sebastian, is found appended to the Humanitas edition of 1990, pp. 256–258.

77. Gabriel Liiceanu, "Sebastian, mon frère" (lecture given at the meeting of the Jewish Community of Romania, April 13, 1997), published in *22*, April 29–May 5, 1997, p. 11.

78. To echo the classic statement in Marc Ferro, *L'Histoire sous surveillance*, Paris, Calmann-Lévy, 1985.

79. On this aspect see Alain Brossat, Sonia Combe, Jean-Yves Potel, and Jean-Charles Szurek, eds., *A l'Est, la mémoire retrouvée*, Paris La Découverte, 1990 (in particular their introduction to the volume, pp. 11–35).

80. This expression comes from Daniel Beauvois, "Etre historien en Pologne:

Les Mythes, l'amnésie, et la 'verité,'" *Revue d'histoire moderne et contemporaine*, July–September 1991, pp. 353–386. On the specific case of Romania, see Alexandru Zub, "History and Myth in Rumanian Society in the Modern Period," *International Journal of Rumanian Studies*, vol. 5, no. 2, 1987, pp. 35–58.

81. On the overly politicized character of the interpretation of recent history in Central Europe, see the two issues of *La Nouvelle Alternative*, "Les Régimes post-communistes et la mémoire du temps présent," no. 32, December 1993, pp. 3–54; and "Mémoire des guerres et des résistances," no. 37, March 1995, pp. 3–36.

82. On this distinction see the discussion between Henry Rousso ("Pour une histoire de la mémoire collective," pp. 243–264) and Marie Claire Lavabre ("Du poids et du choix du passé," pp. 265–278) in *Histoire politique et sciences sociales*, ed. Denis Peschanski, Michael Pollak, and Henry Rousso, Brussels, Complexe, 1991.

83. I adopt here the definition of "habitus" as Pierre Bourdieu expresses it in *Choses dites*, Paris, Les Editions de Minuit, 1987, p. 20: "Behavior can be oriented in relation to certain ends without being consciously directed toward these ends or directed by these ends. The idea of habitus was invented, let me say, to take this paradox into account."

84. Pippidi, "Une Histoire en reconstruction," p. 261.

85. This remark on the innocence complex belongs to the Polish ex-dissident Adam Michnik, who applied it to Poland. "Les Pages blanches" (1989), in *La Deuxième Révolution*, Paris, La Découverte, 1990, p. 173.

Paul Gradvohl

Historians and the Political Stakes

of the Past in Hungary

It is not an easy task to write the history of fascism, of the Shoah, and of Communism in the only Central European country where there is a strong Jewish community and in which the 1970s seemed to be a bright moment. There have already been global approaches attempted by historians on each of these themes and on their relationships or the parallels and similarities apparent between them. But these remain limited. More noticeable is the obstacle presented by the overpoliticization of the reception of historical interpretations. [1] This is the result of a process of political differentiation peculiar to the intelligentsia between 1985 and 1994, [2] a process whose consequences on historiography are even more important because the intellectuals, and especially one group of historians, are very much a part of the political mutations. In this chapter, which is too short to allow an analysis of historiography, three themes have been selected: the relations between a political transition and the handling of the history of Communism and of Nazism/fascism, the evolution in the life of the institutions of historians since the end of the 1980s, and the debate surrounding the comparison of Communism and Nazism/fascism. On these three points the mutations observed in Hungary seem to present characteristics peculiar to this country, which form a rather unique case of continuing resistance, not of political "intellectuals," but of a part of the society of historians and academics to partisan pressures. Hungary in fact has experienced for the first time in the twentieth century a political transformation that has not been accompanied by a collective denial of the immediate past, despite several attempts in this sense at the beginning of the 1990s. This phenomenon has actually benefited the Socialist Party, heir to the previous single party. It happens that a good part of the conservative camp has tried to generate Socialist culpability for the years of Communism, which would be useful in elections. Therefore, maintaining a distance between the "recent" past, which would permit a historical debate and not just politically inspired contests, has become important.

Political Transition and Treatment of the Past

In the middle of the 1980s, at the center of the opposition to the János Kádár regime, tenets of western liberalism were associated with the partisans of national rehabilitation seen as an end in itself. In both cases the concrete goals were unclear, and in fact the two groups could not be cleanly separated from each other. Furthermore, a group of intellectuals close to those in power were looking for a democratic solution to the regime crisis. A rejection of Communism did not allow people to forget how, in Hungary, the regime, sometimes against its will, had permitted the support of differing viewpoints. Writers who came from the populist tradition, sociology or economic critics, liberal historians, Marxist critics or partisans of a national rewriting of Hungarian history, and many others coexisted and published their work. Hindrances to their liberty of expression bore heavily on them, but they were conscious of participating together in a liberating ferment.

The structuring of the political field between 1988 and 1989 and the first free legislative elections in the spring of 1990 put an end to the perspective of an easy dialog on the history of the century. Communism had disappeared and was very soon put to use as a weapon. The conservative government, populated with liberals just as the liberal opposition was, proclaimed itself the only standard bearer for the eradication of Communism. Some years later this sentiment was converted into a political analysis. Maria Schmidt was the historian and advisor to Prime Minister Viktor Orbán (Alliance des jeunes démocrates/Parti Civique Hongrois, FiDeSz-MPP), who was installed July 6, 1998. For her the liberals of the Alliance of Free Democrats (SzDSz) simply refused to accept the 1990 conservative victory, which was that of a "competing intellectual group." As a result they decided to promote the theme of the anti-Semitism of the conservatives and to align themselves with the Communists rather than helping to exterminate them.[3] Such a perception of the political stakes of the Holocaust, which already existed in the "national" right-wing group present in the Democratic Forum at the beginning of the 1990s,[4] made the historical debate difficult. This was reinforced by the feeling of intense frustration by conservative intellectuals between 1994 and 1998, when the liberals benefited from the support of the Ministry of Culture. Furthermore, it gave an exaggerated importance to "intellectual" groups while isolating them from the rest of the population, which from the conservative viewpoint was presented as inert.

At the same time, the weight of "Jews" and ex-Communists (often associated by this school of thought) in the media was emphasized, and the question of the exact nature of the Jewish identity in Hungary throughout the centuries was erased. Yet declarations from Jewish intellectuals, proclaiming themselves as such, were put forward as proof of the special intelligence and capabilities they possessed. In this way we are back to the old ideas of the 1920s, necessary, inevitable, and "natural" separation of Jews and Hungarians, and its corollary, an astonishing view of the passivity of the Hungarians faced with domination by the Jews in a series of sectors of society. But prewar anti-Semitism no longer exists, at least not in the form it took at that time.[5] The subordinate role assigned to the Jews between the two wars is presented as normal in the framework of the "democracy" in power at that time, while the common struggle in 1956 against the Soviets is understood as having reformed the alliance of Hungarians and Jews on a basis of equality.[6] The incoherent logic of the proposition is explained by the political argument set forth: since 1945 the necessary legitimizing of the Left is a condemnation of Miklós Horthy. So if it is recognized that he was a democrat, the Left is in essence lying and antidemocratic. This postulate—Hungary between 1919 and 1944 as a democracy—entails the idea that the historical works written up to now are simple manipulations, and the political designation leads to a (dis)qualification of the historian if he is found to be "on the left."[7] (The characterization reviewed here aims only at taking into account actual Hungarian uses.)

It was on this basis that a group of historians in 1998, having the support of the prime minister elected over the former socialist-liberal majority, decided to put an end to the power of this "clearly definable intellectual group who, for decades, explained to the people that what was normal, good and just, was the way the socialist system—their system—worked. Now [before the legislative elections that gave the victory to the FiDeSz-MPP on May 24 in the second round] once more they want to be the only ones—often these are the same people—to decide for us what we should think about the past: the Communist past, of the period that preceded and the one that followed."[8] Thus the criticism of the Horthy regime on the basis of an interpretation linking it to fascism or the remnant of its anti-Semitism is rejected as being biased in nature. The simple allusion to an eventual responsibility of Hungary in the Russian occupation is condemned because her northern neighbors, although allies of the conquerors, endured the domination of Moscow after 1945, which would mean that Hungary would not have been able to escape a similar fate.[9] It is interesting that Yugoslavia was not mentioned. Also forgotten is the work done in Hungary on Hungarian history since 1945, on Soviet history, or on international relations since 1917, which most often emphasized the uncertainties of the war years and the years 1945–47. The critical studies produced by the "liberals" or even the "Communists" before and after 1989 on Communism or denouncing the outlines of the explanations of Stalinism were passed over without comment. What needs to be pointed out here is the use of extremely simplistic historical explanations. The Jew and the Hungarian are absolutist categories. Horthy is without doubt a hero; Hungary was a democracy under his administration except from the time of the German occupation (March 19, 1944). And outside of these revealed truths, nothing is left to doubt and to research.

It should be noted here that the analysis made by Görgy Földes, the director of the Institute for Political History, agrees in part with that of Mária Schmidt on the proximity (re)created between the liberal intellectuals and the socialists beginning in 1990. He puts the phenomenon on a different level, however. For him the elites of the 1980s were not just cultural, and the population felt a new confidence in them in 1994 because the people were able to demonstrate their capacity to utilize the possibilities that opened up under socialism. The power held by these elites before 1989 was not purely the fruit of a system of manipulation but also of an administrative capacity.[10] This point of view of a militant intellectual at the center of the Hungarian Socialist Party nevertheless also tends to obscure the very slow differentiation at the opposition's center and the hesitations of the intellectual elites of Hungary in the 1980s. The clear-cut positions did not appear in a large way until 1988, when that spring Kádár had to give up power. This perception made people forget the reality of the political attitudes of various intellectual groups under socialism and the fact that the intellectuals of the liberal opposition never set the tone for official propaganda.[11] They were published in samizdat or outside the country, and their support of Charter 77 or of Solidarity met with government disapproval.[12] Yet Westerners approved of their activities while not very familiar with the more nationalist circles.[13] The analysis proposed by Görgy Földes is revealing, however, of the sharpness of the conflicts between intellectuals in the middle of the 1990s[14] and of the precociousness among liberals of the feeling that socialism would disappear, a feeling that allowed them to situate themselves more aggressively against the government than those who had an essentially nationalist viewpoint and remained in retreat until the end of 1989.[15]

The stakes in this battle, whose principle themes put forward by the conservatives were "liberalism" before 1914 (István Tisza), Horthy and "his" period, and anti-Semitism and Communism in Hungary are predominantly political, in the spirit of the initiators. The Hungarian population developed a special view of history. For a majority in 1994 the 1970s represented heights that even the year 2000 would not attain. Only the 10 percent with the most schooling thought then that 2000 would be more favorable to Hungary than 1975.[16] Political conservatives, conscious of this perception of things, avoided using the drastic condemnation of the Communist era in their victorious elections of 1990 and 1998, while after the lost elections of 1994, this very ideological theme was spotlighted.[17] To this perception of the evolution of national history was added a political facet. The Socialist Party wanted to see itself as the representative of the continuity of the evolution and, while recognizing the crimes of the past, demanded that the positive aspects of Kádárism be recognized, thus allowing the population to accept its "adaptation" to overtures offered by that regime. It promoted the idea that a change of administration can take place without a witch hunt or a massive collective denial.[18]

At the beginning of 1999, ten years after the declaration of Imre Pozsgay, who saw 1956 as a "popular insurrection,"[19] the Hungarian intellectual landscape, at least in the area of contemporary history, was destabilized, not so much because of revolutionary works, but because of a break in the dialogue between the majority of historians of the present day and the group close to power, which received important financial aid to create the Institute of Research on the Twentieth Century. This was a purely institutional operation. According to a secretary of state of the Cultural Ministry, this new institute would concern itself especially with the Holocaust, the Republic of Governors (Bélakun, 1919), the period that followed, and the "networks that have remained hidden until now of repressions after 1945."[20] This new situation is paradoxical because since 1989 there has been an important work on post-1945 Hungary and because the Holocaust, in its Hungarian dimensions, has been the object of internationally recognized studies of value. Randolph L. Braham has just published a revised and enlarged version of his general survey in Hungarian,[21] and a volume of proceedings of a 1944 symposium, *The Holocaust in Hungary Fifty Years Later*, appeared in 1997.[22] During the Horthy era, works were many and included syntheses, but on none of the subjects cited have the historians working for the Institute of Research on the Twentieth Century produced reference works. There are no members of the Hungarian Academy of Sciences present, and only one institution, the Catholic University Péter Pázmány, has honored them.[23]

Another paradox resulting from the real pluralism of Hungarian society is that the government of course supports the creation of the Institute of the Twentieth Century, but it has not dissolved the Institute of Historical Sciences of the Academy or the Chairs of Contemporary History at the University, and is content to reduce the funds for the Institute of 1956 and the Institute of Political History.[24] The new institute is the exclusive beneficiary of the creation of a foundation supposedly interested in Central Europe and the Central Orient but that does not include a single specialist of the neighboring countries among its known members. Thus this institute finds itself the recipient of an important amount of money without being able to make offers as an institution, only as a source of financing. It is not the foundation that must send out a call for requests but the Institute of the Twentieth Century (and no calls had yet been made by May 1999). If an institute responds, it will produce results that will be the property of the institute and will appear under its name and under its exclusive ideological control. Although the institutions in place, including the Institute of 1956 and the Institute of Political History, enjoy an ideological pluralism verifiable by their demonstrations and publications, the new authority does not seem to guarantee scientific liberty to the contracting parties.

Conscious of the good reputation of the Hungarian historical school, the government helps its supporters but within certain limits. Yet this operation does not hide the fact that, on the questions that interest us here, there are other lines of rupture in Hungary, especially between liberals and socialists and between groups of historians according to their specializations (economy, military, or international affairs, among others). In attempting a takeover by force, the authorities managed to create a climate of defiance, reuniting most of the contemporary historians whose groups were able to discuss and even cooperate before and after the victory of the socialist-liberal alliance in the elections of 1994. The Institute of 1956, which actively contributed to the uncovering of events that had long been "forgotten," was not threatened by the Socialists, whose party had broken with the Communist heritage. Some representatives of conservative sympathies published or worked with either this center or the Institute of Political History,[25] integrated into the Socialist Party at that time (it has not been since 1998).[26]

Until the end of 1998, the institutions (universities, Academy of Sciences, and various research institutions) had resisted the effects of the overpoliticization of historical themes. The Parliament, directed by the Constitutional Court, had adopted legislation demanding verification of connections between government and parliamentary personalities and the former "general information" Communists, section III/III of the Ministry of the Interior. But the sanction in a case of cooperation, even a limited one, depends on public opinion since the person involved has a choice between resigning or making an announcement in the local *Official Journal* (Magyar Közlöny) of the results of the "bringing to light."[27] In another area the Administration of Scholarly Affairs, in spite of some very tense episodes, had finally managed to find relatively agreed-upon solutions. In the program of elementary and secondary schools, fascism, Nazism, as well as Communism were regrouped under the heading of "Dictatorships,"[28] and the analysis was taken up again by left-wing historians who presented Horthy as a conservative with very limited dictatorial ambitions. In the 1980s[29] we see the beginnings of this analysis and, from 1976, a doubt beginning to form about the fascist nature of the Horthy government.[30] Furthermore, it must be emphasized here that the school texts before 1989 never presented the Hungarian people as guilty and excused them since they fought anti-Semitism in the past; today's texts remain hesitant in their treatment of the genocide of the Jews.[31]

Fascism and Communism in the Historigraphical Debate

The common elements of Communism and fascism have been approached directly by Hungarian historians. Three stages have been evident since the end of Communism.

The first, illustrated here by an article that appeared in 1989, is that of local pioneers.[32] It reminds us of the traits common to the two systems, even to both ideologies. In a review published by reformers of the Socialist Hungarian Workers Party before the adoption of the Democratic Constitution of October 23, 1989, Jószef Vonyó, teaching at the University of Pécs in southern Hungary, compared the Communist Party to those in power after 1947–48 and the attempt of the party of the fascist masses of Gyula Gömbös, a military man of the extreme Right who was once prime minister (1932–36) and tried to overthrow the conservative *establishment*. But this comparison did not work out in the sense that the author shows that the party of Gömbös aspired to being totalitarian (but did not succeed in its ambition to become the only party), while the Communist Party, which claimed to be democratic, found itself alone and did not function democratically at all. Stated in this way, there is no analysis of eventual divergences and convergences.[33]

The second stage is that of the debate in depth begun by Mária Ormos. Her works on international relations after the First World War made her a renowned historian and member of the Hungarian Academy of Sciences. She studied the development of Hungary, but her global perception of the period between the two wars has changed. This evolution is openly admitted, as is frequent in Hungary. What is less frequent is Ormos's desire to take on unhesitatingly an analysis of the subjects about which she has changed her mind. Because of this, she has tried publicly to measure the comparability of the Stalinist and National Socialist systems and to draw up a comparison of these two unique experiences, characteristic of the twentieth century, which have both failed in themselves. The resemblances do not bear on the totalitarian nature of the state, which is still to be shown because, in Germany, a certain institutional chaos prevailed under Hitler, while Stalinism stabilized a hierarchic model clearly defined and dominated by the party. But the two systems aimed at a total dictatorship and revealed numerous traits in common, beginning with a true popularity with the masses, for whom the chief who emerged (Hitler and Stalin verifying the rule) represented a strong symbol that went along with a certain form of security for a majority of the population, who had jobs and who found themselves offered well-chosen cultural references and large public festivals where the masses joyfully shared certain values in following a carefully prepared ritual. But a burgeoning cultural life in the two countries disappeared; deviant works were hidden, exported, or destroyed. The personalization of power was inevitable, but while Hitler probably thought of having a successor, Stalin was determined to liquidate any eventual candidate. Another similarity was the repression that was indispensable to ensure a docile population, but it functioned differently. In Russia it often struck the wrong people because of administrative inefficiency despite a planning with pretensions to being "reasonable." In Germany it sparkled with precision, but there also was an uncertain defining of targets. In both cases the terrorism was necessary even if enemies no longer existed. For Ormos the destruction of the Jews by Hitler brought two neglected lessons: on the one hand, the failure suffered by those in power, for in 1933 and in 1938 their attempts at having the population participate in anti-Semitic violence failed, which explains the secrecy surrounding the Final Solution; and on the other hand, it was a success in the sense that the protestations were finally more limited than in other areas, such as those that affected the Catholics or large German investments. She concludes that the two systems were born and died, each at a steady rhythm, slowly for Stalinism, rapid for National Socialism.[34]

The comparison is carried even further since the results common to these two "adventures" remain to be explained. For Ormos there is a shared meta-

physic whose echo is more resounding the more a population looks to political power for guidance: an earthly paradise can be attained by violence
under the direction of a chosen race or class. Accepting violence goes back
to the laws of nature. Furthermore, in both cases the politics of territorial
expansion is a natural part of the system's function, just as is the nullification
of individual or group rights. The rights themselves become illusory, and
the administrations prevail. If there had ever been a power, there was no
real security, and the discounting of the dead can add nothing more to this
observation. In the same way, the distinction between the claimed humanism
of Communism and the anti-humanism of Hitler does not seem essential to
her. Returning to the present, she explains that these two systems still at-
tract people in 1995 because modern Western democracy also lacks drawing
power,[35] which still leaves a chance for dreams of a guided well being without
the effort of construction. For her history does not have a (pre)determined
meaning.[36]

Such an interpretation, paralleling an analysis of the Horthy era that insists
on the marginalization of the extreme right from 1920 on, no longer comes
from the dichotomy Right/Left, which was taken for granted by the supporters of historical revisionism who launched the Institute of the Twentieth
Century. It also runs counter to Marxist criticism. One of the most faithful
representatives of this, who from the 1980s rehabilitated Trotsky and today
displays a more open ideological confrontation,[37] Tomás Krausz, a specialist
in Russian history, judged it necessary to identify his disagreements with
Ormos.[38] For him totalitarianism is a category that Russian specialists have
not used since the 1970s, political history has lost its monopoly, and social
and economic history show a Russia less controlled than political appearances would suggest. The comparison fascism/Communism was used earlier
against Stalin by Bukharin and Berdiaev in 1923 to denounce a power based
on very limited initial forces, therefore hardly legitimate in itself. Then in the
1930s the comparison served to condemn Stalinist authoritarianism in the
name of democratic socialism.[39] Finally there came a theory of totalitarianism
that had its hour of glory during the early days of the Cold War and again in
the years 1970–90.

For Krausz the aim of this theory is to claim that all forms of socialism lead
to fascism and that the Western bourgeois model is the only viable one. Thus
it is ideological pressure imposed by this new ideological text that makes the
historian's work difficult. His opinion is that the relative differences in social,
economic, and historical origins of National Socialism and Communism,
as well as the opposition between their methods of accumulating capital,

are decisive. It is the same in the area of "catching up," or in other words the accelerated development desired by Russia when confronted with the Western powers. On the one hand, there was the rapid economic progress of certain periods, especially under Stalin (contrary to what Ormos sees from the point of view of the global evolution of the system); on the other hand, Communism massively elevated the cultural level of the population, and there was, contrary to what was found under Hitler, a real cultural creativity, even though those in power hindered it. And as to that repression, Krausz reverses the perspective. According to him it was under Hitler that, along with race, the idea of class played a role in the choice of victims. Under Stalin, from 1934 on, it is impossible to claim this categorization. The system of Soviet concentration camps would be essentially based on economic needs, while its Nazi equivalent would aim first at political objectives. From this came the completely arbitrary nature in Russia of those sent to the Gulag. As for the political essence of the two systems, Krausz sees the *Führerprinzip* as a pillar of Nazism, whereas Communism has as a reference direct democracy, which would come to pass in the form of autonomous worker councils and not under the personal dictatorship of Stalin. Stalin had to hide his misdeeds, Hitler much less so. Therefore, if the Western democracies chose the first in 1941 and not the second, it was not by pure pragmatism or short sightedness.[40]

The Ormos's response shows a very firm desire to transform the paradigms of the debate.[41] For her the historicism and the permanent references to history to legitimize a political stand must be abandoned just as much as the determinism, and therefore a part of the reasoning put forward by her colleague on the development of Russia. The work of the historian is to discover choices and alternatives and to measure the intelligence of the actors in historical situations and the part of the irrational played in decisions made and attitudes adopted. Furthermore, for Ormos the goal of Stalinism was a permanent reinforcement of its military capacities to be used for imperialistic purposes. Terrorism, especially for the peasants, was inevitable, and the fact that Stalin had also liquidated his former friends was secondary.[42] In the two systems an omnipresent state was supposed to bring to the *Volkgenosse*, or to a comrade, whatever was needed.

In reacting in this way, the historian refuses to go into the details of the history of a comparison or of the socioeconomic argument. She rejects the antagonism between affirming a Stalinist lesser evil as opposed to an absolute Hitlerian evil, but she does not take on a gloss of totalitarianism. Having done this, she defends the Hungarian historical school, and alongside the second stage of this investigation of Communism and Nazism, it is the characterization of the situation in Hungary between 1919 and 1989 that is important. Whether it be her own work,[43] that of Zsuzsa L. Nagy,[44] that of Ignác Romsics,[45] or that of Konrád Salamon,[46] citing just a few authors, all of whom use the approach of explanation and not of justification by insisting on the contradictions of the Horthy period—in which the state had the right to make decisions using the antidemocracy of the system, in which a certain liberty of expression existed as counterpoint to the connection of a conservative elite to power, this in the face of threats from the Right—the debates about the years after 1945 are less difficult for historians because of the questions to interpret:[47] the responsibilities of the Soviets and/or Hungarians,[48] the part of choice and of restraints are these days not used much as political themes, and even the Socialist Party does not identify itself with the pre-1989 government.[49] Finally the most difficult question is still that of the fate of the Hungarian Jews.

From this comes the third subject. It had already been outlined in the various approaches of Mária Schmidt, in a provocative way, in an article published in the main Hungarian daily, *Népszabadság*, on March 5, 1999, after several earlier expressions.[50] István Lovas, under the title, "A Morbid Comparative Algebra and the Holocaust" (Osszehasonlító véralgébra és a Holcaust) denied any special value to the Holocaust because the systematic massacres of certain Indian populations in America would take away its specificity, and other genocides are legion. To the contrary, the Holocaust only has a special role because it has become a drama of the conquerors (the State of Israel) legitimized for political ends, including on behalf of Jews in Hungary. The advantage of this article is to make public the argument often heard in snatches in certain circles attracted to the extreme Right, which has put forward this kind of argument for a long time. Perhaps we should point out that Agnes Heller in 1994, in an introduction to a book by Imre Kertész (*L'Holocauste comme culture* [The Holocaust as a culture], Budapest, Századvég Kiadó, 1993), points out that this genocide was not a political myth, that it was not a question of a metaphor of totalitarianism like the Gulag, but a reality in which the good opposed the bad, though probably no one in the purely criminal essence of the project of industrial extermination, but "optimized" economically as much as possible.[51] The rejection by Lovas of the religious dimension, which exists even for nonbelievers, and the philosophic one relative to Hitlerian racism; the quibbling over the statistics; and the attention paid to the ideological uses of the Holocaust more than to the mechanisms that led up to this (nothing is said of this) are the usual indicators of a profound malaise when faced with the question of the responsibilities shared in part by the Hungarians (the French or other nationalities). This last stage on the Jewish question, that is, the Hungarian question (which is Hungarian, what collective behavior characterizes the "Hungarians," and so forth), is only superimposed on the historical debate for political reasons. The work of the historians is hardly touched by these calculations. Yet the question of responsibility is more serious in another way—the part left to the population in the crimes committed before and after 1945 and the eventual rebirth of a dangerous racism in Hungary. Schmidt presents a direct comparison between the relative courage of the Hungarians who saved a good number of Jews in 1944–45 and the passivity everywhere confirmed in the years of Communism.[52] Randolph Braham emphasizes opportunities, taken or not, to save Jews.[53] The waves of repression of the Communist years did not aim, except in special cases, at the physical destruction of the people concerned, and the "stability" of the system is a contrast to the military crisis that shook Europe in 1944–45. How can we interpret the weight of sympathy acquired by the extreme Right in 1939 (19.2 percent in legislative elections)? And how can we fail to take into account the opposition to the installation of Stalinism[54] and of the unending opposition (internal and external) that marks its history? Considering as parallel the two periods of repression and resistance, this seems still closer to an approximation than to a work of serious research. As for the rebirth of racism, it provides an opportunity for Tamás Fricz, a political scientist linked more to conservatives, to remind us that the Hungarian democracy, established in 1989, rests on the confidence between Left and Right. The solution, when faced with anti-Semites like István Csurka, is not legal repression but political isolation.[55] In this way one leaves behind legitimization by history and puts forward partisan struggles in order to succeed in a collective construction of democracy, which furthermore takes nothing away from the sharpness of oppositions between parties.

This brief presentation of the debates about Nazism (fascism) and Communism, of the comparison of these two phenomena, and especially of the conditions in which these developed in Hungary cannot conclude without frankly taking up three points: The debates aroused are due in part to a series of misunderstandings, which are essentially political. Very often the conservatives remind us that the rehabilitation of victims of left-wing Stalinism was premature (funerals of László Rajk in 1956, for example) because they cooperated with the system, and they feel that the attachment to a state of rights on the part of the Left after 1989 is only a clever way of avoiding full justice for victims of the Right. Also for some of them, Jews suffered only from the Germans, and after the war they became Communists and avenged themselves on the Hungarians. In fact the first victims of the Communists in 1944–45 were rebellious Communists, innocents carried off by the Soviets to work in the Gulags, and various conservatives. As for the Jews, their executioners were also Hungarians,[56] and not nearly all of them had benefited from Communism, whatever the definition of the category of "Jew." On the contrary, certain Jews accuse all "Hungarians" of anti-Semitism. In the same way, around 1956, the diversity of forces at one time aligned with each other (Communist reformers, anti-Communists of the Right, partisans of self-governing workers councils, reformed political parties, and others) since 1989 have found expression in the process of assuming their heritage.[57] And the Kádár era contrasts the tenets of the thesis of a dictatorship barely transformed with those of defenders of the hypothesis of an evolution of the regime and of the almost complete exploitation of international conditions of the Cold War period prolonged once more, on a basis more political (conservatives and liberals against socialists) than historical. All the same, it is evident that in Hungary the debates were delayed in relation to older, popular democracies because of the political map of the 1990s and of the specificity of Kádárism.

But there is another reason for the singularity of the Hungarian debate: it is the strength of the community of historians, a strength that also appears when we perceive the internal contradictions between them, in taking up only certain ones who have a recognized body of work. In the case of Tamás Krausz, along with the analyses sometimes characterized by the desire to show the importance of the working class, there are important works that demonstrate that the Right-Left cleavages are transcended in the ideological construction of the Stalinist model.[58] With Mária Ormos we see not only a clear evolution of positions on the political nature of the Horthy era but also a very old concern to always look for multiple causality and complex mechanisms. The work of the Institute of 1956 or of the Institute of Political History is also characterized by the coexistence of divergent points of view and the desire to understand the multiplicity of causalities at work in Communism as it existed in Hungary. One of the signs of the cohesion among historians is, paradoxically, the existence of veiled debates between generations, which shows the social importance of academic positions. This also, however, brings with it a sometimes virulent condemnation from those who do not have access to them. It is one of the aspects of the present conflicts that is less ideological than it appears.

Finally the debate over the responsibility for past crimes benefits from positions taken by nonhistorians on opposite sides, Frigyes Kahler (a conservative jurist)[59] and János Kis (a liberal philosopher), for example, who argue for a renouncement of using the justice system as a way of settling accounts with the past.

Seen from a certain distance, the Hungarian situation in 1998–99 has known only a reorientation due to an attempt to change the rules belonging to the institutional field of history by using political leverage for the profit of a small, marginal group within the community of historians.[60] In democracy the autonomy of the social areas are never complete, and the results of the maneuvers taking place are therefore significant first of all on the sociological level, even if their historiographical effects can be important.[61]

A difference can be noted between the (young) wolves of the end of the 1990s and the conservative prime minister of 1990, Jószef Antall, who reminded us that a number of Communists had been courageous under Kádár and had even contributed to the fall of the regime.[62] It is to be noted also that the community of Hungarian historians functions in a symbiosis with their Hungarian expatriate colleagues. As a consequence, the consciousness it has of the quality of its production is increased, and its ability to resist purely political pressures is also increased.[63]

One of the interests of the small scandal provoked by the concerted action of the government and several historians is to extend the historical questioning relative to the Holocaust to both Communism and Nazism. For almost twenty years historians have publicly participated in challenging the foundations of a national identity on a critical basis;[64] henceforth they will be forced to confront both the imperfections of the democratic present and the troubling realities of the century just past, and this is new. They must learn to distinguish a state of rights and democracy and to take into account the exclusions (for example, in the case of blacks in the United States, mentioned by Mária Schmidt) or limitations on the participation of citizens and that of the articulations between the different groups whose interaction makes up democracy.

For it is not only Stalinism and Nazism, or periods of a more moderate authoritarianism, that are being investigated in Hungary but also the unfinished forms of democracy that have characterized the country throughout the century, even during the "golden age" before 1914.

Translated by Lucy B. Golsan

Notes

1. See Andras Mink, "Történelempolitika" (Politics-History) in the April 1999 publication of *Beszélö, Politikai és kultúrális folyóirat*, pp. 38–41. For this author the history of the present cannot enjoy credibility unless the obstacles to any work of historical analysis connected to the political context and any interpretations of the past received as a heritage are acknowledged.

2. In 1985 at Monor, not far from Budapest, there was an "ecumenical" encounter of the Hungarian opposition, even though the meeting at Lakitelek in 1987, which created the Hungarian Democratic Forum (Magyr Demokra Fórum) no longer counted the "liberal" group among its members. In the spring of 1994, legislative elections ended in a parliamentary majority for the Hungarian Socialist Party, heir of the only former party, the Social-Democrat (Szabad Demokraták Szövetsége), which regrouped the former liberal opposition. The effects of the formation of this coalition government on the ideological landscape are still being felt, although since the end of the spring of 1998, it is a right-wing coalition that has taken power.

3. See her study, dated February 1998, "Az 'anti-szemitizmus elleni harc' szerepe a rendszerváltozás éveiben" (The role of the "struggle against anti-Semitism" in the years of a system change), in *Janus-arcúrendszerváltozás: Tanulmányok* (Change of a biface system: Studies), ed. Mária Schmidt and László Gy. Tóth (Ed.), Budapest, Kairisz Kiadó, 1998, pp. 285–325.

4. This was true of István Csurka, at that time one of the heads of the Hungarian Democratic Forum, which is now at the head of the parliamentary extreme Right (Party of Truth and of Hungarian Life; Magyar igazság és élet pártja, MIEP). Several examples of these discourses can be found in Csurka, *Keserü hátország Tanulmányok* (Bitter back country: Studies), Budapest Magyar Fórum Könyve, 1993 (e.g., p. 31, text of August 20, 1992). He insists on the blocking, between 1990 and 1994 by the liberal and socialist opposition, of the purification law proposed by Zetényi and Takács, voted in on November 4, 1991, and struck down by the Constitutional Court on March 3, 1992, for poorly defined retroactivity. Ibid., p. 90 (the original text appeared on January 23, 1993). See also Frigyes Kahler, "Erkölcsi és jogi igazságtél" (Doing justice morally and legally), in *Janus-arcú*, pp. 158–186; and the 1991 debates in *Magyarország politikai évkonyve 1992*, Budapest, Demokrácia Kutatások Magyar Központja Alapítvány, Economix Rt., 1992, pp. 525–563.

5. There are certainly rather frequent manifestations of anti-Semitism in the press of the MIEP, directed by István Csurka, especially ritual denunciations of the worldwide Judeo-Communist or Judeo-capitalist anti-Hungarian *lobby*, with George Soros as one of its chiefs. Furthermore there are small groups who desecrate Jewish cemeteries or synagogues from time to time.

6. See Maria Schmidt, *Diktatúrák ördögszekerén* (On the panicaut of dictatorship), Budapest, Magvetö, 1998, pp. 54–83, "A Holocaust helye a magyar zsidóság modernkori törtében" (The Place of the Holocaust in the contemporary history

of Hungary). For the use of the concept of democracy applied to the Horthy years, see "Tacitus a négerek Amerikája Károlyi trónfosztása. Schmidt Mária: Szívesen vagyok egy jó király mellett rossz tanácsadó" (Tacitus, the America of the Negroes, Karolyi dethroned [from the national historical pantheon]. Mária Schmidt: I am willingly a bad advisor to a good king), interview with György Balázsi and BélaValancsis, in *Szépszó*, cultural supplement of *Népszava*, May 15, 1999, *http://www.nepszavahu/plusz/szepszo/990515/interju.html.*

7. The obsessive fear of Mária Schmidt for the left-wing intellectuals who, unlike herself, would not come near taking power is expressed with virulence in an interview, *Az (magyar) értelmiség hívatása.Tanulmányok, vallomások, elemzések, levelek (Hetven magyar értelmiségi írásai)* (The Mission of the [Hungarian] intelligentsia: Studies, confessions, analyses, letters [Writings from seventy Hungarian intellectuals]), rev. and ed. Arpád Fasang, pp. 366–367.

8. Schmidt,"Az 'anti-szemitizmus elleni harc' szerepe a rendszerváltozás éveiben," p. 311. According to Schmidt, the struggle surrounding anti-Semitism hides the just demand for change among the intellectual elite, supported by the conservatives who benefit from their lack of shady dealings before 1989. Without going into the subject, it must be remembered here that the dividing line has never been fixed between the camps, and all of the conservatives were not martyred and certainly not imprisoned before 1989.

9. The interpretation of the meeting between Kristóffy, royal legate of Hungary to Moscow, and Molotov on June 23, 1941, which stated that the USSR recognized Hungarian annexes inTransylvania (and foresaw their eventual extension) dependent on the maintenance of neutrality by Budapest, can be contradictory. See *A Moszkvai magyar követség jelentései, 1935–1941* (Dispatches from the Hungarian delegation to Moscow, 1935–1941), ed. Peter Pastor, preface by Gyula Juhász, Budapest, Századvég Kiadó-Atlanti Kiadó, 1992, pp. 344–345 n. 36. See also the analyses ofTofik Islamov published by Múltunk (nos. 1–2, 1994).

10. See György Földes, *Rendszer—hatalom és a baloldal Magyarországon 1994 után* (System—power and the left in Hungary after 1994),Budapest, Napvilág kiadó, 1998, pp. 14–15.

11. In practice Kádár was very soon courting popular writers and firmly opposed left-wing critics of the Lukács school, who had been scattered around the world at the beginning of the 1970s. A large number of conservatives had made fine careers for themselves before 1989, with or without a party card, while more obvious left-wing intellectuals were hindered because of their overly critical stand. For the initial period see Eva Standeisky,*Az írók és a hatalom, 1956–1963* (Writers and power, 1956–1963), Budapest, 1956-os Intézet, 1996.

12.We must point out here the role of the *Magyar Füsetek* (Hungarian notebooks) published in France under the direction of Pierre Kende, which allowed many Hungarian intellectuals to express themselves and be secretly distributed in Hungary.

13. This gap in access to Western intellectual circles between opposing liberals

and nationalists has irritated Mária Schmidt. See "Az 'anti-szemitizmus elleni harc' szerepe a rendszerváltozás éveiben," p. 289. She sees here the proof that the liberal opposition was part of the nomenclature.

14. Görgy Földes rightly points out that the delayed contempt for the works of Communism in Hungary, a contempt expressed as much by conservatives of 1990 as by those of 1998 works as an instrument of political recognition. Thus the simple fact of mentioning an aspect of life in Hungary then seen as positive (before 1989) becomes proof of left-wing sympathies.

15. The campaign for the referendum of November 26, 1989 (on four questions, one of which was the method of electing a future president of the republic) clearly showed that the Hungarian Democratic Forum hesitated over the role to give to Imre Pozsgay, head of the former Communist Party, which had become the Hungarian Socialist Party on October 7, and whom a part of the conservative leaders, grateful for his help in creating the Forum, had made the future president of the republic by universal suffrage. In the end, this method of election having been defeated, Pozsgay's career was ruined. See, for example, the contribution of Miklós Haraszti, "A kiegyezés két taktikája: Ut a négy igenhez" (The two tactics of compromise: The path to the four assents), in *Magyarország évtizedkönyve, 1988–1998: A rendszerváltás* (The Book of the decade in Hungary, 1988–1998: The Change of power), vol. 2, pp. 923–934. For confirmation of this analysis as seen from the opposite perspective, see Csurka, *Keserü hátország Tanulmányok*, p. 27.

16. See György Hunyady, "A XX. Század történetének megítélése a közgondolkodásban: a rendszerváltás tükröződése és hatása" (The Judgment brought by public opinion on the twentieth century: Reflection and influence of the change of regime), in *Vissza a történelemhez: Emlékkönyv Balogh Sándor 70. Születésnapjára* (Return to history: Collection for the seventieth anniversary of the birth of Sándor Balogh), ed. Lajos Izsák and Gyula Stemler, Budapest, Napvilág, 1996, pp. 143–153.

17. See the series *Magyarország politikai évkönyv* (Directory of political life in Hungary) since 1988 (1987 included). This is a publication of the Kemokrácia Kutatások Magyar Központja Alapítvány (Foundation of the Hungarian Center for Research on Democracy).

18. See Paul Gradvohl, Béla Márian, and Ildikó Szabó, "A folyamatosság forradalma, avagy a Kádár korszakhoz való viszony szerepe a magyar politikai Közgondolkozásban" (The Revolution of continuity, or the role of relationships at the time of Kádár in the envisioning of politics by the Hungarian population), *Politikatudomány Szemle*, no. 2, 1998, pp. 5–26. The Socialist Party lost the elections of 1998 while remaining ahead with 32.92 percent of the proportional votes, then 29.59 percent (1st elections on May 10) and 43.04 percent (2d elections, May 24) of the votes by individual conscription, as opposed to respectively 29.48 percent, 9.31 percent, and 37.9 percent for the FiDeSz-MPP.

19. For January 30, 1989, see *Construction de la mémoire du XXe siècle en Hungrie: Sortir de l'image du peuple victime de l'injustice des grandes nations*, Paris, Centre Interuni-

versitaire d'études hongroises, report of the research for MENESRIP, April 1997, ed. Paul Gradvohl, pp. 196–213, "Les historiens hongrois et le XXe siècle."

20. See András Szigethy, "'56-os csizma az asztalon" (The Blow of the boot of '56 on the table), *Népszabadság*, March 27, 1999, p. 12. This article tells of a meeting on financing culture and the European Union in which a director of the Institute of 1956, whose public financing had just been dramatically reduced, had questioned the government representative. The journalist points out that the debate took place without any strong language or bad behavior on either side, which seems to him a point in its favor.

21. *Anápirtás politikája:A Holocaust Magyarországan* (The Politics of extermination: The Holocaust in Hungary), 2 vols., Budapest, Belvárosi Könyvkiadó, 1997 (in English, *The Politics of Genocide:The Holocaust in Hungary*, NewYork, Columbia University Press, 1994). The first edition in Hungarian, under the title *A magyar holocaust* (The Hungarian Holocaust), published by Gondolat in Budapest and Blackurn International in Wilmington NC, is from 1988, and the original English-language edition is from 1981.

22. Edited by Randolph L. Braham, NewYork (Rosenthal Institute for Holocaust Studies and the City University of NewYork), and Attila Pók, Budapest (Institute of Historical Sciences of the Hungarian Academy of Sciences), published by the Europa Institute, Boulder CO (Social Science Monographs) and distributed by Columbia University Press. Remember that Pók is a specialist in Hungarian liberalism in the twentieth century and is one of the directors of the Institute of Historical Sciences of the Academy in Budapest. The Hungarian contributors to this volume are in disagreement over the attitude of the Hungarian authorities over the Jewish question during the war, even before the beginning of massive deportations organized under the aegis of the German occupiers.

23. Maria Schmidt has produced several analyses on the *Judenrat* of Budapest but does not have (to our knowledge) the authorization to direct research. Sandor M. Kiss, former historical counsel of József Antall (prime minister from 1990 to the end of 1993) directs the Department of History of the Catholic University, but he has not written any reference works.

24. See the government decree 1020/1999 of February 24, 1999, for the creation of the "Public Foundation for Research on the History and Society in Central and East-Central Europe" (Közép-és Kelet-európai Történelem et Társadalom Kutatásért Közalapítvány), in the *Magyar Közlöny* (the equivalent of the *Official Journal*), no. 14, 1999, p. 1061. This foundation is financed to the sum of 117 million forints [roughly 500,000 dollars U.S.], by the Ministry of National Cultural Patrimony, which developed out of the separation of the former Ministry of Education and of Culture. It is not connected with the ministry that follows higher education and research. At the same time, the two research institutes mentioned above, which together received a sum equivalent to that attributed to the new foundation, find themselves deprived of public support.

25. See Tamás Fricz, *A népi-urbánus vita tegnap és ma* (The populist-modernist debate yesterday and today), Budapest Napvilág Kiadó, 1997; or the publications of *M últunk*, the journal of the institute.

26. Interview with Görgy Földes, director of the Institute of Political History,April 1, 1999. The institute, created as a foundation in 1990, became a Kôzhasznú Társaság (Society of Social Utility) at the end of 1998, thus guaranteeing its independence from the MSZP, and at the same time refusing any dependence regarding the state imposed by the Hungarian Statute on Public Foundations (Kôzalapítvány). See *A politikatörténeti Alapítvány és a Politikatörténeti Intézet a rendszerváltás után és ma, 1900–1999*. (The Foundation of Political History and the Institute of Political History after the change of systems and today, 1900–1999), Budapest, Politikatórténeti Intézet, January 1999, 35 pp. [reprography]. We note here the support given to the institute by Péter Gostonyi, who emigrated to Switzerland and died in March 1999. He was a specialist on 1956 and not receptive to Communist sympathies. He insisted on the special merits of the institutions, infringed on by the government, faced with the gaps in other centers of research on 1956.

27. On this procedure see András Domány, "Arvilágítás után:Vitya egy Törvény értelmezése Körül" (After the verification:Debate over the interpretation of a law), in *Magyarország politikai évkönyve, 1998* (Political yearbook of Hungary, 1998), Budapest, Demokrácia Kutatások Magyar Központja Alapítvány, 1998, pp. 322–330 [with a summary in English]. The author knew of only one case of an agent of the political-police services discovered in the course of the verification procedure; this deputy (socialist) resigned before the end of the procedure but allowed it to be completed, that is, the publicity from results of the inquest, although he could have blocked it when he gave up his position.

28. Le Nemzeti Alaptanterv (Basic National Program) was adopted by the socialist-liberal majority in power from 1994 to 1998.

29. See, for example, Miklós Szabó (one of the liberals stigmatized by Mária Schmidt), "Politikai évfordulók a Horthy rendszerben" (Political anniversaries in the Horthy regime), in *A két világháborúkozötti Magyarországról* (About Hungary between the two wars), Budapest, Hungarian Workers Party (Kossuth Könyvkiadó), 1984, pp. 479–504, which emphasizes that Horthy was not a dictator and that his cult took on importance in the 1930s to counterbalance the growth of the extreme Right in spite of the reluctance of legitimists (Catholics) who still hoped for a return of the Hapsburgs. Mária Ormos, "Mussolinitól Hitlerig" (From Mussolini to Hitler), in *Diktátorok—diktatúrák* (Dictators—Dictatorships), no. 3 of the collection AKIK NY-OMOT HAGYTAK A 20, SZAZADON (Those who left a mark on the twentieth century), preface by Tibor Erényi, Budapest, Napvilág Kiadó, 1997, pp. 27–47, profited from her contribution to make a detour by Hungary. She emphasizes that the qualification of the Horthy regime remains to be defined. For her it is not a question of a dictatorship, and the fact that the juridical nature of the state is not clearly established still complicates the work of analysis. Let us remember that Ormos is one of the

major historians of the twentieth century in Hungary, and she is an academician who once briefly served as a socialist deputy before giving up her post (1994). After having studied the international relations and foreign policy of Hungary at length, she is currently working on its internal development between 1914 and 1945. She has written *Mussolini* and *Hitler.*

30. See Miklós Incze and Mária Ormos, *Európai fasizmusok, 1919–1939* (European Fascisms, 1919–1939), Budapest, Kossuth Könyvkiadó, 1976, esp. pp. 153–164. The dictatorial qualitative itself is formed by the proposed analyses in the breakdown. Let us note that, from this time on, Ignác Romsics went further in analyzing the limits of the authoritarianism of those in power, especially during the Bethlen era (1921–31). In the eighth volume of *Magyarország története, 1918–1919, 1919–1945* (History of Hungary, 1918–1919, 1919–1945) published by the Academy of Sciences in 1976, the accent is on the counterrevolutionary nature of the regime and on the fact that, given the legal right the state seemed to have, the electoral game ultimately could not question those in power because the system was "closed" (pp. 473–483).

31. See László Karsai, "Tankönyvek a Soáhról" (School texts on the Shoah), *Világosság* no. 7, 1992, pp. 533–537; and idem, "Tankönyvek a Holocaustról" (School texts on the Holocaust), in Braham and Pók, *Holocaust in Hungary Fifty Years Later,* pp. 717–732 [with a summary in English].

32. We have neglected those thinkers inspired by the totalitarian model imported to Hungary, which is based on a general analysis. These are the philosophers who have largely adopted this outlook. An interesting case that illustrates the contemporary liberal Hungarian thought is the development on corporatism (in the fashion of Pétain, Salaz, or Mussolini) as the eventual outcome of Communism for Gáspár Miklós Tamás; see *Idola Tribus, A nemzeti érzés erkölcsi lényege: Vázlat a hagyományról, Az értékválság legendája* (The Idols of the tribe, the moral essence of national sentiment: Review of the tradition, the legend of the crisis of values), Les Livres des "Cahiers hongrois," no. 12, Malakoff, Dialogues européens, 1989, p. 301. In this text, which has not been reprinted in the French translation, Tamás is characterized by original thinking that hopes to go beyond existing models.

33. See *Uj Fórum: Kötzeleti-Politikai Folyóirat* (New forum: Review of public and political life), no. 8, August 11, 1989, pp. 25–27.

34. See "Nemzeti-szocializmus-sztalinizmus," *Historia,* no. 4, 1995, pp. 9–14.

35. See Zsuzsa M. Szabó, "Két elnyomó rendszer Közös gyökerei: Ormos Mária a nemzeti szocializmusról és a sztalinizmusról" (Communist roots of two repressive systems: Mária Ormos on national socialism and Stalinism), *Eszak Magyarország,* November 11, 1995, p. 11. The historian has recently given a talk on this subject at the meeting of the Committee of the Academy of Miskolc.

36. It is interesting to note that László Karsai, a specialist in the Holocaust and the extermination of the Gypsies, reproached Mária Ormos in 1994 for not challenging, beginning with the Holocaust, the ideology of "progress," which came from the Enlightenment, when two years later she joined Karsai, but not on the single basis

suggested by him. For her it is the whole of "historical materials" that leads to this conclusion. See Braham and Pók, *Holocaust in Hungary Fifty Years Later*, p. 728 n. 5.

37. See "A rendszer és polgársága" (The System and its bourgeoisie), *Népszabadság*, February 22, 1999, which condemns the neglecting of workers' councils in the commemoration of 1956 and presents 1989 as the coming to power of a new middle class characterized by a total lack of humanity.

38. The ideological climate in Hungary is nevertheless characterized by a growing tolerance. Mária Ormos and Tamás Krausz are now working on parallel portraits of Stalin and Hitler, which will be an occasion to go further into the debate mentioned here. (*Hitler-Sztalín*, s.1 . . . , Pannonica Kiadó, 1999). In volume 36 of the review *Eszmélet*, the texts referred to in *Livre noir du communisme* (Paris, Laffont, 1997) were translated into Hungarian in order to feed the debate.

39. Tamás Krausz refers here to Attila Jószef, a Hungarian poet active on the Left, who invented the expression "Kommunofasizmus."

40. See "A nácizmus és a sztálinizmus összefüggéséröl (Hét tézis egy régi vitához)" (On relations between Nazism and Stalinism [seven theses on an old debate]), *Magyar Tudomány*, no. 6, 1996, pp. 702–712.

41. Ibid., pp. 712–717. "A történelem 'szemétdombjáról' és a történelmi 'törvénys-zerüségröl'" (About the 'pile of garbage' of history and 'history's laws'").

42. In pointing this out, she avoids the very delicate stumbling block of the ranking of victims, for everywhere in Central Europe there were debates on which victims deserved the most pity, debates that the families of the "bourgeoisie" and other class enemies—often eliminated (physically or socially) before the Communist "purges" began in 1949 (with some exceptions, begun in Hungary in 1945)—protested against the emphasis against the commemoration of former Stalinist partisans. For the case of Czechoslovakia, see Valerie Löwit, "Du passé faire table rase?" *Tumultes: Cahiers du Centre de sociologie des pratiques et des représentations politiques de l'université Paris VII—Denis Diderot*, no. 4, 1994, pp. 121–146.

43. *Magyarország a két világháborúkorában, 1914–1945* (Hungary at the time of the two world wars, 1914–1945), Debrecen, Csokonai Kiadó, 1998.

44. *Magyarország története, 1918–1945* (History of Hungary, 1918–1945), Debrecen, Multiplex Média Debrecen, 1995, TORTENELMI FIGYELO KONYVEK 3.

45. He has just published a history of Hungary in the twentieth century in May 1999, (*Magyaroszág története a XX. században*, Budapest, Osiris Kiadó, 1999), See also Ignác Romsics, "A Horthy rendszer jellegéröl: Elitizmus, tekintélyelv, Konszerva-tizmus" (On the nature of the Horthy regime. Elitism, the principle of authority, conservatism), *Rubicon*, no. 1, 1997 (or on the Web site *www.rubicon.hu*).

46. *Magyar történelem, 1914–1990* (Hungarian history, 1914–1990), Budapest, Nem-zeti Tankonyvkiadó, 1995. Note that this rather conservative author refrains from characterizing the political regimes and remains largely descriptive. The book was released by the publisher closest to the Ministry of Education at the time the socialist-liberal coalition was in power.

47. The historians were helped by jurists, often conservative, who were engaged in a complete reconstituting of the legal procedures of the period; Frigyes Kahler was principal among them. But he still works with (April 1999) the Institute of 1956. Gábor Jobbágyi was one of those who had the crimes committed after November 4, 1956, redefined advancing the idea that, from this date on, there was war, war crimes and crimes against humanity and the prescription was therefore not applicable. He was one of those who had the most difficulty in accepting the 1992 decision of the Hungarian Constitutional Court that put an end to hopes for a purification, especially in accepting the demonstrations of joy from the liberal opposition at that time. See Jobbágyi, *Ez itt a tanúk vére (A 1956 utáni megtorlási eljárások)* (Here is the blood of witnesses) [repressive procedures following 1956]), Budapest, Kairosz Kiadó, 1998, in which the author, besides a brief autobiographical postscript, analyses five affairs. It is especially the political sensibility that changes in relation to certain historians more markedly on the Left, for the work is extremely precise. The demonstration of the illegal and rigged character of the proceedings is clear, but the analysis one can get of the Kádár regime in its early days does not diverge from those in the manuals of the Institute of 1956 or even from works done at the Institute of Political History, notably those of Zoltán Ripp. See, for example, his analysis in *Rubicon*, no. 1, 1998.

48. The "savage" deportations of the Hungarians at the end of 1944 and the beginning of 1945 to the USSR to fill the work camps had many witnesses. See Ilona Szebeni, *Merre van magyar házam? Kénysermunka a Szovjetunióban, 1944–1949* (In what direction is Hungary going? Slave-labor camps in the Soviet Union, 1944–1949), s. 1, Széphalom Könyvmühely, 1992. This book includes a brief study by Tamás Stark, who estimates that there were around 600,000 deportees and 400,000 returned. More recently in Ruthénia (Ukraine), official Soviet documents were published, and a memory park of the Hungarian and German deportation opened in Szolyva in 1994, with help from Hungarian authorities, and later Germany. See György Dupka and Alekszej Korszun, *A 'Malenkij robot' dokumentumokban* (The "Small Work" in documents), Ungvár/Oujgorod, Budapest, Intermix Kiadó, 1997.

49. It is important to note contradictory phenomena in the sensibility of different historians about political repression since 1945. The old guard of 1956 are very divided and rail against each other on the Internet. Attacks suffered by the Institute of 1956, accused of misappropriation of funds and political dishonesty, were supported by certain ones of the group, believed to be on the Right, while others, on their side, signed petitions in favor of the institute. See *Beszélő*, ibid., pp. 8–20. See also the public discussion with György Litván, founder of the institute and a renowned historian of democratic movements in Hungary, who held forth with Eszter Rádai and András B. Hegedüs under the aegis of *Beszélő* on February 18. On the moral and material compensation for damages inflicted on "political" victims and the dispositions taken between 1989 and 1997, see Edit Petri, ed., *Kárpotlás és kárrendezés Magyarországon, 1989–1998* (Compensation and reparation in Hungary, 1989–1998), Budapest, Napvilág Kiadó, 1998, which includes the principle texts. In Hungary the

rehabilitation of victims of 1956 was begun in 1988, though in a very piecemeal way in the beginning.

50. Certain participants at the conference organized by Catholics as a dialogue between Jews and Christians in the large Benedictine Abbey of Pannonhalma November 4–5, 1998,"Hungarian Reflections on the Shoah," viewed the proposals of László Tökécki on the differentiation between Jews and Christians since the nineteenth century as a return to the schema: the Jews are separate, and in exchange for the unequal tolerance of the noble elite, they should have remained politically submissive, but the revolution tempted them. An outline that justifies the implicit maintenance of a Jewish/Hungarian segregation, at least at the center of the elites, even when the "Jew" in question turns out to be Hungarian. Besides the daily press, see the photocopied brochure distributed at the conference under the same title, *Magyar megfontolások a Soáráol*.

51. See *Múlt és Jövö: Zsidó kultúrális folyóirat* (Past and future: A Jewish cultural review), no. 2, 1994, pp. 92–96.

52. See *Diktatürák ördögszekerén*, pp. 84–101.

53. It is pointed out in the account of the last edition of his reference work by Agnes Heller, "A Holocaust Tinódija: Randolph L. Braham, A népirtás politikája" (The chronicler of the Holocaust), *Múlt és Jövö*, no. 4, 1997, pp. 105–110.

54. For a contrasting analysis of the beginnings, see Eva Standeisky, Gyula Koák, Gábor Pataki, and János M. Rainer, eds., *A fordulat évei: Politika, képzömüvészet, építészet, 1947–1949* (The Years of change: Politics, plastic arts, architecture), Budapest, 1956-os Intézet, 1998.

55. See István Csurka, "Van-e nálunk rasszizmus?" (Is there racism among us?) *Magyar Nemzet*, April 20, 1996, reprinted in *Egy következmény nélküli ország* (A thoughtless country), Budapest, Századvég Kiadó, 1998, pp. 240–245.

56. Information on the Hungarian contribution to the preparation of minds and administrations (even if the perspective of the Final Solution was not in everyone's mind) can be found in Catherine Horel,"Avant le pire: La Marginalization progressive des juifs de Hongrie (1938–1944)" (Before the worst:The progressive marginalization of Jews in Hungary), *Cahiers de la Shoah*, no. 4, 1996–97, pp. 11–40.

57. See György Litván, *Az 1956-os magyar forradalom hagyománya és irodalma* (The Tradition and the literature relative to the Hungarian revolution of 1956), Budapest, MTA Történettudományi Intézet, 1992, ELOADASOK A TORTENETTUDOMANYI INTEZETBEN; this volume also includes the debate following the conference from which the title of the work comes.

58. *Szovjet thermidor: A sztálini fordulat szellemi elözményei, 1917–1928* (Soviet Thermidor: The intellectual antecedents of the Stalinist turning point, 1917–1928), Budapest, Napvilág Kiadó, 1996.

59. See *Joghalál Magyarországon, 1945–1989* (The Death of law: Hungary, 1945–1989), Budapest, Zrínyi Kiadó, 1993, esp. pp. 71–72.

60. It should be noted that there are other cases of interference in the institutional

area of history, for example at the university. With the introduction of students on the committee for selecting teachers, the political pressures have greatly eased. On the refusal to offer a professorship to Tamás Krause, see István Riba, "Egyetemitanár-választás as ELTE-N" (The Designation of a professor at the Loránd Eötvös University), *Heti Világgazdaság*, April 10, 1999, p. 119. The historian had received the unanimous support of the commission of specialists, but his competence (and his political opinions) were objected to by the president of the organization concerned with student interests. In this case we find mechanisms that also exist farther west in Europe, independent of the political orientations of those involved.

61. It can be seen here that the ministry, as much as Mária Schmidt, tried to have people forget the measures taken and the accusations brought against the private financial institutions, even though in the spring of 1999 nothing had been settled. See Lajos Pogony, interview by Gergely Pröhle, *Kritika*, no. 5, 1999, p. 28; and "Tacitus a négerek Amerikája Károlyi trónfosztása." It is a question of exchanging forgetting for the advantages of research.

62. See József Debreczeni, *A miniszterelnök* (The prime minister), Budapest, Osiris, 1998, p. 118. Antall had even pointed out that these members of the party had been more courageous than the "pártonkívüliek" (those without a party).

63. The mobilization of Hungarian historians in the United States has been especially rapid regarding the Institute of 1956, for example. But this is only one example.

64. See, for example, "Társadalmi azonosulás és nemzeti tudat" (Social identity and national conscience), *Magyar Hírlap*, November 29, 1981, p. 9, with Ferenc Pataki, psychologist, and Péter Hanák, Miklós Szabó, Miklós Lackó, three historians of the Hungarian Academy of Sciences, a transcript of the televised debate of November 19, directed by Zsolt Papp.

François Frison-Roche

Managing the Past in Bulgaria

The destruction of the Iron Curtain in Bulgaria, as elsewhere, opened the way to creating an important enterprise of exploration that should, first of all, allow the discovery of a "West" whose reality had for a long time remained shadowy but that incarnated the democracy that this "Median Europe" aspired to, to use the apt expression of Fernand Braudel.[1] This discovery had a multipurpose character since it would take place simultaneously in the institutional, economic, political, cultural, and certainly the historical domains, thus making possible an analysis and presentation to the public of the major events that have taken place since the Second World War and even for some countries since the beginning of the century.

With freedom of expression and free access to information, numerous Bulgarian newspapers, magazines, and books were able to discuss current subjects, historical events, or politics such as, for example, 1968 in the West compared to 1989 in the East.[2]

To the discovery of the history of the Western world was also added the necessity of elaborating a new historical method that, during the years of the Communist regime, had been viewed through the prisms of "historical materialism" and "dialectical materialism," which were considered as "the highest point in the development of materialism," to repeat the encyclopedia definition every student would have known by heart at that time.[3]

Even though Bulgaria did not lack qualified researchers, the hold of this exclusive method on research was such that it was possible to find on the history of Byzantium, the powerful neighbor of Bulgaria in the Middle Ages, a voluminous work analyzing this period from the standpoint of "class relationships" and "social movements of the oppressed," which progressively sapped its "feudal power."[4]

The question of the attitude of the historian toward the historical facts and the necessity of an impartial and pluralistic approach was taken up at the beginning of the 1990s in Bulgaria.

The necessity of reexamining Bulgarian history, then, naturally became the order of the day. The "black and white" study in the restrictive forms demanded by the ideology, which presented not only the Communist Party but also the USSR, heir of a liberating Russia,[5] as the principal actors of history, could no longer be perpetuated. The voluntary disregard of the complexity of historical facts and the relegation of all action not coming from the Party to a secondary role, and therefore by definition negative, was already being challenged before 1989. But it was only after this date that many research enterprises that took place during the Communist years could be published. These works concerned areas as varied as the history of minorities, political parties, or key events for the country, such as the Treaty of San Stefano.[6]

Today all of this research work of analysis and discovery continues to be done, though in the uncertain conditions of a society in transition in which difficulties of daily survival and worry about the future have taken hold of minds. Furthermore, since the state is unable to finance sufficient budget support, the most elementary methods for conducting research under good conditions are lacking.

Added to the multiplicity of past and present facts to be considered and reevaluated in an unstable present, along with the necessity of rejecting a whole system of values for the second time (after the rupture of 1945–47) in the space of a half century, is the difficulty of accepting the other traumatic event of the Bulgarian past, nearly five centuries of Ottoman occupation (1393–1878).

This long period of foreign occupation is felt in the collective memory as a national wound that has prevented Bulgaria from following the natural development of other European countries, has slowed the flowering of its culture, and has continued to play its part in the emotional relationships the Bulgarians have with their history.

It is in this context that many Bulgarian historians turn toward both a recent and distant past to wonder about the similarities between the fascist and Communist regimes and bring elements of their thinking to a debate already politicized and whose two components are the totalitarian system and a democratic society. This debate, taking place within a review of past and present, brings to the forefront the necessity of elaborating a new national identity.

History's Stakes in Bulgaria: "Fascism," a Metaphor for Communism

In the years following 1945 and up until the 1980s, historical research in Bulgaria closed in on itself. Cut off from the rest of the world but closely linked to methods and principles adopted in the USSR, it had taken on, as Ivan Itchev rightly says, "an insular aspect."[7] In the grip of ideology, it had to carry out the objectives fixed by the rigid directives outlined in the Party plan. The historical research during this period was largely devoted to the history of the Communist Party, especially the years 1920–30, and to the Second World War, considered the most "glorious" periods. The study of these "subject bearers" could allow the researchers to hope later to rise to positions of responsibility. Furthermore, the Institute of History of the Communist Party exercised a predominant role in the research. Although Ludmila Jivkova had favored a relative opening up of historical research in Bulgaria since the 1970s,[8] it remained based essentially on "the study of Capitalism and the Bulgarian Bourgeoisie."[9]

Even though since the nineteenth century, the mythic writing of history, that which aims at reconstructing the past to forge a national identity, became more and more widespread, the Communist Party did not hesitate to utilize the techniques of manipulation of the past to legitimize its hegemony.

Like the others, the Bulgarian Communist Party justified its power by proclaiming itself the "party of progress, a motivating force in the carrying out of history." The three ideological pillars that legitimized its supremacy and glorified it with the crown of the "martyred Party" were the heroism that it prided itself on during the years of "Bulgarian Capitalism," its combat against "fascism," and its decisive role as the USSR's supporter. The limits were thus clearly indicated to Bulgarian historians and the roles assigned in advance. Until the end of the 1980s, for example, it was impossible to contradict the fact that Bulgaria, in the years before the war, lived under a "monarcho-fascist" regime, a natural ally of Hitler's Germany, and that Tsar Boris III was "under the heel of the Germans."

Any attempt to shed more light on this period was considered a sacrilege and banned. The publication of the work by historian Nicolaï Gentchev on Bulgarian foreign policy from 1938 to 1941 was forbidden in 1968 because he proposed a study accenting the difficult situation in which Bulgaria found itself on the eve of and during the Second World War and emphasized the important role during this period of the prewar political parties.[10] It was not published until 1998 in the original text that was written thirty years earlier.

During the 1960s, at the time of the "thaw" of the Khrushchev period, when the repression of antiestablishment intellectuals became less intense and the regime tolerated a certain liberty of expression, a study on fascism made a conspicuous appearance.[11] The work had been written by a dissident philosopher, Jeliou Jelev, at the time when he had been sent for seven years to a small village in the southeast of Bulgaria. Completed in 1967, it circulated clandestinely for a long time and could not be published in Sofia until

1982. This publication brought about an avalanche of dismissals and various punishments among those responsible at the publishing house and among the universities who, charged with overseeing the ideological conformity of publications, had given approval for its publication.

The author was relieved of his research post, and the book was banned and removed from libraries. But six thousand copies (out of a printing of ten thousand) had already been sold.

The book caused a sensation, not only in Bulgaria, but also in the other countries of the Communist bloc. Even though the Bulgarian authorities had insisted to foreign editors that the book did not exist, in order to keep it from being translated outside the country, several publishers, especially Czechoslovakian and Chinese, showed an interest and contacted the author directly. The book was about to come out in Czechoslovakia when the tanks of the Warsaw Pact brought the Prague Spring to an end, and its translation into Chinese had begun when a campaign against intellectuals began. The book circulated at the time in Russia in the samizdat form.

The official representation of "fascism" in the Bulgarian collective memory, elaborated on in school texts, in sites and symbols of the past, and in books and films having to do with history, can be outlined as follows:

The "reactionary bourgeoisie" and the Tsar Boris had installed a "monarcho-fascist regime" of repression and terror against any free demonstrations of "democratic forces," especially the Communist Party, which brought about the "impoverishment of the deprived peasantry" and of "the working class," which gave rise to a growing discontent and reinforced the positions of the Party.

For its part this last, according to the Bulgarian encyclopedia, with the support of the USSR, had organized the "antifascist struggle." The powerful moments of this effort were of course the Leipzig trial, whose principal accused was Guergui Dimitrov; the aggression by Hitler's Germany against the USSR, which emerged victorious in spite of the devastation of its territory and the suffering of its population, "demonstrating in this the supremacy of socialism";[12] "the historical combat of the Bulgarian CP"; and finally the formation of the "National Front," which under the direction of the Party, unified the "workers," the "poor peasants," and "a large part of the intelligentsia!"[13]

This "theological" vision of fascism, to borrow François Furet's term, orchestrated Communist Party power and ultimately hid the reality from the eyes of public opinion by obscuring the real mode of functioning of the regime. According to Furet, "the interdependence of fascism and Communism, the representation, the passions, and the global historical reality is such that if we know one, we understand the other."[14]

At that time Jeliou Jelev's contribution was to reveal in his study on Nazism, Italian fascism, and Franquism the face that had been hidden by official historiography, that is, the establishment of a one-party system, the fusion of party and state, the conformity of all social and intellectual life, the cult of the leader, the internment camps, the excessive propaganda, the need to isolate the country, and the fear of a foreign menace always lying in wait.[15]

The many Bulgarians who knew how to read between the lines did not fail to make connections with the existing regime. They could even show that certain citations of fascist leaders, reproduced in the book, could have well been pronounced by Communist rulers of their own country. Under the pretext of a study of fascism, Jelev showed not only the totalitarian nature of the Communist regime but also became the initiator of a reflection on totalitarianism by proposing a grid of analysis of its function and asking, in conclusion, the question of the necessity for a dictatorial transition period after the breaking up of totalitarian regimes.[16]

The Stakes in the Debate on Totalitarianism

The debate over totalitarianism (fascism and Communism) versus democracy became open to the public in the early 1990s, fed especially by works such as those of Francis Fukuyama and Furet, to whom a review recently offered an important posthumous homage.[17] But it took a form peculiar to Bulgaria, putting first the debate on the nature of the political regime established in the country from the 1930s to the end of the Second World War. A lively argument developed over the following question: "Did fascism really exist in Bulgaria during this period?"[18] The necessity to be free of the grip of Communist historiography and to recreate history by reexamining historical events brought back into consideration the definition of the characteristics of a fascist regime.

In 1993, only four years after the upheavals of 1989, a work presenting the history of Bulgaria through the eyes of five historians actually dedicated a chapter to this subject. This put seriously in doubt the fascist nature of the regime established after the coup d'état of May 19, 1934, by Colonel Georgiev. It defined that event rather as an authoritarian regime, emphasizing especially "the possibility of public demonstrations of positions taken on important questions about the situation in the country."[19]

In a recent review one historian examined this period.[20] In comparing the restructuring of historical research, the politics of the naming of professors, and the use of racist theories in Germany and in Italy to the situation in Bulgaria, the author concluded that there existed an academic autonomy and a liberal tendency in Bulgarian historiography at this time.

Once the fascist nature of this period's political regime was put in doubt, the existence and the necessity of an "antifascist resistance" was challenged— this resistance was the favorite theme of the Communist Party in order to morally justify its power and its hegemony for fifty years.

Therefore, if fascism had not existed in Bulgaria, the antifascist struggle had no reason to exist either, in any case, in the forms offered during this half century.

By this same token the monuments the Communist regime had progressively erected to celebrate the great moments of its "antifascist" past were deprived of their significance, and another debate began in Bulgaria on their future.[21]

Beginning in 1990, the mausoleum that held the body of Guergui Dimitrov became a privileged symbolic target. Under pressure from the public, Communist authorities still in power, fearing a profanation, had the body quickly withdrawn at dawn, and it was burned and then reburied. The building, a smaller copy of Lenin's mausoleum and a symbol of Communist celebrations, was covered with vulgar and insulting graffiti.[22] It was finally torn down in August 1999. In the political confrontation of the first pluralist elections of June 1990, "a war of symbolic interpretations" began between the partisans of the old Communist Party and those of the Union of Democratic Forces (UFD), each camp defending "their" symbols, going so far as to dig up, literally and figuratively, the bones of "their" dead. This argument, begun over the assassination by the Communists of twenty-two young people in September 1944 to avenge the death of twenty-two Communists killed by the "gendarmerie," was so violent that the entire Bulgarian nation became the prize and was turned into a symbol and place of collective memory. *Démocratsia*, the journal of the UFD, declared that Bulgaria was an "immense Socialist gulag" while *Douma*, the daily of the old Communist Party, declared it "an immense ossuary of pre-1944 Bulgaria."[23]

The disintegration of the Communist legend and the readjustment of fascism and Communism also made necessary the renewal of the contents of school texts destined to "forge the civic and national identity of future generations," according to the formula of sociologist Deyan Deyanov.[24] It is an arduous task to manage to give "a certain picture of the past and of certain telling events"[25] in a period of rapidly changing values in which men and women, of whom many have lived through two transitions in the course of their lives,[26] must face the double trauma of upheavals since the Second World War with all the psychological repercussions that implies.

How does one offer also a picture of a past deprived of the spirit of revenge when the feeling of frustration is always keen and present since, if the positive charge of "Communism" has permanently collapsed, the crimes and the criminals of that regime have been neither judged nor condemned? The task was therefore arduous for the Bulgarian historians called on, as Henry Rousso has said, "to give rational and supposedly truthful intelligibility to the past," even more so since they are themselves taking part in this society in transition.[27]

The textbooks of 1946, 1954, and 1963 called the period before and after the war a "monarcho-fascist" period established by the "reactionary bourgeoisie." Even if for the Bulgarians the text of 1984 marked a timid evolution in outlining the appearance of an opening, it still gave no precise details on the concrete facts and showed instead a new tendency of interpretation. Therefore, the small history textbook that appeared in 1996 offered a double challenge in trying to reconstruct a collective memory and at the same time construct the basis for a civic education suitable for a democratic society. It endeavored to minutely describe the facts in stressing the significance of the constitutional order that "fascism" and "Communism" could only try to impede.[28] Since the debate on the nature of the political regime preceding the coming to power of the Communist Party contributed to the elaboration of a new identity, it found itself thrust into the political arena. Orchestrated by the political movements, it set off a sometimes violent quarrel in the press and led to a confrontation of two views of the history of this period, each of which produced immediate repercussions.[29] These different historiographic interpretations had a direct effect on the private history of individuals in according them or depriving them of notoriety due to the acts they had committed in the past. They justified the more or less prestigious place in the social scale that they could claim in the future according to their role in the political party to which they belonged.[30] Furthermore they could serve to legitimize their political ambitions, that is, facilitate their access to power and to state commands, and as a consequence to the advantages that resulted.

The Bulgarian Socialist Party, epigone of the Communist Party, of course opted for the idea of a "monarcho-fascist" regime, which was a necessary condition for the existence of a "massive antifascist resistance" under the leadership of the Communist Party. This idea morally justified its leadership position and the advantages and privileges enjoyed by the "active fighters against fascism and capitalism," the members of the nomenklatura in general, their children, and even their grandchildren. It was in a way "the red thread," to cite the metaphor of Marie-Claire Lavabre,[31] which allowed them to act.

The other interpretation of historic facts, that is, the thesis that a fascist regime was absent from Bulgaria, implied that the prewar parliamentary system had not been truly eliminated by the political regime and that democratic expression therefore remained possible, although limited. Because of this it stigmatized the actions of the Communist Party as actions above-all unconstitutional and at the same time denounced the interference of the USSR in the internal political life of the country. It not only discredited the Communist Party in this way but also rehabilitated the political parties after 1989, which took up their causes and reclaimed their heritage.

This argument began at the "roundtable" of January 1990 (negotiations with equal participation of the Communist Party and the democratic opposition), when the totalitarian-versus-democracy debate was concretely evident during discussions on the subject of the suppression of multiple tentacled organizations of the Party in Bulgarian society. Certainly traumatized by the images of events in Romania and the brutal end of Ceausescu, one of the Communist negotiators emphasized that they must avoid, in this period of transition from Communism toward democracy, any revenge against the nomenklaturists so as not to repeat the errors of the transition from "monarcho-fascism" to Communism, when adherents of the latter went about punishing "the capitalist and fascist elements in the name of a glorious future."[32]

The totalitarian-versus-democracy debate that quickly intruded on the political sphere in Bulgaria also presented in an urgent way the necessity of a confrontation with the past for motives of a political, moral, and psychological order—the political order first of all because a rigorous and attentive examination of the past would prevent the regular resurgence of those past moments left in shadow to serve as a spearhead for partisan interests;[33] of a moral and psychological order also because the permanent repression of the memory of the past can condition the social behavior of the present.

If this debate was intense immediately after the upheavals of 1989, when it was necessary to denounce the exactions of the Communist system and justify the setting up of new forms of organizing society, when the people came out into the streets en masse to demonstrate their long-withheld indignation and their hopes for liberty, it nevertheless lost its sharpness as years passed. The enthusiasm that had invigorated all these men and women, deluding them with the hope of a free participation in the organization of their society, especially in the political sphere, diminished as time passed.

One researcher has pointed out that everything happened as though the people had made up "an irreversibly disenchanted memory of true socialism, of their past." But caught in the disturbing dynamic of a new society, they were forced to take on a difficult adaptation to new rules and new demands and so had imposed on themselves a withdrawal, cutting themselves off from the political sphere,[34] one that they considered more and more as a "sphere of shady doings" and whose participants, governments and politicians in general, were singled out for defiance as they had been in the past. There are many Bulgarians who believe that the upheavals of 1989 were only a pretense, more like a palace revolution than a real one, which reinforced their conviction that the rejected past had become the discredited present.

This perception of a certain continuity is corroborated by a recent inquest in which one of the people interrogated compared the actual situation in Bulgaria to a piece of theater that would have been in vogue before 1989 and that would continue today to be played by new actors, certainly, but also by former ones who would have donned new costumes.[35]

This feeling of continuity between the society of the past and that of the present, in spite of the difference in their nature perceived by everyone, raises again the question of the moral and psychological effect that would have taken place with a confrontation with the recent past and the necessity of clearly establishing responsibilities for the crimes committed during this time.

The demand for a condemnation of the guilty was delayed many times and was complicated due to the global grip the totalitarian regime exercised on society, which in a way diluted the responsibilities across frontiers, as Vaclav Havel commented, between victims and those guilty, and also even within each individual. This demand, checked also by the widespread idea that the imperatives of the moment demanded a look toward the future rather than toward the past, poses concrete problems about the very necessity of such a judgment, about the way to go about it, and about the opportunity of the moment.

This also explains the difficulty not only of clearly condemning the guilty ones of crimes and persecutions but also of the destruction of civil society and of economic decay. It would manifest itself in Bulgaria by the failure of the case against Todor Jivkov, who was ultimately condemned only for misappropriation of public funds.

This difficulty still exists today, for the torturers of the internment camps, despite overpowering testimonials,[36] have not been brought to trial or condemned. The Bulgarians in 1995 could read interviews with the guards of the Kurtovo camp, in which during the postwar years, the women of "bourgeois origin" who had been officially accused of "depraved behavior and an attack on public morals" were "reeducated." In spite of the cruelty inflicted, these guardians felt they had nothing to reproach themselves for.[37]

In the first pluralist elections of 1990, the anti-Communist coalition of the Union of Democratic Forces mounted on all the walls in the country a poster that pictured the map of Bulgaria with death heads marking the political prisoner camps. This had the opposite effect of what was intended among the population, stirring up a feeling of rejection and fear, for it could be a sign of a new purification like the one following the power takeover by the Communists at the end of the war.

Very recently this difficulty was reaffirmed again when several articles of a law instituting measures of "purification" in the administration, showing contempt for the Constitution and elementary rules of a state of law, were censured by the Constitutional Court.[38]

The confrontation with the past and the condemnation of crimes of the past should have been able to bring a new element into the elaboration of a national identity that seems today to organize itself around a feeling of resignation and fatalism, faced with histories that pile upon each other instead of being sequential, without furnishing any lessons for future generations.

If the necessity of a reckoning with the immediate past is regularly brought up in Bulgaria, not only because of the relaxing of an ideological grip but also because of new political, economic, and geopolitical imperatives, it is nevertheless enclosed within a more general search—that of the need to once again forge a national identity for "all" of the past.

The rigorous examination of the period qualified as "a national awakening,"[39] of liberation from Ottoman rule, which followed it up until the years before the war, cannot just bring new light to the complexity of historical facts and events, but at the same time it must contribute to demystifying the long idealized role of Russia and the USSR in the history of Bulgaria.

Having left the "Communist camp" and the Soviet zone of influence, Bulgaria has, in the last ten years, entered a new phase of its history, one of a return to the Western world. The study of its past and present is explained by the desire to regain, through a recreated identity, the place she once occupied, not only among the Balkan countries, but also in the heart of that Western Europe from which she has been arbitrarily separated for a half century.

A Rediscovered History? The Bulgarian Exception on the Shoah

It was not until February 24, 1993, that a plaque was unveiled in the area surrounding the Bulgarian National Assembly to commemorate the attitude, exemplary in Europe, of the Bulgarian population that opposed the Final Solution.[40] This plaque states: "The 14th of March, 1943, the protests of democratic opinion in Bulgaria, supported by a group of deputies, forced the government to delay the deportation of 8,500 Bulgarian Jews to fascist death camps. These protests, as well as the developments of the Second World War, saved the lives of 49,000 Bulgarian Jews. Unfortunately the Thracian regions of the Aegean Sea and the Valley of the Vardar in Macedonia, territories administered at this time by the Bulgarian authorities, deported 11,396 Jews to the Nazi concentration camps. Only twelve of them returned. The Bulgarian people bow before the memory of those innocent victims."

In April of the same year, during the solemn inauguration of the Holocaust Memorial in Washington, Bulgaria was cited along with Denmark as being among the countries that had saved their Jewish citizens from deportation and death.[41]

In this research to reconstruct a national identity, in reexamining especially the history of the years before and during the Second World War, what is the place attributed in Bulgaria to the Shoah?

To respond to this question, it is necessary to briefly retrace the international context in which Bulgaria first became independent and then found itself drawn into the Second World War, the political situation in the country, and also its national traditions toward its various minorities.

The essential key to the historical development of Bulgaria is found in the years 1860–80. The creation in 1867 first of an exarchat by the patriarch of Constantinople, then in 1870 of a Bulgarian "Millet"[42] by the sultan, who absorbed Thrace and Macedonia, would establish territorial limits to Bulgarian nationalism and contribute in fashioning its dream of identity.

The "Great Bulgaria," created in 1879 at San Stéfano by Russia, was considered the result of this aspiration.

But several months later, the Treaty of Berlin, desired by the European powers, finished the division of Bulgaria by making it an autonomous principality separate from Roumelia (Southern Bulgaria), returning it to Ottoman sovereignty while Thrace and Macedonia remained Turkish.

The Treaty of Berlin was considered a betrayal and a national wound. From then on, the "unification" of all the territories reputed to be inhabited by Bulgarians became the principal objective of Bulgaria, which considered itself a misunderstood victim.

This aspiration conditioned its relations with neighboring countries as well as the great powers of the period and led it first into the Balkan wars of 1912–13, then into World War I. These ended for Bulgaria in a disaster since she found herself in the camp of the defeated. The Bucharest treaties, following the Balkan wars, and then that of Neuilly in 1919 further reduced the size of the country, which led to questioning, with still more urgency, the objective of this unification.

After the beginning of the Second World War, the Balkan countries, situated in a strategic zone and disorganized and divided by old territorial conflicts, became a prize for the great powers. Bulgaria, who also refused the Europe of Versailles, was drawn politically toward Germany and took on closer economic ties.[43] War also served as a catalyst to internal factors that influenced its foreign policy. It revived the mythical dreams of "Great Bulgaria," cultivated especially by the movements inspired by German nationalism. The defeat of France and the Balkan countries allied with Great Britain encouraged Bulgaria to continue to draw closer to Germany.

In the beginning, thanks to pressures from the Reich on Romania, Bulgaria managed to regain the province of Dobroudja South, returned by the Craiova Accords in August–September 1940.

Toward the end of the same year, the weight of the German presence in the Balkans once more modified the actions of Bulgaria. With the failure of Italian troops, especially in Greece, which threatened a reinforcement of English positions in the region, Hitler prepared to intervene and began to exert pressure on Bulgaria to incite it to join the Axis powers.

The first time, in November 1940, Bulgaria managed to reject this proposition, but after the start of Operation Marita, in which Germany transferred troops (around 1 million men) into Romania and concentrated them along the Danube, and after further pressure, coming from not only Germany and Italy but also Great Britain, which tried to draw it into the opposite camp, it finally became part of the Tripartite Pact on March 1, 1941. Bulgaria became what Raoul Hilberg rightly calls an "opportunistic satellite" of Germany.[44]

The signing was followed by the stationing of German troops in the country. After the Nazi victory in Greece and Yugoslavia, Bulgaria was able to partially satisfy its former territorial claims. Germany in fact gave it control of the administration of Aegean Thrace and of Vardar Macedonia without, however, considering them part of Bulgaria since the decision about their final destiny was put off until the end of the war.

While waiting, the administration of these "new territories" was entrusted to the Bulgarian army, and national legislation was extended to include them.[45]

The nature of the regime established in Bulgaria, especially since the coup d'état of May 19, 1934, until the end of the war is exactly what provokes a lively polemic today.

As happened simultaneously in several countries, the regime established a hypertrophy of executive power. Essentially it based the legitimacy of its action on Article 47 of the Constitution of 1879, called the Véliko-Tarnovo,[46] at the same time allowing in Sabranié, the National Assembly, a legislative function and manifest control.

All of the administrations of this period relied on Article 47 in one way or another in order to govern. They were thus able, from 1934 on, to suspend the activities of certain political parties and organizations and limit public liberties, especially freedom of the press, which allowed them to forbid during the war the "antibolchevik propaganda," especially that directed against Stalin.[47]

Boris III, who, it must be emphasized, could not act alone according to the terms of Article 47, nevertheless benefited from it in order to fully exercise his powers by relying on the successive governments of one of his close friends, Gueorgui Kiosseivanov,[48] on the margins of more and more limited maneuvers as events accelerated.

To facilitate the adoption of government edicts and to give a more legitimate foundation to the regime, parliamentary elections were organized in March 1938, and the electoral law was modified. The right to vote was given to women, and the age of majority was lowered. The electoral districts were redrawn and reduced from 274 to 160 in a way that favored candidates "without a party" who ran on the slogan of "civil solidarity." These elections took place in a climate of violence and confrontation; the pro-government candidates carried out a campaign of "renewal of Bulgarian democracy, or of ridding the country of "partisan behavior," which, it is true, the country had suffered from for many years.

The government was able to unite a heterogeneous majority of ninety-seven seats against sixty-three for the opposition, but in the autumn of 1938, a motion of censure failed by only two votes.

In December 1939, in a very unusual international context since Nazi Germany had just invaded Poland, new elections were organized, after which the tsar dissolved the preceding assembly, as the constitution allowed him to do (Article 136). This time the government held a crushing majority of 140 seats. In February 1940 a new "government of technicians" was formed by a historian without political experience, Prof. Bogdan Filov. The executive power was even more concentrated in the hands of King Boris, whose power was reinforced by new laws such as "civil mobilization," which aimed at "preserving the population from spiritual and material pollution."[49]

In the autumn of 1940, a proposed law on "the protection of the nation"[50] was presented to the assembly and made public on October 21. The first part of this law had as its object the interdiction of "secret organizations." Articles 15 and 33 concerned "persons of Jewish origin" and the stripping away of their fundamental rights. They could not have Bulgarian nationality, had to pay exorbitant taxes, and were forbidden to practice certain professions.

The project immediately provoked great indignation in Parliament and among the population. Personalities such as the deputy Nikola Mouchanov, one of the leaders of the Democratic Party, opposed the proposal by denouncing it as anti-constitutional and contrary to national traditions.[51]

Situated in the heart of the Balkans, for many centuries Bulgaria experienced great ethnic and religious diversity. Bulgarians cohabitated especially with Turks, Greeks, Armenians, Jews, Tartars, and Valaques, with whom they kept up neighborly relations. This tolerance toward minorities was even written into and supported by the Constitution of 1879 (Articles 40, 57, and 82 particularly). Bulgaria had generally welcomed Armenians who fled the genocide perpetrated in Turkey at the end of the nineteenth and beginning of the twentieth century. Many Jews had come to find refuge on Bulgarian territory after their expulsion from Spain at the end of the fourteenth and beginning of the fifteenth century as well as at the end of the nineteenth century, when they fled the pogroms in Russia.

At the time of the census of 1934, Jews numbered 48,565. They enjoyed great autonomy, had their own schools, and were largely integrated into the social, cultural, and economic life.[52]

The announcement of this proposed law on "the protection of the nation" raised heated protests, and many petitions were presented to the National Assembly. According to the archives, which can be consulted in Paris, these came from groups of teachers and workers of Plovdiv,[53] adolescents and shopkeepers of Sofia,[54] or yet again from lawyers from the town of Vidin.[55] All of these protests expressed feelings on the part of the public of consideration for their fellow citizens of the Jewish faith, who, having shared the fate of the Bulgarian population since the Middle Ages, "its joys and sorrows," were deeply rooted in the country.

The association of Bulgarian doctors was indignant at the restrictive measures that were going to be imposed on Jewish colleagues, who were prevented from practicing their profession, and insisted they would "tarnish the reputation of Bulgaria."[56] The association of lawyers asked that the proposal be abandoned, for it was contrary to Article 60 of the constitution.[57] Many intellectuals also showed their opposition to the law, and the Saint-Synod addressed a letter of protest to the prime minister and to the deputies.[58]

Elsewhere, several newspapers of the extreme Right, such as *Ataka* (The Attack) or *Stoudenska douma* (The Word of the students), published anti-Semitic articles accusing the Jews of having committed exactions counter to the Bulgarians.[59] In spite of this, these incitements to racial hatred found very little response in the population.

It can also be noted that, according to these same archives, the Communist Party daily, *Rabonitchesko delo* (Workers' cause), cautioned prudence, and the Party distributed "calls to the population" in their favor.[60]

Despite all of these protests, the government and its parliamentary majority approved the law on December 24, 1940, promulgated by a decree of King Boris on January 21, 1941.

Once the repressive measures against the Jews were made legal, they were put into practice under pressure from Germany. An administration for Jewish questions was created in 1942, and its director, Alexandre Belev, set about preparing to confiscate Jewish property and organizing deportations to Poland. Yet it is important to note that this administration was limited in its action since it was part of the government and needed legal authorization to act. Since Bulgarian law was able to send back government decisions, and these actions were contested by the king, "the Bulgarian setup thus became an instrument adapted to stalling tactics, which the Germans did not immediately understand."[61]

Developed in 1942, a ruling on the nationalities of the populations of the "New Territories" refused to Jews what was authorized for Greek and Yugoslav inhabitants:[62] to obtain Bulgarian nationality if they did not show an intention to keep their nationality of origin and leave the territories.[63]

In February 1943, under strong German pressure, an accord was signed by Belev and Dannecker, the Gestapo representative in Bulgaria,[64] which planned the deportation of 8,000 Jews from Macedonia, 6,000 from Thrace, and 6,000 from Bulgaria.

This agreement laid out plans for the operation of trains leaving cities such as Skopje, Douptnitza, or Radomir with 1,000 persons per train, the Nazis billing the Bulgarians for transportation furnished by the Reichsbahn.[65] At the end of February and the beginning of March, the accord was implemented for the 11,343 Jews[66] of the New Territories, who were deported to the camp at Treblinka.

In the springtime of 1943, the dangers threatening the Jews of Bulgaria intensified, and the preparations for their deportation mobilized public opinion. In a petition forty-three deputies made known their refusal to support "the sending of Jews outside of Bulgaria."[67]

The Bulgarian Orthodox Church, through natives such as Stéphane de Sofia and Cyrille de Plovdiv, protested to King Boris.

The vice president of the National Assembly, Dimiter Pechev, made a request to the interior minister and offered a motion of censure accusing the government of atrocities. The motion was not adopted and he resigned. A little later an intervention "coming from high up" was carried out to suspend all deportation. The 6,000 Bulgarian Jews who then were supposed to leave were released.[68]

In a report of an interview dated April 4, 1943, Joachim von Ribbentrop emphasized that King Boris was ready to authorize deportation of Macedonian and Thracian Jews but that he was firmly opposed to the deportation of Jews living in Bulgaria.[69]

Caught in a stranglehold between the pressure from the Nazis, who insisted the deportations be carried out, on the one hand and the indignation of public opinion on the other, King Boris, on Belev's proposition,[70] decided to have 25,000 Jews transferred basically from the capital and the large cities to work camps in the provinces rather than deporting them to Poland. This decision was taken on the eve of the festival of Saints-Cyrille-et-Méthode, which celebrates the creation of Slavic writing, and the traditional parade that year was transformed into a protest against this new measure.[71]

After the Nazi defeats on the eastern front during the summer of 1943, Bulgaria found itself in an increasingly unsolvable situation and tried to establish contact with the Allies.

According to certain witnesses, Hitler was supposed to have asked Tsar Boris, without success, during an interview on August 14 to send Bulgarian troops to the Russian front.[72]

King Boris died suddenly in Sofia on August 28. Since his son, Siméon, was a minor, a Council of Regency was organized and approved by the Assembly, with no regard for the constitution (Chapter 6, Articles 25–33). This council was made up of the prime minister, Bogdan Filov; Prince Cyrille, brother of the dead king; and Nikola Mihov, a former war minister. The double unconstitutionality, the presence of a member of the royal family at the heart of the council and the approval of its formation instead of its election by the Assembly, were further symptoms of the gravity of the crisis throughout the country and in its government.

The developments of the war also weighed heavily on the political situation in the country. The government showed a willingness to give amnesty to the resistance, calling on them to give up their "illegal" activities while establishing a special militia (gendarmerie) in an attempt to halt guerilla activity, which was intensifying. The resulting toll on all sides was heavy; the civilian population suffered the most from fratricidal combats and the settling of scores between armed groups in addition to Allied bombardments of the large cities.

On June 1, 1944, the Bagrianov government, which had just been formed, began to distance itself from Germany and accepted several suggestions of a legal opposition established several months before. At that time Russian troops were at the doors of Bucharest.

On August 26 Bulgaria declared its "total neutrality" in the German-Soviet conflict while pursuing diplomatic steps with Great Britain.

On September 4 the new government formed by Constantin Mouraviev, which only lasted a few days, suspended all death penalties for partisans and proclaimed a general amnesty. It was also forced to dissolve the Assembly, outlaw extreme right-wing organizations, and repeal the "law of protection of the nation." In a final attempt he proceeded to reverse alliances, retracting the declaration of war against Great Britain and the United States and declaring war on Germany on September 6—on the fifth, however, the Soviet Union had declared war on Bulgaria, and its troops crossed the Danube three days later.

During the night of the eighth, a coup d'état was organized. The government was arrested and the Regency Council dissolved. A government of the "National Front" was formed, which included four Communist ministers. Bulgaria turned a page in its history and was to enter into the Soviet orbit.

A Recovered Identity?

The imperatives of Communist historiography in Bulgaria hid the question of genocide of the Jews in Europe and its particulars within the country.

Thus, even if under the entry "Jew" the 1963 encyclopedia does not give a special place to the Jewish genocide in Nazi crimes, it does recognize that during the Second World War, the Nazis assassinated around 6 million of them.[73]

The heading "Concentration Camp" does not exist. But a "prisoner of a concentration camp" is defined as "a political prisoner of a concentration camp, deprived of his rights and his liberty for an undetermined duration and without legal decision."[74] "Auschwitz" is defined as a southern city of Poland where Nazis had organized the largest concentration camp for a massive extermination of people, a "killing factory" where "4 million prisoners of all nationalities" died of disease and hunger and were gassed and burned.[75] "Buchenwald" is defined as a concentration camp where more than fifty-five thousand people of "different nationalities" died,[76] the entry adding that a monument was erected in this location in 1958 in memory of the "antifascists" who died there. Treblinka, the camp where the Jews of Macedonia and Thrace were exterminated, is not even mentioned.

It is also to be noted that, although until the 1980s at least, the history texts of the terminal classes devoted several chapters to the "antifascist struggle of the Bulgarian people" and of the Communist Party against "monarcho-fascism," it only mentioned in two lines the existence of the "law of the protection of the nation" without reporting any facts about its application in the country.[77]

The history of the repression against the Jews of the New Territories and of the rescue of Bulgarian Jews and the support offered them by the population still includes many facts that remain scarcely known in Bulgaria and the world.[78] Important documentation is kept in the Bulgarian archives.[79] A study of those papers could certainly shed new light on the exact role of King Boris and could clarify conditions under which the deportation of Jews of the New Territories was organized as well as the negotiations in 1943 between Bulgaria and Great Britain, the United States, and the Swiss for the emigration of Jews to Palestine. In a letter addressed to Ribbentrop, Grand Mufti Amin El-Hussein protested against the emigration and the transfer to Palestine of four thousand Jewish children accompanied by five hundred adults after Anglo-Bulgarian negotiations. Dated May 13, 1943, the same day Bulgarians had been mobilized to come to the aid of their Jewish compatriots, this letter explicitly asks Germany "to do all it could to have Bulgaria give up . . . the execution of the Judeo-Anglo-American plan."[80]

A more thorough study of little-known facts, such as the repression against Jewish Bulgarians, the deportation of those from Aegean Thrace and Vardar

Macedonia, and the reactions they stirred up in Bulgaria, will bring with
it new elements in the reassessment of the nature of the regime Bulgaria
on the eve of and during the Second World War. The return to this period
in Bulgarian history lies within a more general movement of rewriting the
history and a reconstruction of national identity. This task should extend to
all of Bulgarian history since, under Communism, it was the entire history
of the country that was manipulated to try to impose the scientific rigor of
historical materialism. But this task will certainly be made more complex by
a psychological resistance, particularly regarding those events of the Bulgarian
past that are still painful.

To the reticence of confronting the recent past of the Communist era is
added, as we have pointed out, the more passionate approach to the distant
past of the Ottoman occupation and its consequences, felt in the collective
memory to be "a history deferred," to use the words of François Thual.[81]

As has already been touched on, the traumatism of this thwarted history
is so tenacious that the memory of unhappiness suffered during this period
can even be found extended to a still earlier period, when the Bulgarian
kingdom fell under the influence of Byzantium during the Middle Ages and
was integrated into its empire for two centuries.

The journal *Kultura* published a "summary" of Bulgarian history as described by a child:[82] "First Bulgarian Kingdom, Byzantine enslavement! Second Bulgarian Kingdom, Turkish enslavement! Third Bulgarian Kingdom,
Communist enslavement!"[83]

This perception of a national history regularly punctuated by periods of
enslavement, and therefore of retreat, is very revealing of the imperatives
imposed on Bulgarian historians. To the range of their research task is added
the necessity of surmounting national emotions, cleverly encouraged in the
period of Communist historiography.

This is why in Bulgaria, contrary to other European countries, participation in the Shoah can appear to be minor; but it is also considered by
Bulgarians an imported event imposed by an international condition, a specific geopolitical position, which was not related to this mythic objective of
unification of "Bulgarian lands." There was no reference to anti-Semitism
in national traditions of the welcoming of minorities in general and Jews
in particular. Although Bulgaria was an ally of Hitler's Germany, Germany
did not gain the benefit of a society favorable to the implantation of anti-
Semitism.

The evocation of this attitude, which refers to a tradition of tolerance toward minorities, can today be considered valuable in Bulgaria, even if the Communist regime in its time had put it to the test in undertaking a policy of forced assimilation aimed at the Muslim minority.

The memory of Jewish genocide in Europe and of the attitude of the Bulgarian population can also seem to be an important element in the reconstruction of a national identity through this debate on totalitarianism and democracy.

Finally, and hopefully, it is useful to say here that, in the conflicts that affect the Balkan region today, Bulgaria can also appear a successful example of interethnic cohabitation.

Might not this image of a past recovered in all its dimensions be finally a determining factor that would help Bulgaria accomplish its integration into the democratic Europe to which it aspires?

Translated by Lucy B. Golsan

Notes

1. Fernand Braudel, preface to J. Szúcs, *Les Trois Europes*, Paris, L'Harmattan, 1985, p. 6.

2. Gueorgui, "68, 89, otsamnitchestvoto" (68, 89, with them and with us), *Kultura*, no. 33, August 21, 1998, p. 9.

3. *Petite Encyclopédie bulgare*, Sofia, Editions de l'Académie des Sciences, vol. 3, 1966, p. 369.

4. Dimitar Anguelov, *Vizantia vazhod i zalez na edna imperia*, Sofia, Editions of the University Kliment Ohridski, 1990.

5. Bulgaria was liberated from Ottoman rule after the Russo-Turkish War of 1878. The myth of the USSR is part of the continuum of deliverance by Russia.

6. The Treaty of San Stefano (today Yecilköy, in the Istanbul suburbs) of March 1878 ended the war between Russia and the Ottoman Empire and permitted independence for a "Great Bulgaria" of 164,000 square kilometers, headquarters for the Russian expansion in the region. In reaction to this Russian influence, the western powers who supported the other Balkan countries revived the Congress of Berlin (June–July 1878), which redivided the map of the Balkans and reduced by half the area of Bulgaria.

7. Ivan Ilchev, *La Science historique bulgare au cours des années 70–80: Histoire et pouvoir en Europe Médiane*, Paris, L'Harmattan, 1996, pp. 171–187.

8. Ludmila Jivkova, daughter of the secretary general of the Communist Party, Todor Jivkov, was from 1975 chief of the Committee for Culture and the Arts. This

238   *François Frison-Roche*

body was later renamed in 1977 the Committee for Culture, which directed and oversaw the ministers and organizations in the cultural sector, including the various "unions of intellectuals." She died suddenly in 1981.

9. Boris III, Bulgarian tsar (1894–1943), son and successor to Ferdinand I. He ascended the throne in 1918 after the abdication of his father. After Bulgaria joined the Axis in 1941, he authorized German troops to penetrate Bulgarian territory. He died of a heart attack in Sofia after returning from an interview with Hitler in Germany.

10. Nicolaï Gentchev, *Vanchnata politika na Balgaria, 1938–1941*, Sofia, Editions Vector, 1998, 190 pp.

11. Jeliou Jelev, *Le Fascism, État totalitaire*, Geneva, Editions Rousseau, 1990, 204 pp.

12. *Petite Encyclopédie bulgare*, vol. 3, p. 102.

13. Dimitar Kossev, Christo Christov, and Dimitar Anguelov, *Précis d'histoire de Bulgarie*, Sofia, Editions en langues étrangères, 1963; and Alexander Bourmov, Dimitar Kossev, and Christo Christov, *Istoria na Bulgaria*, Sofia, Editions Prosveta, 1967.

14. François Furet, "Un sujet tabou," in Furet and Ernst Nolte, *Fascisme et communisme*, Paris, Plon, 1998, p. 39.

15. Jelev, *Le Fascism*.

16. Ibid., pp. 178–183.

17. *Revue democratique*, no. 33, autumn 1997, pp. 660–681.

18. Nina Nikolova, "Imalo li e fachisim v Bulgaria?" *Kultura*, no. 18, May 5, 1995, p. 12.

19. Ivan Bojilov, Vera Mutaftchieva, Constantin Kossev, Andrei Pantev, and Stoïtchko Grentcharov, *Istoria na Balgaria*, Sofia, Editions Christo Botev, 1993, p. 653.

20. Nicolai Prodanov, "Sachtestvuva li 'fachistki périod' v évolutsiata na balgarskia istoriopis," *Revue démocratique*, no. 35, spring, 1998, pp. 217–231.

21. "Trudnosti c nasledstvoto," selections from a discussion on the theme "Symbol of Totalitarianism or Historical-Artistic Heritage?" *Kultura*, no. 13, March 27, 1992, pp. 4–5.

22. Vladimir Gradev, "Le mausolée de Dimitrov," *Communications*, no. 55, 1992, pp. 77–88.

23. Deyan Deyanov, "La Guerre des interprétations symboliques," *Communications*, no. 55, 1992, pp. 55–65.

24. Deyan Deyanov, "Outchebnitsité po istoria i obchtité mesta na pametta," *Kultura*, no. 18, May 5, 1995, p. 9.

25. Henry Rousso, "Pour une histoire de la mémoire collective: L'Après Vichy," *Les Cahiers de l' IHTP*, no. 18, June 1991, p. 168.

26. Bernard Lory, "La traversée du communisme en Bulgarie par quatre classes d'âge," *Balkanologie*, vol. 1, no. 3, December 1997, pp. 57–70.

27. Rousso, "Pour une histoire de la mémoire collective," p. 169.

28. Nina Nikolova, "Fachism ili nesastojalata se democratia," *Archiv: Buletin za grajdansko obrazovanie po istoria*, nos. 1–2, Sofia, 1996, pp. 15–25.

29. Liliana Deyanova, *Traumatic Places of Collective Memory, Balkan Transition*, Sofia, Access/BCN, 1997, pp. 85–89.

30. Andreï Boundjoulov, "Imalo li e fachism i antifachistka saprotiva v Bulgaria?" *Archiv*, pp. 39–49.

31. Marie-Claire Lavabre, *Le Fil rouge: Sociologie de la mémoire communiste*, Paris, Presses de la FNSP, 1994.

32. Jeliou Jelev, *Kraglata masa*, Sofia, Ed. Biblioteka 48, 1998, p. 170 [A report from stenograms of the negotiations of the Bulgarian Round Table of 1990].

33. Timothy Garton Ash, "Les Séquelles du passé en Europe de l'Est," *Esprit*, no. 246, October 1998, pp. 45–66.

34. Alain Brossat, "Perception et mémoire du 'socialism réel' en Europe central et orientale," *MSH informations*, no. 74, winter 1997–98, pp. 11–15.

35. "Enketa: Kakvo se slutchi c vas prez tési desset godini? Kakvo se slutchi c Bulgaria prez tési desset godini?" *Kultura*, no. 44, November 6, 1998, pp. 12–13.

36. Tsvetan Todorov, ed., *Au nom du Peuple, témoignage sur les camps dans les anciens pays communistes*, Paris, Editions de l'Aube, 1992; and Stéphane Botchev, *Béléné: Souvenirs du goulag bulgare*, Editions Noir sur Blanc, 1998.

37. Emilia Choucharova, "Za lagera v célo Kurtovo-Konaré," *Kultura*, no. 35, September 1, 1995, pp. 10–11.

38. Décision no. 2 of January 21, 1999 (*Journal officiel* du 29 janvier 1999, pp. 1–6).

39. This term designates the process begun in the eighteenth century that resulted in the conscious recognition of a national identity that, through the struggle against the Ottoman Empire and the desire for emancipation of the Bulgarian church from the Greek yoke, affirmed a national unity, a Bulgarian language and culture, and concluded with the formation of the Bulgarian nation, the essential objective—the independence of the country.

40. Few French works mention the fate of the Bulgarian Jews during the Second World War. See, however, Raoul Hilberg, *La Destruction des Juifs d'Europe*, Folio-histoire, Paris, Gallimard, 1997, pp. 643–655 (1st ed., Paris, Fayard, 1988); Magdaléna Hadjiisky, "Le Sauvetage des Juifs bulgares de la Shoah en 1943," *La Nouvelle Alternative*, no. 34, June 1994, pp. 54–56. In English one can consult Frederick B. Chary, *The Bulgarian Jews and the Final Solution, 1940–1944*, Pittsburgh, Pittsburgh University Press, 1972. On a more general level, see Esther Benbassa and Aron Rodrigue, *Juifs des Balkans: Espaces judéo-ibériques, XIVe-XXe siècles*, Paris, La Découverte, 1993.

41. Jeliou Jelev, *Bulgarie, terre d'Europe: La politique étrangère de la Bulgarie postcommuniste*, Paris, Editions Frison-Roche, 1998, pp. 113–114.

42. A Turkish word coming from the Arabic and signifying "people."

43. The exterior commerce of Bulgaria with Germany "in 1933 was still only 25% of its total trade, which grew to 48% in 1936, and to 70% during 1940–1942."

Simeon Angguelov, "La Bulgarie, un pays ayant le francais en partage," in *La Bulgarie en mutation, 1989–1999*, Editions Frison-Roche, forthcoming.

44. Hilberg, op. cit., p. 642.

45. Georges Castellan, *Histoire des Balkans XIVe–XXe siècles*, Paris, Fayard, 1991, pp. 450–453.

46. Article 47: "If the State is threatened by some interior or exterior danger and the National Assembly cannot be convened, then, and only then, the King can, on the presentation of the Council of Ministers and under their collective responsibility, publish edicts and take extraordinary measures that will have the same authority as laws. These edicts and these extraordinary measures will be submitted for the approval of the first National Assembly subsequently called into session."

47. Hilberg, op. cit., p. 655.

48. Gueorgui Kiosseivanov, prime minister from November 23, 1935, to February 16, 1940, was a career diplomat and former chief of the Chancellery of the Palace. He resigned officially for reasons of health and was named ambassador to Switzerland. His resignation was also interpreted as a taking over of affairs by Tsar Boris III.

49. Bojilov, Mutaftchieva, Kossev, Pantev, and Grantcharov, op. cit., pp. 656–679.

50. "Zakon za Zachita na Natziata" of December 24, 1940 (Archives of the Centre de Documentation Juive Contemporaine de Paris [CDJC], document ref. CDLXXIX-161), promulgated by Decree no. 3 of January 21, 1941.

51. Maya Nyagolova, *Le Sauvetage des Juifs bulgares pendant les années de la Second Guerre mondiale*, Editions Shalom, communauté des juifs de Bulgarie, 1993, p. 7.

52. Antonina Jeliaskova, "Les Minorités en Bulgarie," in *La Bulgarie en mutation, 1989–1999*.

53. Archives of the (CDJC) document ref. CDXXIX-116, 142.

54. Ibid., document ref. CDLXXIX-136.

55. Ibid., document ref. CDLXXIX-138, 139.

56. Ibid., document ref. CDLXXIX-130.

57. Ibid., document ref. CDLXXIX-131.

58. Ibid., document ref. CDLXXIX-133.

59. Ibid., document ref. CDLXXIX-127, 128.

60. Ibid., document ref. CDLXXIX-147, 150.

61. Hilberg, op. cit., p. 645.

62. Nyagolova, op. cit., p. 10.

63. Dimitar Yontchev, *Balgaria i bélomoriéto*, Sofia, Editions Dirum, 1993, p. 92.

64. Theodor Dannecker, chief of the Service IV-S at the heart of Sipo SD, responsible for the anti-Jewish service of the Gestapo in France, arrived in Bulgaria in January 1943.

65. Archives of the CDJC, document ref. CDLXXIX-175.

66. The figures differ according to the source. See Hilberg, op. cit., p. 653 n. 49.

67. Nyagolova, op. cit., p. 12.

68. Hilberg, op. cit., p. 653.

69. Archives of the CDJC, document ref. CXX-9a.

70. Hilberg, op. cit., p. 654.

71. Archives of the CDJC, document ref. LXX-105.

72. Bojilov, Mutaftchieva, Kossev, Pantev, and Grantcharov, op. cit., p. 717.

73. *Petite Encyclopédie bulgare*, vol. 2, p. 258.

74. Ibid., vol. 3, p. 124.

75. Ibid., vol. 4, p. 22.

76. Ibid., vol. 1, p. 318.

77. Bourmov, Kossev, and Christov, op. cit., p. 300ff.

78. Mentioned by the former president of the republic, Jeliou Jelev, in *Bulgarie, terre d'Europe*, pp. 113–117.

79. Bogidar Evtimov, "La Question juive en Bulgarie, 1940–1944," in *Les Archives de la Shoah*, Paris, L'Harmattan/CDJC, 1998, pp. 219–224.

80. Archives of the CDJC, document ref. CCXXVIII-14.

81. Francois Thual, *Le Douaire de Byzance: Territoires et identités de l'orthodoxie*, Ellipses-Marketing, 1998, p. 59ff.

82. Deyanov, "Outchebnitsité po istoria i obchtité mesta na pametta," p. 9.

83. Founded in 681, the "first Bulgarian kingdom" fell under the influence of Byzantium in 1018 and was integrated into the empire until 1186. A "second Bulgarian kingdom" was proclaimed in 1186, which was then invaded by the Ottoman Empire in 1396. Liberated in 1878, Bulgaria became a monarchy (the "third Bulgarian kingdom" for this child) from 1879 until the rise to power of the Communists.

Andrzej Paczkowski

Nazism and Communism
in Polish Experience and Memory

Poland is one of those nations that has behind it the experience of both Nazism and Communism. But these are not equal experiences, and society's memory of them is very different. If we could carry out experiments on the living body of history, in changing at will the course of events, perhaps we could obtain an equal effect for a short fragment of the most recent history, for the period that stretches from mid-September 1939 to June 1941, during which time the partitioning of Poland between two totalitarian nations was consummated, one "brown" and the other "red." To do that, however, we would have to "stop history" in June 1941. But since this is not possible, the distinctions that influenced and continue to influence the different memory of these two experiences once more become important.

The Nazi Experience and the Memory of Evil

The Nazi occupation was incredibly brutal and bloody, even outside the Holocaust and even if we restrict ourselves to Polish "ethnics," though that is not really justified. Truthfully up to the present, there have been no statistically reliable figures, but in general it is held that no less than 1.5–2 million Poles (and more than 2.5 million Jewish Poles) died at the hands of the Germans and as a result of war actions carried out by them. In Warsaw from October 1943 to July 1944, at least 8,000 people were shot, which means that (on average) 25 people died each day. The losses for the armed resistance for the period from the autumn of 1939 to July 1944 (until the explosion of the Warsaw insurrection) in territory occupied by the Germans alone are estimated at around 60,000–70,000 people. In the years 1940–44 around 100,000 people a year were sent to concentration camps. In the autumn of 1939, the evacuations of populations from occupied countries to the Third Reich had begun, and during the first six months, 400,000 were deported. At the same time, the "roundups" began and also the deportations to forced labor camps. In the summer of 1944, around 1.3 million Polish slaves were working in the Third Reich. It is superfluous, no doubt, to continue this enumeration of atrocities, even though these examples are far from exhausting a list that should also include such acts as the expatriation of children (according to some calculations around 200,000) or the exactions carried out in particular against the intelligentsia, from priests and landowners to schoolteachers and professors. In certain professions of the intelligentsia, the losses were as much as one-third.

Although the experiences of the years from 1939 to 1944 were terribly tragic, the Warsaw massacre—first of the population (180,000) and after that the crushing of the Warsaw uprising and the burning of the city, house after house—constitutes in a sense the final act of Polish martyrdom.

It is evident then that Nazism was a traumatizing experience as much on the individual level as the collective. And since from 1941 all the lands inhabited by the Poles were occupied by the Germans, this experience is common to a great majority of the population. It is therefore a national experience lived by 20 million Poles. Those who did not experience it may perhaps number a million, some tens of thousands who in 1939 and 1940 managed to escape into Allied countries, as well as the hundreds of thousands who found themselves in distant parts of the Soviet Union before the German-Soviet war, where they suffered various forms of oppression.

Although a very extreme nationalist right wing had existed in Poland before the war, and the admirers of the Hitlerian model of political efficiency were not lacking (in reality Mussolini was more often the one admired), the experience of Nazism was seen largely as an occupation experience. No important personality and no political group decided to collaborate with the Third Reich. It is difficult to evaluate this absence of political collaboration because the Nazis in Poland did not in fact look for forces ready to collaborate, nor did they try to create such groups. Only one attempt, in 1939 by a fraction of a party of the extreme Right (ONR-Falanga), was ended after several weeks because its members were arrested. The only political figure known to have presented a memorandum to the Germans, an old Germanophile politician known since the First World War (Wladyslaw Studnicki), found himself under house arrest. Only one known journalist (Emil Skiwski) undertook a long-range collaboration, and that only when Goebbels launched the defensive slogan of *Fortress Europe*. The extreme right-wing parties, like all the others, were considered a conspiratorial opposition by the Nazis and were persecuted as forcefully as the others. This state of affairs did not change when, in January 1945, the Soviet army crossed the line of the Vistula. There was only one of the extreme-right formations of the resistance (la Brigade Swietokrzyska) that left for the West under the cover of the Wehrmacht in retreat, thus arriving in Czechoslovakia and, according to plan, arriving in territories controlled by the American army.

In the memory of the Poles and in terms of the realities of the war years, Poland was the only nation not to be tainted by collaborating with the Nazis. Without mentioning the regimes of Vichy, of Quisling, of the Walloon, or the Flemish or Latvian Waffen ss, let us point out that even among neighbors to the east, Ukrainians, Byelorussians, and Lithuanians, certain political groups of influence and importance had (even before the war) counted on the Third Reich to protect them in their struggle against Poland and against the Soviet Union. The occupying German powers offered them certain possibilities of action (for example, the Ukrainian ss Division "Halitchina" or the Lithuanian troops of General Plechavicius). Even the Russians had a general, Andriej Vlassov, with armed troops who fought beside the Wehrmacht; and on occupied Polish territory also, hundreds of thousands of Soviet citizens of various nationalities served in secondary units.

The Nazis were perceived exclusively in terms of a brutal occupier, and Polish condemnation of the Occupation was therefore absolute and unequivocal. It was accompanied by an unassailable hatred and a desire for revenge. Although after the defeat of the Third Reich there were almost never acts of summary judgment on a grand scale, and the deportation of Germans (more than 2 million) took place without demonstrations, tens of thousands applauded, at least a few times, at public executions of war criminals. Some of the executions were carried out by former prisoners of concentration camps dressed in their striped uniforms from the camps.[1]

In general Poland appears not only as an innocent victim but, because of its martyrdom and lack of collaboration, as saintly in its suffering. Moreover the Poles are universally convinced that Poland was not only badly treated by Nazism (then by Communism) but also *betrayed* by its allies—and at least twice. The first time was in 1939, when neither the French nor the English lifted a finger to help them in their struggle against the Third Reich. The second time was at Yalta, when Poland was "abandoned" to Stalin. And yet it was Poland—and this is widely emphasized—who, alone at the side of Great Britain, struggled from the first to the last day against Nazism on dozens of fronts, the bloodiest of which was the resistance.

This opinion, with a few small variations, is still widespread today. The Poles are proud of their participation in the war, convinced they suffered the worst losses. They do not like to say—or to hear—that the saintly image could be tarnished in spots. To this day there has been no monograph on the "daily collaboration" that was necessary, however, in order to survive. Railroad conductors drove German trains, workers worked in German factories, shopkeepers sold products to the Germans, and prostitutes practiced their trade equally (and perhaps especially) with officers of the Wehrmacht. Journalists—certainly not numerous but they existed nevertheless—wrote for German papers published in Poland. And a few rare performers acted in vaudeville despite a boycott. For these acts spectators, also ignoring the boycott, were not lacking. It was the same with movie audiences or with those who read the press, which, however, was under the control of the enemy. To this day only one monograph has been written on the Polish police, a security service that more than once found itself assigned missions going beyond the simple pursuit of thieves, such as lending assistance during the roundups, the pacification of the countryside, and the deportation of Jews to the ghettos. There exists no systematic study of those who denounced hidden Jews to the Germans, nor about those who used the threat of denunciation for lucrative ends, nor on the way the Poles appropriated the possessions of Jews sent to ghettos, nor on the pillaging of abandoned houses and stores. There are no studies on the denunciations to the German police (Gestapo, Kripo, Sipo, and others) of "suspect" persons who gathered in apartments, participants in the resistance, or the peddlers of clandestine newspapers, and these were so thoroughly carried out that the commander of the Army of the Interior, General Rowecki, was arrested thanks to Poles who were secret collaborators with the Germans. People denounced each other to hurt a neighbor they disliked or to have access to his belongings. There is no study of the banditry that proliferated enormously during the war. War is often a period of profound social transformations: certain groups lose, while others gain. Among those who gain are the ones who accumulated the profits of doing business with the Nazis, those who agreed to become stewards of properties, and those who speculated and practiced corruption with the occupiers. No one has written on this subject.

No publication has appeared on what happened after the war to those who denounced others, to the police, or to the Polish collaborators with the Gestapo, although a part of them had been condemned by the courts to prison sentences or to a cessation (partial or temporary) of the practice of their profession by professional organizations.

Certainly we can say that these omissions are made by historians, and there is a large part of truth in this. Polish historians rarely study social history and rarely do they write "micro-history," especially sensitive to problems of behavior and attitudes. The real reasons are found elsewhere. Historians, contrary to their vocation as intellectuals, react in the same fashion as society in general. Since the Poles (as no doubt most nations) do not like to hear talk of what was hateful or unworthy in their past, historians do not like to talk about it, or perhaps they do it only half-heartedly.

Postwar events also had an influence on all that made for the complexity of questions about the war and the Occupation, those that concerned negative phenomena (for example, denunciations and anti-Semitism), and those considered positive (for example, the resistance and participation in the fighting). It is difficult to treat them here in an exhaustive fashion, which would require a much larger study, and that is why I will just mention them here.

In the forefront, no doubt, we find the official version (Communist) of the past imposed by the medias, controlled and directed by the central power; by the propaganda; and by the schools. One of the essential elements of this version was the denigration of the military efforts of the resistance other than those of the Communists themselves. Beginning in 1944, the official propaganda claimed that the Army of the Interior and the other armed organizations that were non-Communist acted on behalf of the Third Reich, uttering direct accusations of collaboration against them. Between the years 1940–50, during the period of the intensification of the Sovietization and Stalinization of Poland, death sentences were pronounced against officers and activists of the resistance for their presumed collaboration with the occupiers.

These were less-than-effective campaigns of persuasion on the part of those in power. As a consequence, however, especially in social or family transmission, public opinion glorified not only the supposed collaborators but also the attitudes of the whole nation.

When Communism became entrenched and the process of acceptance of the system was well under way, people began to insist on "the moral and political unity of the nation." It was at that time in the interest of those in power to emphasize the elements of solidarity and to point out the universal participation in the struggle against the occupier and the dignity with which the Poles endured this terrible occupation. The attitude toward the non-Communist resistance changed. What was now emphasized was much more the enormity of the losses and the moral values of the entire nation, which united opposed the invader.

Another change occurred in the insistence that Nazi crimes be more emphasized in official propaganda and in public opinion. This of course was normal for a Polish nation that found itself under Soviet occupation. To emphasize Nazi crimes was a way of suppressing the memory of what had happened in the years 1939–41 and 1944–45 to the east of Poland. The more impossible it became to speak of these events, the more loudly one spoke of the nightmare of the German occupation.

Other important campaigns of persuasion, which influenced as much the memory of the recent past as the ways of describing the war and the Occupation, derived from the fact that one of the most important elements in legitimizing the Communist system was the feeling of danger from the Germans, linked to the conviction, constantly reinforced, that only the neighboring Soviet Union could protect Poland from a vengeful Germany. This reinforced not only the conviction of the enduring hostility of Germany for Poland but also the constant effort to recall Nazi crimes and, finally, the notion that the nation had united and was unwavering in its opposition to the Nazi occupant. These perspectives never wavered, even with the creation of the GDR, although minor shifts did occur as a result that helped change what was emphasized. Since a German Communist state existed, a state peaceful and democratic by definition, it became more difficult to speak of crimes committed by Germans in general. Poles were confronted with a kind of "Marxization" of the German problem that had to be resolved in terms of classes: in the east were the good Germans because they were progressive; in the west, the bad Germans, reactionaries, heirs of Nazism, even more-or-less camouflaged Hitlerians. This nuance is easily detectable in the changed name of the institution charged with the pursuit of war criminals: the original name spoke of "German crimes," but later it was changed to "Hitlerian crimes." Yet even during the times when relations between Communist Poland and the FRG were relatively good, principally for economic reasons, a strong anti-German attitude was always present.

Most historians who studied contemporary history were in agreement with these tendencies. In the first postwar years, they devoted themselves to analyses of losses and with those caused by the Third Reich exclusively. Although I am not a demographic specialist, in reading these works I cannot help noticing the many imprecisions in terminology and the lack of clear definitions in discussions of demographic losses. Were the historians speaking of Poles ("ethnic") or citizens of the multiethnic prewar Polish state? It is not easy either to know which losses are being discussed because nowhere in the studies based on the comparison of the census taken in 1931 and that of 1946 is it clear which losses were the work of which occupant. They were all attributed uniquely to the Germans.

Following these initial studies, research is more often and more completely concerned with resistance movements, although research about non-

Communist resistance groups did not begin until after 1956, and even then with numerous biases operating. These biases consisted of comparing "the reactionary elite" (the Army of the Interior command and the leaders of the Republic of Poland in London) with the "patriotic masses of soldiers," or of ignoring or completely distorting the activities of the right-wing resistance. These biases continued to hold sway when even the spectrum of legitimate organizations was widened and the national, even nationalist, tradition made its presence felt. This occurred in the middle of the 1960s in relation to the activity of the partisan group of the Communist Party (under General Miczar). The consistent efforts to insert nationalist elements into Communism led, by force of circumstances, to the consolidation of the social memory that the collectivity accepted the most easily: the conviction of its own innocence. The great majority of historians supported these tendencies, some out of simple opportunism, others from an ideological viewpoint because they were nationalists or felt uncomfortable in the corset of "proletarian internationalism," others finally felt that it allowed them to express, however limited in scope, a part of the truth about the Second World War.

For society as a whole, problems linked to the war and the Occupation became less and less important. This resulted from, among other things, not only the natural rhythm of the generations (fewer and fewer Poles remembered the war personally) but also from an "overemphasis" on Nazis crimes. In certain groups the "boomerang effect" could be observed. The official version was too often expressed and with too much insistence. With the weakening of social control, it also became easier and easier to ask—of oneself or of others within limited circles, of course—if the war or the Occupation was uniquely a Polish-German conflict and a betrayal by the Anglo-Saxons.

Whatever the circumstances the Nazi experience was above all, and no doubt exclusively, an existential experience, one of life or death. The German occupation did not constitute an intellectual challenge except as a study of the questions of the evil that exists in human beings. Yet even in this case, the issue was the evil of others, of the foreigner, the enemy. The question of the state of the Polish "National Soul" did not necessarily follow from this question. "Evil is not us" was always (and still is) the most frequent response. The moral dilemmas, especially the dilemma of collaboration, were pushed to the edges of consciousness, and even perhaps beyond the subconscious into nonbeing. This is also reinforced by the natural tendency to remove from memory anything that is bothersome. Too, and largely due to the intellectual elite, this is because of the fact that, after the war and the Occupation, a majority (no doubt a crushing one) of Poles were introduced into a system that the nation had not chosen itself, a system against which it had strongly resisted for several years. This system had established a false settling of scores with the recent past that was both selective and unjust. This did not encourage self-evaluation and self-criticism.

The First Communist Experience and the Forbidden Memory

The first encounter of the Polish people with Communist power, that is, with a state founded on Communist ideology, took place just after the creation of the Soviet Union in the years 1919–20. The crucial encounter, which had the greatest influence on social attitudes and consequently on the national memory, was the Red Army offensive in the summer of 1920, which was defeated with great difficulty. This campaign began with the famous appeal of Tonkhatchevski, "Pass over the body of Poland to go toward the heart of Europe," but it also included the efforts of the Provisional Polish Revolutionary Committee (with the participation of Feliks Dzierzynski). Thus began a weak and happily short-lived attempt to transfer to Polish territory the methods of the Russian Civil War: the executions, the expropriations, the Tcheka, and the "brain washing."

On September 17, 1939, when Soviet divisions crossed the frontiers of Poland, the memory of this episode was reawakened, although Lenin was not there to call the Polish proletariat to revolution. This time the "Polish proletariat" along with the "Polish lords" were the enemy. The Soviet occupation of 1939–41 can be compared to the German occupation in the same years, at least from the point of view of Polish "ethnics." In four waves of massive selective deportations, 350,000 persons were sent to the backwaters of Russia, and from all reports these deportations were harder to endure than the German ones.

Poles expelled from territories annexed by the Third Reich found themselves with their compatriots in central Poland. They remained in the same climate and in a familiar environment. Those deported from territories annexed by the USSR ended up on the steppes of Kazakhstan or in the taiga of the Komi Republic. They found themselves among other deportees and surrounded by a totally strange and hostile physical environment. The mortality rate in the convoys and in the lodgings was very high, more than that of the non-Jewish population under the German occupation.

Besides these four waves, there were other deportations on a smaller scale and not as far, though always to foreign lands. They included, according to the estimates, at least 50,000 people. The young people were forcibly enrolled in the Red Army, tens of thousands of prisoner-soldiers were attached to forced-labor groups, the same number left to work—more or less voluntarily—in the Donbass mines.

On March 5, 1940, the Political Bureau of the Central Committee of the Bolshevik Communist Party decided to execute 25,000 persons, of whom 14,700 were prisoners and internees. Although this order was not entirely carried out, for reasons still unknown today, it did result in the execution of 21,900 people, of whom 4,400 were executed in the Katyn Forest. Most of them belonged to various groups of the intelligentsia. These were not the only executions. During the retreat after the German offensive of June 1941, 10,000 prisoners were assassinated, most of whom had not been condemned to death or even accused according to the "paragraph" that set out this punishment. Around 100,000 Poles passed through the prisons, many of them serving their sentences in the hundreds of "islands" of the Gulag archipelago.

Experiences of daily life were tragic too. Factories of every size were nationalized and the same took place with landed property. Artisans had to "enroll" in cooperatives; classes in the schools were taught in Russian or Ukrainian. All of the newspapers and media organizations were suppressed; directors of the NKVD controlled everything, everyone, and were present everywhere in a much more "hermetic" way than the Gestapo. Commodities were suddenly missing from the stores and food from the markets. In 1941 preparations for collectivization began and arrests and deportations spread terror.

Certainly most Polish Communists were ready to collaborate, but Moscow did not seek out their services. Although posts not occupied by people from Kiev, Minsk, or Moscow were passed down to them, there was no question of a Polish Soviet Socialist Republic that could have governed along with them. Stalin had resolutely rejected the German propositions, certainly imprecise, of creating a Polish semi-rubber-stamp state.

Therefore, in many crucial respects, such as the extent and nature of the repression, Soviet occupation was not very different from that of the Germans. The system of occupation was certainly different. Participants included not only those who came from the USSR and Polish Communists but also Ukrainians, Jews, and Byelorussian locals. Moscow had also allowed a certain margin of flexibility in the cultural domain, which attracted a group of writers, artists, and scientists. The former prime minister Kazimierz Barlel, a professor at the Polytechnic School of Lvov, continued to hold his chair. Although the University of Lvov was "Ukrainized," most of the professors were kept in their posts (the Third Reich had eliminated all the advanced schools and deported a part of the faculty at Sachsenhausen). The barriers between the occupiers and the occupied were not as visible as "under the Germans," which resulted in a linguistic proximity. Despite these differences, the feeling of being truly occupied was unanimous among the Polish population.

It was an experience of *Communist occupation* that, just as in the case of Nazism, was considered a foreign body, an enemy. While occasionally some forms of adaptation were evident, they had a passive character, although the occupier leaned more and more toward Sovietization of the local population and of all nationalities and religions. It undertook actions that had no equivalent in the German occupation system. Children had to sing Soviet songs at school, workers were supposed to participate in political meetings, those who lived in towns were to take part in the May Day marches, and the peasants took part in ceremonies for the delivery of conscripts. "Elections" were even organized in which participation was practically obligatory and in which everyone had to vote for a single list without crossing out names. Special services and trusted persons in the commissions that counted the votes oversaw the elections. One Polish observer estimated in 1941 that society began to adapt to the new conditions, as more and more informers in the population materialized (and not only in the Communist groups) as well as those who were ready to conform to everything.

The Soviet occupation of 1939–41 concerned a minority of Poles, only one-fifth of the Polish population lived in the territories incorporated into the USSR. For a great number of those who "lived" the Soviet experience, the terror of the NKVD was largely exceeded by the German terror and, in most of the territories of the east, by the bloody and drastic "ethnic purification" carried out by Ukrainian majorities. It is a paradox that many Poles had welcomed the "second entry" of the Red Army as a liberation from the terror of Ukrainian battalions, while the Polish battalions of local self-defense forces received a formal designation as *istribitielnyje bataliony NKVD*. Furthermore, during the transfer of populations undertaken in the autumn of 1944, most inhabitants abandoned their "little countries" to follow the exodus toward former German territories.

There was no subject in Communist Poland (and this since the beginning of its existence) more under official taboo than the affair of the extermination of Polish officers, internees, and prisoners of the deportation and the gulags. It was permanently present in the collective conscience, but for a long time it was ruled out in conversation groups and in the most intimate exchange of confidences. The word "Katyn" was repressed to such an extent in public vocabulary that, for a certain time, it was completely eliminated. There was not even an attempt to put the blame on the Germans. Kazakhstan and Siberia were spoken of in an enigmatic way when, from deepest Russia, came Polish soldiers being celebrated and honored as fellow soldiers of the Red Army and founders of the Polish Popular Army. The fate of Poles under Soviet occupation was mentioned only in the emigrant press, and these texts got into Poland only with the greatest difficulty and in small quantities. It was still possible to count on news from Radio Free Europe, while official radio broadcasts from Voice of America or the BBC, influenced by English politics, rarely mentioned these things.

This experience was less universal than that of the Nazi occupation in as much as, since 1944, it foundered on a forbidden memory. As a consequence, for many years it became a lost memory. Then with the appearance of a line of independent (and clandestine) publishing and with the sudden social and political awakening that followed the creation of Solidarity, a reconstruction of this memory, dynamic and beyond the control of those in power, was undertaken on a massive scale. During this period the mention of the experience constituted an element of deligitimatizing the Communist system that, in the Polish context, was founded on "the lie of Katyn." Actually, accusing the Third Reich of the crime in 1943 had given Stalin an excuse to break relations with the legal Polish government (in London) and to construct an alternative center of power, an embryo of the Communist state. Formerly, especially in 1945–46, the trauma felt by the Poles following the two entries of the Red Army (1939 and 1944) made up, along with the activity of the National Security Services and terrorism, one of the elements of the system of terror that was itself an essential element of the attempt of those in power to subjugate society. It can be advanced, therefore, that paradoxically, the "forbidden memory of this experience" served Polish Communism well and facilitated the exercise of power.

Communism in Poland and Memory Divided

As previously noted, these two experiences were, in spite of the signs of adaptation and the phenomena of collaboration, above all experiences of an occupied nation, and therefore, in a way, both were "exterior" to it. Furthermore it is clear that the experience of the Nazis was primary and unique. But though there was recourse during the years of Communist Poland to reference a permanent threat of revenge and a possible reemergence of a

German neo-Nazism, even those who created the propaganda no doubt did not completely believe in a return of Nazism nor in the possibility of the creation in Germany of a "Hitlerian state without Hitler." It was otherwise with Communism.

One can say that the real experience of Communism began only with its actual establishment in Poland. The fact that it was "established," or (as it is often asserted) "brought in on Soviet tanks," had a considerable influence on how it was perceived and installed. Although the degree of autonomy in Communist Poland varied during the forty-five years it existed, with a general tendency toward enlarging this autonomy beginning in 1956, it nevertheless remained a Soviet satellite. It was not only dependent on an ideological plan, and equally on an economic or military plan, but also, without the help of the power of the Soviet Empire, it could not have been maintained. The following question is therefore extremely pertinent: Was this Communism in Poland or was it Polish Communism?

Certainly many historians, political scientists, and Polish journalists summarily describe the state of dependence on Moscow in terms of an "occupation." But even these are conscious of the fact that, even if one dismissed members of the Communist Party as collaborators, there were still several million Poles who cooperated with the occupier. One must therefore speak of a very particular form of occupation, perhaps even an "auto-occupation." Even if this expression seems (more than) paradoxical, it takes into consideration, at least in part, a certain state of things in Poland from 1944 to 1989 and of a state of mind of a portion of the Polish population.

Moreover, during the first years, the real state of affairs justified this opinion. In 1944–45 a Soviet army of several million men was stationed on Polish territory. In the days following Yalta, its soldiers and officers behaved well, as often happens in occupied territory in countries exposed to violence and pillaging. Independent units of NKVD armies, made up of at least 15,000–20,000 men, spent time in Poland. Later the Soviet Northern Army Group, which had more than 100,000 men, was stationed in Poland, and Soviet advisers and officers were present in all the structures of the security apparatus and the army (between 1949 and 1956 the minister of national defense was a Soviet marshal—also Polish—Konstantin Rokossowski). After 1956 the physical presence of Moscow became more discrete, but armies in Poland had at least twice (1956 and 1980–81) been ready for a direct intervention.

In the years 1944–56 the opinion that Poland was an occupied country was widespread among the population, indeed even preponderant. It is true that no public-opinion poll exists for this time, but thanks to a knowledge of the results of a referendum of June 30, 1946, we know that the Communist Party, with its three allied parties and various "transmission belts," even if they held a crushing majority because of their propagandizing and apparatus of repression, hardly garnered a total of more than one-quarter of the votes. There were not many (even among the Communists) who believed themselves able to sustain commands without the presence in Poland of Soviet armies and without the country being kept in a military stranglehold, for there were at least a half million elite troops stationed in the Soviet zone at that time.

To try to summarize the problem that interests us here, I will risk a hypothesis. It seems justifiable to summarize Polish attitudes toward Communism (Polish? In Poland?) as consistently of four principal types: *resistance* (or *rejection*), *adaptation*, *acceptance*, and *approval*.

As with all attempts at rapid typology, this surely possesses more faults than virtues. But it does allow a demonstration of a certain differentiation and a dynamic of change, for—and this is my second hypothesis—these attitudes do not organize themselves in a chronological succession ("resistance" first, then "adaptation," and so on), but they appear simultaneously; only what is dominant changed. It was first one and then the other attitude that dominated. It would be altogether false to say that it is possible to present in a precise and dependable way the proportions of each attitude at different periods. We are in fact condemned—which often happens to historians and not just to those who study contemporary history—to calculations. In any case this is true concerning the period up until 1980, when serious and representative studies of this problem were first undertaken.

While I am conscious of a major simplification, I would nevertheless put forward the following conclusions.

In the beginning, *the attitude of resistance and rejection* prevailed. It was embodied in an armed and clandestine resistance, and at the same time, it was openly given voice by legal political forces, first and foremost by the Polish Peasant Party. On a national scale, alongside this attitude of resistance—and perhaps equal to it—the attitude of adaptation also made itself felt in efforts to secure social footholds, to meet daily material needs, to assure the future of children and the security of the family, and to pursue a profession. From 1947 the legal and clandestine suppression by force of the opposition movement and a growing feeling of impotence in the face of the power of the system led to the transformation of the opposition, which went from collective action (participation in partisan battalions, clandestine groups, or opposition parties) to stands taken by individuals in opinions presented in very limited circles. This included reading forbidden books or listening to foreign radio broadcasts. Even though there were always individual acts of opposition, they were dispersed and tended to diminish. This contributed to the development of attitudes of adaptation that, with time, became dominant. Although it was difficult to evaluate the influence of the Catholic Church, it seems that its activity in pastoral as well as social functions encouraged adaptation rather than resistance. The appeals for the defense of the faith and of the church were not absent, especially in 1945–47 or in the dramatic *non possumus* of the primate Wyszynski in 1953. Yet the church never called for uprisings or for civic obedience. It had in fact adopted a tactic of survival and applied it even during open conflicts with the government. This was the way it functioned at the time of the *Kulturkampf* of Gomulka from 1958 to 1968.

It is equally possible to put forth the hypothesis that, after 1956 and the triumphant return to power of Wladyslaw Gomulka, the *attitude of acceptance* was quickly propagated. It was manifested by, among other things, the rapid increase in the number of adherents to the Communist Party, which from 1960 to 1970 doubled the number if its members. This shift was facilitated by the distance taken by Gomulka in relation to crimes of the Stalinist period and by the emphasis placed on the notion of national sovereignty, even though this was sovereignty in name only. The attempts to implant in official ideology more and more elements of national tradition, indeed even of nationalist motifs, came within the framework of a "Polonization" of the system.

The spontaneous demonstrations of resistance (1956, 1968, 1970, and 1976) in the form of strikes, street demonstrations, and confrontations with the police (militia) do not, I would argue, call into question the proof of the widespread but not universal support for an attitude in favor of acceptance of the regime. This is supported by the fact that between these uprisings, the "social silence," which is a symptom of adaptation and/or acceptance, continued.

The *attitude of resistance* (of rejection) on a massive scale took an important turn for the better beginning with the end of the 1970s and reaching national dimensions after the creation of Solidarity. The repressions that can be associated with a state of war greatly reduced its size, but the seed of resistance-revolt had taken hold and was a sentiment widely shared until 1989. It was a visible component of the social and political situation.

I have not yet mentioned *the attitude of adhesion*, though not because I deny its existence or overlook it. It certainly deserves special attention, if only because it was an attitude that characterized the majority if not the totality of those in the category one could label, following George Orwell, the "interior party" as well as persons concentrated in the top institutions of power (the security services, officers, and others). Sincere approval was, I think, more widespread in the years when the Communist Party linked its capacity to mobilize and motivate to a vision of revolution and social utopia. Also, later, when other factors of legitimization were advanced, hundreds of thousands of Poles actively and with conviction supported the system and, even more, believed in the ideals on which it was founded. This does not belie the fact that even in the highest echelons of the apparatus of power and the party there were cynical technicians of power who made ritualistic declarations and carried out ritual actions, using ideology as a shield and as a painful but useful instrument.

All of this does not mean that "mixtures" of these attitudes was impossible, especially for neighboring attitudes (resistance-adaptation, affirmation-acceptation), or for "turncoat" individuals, passing from one extreme to the other.

The debate over decisive factors determining proportions of these attitudes/types would be too long. To take the shortest route, I will mention these factors in two sequences, which does not mean that their results cancel out each other. To the contrary, certain factors were often reinforced by others belonging to the same group. These groups are obviously not exhaustive, but rather examples.

Positive factors of legitimization:

The social rise of numerous groups traditionally neglected, which provoked a strong feeling of loyalty toward the system as such, as much with the direct beneficiaries as in the milieu that formerly deliberated on their fate.

The leveling of differences between social groups that resulted as well as the creation of a society relatively homogeneous, which for many was a value in itself independent of Marxist-Leninist convictions or the lack thereof.

The industrialization and urbanization of a country of retarded development, which was widely viewed as a process of modernization leading to technological development and growth.

The power of persuasion of the ideology as well as the great efficiency of some of the efforts at legitimization, which depended largely on the demonstration of the efficiency of the power of the Communist Party.

The argument, endlessly repeated, that Communism alone guaranteed Poland the support of the USSR linked to the conviction that the division of the world into two camps would last.

The factors of oppression:

The period of terror that lasted a little more than ten years (1944–55), including an intense, massive, and generalized terror (1949–54). More than 15,000 people were victims (killed, executed, or died in prison); no less than 200,000–250,000 persons were sent to prison.

For many years this system of terror effectively terrorized a majority of the population. Moreover it eliminated a part of the existing and potential elite, a possible alternative to the Communist rulers.

During this same period the construction of an immense system for controlling the population was created, consisting of networks of agents, the censorship of letters, wiretapping, personnel services, and the development of Communist Party cells in all institutions and enterprises.

An efficient apparatus of professional promotion (the nomenklatura) and of forced dependence of citizens on the state, notably through a general nationalization of industry and commerce, was implemented along with the development of a bureaucracy and the unification of all social organizations.

Despite the changes after 1956, the Communist system did not give up any of these institutions of terror, control, promotion, and dependence, and although terrorism per se was limited, the other elements of oppression, control, and surveillance were reinforced.

Thus a majority of Poles remember the period 1944–55 as the *Stalin trauma*, either because they were victims of extortion or because they knew of victims firsthand. Fear for their lives, their social position, the future of their children, and their possessions (painfully accumulated by past generations) taught them submission and urged them to conform. During the years following (1956, 1968, 1970, 1976, 1981, and so on), hundreds of thousands of strikers and demonstrators knew the power and intransigence of the apparatus of repression (several hundred dead, thousands wounded, and tens of thousands arrested and fired from their jobs). They knew that if the need arose, the government would not hesitate to call out the army. Feelings of humiliation and powerlessness were widespread as much in cases of street confrontations with superior forces as in daily life, especially in businesses and administrations. The clear and unique question then remains unanswered: Why did the Poles rebel and why so often?

It is also important to remember that not everyone rebelled. Even worse, those who crushed the rebellions were Poles (and one should not forget that opinions very close to anti-Semitism were widespread concerning the role of the Jews or persons having Jewish origins who were linked to the establishment and maintenance of Communism). This is where the problem of the Poles with Communism lies. Actually the relationship cannot be explained simply through recourse to words like "foreigners," "NKVD agents," "janizaries," or "traitors." The Poles played the role of victim and executioner, of administrator and comrade (*kleines parteigenossen*), of the "for" and the "against," of those who won and those who lost, and of resistors (in acts and words) and informers. This state of affairs lasted more than four generations. Several generations and thousands of Poles found themselves on both sides. It is difficult to say today with certainty which side prevailed. Without doubt the most numerous were those who chose the strategy of adaptation and formed part of what is generally called the "silent majority."

It is no doubt surprising that this division still exists today, ten years after the defeat of true socialism. It has appeared in the political options available, in attitudes toward the past and its symbols—for example, the anniversaries, the monuments, the heroes—and also in attitudes toward the present. It derives largely from the position occupied before 1989. According to a recent public-opinion poll (December 1998), a positive attitude toward the former Communist Party was expressed by 34 percent of its former members, though by only 8 percent of nonmembers and 10 percent of those who were too young to join.

If these percentages are thought high, it is even more astonishing that the poll took place after everyone had heard about Katyn, the gulags, deportations, strikers shot, executions of heroes of the anti-Stalin resistance, electoral manipulations, and abuses of power. Everyone also knew that the ideological project of Communism turned out to be not only an impossible utopia but also a bloody one. It is difficult to say at what point these opinions are influenced by personal experience, by the nostalgia for a bygone time that today appears to be a period of stability, or even by a sense of loyalty to oneself and especially to one's earlier beliefs.

Communist Poland received negative opinions from the public after 1989. For example, in a poll taken in 1996, nearly one-third of those polled on "occurrences that were detrimental to the Poles" mentioned different events and happenings linked to the Communist regime. According to the same poll, on "facts that the Poles can be proud of," 29 percent of those questioned chose the fall of Communism and the creation of a democratic state. This figure exceeded the one established for Polish participation in the battles of the Second World War (28 percent).[2]

The official discourse on historical events and their interpretation during the Communist era was an important instrument in controlling the population, although it is difficult to measure its precise usefulness. The content of this discourse changed during the years of Communist Poland, especially in the growing introduction of non-Communist elements, indeed even non-Leftist, of the national tradition. These included the abandonment of a one-sided evaluation of the Polish state during the years 1918–39 and the rehabilitation of a part of the resistance and of the Polish army that had fought alongside the Western allies. This part of the record was the most tightly controlled, which was natural in that it concerned the history of Communist Poland itself (and, as I mentioned, questions linked to repressions against the Poles by the Soviets).

With the help of indoctrination, the task was not so much to control by censorship, which had a secondary character, but rather to direct the subjects of research, the subsidies, and the selection of those who could direct it and who would be allowed to consult the archives, in reality only a very few. Most of the historians wrote in agreement with the political line in force in the Party, sometimes even with the detailed "directives" provided at the behest of the Party (for example, by the Department of Science of the Central Committee). In light of the total centralization, it is clear that the authors of school texts received the same instructions as did the journalists and the publicists specializing in the popularization of history. Thus both school and television diffused a homogeneous image of recent history. A great proportion of the historians were members of the Party, and many, especially among those who studied contemporary history, worked in Party institutions that were well financed. The salaries were higher and the working conditions were better.

As a result, for many years the only work independent of Party direction appeared among those who had emigrated. Yet this was primarily concerned with the war period and the Second Republic. It was only in the 1970s, with the appearance of small groups of independent historians and the general autonomy of researchers, that the first analyses of postwar Poland appeared. The emergence of these tendencies forced those in power to "loosen the reins" on their own historians. This resulted from the fact that the leadership of the Communist Party was disturbed to see that the genealogy of the system and its own tradition, an element so important for legitimization, was coming under increasingly virulent attacks. Furthermore, the existence of clandestine editions favored a diffusion of this "opposition history."

Barbara Szacka, in her many sociological studies undertaken since the 1960s, has come to the conclusion that the "decline of popular Poland" began in the second half of the 1970s. Even before the fall of the Communist system in Poland, "the current social memory had been emptied of all that could have been used in legitimizing the Communist State," she writes in her 1998 study.[3] We can cite, for example, a 1965 poll in which 29 percent of those surveyed "hoped" to celebrate the creation of a popularly governed Poland (on July 22), while in 1988 only 6 percent shared this opinion. Thus *dixit* Szacka, Communism had collapsed in the minds (and hearts) of the great majority of Poles even before its final collapse.

Communist Poland is "not well regarded," but that does not mean that the Poles should necessarily also have a bad opinion of themselves, even those—and there were millions—who had accepted or supported the Communist system or others who had in various ways contributed to its establishment, its consolidation, and its maintenance, including its faults and its crimes. The settling of accounts with Communism is in reality often an examination of conscience too. It is much easier for those who resisted, struggled, and suffered. It is less easy, but also less complex, for those who actively participated, who were militants, directors, and ideologues. They believe they should not be called to account, and they protest when others want to undertake in their place a reckoning with the past. Matters are complicated in a different way for those who carried out orders without believing in the radiant future promised by the ideology, those who did not emerge from the adaptation strategy. The best escape for them is to forget or to point a finger at others.

Nazism was not and is not considered by the Poles as being their problem, and even if it were, it is only in isolated cases that happened a long time ago. From their point of view, they have nothing to account for, and a sense of common responsibility is not a factor. A large number of Poles also think that Communism is not a "Polish problem." The guilty ones, they believe, are somewhere else—or they maintain that no one—unless it is destiny—is guilty.

Translated by Lucy B. Golsan; text translated from Polish to French by
Justine Balasinski

Notes

1. These matters are the subject of an interesting monograph by Edmund Dmitrov, *Niemcyiokapacja hitlerowska w oczach Polaków: Poglady i opinie z lat 1945–1948* (The Germans and the Hitler occupation seen by the Poles: Opinions from the years 1945–1948), Warsaw, 1987.

2. Tomasz Zakowski, "Swiadomosc historyczna Polaków w polowie lat dziewiecd-ziesiatych" (The Historical conscience of the Poles in half of the 1990s), in *Ofiary czy wspólwinni: Nazizm i sowietyzm w swiadomosci historyczne* (Victims or accomplices: Nazism and Communism in the historical conscience), Warsaw, 1997, pp. 65–76.

3. Ibid., p. 59.

Étienne François

An Archive's Revolution

and the Rewriting of History

East Germany

The emblematic moments of present-day European history, the fall of the Berlin Wall in November 1989 and then German reunification the following year, extending the West German model to a crumbling GDR, escape ordinary classifications. These uncertainties and hesitations were each qualified as a "revolution," which was in current usage at the time, but this rapidly gave way to the word *Wende*, a purely descriptive neutral term deprived of any analytical or normative value. In one area, however, that of the archives, the term "revolution" is necessary: in the space of only a few months, Germany has actually lived a revolution of archives as rapid as it is complete. What were the real dimensions of this advancement, whose true measure has never been taken? What were its consequences in the short or middle term? Has it begun to make its effects felt in depth, and if so, where and how? And finally, how has it affected the way the Nazi period and the German past in general are viewed? These are the kinds of questions to which this article brings a few elements of response.

This archival revolution is first of all a quantitative one. Enormous masses of documents, which had been very difficult to get to or were totally inaccessible and which no one could imagine would ever be available, were opened and put at the disposition of the public.

The safeguarding and the opening of the most secret archives of the GDR, the archives of the Ministry of State Security (Ministerium für Staatssicherheit, or Stasi), with its millions of individual files, represent the best-known and most extreme example of this true revolution. In November 1989 the civic movements (*Bürgerbewegungen*) that made up the avant-garde of the political opposition occupied several regional offices of the political police in Erfurt, in Dresden, and in Leipzig in order to create an obstacle to any attempts to destroy the documentation that had been gathered. The movement, which spread over the entire GDR, ended in January 1990 with the occupation in Berlin of the central seat of the political police in the Normannenstrasse. In the space of only a few months, before widespread destruction could take place, almost all of the information amassed in forty years by a political police force as tentacular as it was methodical, 180 kilometers of archives, was protected and made accessible.[1]

As spectacular as it was, this opening of the Stasi files was only a part of a more far-reaching movement. The protection and freedom of access actually includes the entire archival inheritance of the fallen regime—state archives, those of ministries and administrations and large companies as well as of political parties and organizations of the masses—beginning with the records of the Sozialistische Einheitspartei Deutschlands (Unified Socialist Party of Germany, SED). Placed end to end, these resources represent, as a total, a mass of documents even more impressive because here too there is very little destruction and, in the case of the GDR, we are dealing with a particularly bureaucratic regime that had a mania for secrecy regarding the archives and their conservation.

This review would not be complete if it did not mention access to older archives that, until then, had been difficult if not impossible to get to. A first category of archives includes archival holdings on German history in its entirety conserved in the GDR depositories (for example, the Central Archives of Prussia at Merseburg before the fall of the wall); regional and local archives (such as those of Saxony); archive holdings from former eastern provinces of the Reich (Silesia, Pomerania, and Prussia) that had never been moved and were preserved by Poland and Russia; and more generally the archives of Central and Eastern European countries occupied by the Reich during the war. The second category concerns the German archives seized by the Soviets and their allies during the Second World War, most of them transferred to Soviet depositories (beginning with the famous Sonderarchiv of Moscow) and kept secret until that time.

Quantitative in the mass of documents that it has opened and safeguarded, the archival revolution of 1989–90 was also qualitative in the radical newness of the conditions of access that it created. Since the autumn of 1989 and the first occupations of regional offices of the political police, the demand for totally free access to the Stasi archives has been answered. This claim, directly linked to the demands of political combat (it was necessary above all to keep former leaders of the political police from profiting from the uncertainty of the moment and their own accumulation of knowledge to sink the opposition movements by erasing the traces of their former activity and thus assure, at best, their conversion [to legitimate politics]) was advanced by a political-ethical ambition of a more fundamental importance: in order to more easily eradicate the reign of secrecy and denunciation, it demanded that all those who were observed (often without their knowledge), pursued, and persecuted by the political police, and therefore deprived of their identity by the regime, be given the right to free and complete access to their file and to knowledge of who observed and denounced them so that they might take back their past and their stolen identities. Putting the finishing touches to the dissolution of the political police, a law to this effect was approved in August 1990 by the Chamber of Deputies (Volkskammer) elected in March 1990, the first free elections in the GDR. It laid plans for the creation of an institution charged especially with conserving the archives of the political police and assuring access to the victims of the regime, and this responsibility was entrusted to the pastor Joachim Gauck, a native of Rostock, who was already responsible for the commission charged with controlling the dissolution of the Stasi. After the unification of October 3, the Bundestag, as agreed in the treaty of unification, confirmed and identified the choices carried out by the GDR in the last months of its existence. The law of December 20, 1991, passed by a large majority, outlined the scope and missions of the administration in charge of the archives of the Stasi, approved Pastor Gauck in his functions (this is the source of the name Gauck-Behörde, given to the new institution), and reaffirmed in particular the recognized right of anyone who asked to have free access to all the secret information gathered on him by the political police.[2]

This principle—which takes exception to the thirty-year rule—was also taken advantage of by the principal institutions of historical research. Beginning in the summer of 1990, these centers published a manifesto demanding that all available holdings of the former GDR be saved and protected, that the archives and the documentations be confined to competent services, that documentary and archival holdings not be dismembered, and especially that the whole of this material be made freely available without any time limits. This request was accepted by the authorities of the reunified Germany and extended to almost the entire archival and documentary heritage of the former GDR. This extreme liberality nevertheless had two reservations: it did not apply (except for special dispensations) to legal archives or to the archives of the Ministry of Foreign Affairs of the GDR; and it did not extend to the FRG archives, which remain under the thirty-year rule with, as a consequence, a serious "asymmetry of documentation and research" on the history of present-day Germany.[3]

Following reunification, an enormous work of inventory, filing, and restructuring was undertaken by the archive services of the Bund and the Länder. The principal steps were the combining in 1990 of the Bundesarchiv with the Central Archives of the GDR; the removal of regional and local GDR archives to the Länder (Staatsarchive); the regrouping in Berlin-Lichterfelde of all the central archives of Germany from 1871 to 1945; the regrouping of Prussian archives at Berlin-Dahlem; the creation in 1993 of a foundation "archives of parties and mass organizations of the GDR," reattached to federal archives and charged in particular with the conservation of the archives of the SED;[4] and the return, finally, in 1994 of the Bundesarchiv, Nazi archives held by the Americans in the Berlin Document Center.[5] Here also the institution created especially to manage and care for the Stasi archives can serve as an example of the effort undertaken to deal with the material. This federal institution, with its own statute since it comes directly from the Bundestag and is not under any other control than that of the law of Parliament and its scientific adviser, actually employs not less than 3,000 associates and has an annual budget of around 200 million marks (about 114 million dollars U.S.). From its beginnings, the Gauck-Behörde had funding from a service specializing in research, which is employed by way of the publication of guides, catalogs, and studies and in facilitating the historical use of the enormous documentation that it deals with and preserves.[6] Following this example, the different archives and documentary institutions created or organized since 1990, in their turn, multiply the publication of inventories and work resources intended for researchers.[7]

This effort was finally completed by two types of supplementary initiatives: first, the protection, creation of inventories, and beginning of use of the important documentation of a sociological nature, most often unpublished, developed by the GDR itself for its own research institutions and that in a way constitutes second-degree archives (opinion polls; investigations of a sociological nature, of enterprises and population groups, and of regions; and studies bearing on the whole of society);[8] second, the production of new archives through the work of investigation and documentation led in particular by the Commissions of Enquiries set up in 1992, then in 1995 by not only the Bundestag but also the Commission for the Study of Political and Social Change (Kommission für den Sozialen and politischen Wandel), created following reunification in order to analyze "while still warm" the transformations then going on and to serve as a substitute institution for the researchers of former research institutions of the GDR.[9]

These few examples will have sufficed to make evident that Germany after 1989–90 has been through a real archival revolution, characterized not only by making accessible to researchers and society in general impressive amounts of documents but also by the installation of conditions of access of a rare freedom to records entrusted to competent administrations who are professionals and equipped with good working conditions. Without equal in the rest of Europe—both East and West—this unusual situation is itself the result of a unique combination of factors. These include the power of the internal opposition movement in the GDR, beginning in the autumn of 1989, and the importance of its ethical and political motivations (the desire to open up everything to the light of day being in inverse proportions to the practice of secrecy and suspicion that had belonged to the former regime); the rapidity of the political, administrative, and state implosion of the GDR; the desire of the FRG to better emphasize the irrevocable rupture with the former regime, and the fact that the GDR had been only a parenthesis in German history; the shared desire of research institutions and those who protected the archives to better seize the chances offered by an unprecedented situation in putting forth new solutions themselves; the existence in the FRG of institutions ready immediately to take over; the professionalism that allowed the enormous documentation to be made available almost from one day to the next; and finally the desire, not free of a bad conscience, not to repeat the errors committed after 1945 and to act so that the release of what one hurried to call a "second German dictatorship" operated under conditions of absolute democratic transparency.

The opening of the archives, and especially the complete freedom of requirements for access and use, at first caused a regular stampede. One statistic will suffice to show the extent of this: for the year 1992, the year following the vote and execution of the law stating conditions and functions, the Gauck-Behörde received no fewer than 1.2 million requests for information and consultation and this caused enormous problems in answering this unexpectedly large demand and at the same time carrying out its other duties.

  With this stampede it is not surprising that "historical" motives in the usual sense of the word came in last. In going to the archives, two purposes dominated all the others: the desire to settle scores with the fallen regime, to make the break with it final and carry out revenge on an entirely rejected past, and the quest for sensational revelations. The largest number of requests to consult the archives, to have access to the documentation and information, came from administrations and the courts. Requests for verification addressed in 1992 to the Gauck-Behörde by public administrations and other institutions (churches and political parties, among others) in order to learn whether or not the persons they employed or intended to recruit had worked for the political police, represented more than half the total for the year, about 623,000—without counting the demands from the courts and the judiciary for use in trials as well as procedures of rehabilitation and restitution. In second place we find the individuals, mostly those opposing the regime and its victims, demanding to see their personal files, with the double concern of taking back their own past and discovering the identity of those who had pursued or denounced them or had spied on them (522,000 demands). Far behind these came the publicists and journalists who devoted themselves to bringing to light unpublished proof to support the misdeeds of the fallen government and the compromises and support that allowed it to last such a long time and to raise the tone of public denunciation and the stigmatization of all the personalities in political, literary, and public life (not only from the East but also the West) suspected of having sympathies at one time or other for the GDR or, even worse, having worked in the shadow for the political police as "unofficial informers."[10]

In this group the professional historians are only a tiny minority. The most active and quickest to publish claim a militant conception of history that brings the function of the historian closer to that of the prosecutor. Taking inspiration from the theory of totalitarianism, to which this offers a second youth, they emphasize the complete power of the regime, insisting first on its repressive nature and multiplying the comparisons with Nazism to better emphasize the resemblances and the continuities between the two regimes. Denouncing, globalizing, and politicizing, this first-hour historiography makes the East German Communist Party the principal, if not the only, actor in the history of the GDR; it sees the forty years of its existence as a whole and searches in its politics and ideology for explanations of a final proof of its reality. This attitude is shared by the first commission of inquiry of the Bundestag as well as historians coming from the opposition, such as Armin Mitter and Stefan Wolle,[11] or again by "militant" Western historians, such as the religious history specialist Gerhard Besier, who published almost "on the spot" three volumes of documentation denouncing the collusion of the Protestant Church with the regime and its infiltration by the political police.[12] The dominant attitude, directly linked to the political, ideological, and media context of the years immediately following the collapse of the GDR, found its expression in the four qualifiers created at that time to define the GDR as the object of inquiry: "The ex-GDR," "the second German dictatorship," "the State-SED," and "the State of no-law of the SED." The first qualifier (in German, *die ehemalige Deutsche Demokratisch Republik*) expresses a finalist vision of things that, beginning with the end, interprets the entire history of the GDR in the light of its final failure and emphasizes that this footnote in German history is totally and irrevocably closed; the second (in German, *die zweite deutsche Diktatur*) is a qualifier directly inspired by the theory of totalitarianism, which places the GDR as a prolongation of Nazism, insists on the structural resemblances between the two regimes, and defines the GDR, not in relation to itself, but in reference to a democratic and liberal model; the third (in German, *der* SED-*Staat*) goes back to an exclusively political and ideological definition of the GDR, which reduces it to being nothing more than a prolongation of power exercised by the Communist Party and calls into question its reality as a state; and the last (in German, *der* SED-*Unrechtsstaat*) goes the previous definition one better and insists even more firmly on the absence of legitimacy of the regime and on its deep-seated evil.[13]

Dominant up until the middle of the 1990s, this way of taking over the use of the archives and the history of the GDR is now very much in retreat. There are several reasons for this: overwhelming and urgent necessities following the fall of the wall, the renewal of the elites and the purification both carried out on a grand scale (thanks, among other things, to recourse to the archives) are now completed;[14] the attempts to have legal rulings on the past met largely with failure and the effects of prescription began to be felt;[15] the reunification was no longer questioned by anyone and the fact of political bankruptcy, both moral and even more economic, of the GDR was the object of a general consensus, favoring by this an even more distant and differentiated assessment of the GDR; but the difficulties and the unfolding, often surprising, of the reunification—beginning with the appearance of a new East German identity and the success of a post-Communist party, the PDS, which received 20 percent of the vote in the "new" Länder and whose attitude adroitly mixed a critical distance with a claim of continuity (in particular, among its militants and its constituents)—demonstrating the limits of an exclusively political approach to the history of the GDR, reminded everyone that the archives did not have an answer for everything and encouraged researchers and historians to diversify their approach, to go more deeply into their problem situations, and to better take into account the social and cultural dimensions of the East German past.[16]

In contrast to fewer and fewer institutional demands for information and consultation addressed to the Gauck-Behörde—in 1996 one counted only 62,000 coming from public administrations—the number of research projects undertaken by German and foreign historians continued to increase: an institute of the University of Mannheim, which drew up an inventory and keeps it regularly up to date, counts nearly 2,000. This progression of research, which itself goes along with a new balance in the direction of a more "historian" approach, was helped by the creation of several specialized institutes that, despite their differences in orientation and profile, have in common a desire to reunite native eastern German historians as well as those of western Germany and to carry on coordinated political activities of research and publication (sources, monographs, and collective inquiries). The most active and most original institution is the Center of Research of Modern Day History (Zentrum für Zeithistorische Forschung) in Potsdam. Created in the days following reunification to welcome the historians of the former Academy of Sciences of the GDR, this center specializes in social and cultural history (in a broad sense of the term), makes an effort to combine recognizing structural realities (of a political and social order) and subjective experiences (individual and collective), and is particularly careful to place its inquiries in a comparative and international perspective.[17] Three other institutions, created after 1990, are also worth mentioning: the branch first situated in Potsdam, then transferred in June 1996 to Berlin, of the Institute of Contemporary History (Institut für Zeitgeschichte) of Munich;[18] the new Hannah Arendt Institute for Research on Totalitarianism (Hannah-Arendt-Institut für Totalitarismus-Forschung), attached to the Technical University of Dresden;[19] and the Research Section (Abteilung für Bildung und Forschung) of the Gauck-Behörde.[20]

The first assessments compiled by Alf Lüdtke[21] and Ulrich Mählert[22] help take the measure of the effort accomplished and the reorientation of research in the direction of a "historization" of the GDR. Defiant in regard to grand schemes of theoretical explanation, based on a thorough study of extensive archives, conscious of the risks from both the enormity of the available documentation and its limits,[23] and careful about contextualizing, these inquiries have systematic recourse to comparisons in time (principally with Nazism) and in space (not only with other socialist countries but also with the FRG) to better bring out the specificity of the GDR and avoid too great a splitting up of the research. Chronologically the most numerous inquiries focus on the immediate postwar period, that is, on the Soviet occupation zone (from 1945 to 1949); then on the early days of the GDR (until the end of the 1950s), especially the installation of the new regime; on the coming to power of the Communist Party and the progressive extension of its grip on the state and society; and on the increasingly profound restructuring of the economy and society. Equally numerous are the investigations of the last years of the regime, of its fall, and of the beginnings of reunification.[24] The years between these two periods, however, have been less well studied, and the political history of the Honecker era, like the erosion of the interior of the regime in the 1980s, represent sectors still neglected in the research. Thematically the studies now being done and the first results, which have already appeared, are characterized not only by a real desire for expansion and diversification but also by a willingness to take into account the interactions between various demands of reality and finding the modes of functioning and the autonomy of a society that, however, is infiltrated by those in power.[25] For now a large place is given to social, cultural, and religious history;[26] to the history of daily life; to a study of specific groups and of local and regional communities; and the only areas in which research remains rare are, on the one hand, economic history and, on the other, the history of the foreign policy of the GDR and its place in the arena of international relations. From 1994 the collection of studies published under the direction of two West German historians Hartmut Kaelble and Jürgen Kocka and an East German historian, Hartmut Zwahr,[27] indicates the directions taken by this reorientation of research. A special issue of the review Annales, devoted to the social history of the GDR, has made this available to the French public.[28]

In fact it has been only a short time since the effects of the impetus of the opening of the archives on other areas of historical research have begun to make themselves felt. The sector in which this was the most immediately perceptible is the history of Nazism and the Second World War. It is still only an inclination: the principal orientations of research and the dominant paradigms are earlier than 1989–90; the most influential historians and in particular those who head specialized research institutions are all Western; and recent publications, in the majority, are situated in the line of investigation begun long ago and are based on documentary reserves already accessible before 1989. The example of these continuations not affected by the recent transformations is that of the new and remarkable biography of Hitler by Ian Kershaw, begun in the early 1980s, and whose first volume was recently published.[29] This being true, several changes are already apparent. The systematic comparison between Nazism and the GDR—a comparison that demands attention even more because the GDR is even more clearly defined than the FRG by its radical opposition to Nazism and has made "antifascism" its true "founding myth"[30]—has not only had the effect of having the study of the immediate postwar years and the early years of the GDR profit from all the conceptual and methodological acquisitions of the historiography of Nazism, but it has also had the effect, in the opposite sense, of bringing out the specificity of the Nazi period; far from having led to a relativization of Nazism, as was feared in the beginning, it has, to the contrary, contributed to making more apparent its monstrous singularity. To take only one example, the more research on the GDR revealed the growing importance of its repressive apparatus, its desire to control everything, and to make everyone toe the line—therefore its dimensions of a "dictatorship without the people"—the more it brought out the opposite, to what extent Nazism was a "dictatorship with the people" marked by a mixture of extreme violence (whose equivalent is not found in the GDR) and of support spread among the population and carried along by the adherents, the support and enthusiasm of wide and varied sectors of society. The archives of the Nazi period, preserved in the GDR, in occupied countries, and in the Soviet Union, led also to a reinterpretation—worse and more explicit—of the war and more particularly the policies of Nazi Germany throughout the eastern front: population transfers, expropriation and colonization, exploitation, destruction, massacres, and implication of the Wehrmacht in genocide.[31] The historiographical debates surrounding the Nazi affiliations of a number of German historians (in particular, several of those who after 1945 contributed to the resumption of historical research in the FRG, such as W. Conze and T. Schieder);[32] or on the genesis of the instigation of the Shoah, and on the role played personally in the matter by Hitler;[33] or about the implications of banks and large German companies in the functioning of the government, in the policies of the war, and in the genocide are some examples of the development of the view of Nazism under the double effect of the archival revolution and of the comparison with the GDR,[34] and everything leads us to believe that this movement of reinterpretation is just beginning. All of these debates, moreover, are followed with passionate interest by public opinion and the media, for their fundamental stakes are political, directly and visibly affecting the identity of reunited Germany, whether it is a question of the restructuring of the memorials set up in the concentration camps at Buchenwald, Sachenhassen, and Ravensbrück,[35] as it was several years ago, or of recent discussions about construction beside the Brandenburg Gate in Berlin of a memorial to victims of the Shoah.[36]

On the contrary, the area least affected by the fallout from the opening of the archives is the history of the FRG, for this last was protected both by the maintenance of the thirty-year law for all the archives concerning it and also by the idea that the fall of the wall and reunification would be the ultimate proof of the superiority of its model. Research on either the history of the FRG from GDR sources or from a perspective of the whole, which mixes both comparative analysis of the development of the two societies and that of their interaction, are very rare in the pioneer publications of Christoph Klessmann.[37] The recent essay published by the Munich historian Gerhard A. Ritter on the history of Germany from 1945 to the present, which offers a nuanced and open assessment, both diversified and balanced, of the evolution and the interactions of the two states and their two societies, then of the first years of a reunified Germany, presents a principal example of what could be done with the material.[38] But for the moment these are still exceptions, and it is to be feared that the climate of commemorations in 1999, celebrating in the same movement the fiftieth anniversary of the founding of the FRG and the tenth anniversary of the fall of the Berlin Wall, and in this way the glory and the success of the democratic and liberal model of West Germany, is not favorable to such a development.

Even though it is not surprising, the contrast between the rapidity and the extent of the archive revolution, on the one hand, and the slowness and limited number of historiographical transformations, on the other, is the undeniable record we face at the conclusion of this rapid overview.

But the movement has been launched. Thanks to the archive and document revolution of 1989–90, though thanks also to the creation of new institutions where historians from both East and West, Germans and foreigners,[39] work together, the history of the GDR is on the way to becoming one of the most dynamic subjects for research. This activity is measured not only by the number of projects going on but also by its experimental and innovative character. The history of the GDR is actually the privileged area where researchers have passed beyond the confrontations that ten years ago had unfailingly pitted the tenants of a history of daily life being demanded by historical anthropology and microhistory against the tenants of a global social history putting the emphasis, as a priority, on structure and process. It is the field where a rethinking and a productive deconstruction of huge theoretical and conceptual edifices are being carried out, theories such as modernization of totalitarianism, by which attempts were made to account for the enigma of the GDR before having recorded facile tautological drifting;[40] it is one of the sectors in which the richness of the comparative approach—in time as in space—stands out the most clearly; and it is finally the area in which, in feeling its way, it frees itself from the yoke of unsuitable theories by beginning with the minute analysis of concrete situations, of new ways of thinking and understanding the connections and the interactions between the private and public spheres, between those in power and society, and between practices and appearances. Directly affected not only by the opening of archive holdings formerly inaccessible but also by the systematic recourse to comparativism to better tell the history of the GDR, the history of the Nazi period and of the Second World War is the second area of research in which the repercussions from the upheavals of 1989–90 are the most evident—even though here too there is every reason to believe that we are only at the beginning.

In other areas, however, the transformation is hardly perceptible. Although indispensable for counterbalancing the negative effects of what the Berlin historian Edgar Wolfrum called the *Bundesrepublikanisierung* of the research on German history—that is, its concentration in the form of a return to the regions corresponding to the territory of the former Federal Republic, the rebalancing of German history (from the Middle Ages to the beginning of the twentieth century) beyond the former Germano-German frontier and the Oder-Neisse line to include the totality of what was at one time or another German land—has not gotten past the stage of pious wishing. The history of the FRG, however, appears to continue undisturbed according to its pre-1989 launching. The modes of writing history have not yet been affected by the change either; and even if certain historians wonder about the necessity of inventing a new way of writing adapted to the new "historicity regime" (F. Hartog), which we have supposedly entered into since 1989–90, and plead in favor of a more open and less determinist history, making a large place for contingency, surprise, and the event itself without, however, questioning its scientific and ethical demands, the concrete reactions to this thinking on historical production are as yet not very strongly felt.[41] On one point we can even speak of a regression: the rapid development of research on the GDR and the sustained attention of the scientific community and public opinion, without being deliberately sought after, contributed to reinforcing the already pronounced disequilibrium in German historical research between contemporary history and the whole of all other historical periods.

If we compare the way in which society and German historians reacted to the upheavals of 1989–90 to what happened after 1945, the contrast is glaring. The exceptional opening of the archives and the documentation, the intensity of the debates, the liveliness of the challenges, the multiplication of the research projects, and the early attention to a "historization" of the history of the GDR are actually the opposite of the limits imposed on the opening of the archives, of the brevity of the period of serious debates on Nazism and the German past, of the slowness of historiographical challenges, and of the tardy character of the institutionalization of research on contemporary history in Germany after 1945.[42] What is the long-term fallout of this contrasting attitude on cultural policy and the memory of what we habitually call the "Berlin Republic"? It is still too soon to say, but everything leads us to believe that it will be all the more important since, besides the debates that hold the attention of public opinion and the media, we should be able to measure the depth of the effect of the confrontation with their own past for the 1.3 million people who, since the vote on the law of 1991, have access to the personal file the Stasi had established on them.[43] Everyone agrees to recognize the trying character of this confrontation with a past that is difficult to accept and with portraits most often negative of themselves and those around them, which these documents reflect, and the vast majority also agrees to recognize the beneficial effects of this work of self-reappropriation with, as a consequence, a modification not only of the way they see their own history but also of the GDR. Contrary to what was feared in the beginning, these numberless recollections have not had the feared destabilizing and disintegrating effects. But we certainly remain incapable of saying in what way this experience, without any other comparable example in history, has modified the relations between East Germans themselves (in particular between "victims" and "executioners") or the relations between East Germans and West Germans. Is it possible to hope, as certain witnesses encourage us to do,[44] that despite its imperfections and its limitations, this represents for present-day Germany an opportunity that is also without precedence?

Translated by Lucy B. Golsan

Notes

1. The members of the political police grew as the alienation of the population from the regime became worse. At the end of its existence, the Stasi had 90,000 full-time employees plus about 170,000 "unofficial collaborators" (*Inoffizielle Mitarbeiter,* abbreviated IM), recruited from all sectors of the population by signing a letter of personal engagement, working in secret, and each having a codename known only to the police. Between the moment of the collapse of the regime and that of the occupation of offices of the political police, the employees of the Stasi had begun to shred some of the archives. These last were seized and are being reassembled. The only documentary holdings of the political police destroyed were those concerning espionage in West Germany—with the exception of documents and files passed to the U.S. Secret Services and for which German authorities were never able to obtain restitution. I thank Marie-Bénédicte Daviet for the documentary and bibliographical help she gave me in the preparation of this article.

2. Hansjörg Geiger, *Stasi-Unterlagen-Gesetz (StUG): Textausgabe mit ausführlichem*

Sachregister, Munich 1994; Albert Engel, *Die rechtliche Aufarbeitung der Stasi-Unterlagen auf de Grundlage des StUG,* Berlin, Dunker and Humbolt, 1995.

3. See on this subject the pertinent remarks of the "dean" of German research on the GDR, Hermann Weber, "'Asymmetrie' bei de Erforschung des Kommunismus und der DDR-Geschichte? Probleme mit Archivalien, dem Forschungsstand und bei de Wertungen," in *Aus Politik und Zeigeschichte, Beilage zur Wochenzeitung "Das Parlament,"* B 26/97, June 20, 1997, pp. 3–14.

4. Elrun Dolatwski and Anette Merburg, "Die Stiftung Archiv de Parteien und Massenorganisationen der DDR im Bundesarchiv," *Der Archivar,* no. 50, May 1997, pp. 288–300. The foundation has published a brief inventory of its holdings: *Die Bestände der Stiftung Archiv der Parteien und Massenorganisationen der DDR im Bundesarchiv,* Berlin, Kurzübersicht, 1996.

5. A good view of the entire collection on the restructuring of the archives in the eastern part of Germany is found in a recent article by the director of the central archives of Lichterfelde, Hermann Schreyer, "Entwicklungen im ostdeutschen Archivwesen seit dem 3, Oktober 1990," *Der Archivar,* no. 50, May 1997, pp. 494–516.

6. At the time they were seized, only 58 linear kilometers of the archives, out of a total of 180, were immediately available. Eighty-five percent of the total is now usable. The conservation and treatment service of these archives is overseen by a *Beirat* of 15 people presided over by a representative of civic movements of the GDR, Ulrike Poppe. Of the 3,000 employees of the Gauck-Behörde, 1,700 are in Berlin; the others are divided among the fourteen regional and local branches of the institution. Ninety-five percent come from the "new Länder." The *Unterlagen des Staatssicherheitsdienstes der ehemaligen DDR,* that is, "The federal agent in charge of the documentation of the Security Service of the former GDR."

7. For a detailed and complete presentation of the archival institutions and of documentation and research on the GDR, see the list in Uhlrich Mählert, ed., *Vademekum DDR-Forschung: Ein Leitfaden zu Archiven, Forschungseinrichtungen, Bibliotheken, Einrichtungen der politischen Bildung, Vereinen, Museen and Gedenkstätten,* Bonn, 1997.

8. For one example see the bibliography and collection of studies *Materialien zur Erforschung des DDR-Gesellschaft Quellen: Daten, Instrumente,* Opladen, 1998, published by the Gesellschaft Sozialwissenschaftlicher Infrastruktureneinrichtungen in partnership with the Institute of Sociology of the University of Iéna and the Center of European Sociology of the University of Mannheim.

9. In 1992 the Bundestag voted for the creation of a commission of inquiry of "the history and the consequences in Germany of the SED dictatorship" (Enquete-Kommission Aufarbeitung von Geschichte und Folgen der SED-Diktatur im Deutschland). Directed by Gernd Faulenbach, a historian at the University of Bochum, specialist on the history of the workers' movement, and close to the Social Democrat Party, this commission has carried out an enormous work of documentation

10. On the Stasi, its activities, its archives, details of the conditions of access

and utilization of the documentation, and more generally on the question of the treatment of the past, see the excellent special issue (in French) of the review *Allemagne d'aujourd'hui*, no. 136, April–June 1996, "La 'déstatification': Problématique et dimension idéologique de la confrontation au passé en Allemagne de l'Est"; and *Gauck-Behörde: Dritter Tätigkeisbericht des Bundesbeauftragten für die Unterlagen des Staatssicherheitsdienstes der ehemaligen Deutschen Demokratischen Republik*, Berlin, 1997, its last activity report. Since the creation of the institution, more than four million demands for information and consultation have been addressed to it. This research has uncovered strong differences in degree of collaboration with the political police of different circles and professions. Only 1 percent of Protestant pastors had agreed to work as "IM," as opposed to around 5 percent of East Berlin teachers and more than 20 percent of police officers. The Gauck-Behörde was satisfied to send the results of its investigations to the administrations and institutions that requested it, leaving to these last the task of drawing from it the consequences each thought necessary. As an illustration of the good historical use that can be made of the archives of the Stasi, we particularly recommend Sonia Combe, *Une Société sous surveillance: Les Intellectuels et la Stasi*, Paris, Albin Michel, 1999. Well informed, measured, subtle, sensitive, and intelligent, this book, composed of twenty files established by the political police from 1950 to 1989, allows us to grasp in a concrete way not only the repressive practices of the GDR but also the forms of resistance to control or, the opposite, the different modes of collaboration with the Stasi. It contains an excellent introduction to the understanding of the manner in which the Stasi exercised its power and, more generally, an invitation to examine the question of the ties intellectuals were led to keep with the state.

11. See, as an example, their book, actually enlightening and well documented: Armin Mitter and Stefan Wolle, *Untergang auf Raten: Unbekannte Kapitel der DDR-Geschichte*, Munich, Bertelsmann, 1993.

12. Gerhard Besier, *Der SED-Staat und die Kirche*, 3 vols., Munich and Berlin, 1993–95.

13. The same observations can be stretched to the concepts and approaches used after 1989–90 by the majority of sociologists and economists to analyze the "transformations."

14. Several recent publications have drawn up a balance sheet: Gert-Joachim Glaessner, "Regimewechsel und Elitentransfer: Parlamentarisch-politische und Verwaltungseliten im Ostdeutschland," *Deutschland Archiv*, no. 6, 1996, pp. 849–861; Heinrich Best and Ulrike Becker, eds., *Elites in Transition: Elite Research in Central and Eastern Europe*, Opladen, 1997; Wilhelm Bürklin and Hilke Rebenstorf, eds., *Eliten im Deutschland: Rekrutierung und Integration*, Opladen Leske u.B., 1997; Hans-Ulrich Derlien, "Elitezirkulation im Ostdeutschland, 1989–1995," *Aus Politik und Zeitgeschichte*, no. 5, 1998, pp. 3–17.

15. See the ever timely essay that appeared five years ago by Jacqueline Hénard, *Geschichte vor Gericht, Die Ratlosigkeit der Justiz*, Berlin, Siedler, 1993.

16. I addressed these questions in a previous article: Étienne François, "Les 'Trésors' de la Stasi ou le mirage des archives," in Jean Boutier and Dominique Julia, eds., *Passés recomposés: Champs et chantiers de l'histoire*, Paris, Autrement, 1995, pp. 145–151.

17. Information taken from the 1997 report of activities (*Tätigkeitsbericht 1997*) of the center. The series of publications of the center published by Akademie-Verlag in Berlin comprises eleven volumes.

18. Horst Möller and Hartmut Mehringer, "Die Aussenstelle Potsdam des Instituts für Zeitgeschichte," *Vierteljahrshefte für Zeitgeschichte*, 1995, pp. 3–16.

19. This new research center is directed by the historian Klaus-Dietmar Henke, who was formerly assistant director of the Institut für Zeitgeschichte of Munich, then director of the research section of the Gauck-Behörde.

20. This section publishes a series, Analyses and Documents, through Ch. Links in Berlin (thirteen volumes have appeared). Let us also point out that the Bundestag decided in April 1998 to create a "foundation for the study of the history and the consequences of the SED-Dictatorship in Germany," which began operation in November 1998.

21. The best presentation in French of the state of research on the GDR is in the article–balance sheet of Alf Lüdtke, "La République démocratique allemande comme histoire: Réflexions historiographiques," *Annales*, no. 53, 1998, pp. 3–39 (special number on the social history of the GDR); to supplement with idem, "Die DDR als Geschichte: Zur Geschichtsschreibung über die DDR," *Aus Politik und Zeitgeschichte*, no. 36, pp. 3–16.

22. As a useful introduction, see the concise and well-informed clarification of Ulrich Mählert, *Kleine Geschichte des DDR*, Munich, Beck, 1998.

23. Beginning with the difficulties of gaining access to Soviet archives of the military administration, of the commission of control, of the top police bureau, of the embassies, of the occupation troops of the Party, and of the government.

24. For an overall view that is particularly clear sighted and thorough, see the work of the American historian Charles S. Maier, *Dissolution: The Crisis of Communism and the End of East Germany*, Princeton University Press, 1997.

25. See, as an introduction to this question, the study of Sigrid Meuschel, *Legitimation und Parteiherrschaft: Zum Paradox von Stabilität und Revolution im der DDR, 1945–1989*, Francfort Suhrkamp, 1992; as well as the collection of essays in Richard Bessel and Ralph Jessen, eds., *Die Grenzen der Diktatur: Staat und Gesellschaft im der DDR*, Göttingen, Vandenh.u.R., 1996.

26. On the religious history of the GDR, see especially the study of East German sociologist Detlev Pollack, *Kirche im de Organisationsgesellschaft: Zum Wandel der gesellschaftlichen Lage de evangelischen Kirchen im der DDR*, Stuttgart, Kohlammer, 1994, who, adopting an approach radically different from that of Gerhard Besier, represents the best clarification of the place and the evolution of Protestant churches in East German society.

27. Hartmut Kaelble, Jürgen Kocka, and Hartmut Zwahr, eds., *Socialgeschichte der DDR*, Stuttgart, Klett-Cotta, 1994.

28. This special issue, appearing in January–February 1998, contains, besides the historiographical balance sheet of Alf Lüdtke (cited in note 11), two articles by Peter Hübner and Petra Clemens on feminine working conditions (pp. 41–89) and two articles by Ralph Jessen and Thomas Lindenberger on Communist dictatorship and social control (pp. 91–152).

29. Ian Kershaw, *Hitler, 1889–1936: Hubris*, London, Allen Lane, 1998. [The second volume of this study has been published recently: Kershaw, *Hitler, 1936–1945: Nemesis*, New York, W. W. Norton, 2000.]

30. Jürgen Danyel, *Die Geteilte Vergangenheit*, Berlin, Academie-Verlag, 1995.

31. Edouard Conte and Cornelia Essner, *La Quête de la race: Une anthropologie du nazism*, Paris, Hachette littératures, 1995. The exhibition "Vernichtungskrieg: Verbrechen der Wehrmacht, 1941–1944," on the war crimes perpetrated by the German army on the eastern front, fits into this same context. Created by the Institute für Sozialforschung of Hamburg, this itinerate exhibition was inaugurated in March 1995 and was accompanied by intense debates in public opinion. In the spring of 1999, it had been shown in almost thirty German and Austrian towns and seen by more than 800,000 visitors.

32. See as introduction Götz Aly and Suzanne Heim, *Vordenker der Vernichtung: Auschwitz und die deutschen Pläne für eine neue europäische Ordnung*, Hamburg, 1991; and Peter Schöttler, ed., *Geschichtsschreibung als Legitimationswillenschaft, 1918–1945*, Frankfort, Suhrkamp, 1997.

33. The indications contained in Himmler's service agenda found in the Sonderarchiv of Moscow have led historian Christian Gerlach to believe that Hitler personally gave the order to massacre the Jews, dating this order December 18, 1941. Himmler's agenda has become the subject of a critical edition by a group of eight historians of the Forschungsstelle für Zeitgeschichte of Hamburg: Peter Witte et al., eds., *Dier Dienstkalender Heinrich Himmlers, 1941/42*, Hamburg, 1999.

34. An expression frequently used by journalists sums up very well—even though it is a bad wordplay—the contrast between Nazism and the GDR: while one accumulated "piles of cadavers" (*Leichenberge*), the other only accumulated "piles of files" (*Aktenberge*).

35. The double challenge that confronted the restructuring commission was, on the one hand, the necessity of taking into account the reutilization of the camps of Buchenwald and Sachsenhausen without, in doing this, putting Nazism and Communism on the same footing and, on the other, that of proposing a critical and objective vision of the ideological utilization of the camps, which the GDR had undertaken. On the "special camps" of internment in the Soviet-occupied zone, see Jörg Morre, *Speziallager des NKWD*, Potsdam, 1997; and Sergej Mironenko, Lutz Niethammer, and Alexander von Plato, eds., *Soujetische Speziallager ind Deutschland 1945 bis 1950*, vol. 1, Berlin Adakemie-Verlag, 1998. I took up the question of the posterity and the recon-

sideration of these camps in an article, "La Postérité des camps en zone soviétique et en Allemagne de l'Est," in *La Déportation, le système concentrationnaire nazi*, ed. François Bédarida and Laurent Gervereau, Paris, La Découverte, 1995, pp. 228–233.

36. Michael S. Cullen, ed., *Das Holocaust—Mahnmal: Dokumente einer Debatte*, Zurich, Pendo-Verlag, 1999.

37. Christoph Klessmann, *Die doppelte Staatsgründing: Deutsche Geschichte, 1945–1955*, Göttingen, Vandenh.u.R., 1991 (5th ed., augmented and revised from a book whose first edition goes back to 1982); *Zwei Staaten, eine Nation: Deutsche Geschichte, 1955–1970*, 2d ed., Bonn, 1997.

38. Gerhard A. Ritter, *Uber Deutschland: Die Bundesrepublik im der Deutschen Geschichte*, Munich, Beck, 1998.

39. Indicative of this, the Center of Contemporary History of Potsdam is directed jointly by a German historian, Christoph Klessmann, and a German-American historian, Konrad Jarausch.

40. On this subject see the insightful article of Thomas Lindenberger, "Altagsgeschichte und ihr möglicher Beitrag zu einer Gesellschaftsgeschichte der DDR," in Bessel and Jessen, *Die Grenzen der Diktatur*, pp. 298–325 n.25, which shows very well that if the GDR, when it is studied according to the program elaborated by its leaders, is actually a totalitarian state carried along by an ambition for total control of society, it is, however, made up of compromises, of negotiations, and of constant turnabouts of society when its everyday functioning is examined.

41. One of the first historians of the German language to have felt the necessity to rethink, with added cost, the links between event and structure in the light of the "events" of 1989–90 and to have modified, as a result, his historical practices in applying it to a dossier of modern history, in this case the peasant war of 1653 in Switzerland, was the Swiss historian Andreas Suter, *Der Schweizerische Bauernkrieg von 1653: Politische Sozialgeschichte—Socialgeschichte eines politischen Ereignisses*, Turbingen, 1997, ("Frühneuzeit-Forschungen," vol. 3). See also, by the same author, his article in French, "Histoire sociale et événements historiques: Pour une approche nouvelle," *Annales*, May–June 1997, pp. 643–667. Comparable reflections on the relationship between long time and short time, and the consequences from it for the way of writing history, can be found in the preface and throughout Maier, *Dissolution*. The echo of these reflections can be found in two recent syntheses of the history of Europe: Hagen Schulze, *Phoenix Europa: Die Modern, von 1750 bis heute*, Berlin, Siedler, 1998; and Heinz Schilling, *Die neue Zeit: Vom Christenheitseuropa zum Europa de Staaten, 1250 bis 1750*, Berlin, Siedler, 1999 ("Siedler Geschichte Europas," vols. 3 and 4).

42. As an introduction to this subject, see Winfred Schulze, *Deutsche Geschichtswissenschaft nach 1945*, Munich, DTV, 1989; and Jean Solchany, *Comprendre le nazisme dans l'Allemagne des années zéro*, Paris, PUF, 1997—while waiting for the appearance of the still-unpublished thesis of Sebastian Conrad, "Auf des Suche nach verlorenen Nation," defended at the Free University of Berlin in February 1999, which compares

the evolution of West German historiographies with Japanese between 1945 and 1960.

43. After the stampede of 1992, which registered 552,000 requests for consultation coming from private individuals, the total number of requests has since stabilized at about 200,000 each year. Since July 1995 the Gauck-Behörde has also registered a few more than 5,000 requests coming from researchers, journalists, and publicists.

44. On this subject see the sensitive and measured personal testimony, Timothy Garton Ash, *The File: A Personal History*, London, Flamingo, 1997, in which the British historian recounts what the reading of his personal file meant to him, then the encounters he had later with almost all of those who had observed him and followed him for the GDR.

3. Commentaries

Pierre Hassner

Beyond History and Memory

Has the study of Communism and fascism (or more precisely—a distinction we will return to—of Stalinism and Nazism, therefore of totalitarianism) arrived at a positive stage? After the theological stage, represented by the confrontation of secular religions, and the metaphysical stage, whose theme seemed to be the essence of Communism (criminal, according to some, and innocent, according to others, of all contamination by the crimes committed in its name), we could be finally at the stage of empirical comparisons, characterized by a precise definition and periodization of competing terms and by an effort to get past sterile polemics and unbending positions.

In any case this is the largely realized ambition of this volume. Henry Russo's introduction keeps its distance, calmly, judiciously, and most often with an irrefutable precision, in dealing with the great French debates occasioned by the books of Karel Bartosek and François Furet, and especially *Le Livre noir du communisme* (The Black Book of communism). He definitively establishes that the comparison serves to mark the differences as much as the similarities, indeed that, according to the formula of the Anglo-American predecessors of this book, Ian Kershaw and Moshe Lewin, "only comparison allows us to understand uniqueness."[1]

The authors of two parallel studies in part 1, Nicolas Werth and Philippe Burrin, have introduced the comparative study of totalitarian phenomena in its third period by going beyond traditional arguments in their respective areas in two ways: those of the totalitarian model, or the primacy of ideology in opposition to the revisionist school, and the primacy of social forces in the Soviet case, and those of "Intentionalists" and "Functionalists" in the case of the Germans.

In a sense the present volume marks a clearer step forward than does the book by Ian Kershaw and Moshe Lewin, editors who have subscribed to a camp and whose entire undertaking is inspired by their intention to combat the totalitarian model. On the contrary, Burrin clearly challenges the idea of the inflexible character and the inevitable self-destructive anarchy of the Hitler regime, defended by Hans Mommsen in an earlier work. For his part Werth emphasizes, as he has already done in *Le Livre noir du communisme*, that the initiative for terrorism under the Stalin regime came from above, that is, from Stalin himself. But in the two cases, they both acknowledge that a part of the truth belongs to those they criticize and to those with whom—in the case of Werth at least—they felt intellectually sympathetic in the beginning.

If there has ever been a successful effort to have a new and equitable look at such sensitive and complex subjects, burdened with the weight of past quarrels, it is surely accomplished in these two parallel studies.

In a sense they refute the skepticism I expressed fifteen years ago about the possibility of an objective or "scientific" study of totalitarianism. In a work on "totalitarianism as seen by the West,"[2] I had tried to show that the development of Sovietological approaches to the idea of totalitarianism and its application to the USSR depended at least as much on the development of East-West relations, on the prestige of the social sciences in the eyes of Sovietologists, or on personal political history as on the development of Communist regimes themselves. It is only in this way that one could explain the crossfire between the dominant tendency of American Sovietology, first centered on the totalitarian mode, then rejecting it as nonscientific, and the discovery of this model (and that of Hannah Arendt) in France at the very moment when its application to the Soviet Union and to Eastern Europe became less defensible. I concluded that the concept of totalitarianism was the opposite of an acceptance of democracy and human rights and became more political philosophy than political science.

The studies in part 2, by contrast, strongly reinforce this interpretation. Except to a certain extent in the case of Hungary, where the corps of historians, according to Paul Gradvohl, seem to have resisted overpoliticization more than elsewhere, they show that most often in the transposing of debates on relations between fascism and Communism, and especially between the Holocaust and the Gulag, it is really about the self-justification of the peoples concerned. Andrzej Paczkowski, in a chapter that is both a contribution to our knowledge of the specificities of the Polish regime and its development as well as to our understanding of what forms of acceptance and refusal concerning the past characterized the population, also shows the correlation of these factors with positions adopted on the problem of the equivalence, and thereby exposes the strategies of forgetting and sidestepping guilt. Alexandra Laignel-Lavastine, in an exhaustive study both subtle and passionate, shows how the transposition of the theses of François Furet, Alain Besançon, and of *Le Livre noir du communisme* in Romania and the popularizing of the idea of a "Red Holocaust" have served to shortchange any critical review of the past and to falsely portray the Romanian people as the collective and innocent victims of a foreign regime and as victims whose sufferings would have paid for any crimes committed in their name during the Second World War. Although she is entirely convincing when she demonstrates and denounces the equivalence strategy, indeed the inversion, she perhaps gets carried away by her argument to the extent of passing a bit rapidly over the legitimate reasons for undertaking a comparison of the two totalitarianisms and the horror of the fate inflicted on prison-torture victims of the Communists, whose history—as well as the memory of it—are worthy of being preserved and discussed independently of those of the Shoah.

Perhaps a useful bridge between the first and second part would have been to analyze the German debate, which the reader must be content to find in the excellent study by Étienne François, of the revolution provoked by the opening of the GDR archives. But it is certainly in Germany and about Germany that the debate came into being. It is there first because of the existence of the two Germanys, and then as a consequence of the parallels between de-Nazification and de-Communization, that it found its most direct and concrete translation. Here also the connections between the debates on history and political developments would be interesting to study and would illuminate a number of paradoxes produced by the success or alternating use of fascism or Communism as the crucial element, leading to a correct interpretation.

This is why the important book by Ernst Nolte, *Der Faschismus in seiner Epoche*,[3] appeared, in 1963, to present an alternative paradigm to the totalitarian model. This was of course before its author changed his idea of fascism, coming to see it subsequently as a reaction to Bolshevism, to the peaceful uniformity of society, and to the idea of universality itself, as well as ultimately a sort of "historical-genetic theory of totalitarianism," with Nazi crimes appearing as simply a response to those of Stalin. It is to François Furet's credit that, in his debate with the German historian, he clearly distinguished the reality of what Raymond Aron called "the dialectic of extremes" and the fantasies of this causal, if not apologetic, approach.[4] Was it possible to go further with this type of discussion to extract the "rational core" from the self-serving interpretations? Was it possible to directly confront history and memory, or at least within each category, to proceed directly to a comparison, on the one hand, between the two regimes or movements and, on the other, between the different collective ways of "managing the past?"

This is finally the undertaking of the present volume. Its quality and, in a way, its charm come from the multiplicity of its levels and tonalities, from its "soundings" rather than the systematic nature of its construction. Furthermore it is obviously not a question of impressionism or pointillism in the present volume. The choice of three themes—dictator, violence, and society—for a parallel treatment is more methodologically rigid than the approach taken in the book of Moshe Lewin and Ian Kershaw. But this allows for a combined response to the question asked, and while the present work leaves us not entirely satisfied, it at least invites us to draw our own conclusions.

Evil in Politics

I do not wish to draw these conclusions here. But I would like to share a general impression that is very similar to the one offered by the British historian of power Michael Mann, a participant in the work of Ian Kershaw and Moshe Lewin,[5] on the volume by his coauthors. Mann feared that, on the one hand, they had insisted too much on the differences between the two regimes and, on the other, that they had exaggerated the suicidal incoherence of the Nazi regime. This perspective runs the danger of missing the essential, which is the Nazis' and Soviets' search for a continuing revolution, their refusal of any compromise other than tactical and temporary, and the tension (self-destructive in the long run) between ideology and bureaucracy, between institutionalization and revolution, and between the arbitrary and orderly administration. In presenting the character of the two regimes as anarchic or chaotic, there is a risk of forgetting their frightening efficiency, at least in terms of conquests and exterminations. In insisting on the difference between the origins and objects of their frenetic genocide, we might forget what they have in common, this frenzy itself. As Pierre Bouretz has responded to Kershaw, almost in the same words as Mann, one avoids facing the problem of evil in politics.[6] There is a risk of minimizing the common enormity (beyond their sociological differences, even their unequal degree of radicalism) of what Kershaw and Lewin called "the massive sacrifice of human beings on the altar of political myth," which Henry Rousso's introduction describes as "the two great scourges of the century."

Although my general position is almost the same as Mann's, I will have to be careful about applying these critiques to the analyses of Philippe Burrin and Nicolas Werth, who appear to me to admirably hold both ends of the chain. But these preliminary remarks are worth making because in places the introduction and the very concept of this book present two problems. On the one hand, the postulate that it is possible to separate empirical analysis and moral evaluation (especially in the case of victims of terrorism and the problem of equivalency) is troublesome. On the other, certain remarks by Rousso at times go beyond methodological issues and intervene in the debate by attributing a greater importance given to the differences between Nazism

and Stalinism than to their common character. But a careful reading of part
I seems to me to point in the opposite direction.

Let us begin with the lack of symmetry indicated by the title. Why "Stalinism and Nazism" rather than "Stalinism and Hitlerism" or "Bolshevik and
Nazism"? The answer calls for a differentiation between Stalin and Hitler:
"the first inherited a system that survived him; the second founded a system
that died with him."[7]

True, but this identification of the man and the system would just as
easily justify the term "Hitlerism." Moreover, and more importantly, there
is a danger of accepting as fact two defensible but unproven theories: first,
that of the necessarily self-destructive character of Nazism, which made it
both ephemeral and historically unique; and second, the exceptional nature
of Stalinism within Bolshevism. It is probable in fact, as Krzysztof Pomian has
remarked, that in unleashing its violence externally more than domestically,
Nazism more than Stalinism risked hastening its own ruin. And it was beaten
militarily, from the outside. It did not collapse under the weight of its own
anarchy or contradictions. Moreover, even though Hitler and the fiery phase
of Nazism were incompatible with the international system, nothing proves
that, given its maintenance of economic and social capitalistic structures, his
successors would not have been able, with time, to integrate themselves into
this same system at the price of an erosion of their deadly adventurism. Yet
if Stalinism was followed by a de-Stalinization—a necessary argument for
those who refuse to identify him with Communism—and if it is true that
the post-Stalin regimes of Central Europe had abandoned the excesses of
totalitarian violence, it is just as true and important to remember that these
same excesses were not only prepared by Leninism, but have reappeared
in China, North Korea, and Cambodia. It must be admitted therefore, that
Stalinism is much more than Stalin, and we must ask ourselves what it was
in Stalin that came from the personality of a tyrant and what belonged to a
dynamic or an internal logic of the system.

The two studies on "the dictator and the system" call for analogous reflection. Each describes both the central role of the dictator and the manner
in which the dynamics he put into action escaped him (but only to a certain
extent, for it was always within his power to stop them). Each study describes the way relations with the bureaucracy and with society developed in
a contradictory and complex way. Thus Werth reemphasizes the opposition
between the revolutionary Stalinism of the 1930s and the conservative and
nationalistic Stalinism of the war and postwar years, which paved the way for
the post-Stalin bureaucratization. But the paranoia of the dictator in the last

years also led the regime to slide into episodes like the trial of the "White Shirts" and the projects for the deportation of Jews, excesses as frenzied as those of the 1930s.

The differences are self-evident in the structure of the Party (centralized or decentralized); in the respective style of the dictators, one anxious to control everything and the other prone to giving free rein to cronies; in the charismatic character of one's power and the manipulative nature of the other; and in the wild fanaticism of Hitler and the calculating, suspicious, cruel cynicism of Stalin. But the similarities, especially in the absence of scruples; the preference for police and populist strategies over institutions, including those of the party; and especially in the cults of which they were the respective objects, are no less striking. What is particularly problematic is the parallelism implicit in the results despite the opposite points of departure. It is certainly true that the cult of the leader is central and fundamental to Nazism and not necessarily to Communism. Hitler had a personal charisma that created a mystical communion, or at least an irrational one, with his acolytes and was aimed at the entire German population. Stalin, however, ruled by manipulation and fled contact with crowds. But the interesting point is that Stalin still managed to create a kind of charisma from a distance, and his cult reached the same religious heights as Hitler's and as did, after him, Mao, Kim Il Sung, Tito, and Ceausescu.

At this stage we arrive at the dimension that seems central to me, that of violence. From the title of the two studies, it is clear that there is a fundamental difference: violence is congenital to Nazism, while in Stalin's USSR it is the result of several different motivating factors that, as Nicolas Werth had already shown in his brilliant contribution to the *Livre noir du communisme*, follow and fit within each other, producing an unequaled brutalization of political and social relations and a permanent war of the regime against its own people. This points to the difference in violence between the two systems. Nazi violence was more targeted and more limited in its reach (because it essentially aimed at the Jews, the Gypsies, the homosexuals, the handicapped, and in a less radical manner the members of those peoples judged inferior), but it was also more extreme (in its unparalleled effort to eliminate an entire people and its descendants). Stalinist violence was more diffused, more omnipresent, and more unpredictable.

There are also similarities in the violence of the two regimes, beginning with the excess and unlimited nature, which has a significance other than quantitative. It is here that the studies seem to me not to agree with certain statements in the introduction.

Where Henry Rousso speaks of "superficial resemblances" and indicates that making an equation of the number of victims "does not help at all in understanding the nature of the political, social, and cultural processes set in motion" (p. 13), Philippe Burrin stresses "the crucial role that categorization played in Nazi violence, as in Stalinist violence" (p. 13). "The definition of target groups," which is necessary in both cases, is certainly more vague and, in any case, less directly biological or ethnic in the case of Stalinism. But as Nicolas Werth points out, the decision to eliminate the Cossacks dates from the beginning of the regime, and the "second Stalinism" aimed more and more in its deportations at entire populations defined by their ethnic character. Rousso repeats with approval the traditional affirmation, formulated by Ian Kershaw and Moshe Lewin, that, contrary to the physical elimination of entire ethnic groups by Hitler, "among Stalin's victims, an especially heavy tribute was, we know, exacted from the government and from the party" (p.8). Werth, however, emphasizes, "the large campaigns of mass repression during 1937–38 [had] . . . as their goal the conclusive eradication (that is, the physical elimination of more than 680,000 people) of all elements judged 'foreign' to the 'new society' under construction" (p. 85).

He continues: "Contrary to a still widely held opinion, recently available documentation on the sociology of the victims of the Great Terror shows that Party and economic cadres, military personnel, diplomats, members of the intelligentsia, and administrators and functionaries of all ranks only represent a small minority of the 680,000 people executed in 1937–38. As spectacular and politically significant as it was, the often high percentage of arrests of the Communist nomenklatura (from 50 percent to 95 percent) of a given region represented only a small fraction of the entire number of arrests" (p. 85).

Werth also stresses that the character and targets of Stalinist violence could vary according to the events, sometimes striking at political rivals, at others, certain social categories such as the kulaks. Sometimes it attached a particular criminalized social behavior, at others, certain ethnic groups were considered foreigners or traitors in spirit or deed. Both regimes selected according to their respective mythologies—in the one case, that of a racial purification carried out by experts turned witches and torturers, in the other, that of a political purification in the framework of planning gone berserk. An example of the latter can be seen when Comrades Anastas Mikoyan, Malenkov, and Litvin wrote to Comrade Stalin on September 22, 1937: "To assure a real cleansing of Armenia, we request the authorization to shoot a supplement of 700 (seven hundred) individuals arrested among the Dachnaks and other anti-Soviet elements. The authorization given for 500 individuals of the first category is on the point of being fulfilled." But is not the essential point the common idea of cleansing, evident in the image used by both regimes of the elimination of harmful insects, and also in the dialectic between, on the one hand, abstract categories or impersonal murder, and on the other, the manipulation and unleashing of passions, such as suspicion, jealousy, hatred, fear, the intoxication of domination, and that of cruelty?

Certainly it is not a question of either comparing victims quantitatively, denying the uniqueness of the Shoah, or pretending that the Soviet camps had the same final result of extermination and dehumanization as the Nazi camps (and yet in the matter of systematic dehumanization, the prison at Pitesti, described in the fine book by Virgil Ierunca,[8] managed to be innovative even in comparison to the Nazi camps). It is a question of studying the specificities and the differences between the regimes, beginning with a problem that cannot be other than common to both: violence without limits.

The third pair of parallel studies, dealing with power and society, calls for less discussion, even though it is perhaps the one that shows the most obvious progress in our instruments of analysis. Here the suitability of the same categories for studying the two regimes is both affirmed and illustrated, for the two authors rely on the distinction offered by Kershaw concerning the degrees of adhesion or opposition to Nazism in German society. It is the occasion for Burrin to move beyond the German quarrels rekindled by Daniel Goldhagen's thesis and for Werth to highlight in his analysis the changing role of Soviet society and its forms of resistance to power, a role that was asserted but not analyzed in his previous writings.

It seems to me that in the binomial "power and society," if the form, range, and even nature of power are basically different in Nazism and Bolshevism, the reactions of society, on a scale from enthusiastic acceptance to organized resistance, can vary at least as much within each type of regime, depending on the time and the country, as they can between these two countries themselves.

The Totalitarian Dynamic

Let us return to the first two themes in order to understand the dialectic already outlined. The more the differences that separate Communism and Nazism are emphasized, the more their unquestionably converging elements become obscure and demand reflection. How did it happen that an egalitarian and universalistic doctrine declaring "there is no supreme savior, nor God, nor Caesar, no tribune," and "proletarians have no country," and drawing a large part of its historical success from its pacifism in 1914, could end up in several instances, in different countries and historical moments, as an insane cult of personality, excessive nationalism, and massive, prolonged violence, finding itself always with new enemies and new victims? How, beginning with such contrasting ideological intentions and social conditions, could it end with results comparable to those that naturally belong to national socialism in the double sense of the nationalization of socialism and of the Nazi monstrosity itself?

There must be a dynamic or a logic that accounts for this reversal, and this is what historians, politicians, and philosophers should make an effort to uncover, rather than confronting each other over problems of definition or of classification.

Today there should be few disagreements on the facts. The debate is more about their respective degrees of importance. It is thus that a partisan of the idea of totalitarianism, like the author of these lines, finds himself almost agreeing with the most systematic critic of this very idea and of the rapprochement it implies between Nazism and Bolshevism, namely Ian Kershaw. Following other authors such as myself, he distinguishes between the definitions of totalitarianism centered on the state and those centered on the movement, recognizing no partial validity except in the case of the second category. What Nazism and Communism have in common is "a total or totalitarian aspiration that has consequences for both the mechanics of power and the behavior—enthusiastic acclamation or opposition—of the subjects."

He has spoken of "new technologies of power combined with an ideological dynamic and monopolistic demands addressed to society. . . . On this basis," he concludes, "it is legitimate to compare the forms of power in Germany under Hitler and in the Soviet Union under Stalin, even if this comparison is destined from the beginning to be superficial and unsatisfying. Moreover, the idea of totalitarianism, if one insists on using it, should be limited to passing phases of extreme instability reflected in the paranoid feeling of insecurity of these regimes, rather than seen as a durable structure of government. In a long-term perspective, the entire Third Reich period and most of the Stalin period should fall into this category. This would be one more reason to exclude the application of the concept of a comparative totalitarianism to post-Stalin Communist systems, an approach that borders on futility if not absurdity."[9]

It seems to me that one can accept these proposed limits (with the reservation that it remains strange to qualify the Stalin and Hitler periods as "passing phases of extreme instability") on the condition that we add that it would be just as absurd to exclude, on the one hand, Lenin's Russia and, on the other, Mao's China, Pol Pot's Cambodia, and Kim Il Sung's North Korea.

From here we are led to take the "total aspiration" and the "technology of power"—which Kershaw acknowledges rather disdainfully in the regimes of Stalin and Hitler as well as the "paranoid feeling of insecurity" of each— rather more seriously than he does and reflect on their double heritage: on the one hand, "the post-totalitarian authoritarianism" (to repeat the term introduced by Juan Linz), that is, regimes that abandon totalitarian violence but are always influenced in their nature and development by their violent origins; and on the other, movements and regimes that, in other countries and at other times, from Yugoslavia to Rwanda or Sudan, reproduce their frenetic push toward the extermination of millions of people without necessarily basing it on a developed ideology or on a positive utopia.

I am tempted, in an obviously "superficial and unsatisfying" way for those who refuse to take up the entire question of the "scourges" or "unhappiness" of the century, to search for the key to this totalitarian dynamic in three associated ideas:

First, one wonders, contrary to Ernst Nolte's last work, in which Nazism is essentially a defensive and mimetic reaction to Bolshevism, if it is not this last that is a hybrid compromise between old and modern values, be- tween democracy and dictatorship, between universalism and nationalism. One wonders as well if the natural inclination in situations in which tradition and modernity are equally in crisis, in which neither democracy nor empire are recognized as legitimate authorities, is not something, as in William Gold- ing's novel *Lord of the Flies*, that is much closer to Nazism, with its emphasis on the power of a leader and an elite who oppress or exclude some and combat others, than the Communist ideal. In other words Nazism, far from being a reaction to Communism, would risk becoming the natural inclination of Communism once both traditional beliefs and liberal institutions have been rejected.

The second idea can be seen as a less paradoxical formulation than the first. It is considerably encouraged by Nicolas Werth's insistence, both in *Livre noir du communisme* and in this collection, on the dynamic of violence. It consists in suggesting that totalitarianism is founded first on the identification of politics with war, or more precisely, on the inversion of the Clausewitzian formula in a combination common to Lenin and Ludendorf, according to which "politics is the continuation of war by other means." It is the notion of a "struggle to the death," of a final reckoning, of a total destruction of the adversary, that brings about the rest.

No one has explained this relationship better than Carl Schmitt in his formula: "Total enemy, total war, total State."[10] At the center of this triad is the total enemy: "The basis of the problem is found in war. The kind of total war in question determines the kind and form of the total quality of the State, but total war takes its meaning from the total enemy."

In this text Schmitt is speaking just as much about an external war as of one waged within. But of course the perfect total enemy for Nazi totalitarianism was the Jew (and other groups slated for extermination). The idea of the indispensable and unproblematic nature of collective extermination seems central to totalitarianism in its two major interpretations: in Hannah Arendt's "the logic of an idea," in which terrorism begins by being at the service of the ideology and ends by replacing it, and in Claude Lefort's interpretation, according to which it consists in the attempt to restore by modern means, in a world where individualist and bourgeois revolutions have already taken place, the premodern primacy of the total community and the suppression of the distinction between the state and society. In the two cases the resistance of a complex reality produces the need for a scapegoat whose elimination, never perfectly achieved, serves to mask the failure of the plan and to direct the mobilization of fear and hate.

Certainly fear and hate do not necessarily need a totalitarian ideology to be provoked or unleashed. But the main point (and this is the third dimension of the same idea) is that the essence of totalitarianism lies in its complete rejection of all barriers and all restraints that politics, civilization, morality, religion, natural feelings of compassion, and universal ideas of fraternity have constructed in order to moderate, repress, or sublimate the human potential for individual and collective violence. Once these barriers are removed or the brakes released, violence can either, as in the case of Nazism, be more easily cultivated as an end in itself and assume more extreme forms or, as in the case of Communism, be seen initially as a possible way to a peaceful end and thus take on a life of its own, diffuse and unpredictable. But these differences are less important than the dynamic of a continual revolution unleashed by the cult of an iron will, a hatred of compromise, and a contempt for civility, which together create less a regime than a state of paroxysm—like the plague and the *Stasis* described by Thucydides—where literally anything is possible.

In this sense it seems to me that we must accept, reclaim, and enlarge the criticism that claims that totalitarianism is a concept that cannot be defined except negatively, from a liberal point of view. Yes, what Bolshevism and Nazism have in common is essentially negative; it is the rejection of pluralism, of a state of laws, of Judeo-Christian morality, and of the established principles of civilization. They also have in common a rejection of man's recognition by other men and promote the exclusion from the human species of entire categories of people. The eventual result is their dehumanization and the negation of humanity in a double sense of the word.

It is here that I cannot entirely agree with Henry Rousso when he believes, on the subject of violence, that he can separate an empirical analysis from moral judgment. To place crime, as does *Le Livre noir du communisme*, at the center of Bolshevism (rather than of Communism in general or Stalinism in particular) as well as Nazism and, in a more general way, totalitarianism seems to me justified as long as we understand that it is not necessarily a question of ordinary criminality (even though recent research shows, in the case of the Soviet Union as in that of Nazi Germany, the role of gang warfare and the widespread use of common-law criminals). But just as importantly we must recognize the role played by the intoxication of the transgression in the name of what Hegel called "the law of the heart and the delirium of presumption," or more oppositely, "absolute liberty and terror."

The reference to Hegel, even if misguided, is not due to chance. I hope it will indicate the sense of my interest in the enterprise of the present volume and the collaboration among disciplines on subjects that concern us all. To paraphrase one of Kant's most quoted phrases: philosophical concepts cut off from historical experience are empty; historical analyses cut off from philosophical questioning are blind.

Translated by Lucy B. Golsan

Notes

1. Ian Kershaw and Moshe Lewin, eds., *Stalinism and Nazism: Dictatorship in Comparison*, Cambridge, Cambridge University Press, 1997, p. 1.

2. Pierre Hassner, "Le Totalitarisme vu de l'Ouest," in *Totalitarismes*, ed. Guy Hermet, Pierre Hassner, and Jacques Rupnik, Paris, Economica, 1984, pp. 15–41. Reprinted in Pierre Hassner, *La Violence et la paix: De la bombe atomique au nettoyage ethnique*, Paris, Ed. Esprit, 1995, pp. 221–258.

3. French translation, *Le Fascisme en son époque*, 3 vols., Paris, Julliard, 1970.

4. François Furet and Ernst Nolte, *Fascisme et Communisme*, Commentaire, Paris, Plon, 1998, chaps. 4–5.

5. Michael Mann, "The Contradictions of Continuous Revolution," in Kershaw and Lewin, op. cit., pp. 135–157.

6. Pierre Bouretz, "Penser au XXe siècle: La Place de l'énigme totalitaire," *Esprit*, January–February 1996, pp. 122–134.

7. Henry Rousso, in this volume, p. 7.

8. Virgil Ierunca, *Pitesti, laboratoire concentrationnaire*, preface by François Furet, Paris, Ed. Michalon, 1996.

9. Ian Kershaw, "The Essence of Nazism. Form of Fascism, Brand of Totalitarianism, or Unique Phenomenon?" in *The Nazi Dictatorship: Problems of Perspectives of Interpretation*, 2d ed., London, 1989, pp. 40–41.

10. Carl Schmitt, "Totaler Feind, totaler Krieg, totaler Staat" (1937), in *Positionen und Begriffe*, 1939, p. 236.

Krzysztof Pomian

Postscript on the Ideas of Totalitarianism and of the "Communist Regime"

The typology of political regimes set out in antiquity seemed definitive for a long time. It is true that the ideas introduced changed in content several times. The Roman Republic was different from that of Athens; a republic of nobility that existed in Poland from the sixteenth to the eighteenth century was very different from the Roman Republic, which nevertheless was considered as the model; and the French Republic had little in common with Poland. Medieval and modern monarchies were different in several ways from those of the Greeks and Romans. Slavery disappeared in Europe, countries became more vast than the ancient cities, the economy played a much larger role, and the individual was liberated from the complete dominance of a social body.

These differences were clearly pointed out, most recently, at the beginning of the nineteenth century in the celebrated discourse of Benjamin Constant on the liberty of the ancients as compared with that of the moderns. At the end of the nineteenth century, it was also evident that an extended modern democracy on the scale of a large country and based on universal suffrage, even though only masculine, was far from being a simple copy of ancient democracy. But that in no way precluded thinking that such categories as "republic," "monarchy," and "tyranny," and where republics are concerned, "democracy," "oligarchy," and "aristocracy," could not recreate in an exhaustive fashion, with several additional distinctions, all the political regimes known to history, if not all those that could possibly be conceived.

The twentieth century has scrambled this beautiful layout. To be convinced of this, one has only to note that the introduction of universal suffrage in Great Britain, the Netherlands, or in the Scandinavian countries gave birth to the unexpected case of a democratic monarchy. But the question became especially pertinent beginning with the 1920s and the establishment of regimes by the Fascist Party in Italy, by the Nazi Party in Germany, and by the Bolshevik Party in the former Russian Empire, which of course became the Soviet Union. Is it possible to include them within the frame of a classical typology?

Whoever answers this question in the affirmative must characterize the nature of each one of these regimes in order to see if it is legitimate to include them all under the same heading or if, on the contrary, they differ among themselves in their very nature. Whoever answers in the negative finds himself obliged to explain the new characteristics each one has introduced and whether or not these are important enough not to be considered a variant of established models. Then the question arises of knowing if these three regimes are creations of the same type or if they must be treated separately. If we opt for the first solution, this type must be given a name. It is then and then only that we run into the term "totalitarianism," which since the 1920s has been the principal candidate for this role.

It is useless to retrace here the events of the controversy that the use of this term has stirred up and that are not over; references are found in the introduction by Henry Rousso. Although this has also been done before, let us again point out that the ideological and political assumptions have interfered constantly in this controversy, relying in their arguments on data from history and other social sciences. Today, over ten years after the fall of the Berlin Wall, the subject seems to be treated with more detachment, even though the ideological and political stakes are far from disappearing.

New Forms of Tyranny

Let us begin then by emphasizing that the term "totalitarianism" is not worth being introduced unless we admit that regimes imposed by the Fascists in Italy, by the Nazis in Germany, and by the Bolsheviks in Russia—perhaps only by the last two and certainly also by other forces in other countries— were characterized by political features that logically prevent or at least make it difficult to think of including them in the traditional typologies. Otherwise "totalitarianism" would be only a word that allows, certainly, the expression of a judgment of negative value on such and such a political regime but would add nothing to the understanding of the facts. It is up to those who claim that political regimes appeared in the twentieth century that were characterized by new ideas that were clearly political and were without precedent to prove this: they ought to identify these new characteristics and show that their presence defines a type of political regime unknown in the past.

Without going into details, we will mention two of them. The first new characteristic trait of the governments in question is that these are *revolutionary regimes*. As for the objectives they aim at, they refuse to be bound by any preestablished norms, or at least to be constrained by any dealings with forces unfavorable to them. Even Mussolini and Hitler, who came to power through elections, rapidly broke loose from legal constraints. Lenin and Stalin never had to worry about them. As to the political sphere in general and, in particular, the treatment inflicted on those who were considered enemies by those in power, the idea of legality loses any significance.

As for legitimacy the three regimes discussed here do not even try to base themselves on such a tradition, real or cobbled together. It does not matter even if the first speaks of the Roman Empire, the second of ancient Germany, and the third—in its later years, it is true—of the glories, especially military, of Russia. But in the eyes of their spokesmen and those who support their objectives, the legitimacy of these regimes results, not from their roots in the past or in the great beyond, but in the future to which they are supposedly bringing great promise. These are future-centric regimes that will transform their countries, even the entire world, radically and very quickly by way of a rupture with the established order—whether internal or international—and that, to realize their ambitions, make a large-scale commitment to violence— to terrorism or to war, the two are not mutually exclusive.

The second original and characteristic trait of the regimes under discussion is that they *react against modern democracy*, a system based on universal suffrage, which thereby necessarily involves the masses in political life. Directed by their revolutionary orientation, this presents them with problems that no other tyranny in the past has had to resolve. In fact they must maintain the participation of the masses in political life and at the same time manipulate them for their own exclusive profit. As a consequence, as much for Fascists as for Nazis and Bolsheviks, it is a matter of setting up, first in their respective countries, a monopoly on the organization of the masses, which means that they must destroy any political force likely to compete with them. This is the first function of state terrorism. They must then stifle the very possibility of a spontaneous action from the masses, which necessitates creating a system of enclosure that leaves no form of activity, no stage of life, no place outside and that produces a state of permanent mobilization. They must at the same time impose a common belief on the masses and direct their emotions along the same path in presenting them with examples to admire and follow, having in the lead an infallible ruler. The masses must also be given targets for their hatred. From this develops a multiplication of unions, associations, and committees and uses the media on a huge scale: radio, the printed press, and the cinema along with the deployment of propaganda by banners, flags, slogans, and images. There must also be reunions, gatherings, and parades.

These summary remarks allow us, I believe, to state that before the 1920s there had never been a political regime conceived as a revolutionary reaction against democracy of the masses. No regime prior to 1920, therefore, revealed the characteristics that have just been mentioned. It is obviously possible to reject this assertion, but it would be a difficult case to prove. Until counterevidence is provided, it is reasonable to contend that the political regimes that are revolutionary reactions against democracy of the masses have no place in the traditional typology of political regimes, and it is, therefore, desirable to give them a different name. Good reasons exist, therefore, for calling them "totalitarian." The term "totalitarian" designates the inherent tendency or impulse of these regimes alone to submit the totality of personal, family, and collective life to the surveillance of their administrative, political, and police organs to the point of abolishing the boundaries between the public and private spheres. This tendency results from the recognition of the necessity to mobilize the masses while controlling them, unrestricted by any barrier inherited from the past, whether it be legal, customary, religious, or moral. But this impulse cannot be realized unless social conditions and technical methods allow for it.

The addition of the category "totalitarian" to the typology of political regimes makes it possible to highlight the historical origins of certain forms of tyranny that have appeared in the twentieth century. But this applies only to certain ones, for there have also been tyrannies that constituted more-traditional reactions against mass democracy and that as a consequence, while having affinities with the totalitarians, did not belong to the same family. Horthy, Salazar, Pilsudski, Franco, and a number of others had established dictatorial or tyrannical regimes. But they did not attempt or implement a total mobilization of the masses: to the contrary, they did everything to keep them in a passive state. And their aim was not to carry out a revolutionary rupture. Rather, they wanted to restore the political hierarchy that had existed before democracy and that had been dismantled by the masses. The distinction between such authoritarian regimes and totalitarian ones is important. Without this, it is as difficult to understand the internal conflicts of the Iberian countries and most of the countries of Central and Eastern Europe between the 1920s and the end of the Second World War as it is the development of international relations during these decades.

Two Communist Regimes

But the distinction between totalitarian and other authoritarian regimes is important for yet another reason. It suggests that we make other distinctions in our typology of political regimes as well. For example, we currently use expressions such as "fascist regime," "Nazi regime," and "Communist regime." The first two denote relatively short temporal sequences: respectively of twenty and twelve years. It is otherwise with the third one. The "Communist regime" has lasted sixty-four years in the former Russian Empire and forty-five in the Communist bloc. So the question arises: has it changed during these decades or has it remained the same?

It is in attempting to respond to this question that we find ourselves caught in the trap of an inadequate terminology, for in one sense, the "Communist regime" has not changed: it has remained Communist throughout in that it has maintained for itself, in the USSR as it has in the "Socialist countries," a monopoly on political, economic, and cultural power. It is no less obvious that this regime has changed, that it has even changed profoundly; the populations of the countries involved have not failed to notice this. Just the same, if it had not changed, it would not have collapsed without encountering any opposition, to the amazement of all the Sovietologists who were ready for anything but that.

The only way to avoid a futile debate over the evolution of the so-called Communist regime is to use the expression only under very limited circumstances. Strictly speaking, there was actually no "Communist regime" in the singular. In the course of its long history, Communist domination was carried out under two different forms. It would also be well, at least in a discourse aimed at being historical or scientific, to clarify when we speak of a "Communist regime" which of the two forms of domination we are discussing.

The Communist totalitarian regime that lasted in the USSR until the death of Stalin was, from that moment on, more and more in a state of crisis. The Communist Party, which alone held power, began by abandoning mass terrorism and then later discarded the idea of mobilizing the masses to whom it ceased, first, to propose enemies to hate and, then later, to offer objectives to be enthusiastically attained. The idea of the "worsening of the class struggle," the insistence on hidden enemies of the people, and the daily incitement to unmask and exterminate them was replaced little by little by the emphasis on the "moral and political unity of the people." Elsewhere the Party set about celebrating the defining character of the regime, of pointing out its legality, which it had ignored until then. It then attempted to exclude any further change in its structures, to treat the revolution itself as a thing of the past, and to present the future as a simple continuation of the present. In other words, from being revolutionary, the regime transformed itself more and more into a traditionalist one, from being future-centric it became backward-looking:

in a word, without ceasing to be Communist, it acquired the characteristics of an authoritarian rather than a totalitarian regime, although it is impossible to point out a date that marked the passage from one to the other.

Nevertheless this transformation had progressed enough in the USSR during more than thirty years for a peaceful exit from the Communist period to take place. It began with *Perestroika*, but it had not been able to install an authoritarian regime purged of the last residue of totalitarianism, which in Russia would have led to redefining relations with a nationalist past and with the Orthodox Church, while in other republics with opening the field to the action of centrifugal forces. And when it almost managed to do this, it provoked the disappearance of the USSR itself and the installation in Russia of a political regime difficult to characterize. This government united unquestionably democratic elements with others that were not. Given these developments, even in the case of the USSR, one cannot speak of an unchanging political regime in all the sixty-five years of Communist domination.

In the Communist bloc countries, the changes in the nature of the regime began in sync with the USSR. But they have since acquired a different rhythm, which varies according to the country; in certain ones it was more rapid, in others it seems to have been slower. Thus Poland, from 1956 on, became an authoritarian regime. Even though it still held economic and political power, the Communist Party abandoned the collectivization of agriculture while losing the monopoly on collective beliefs and culture since it was forced to leave a larger and larger place to the Catholic Church and open itself up to influences from the West. Beginning in the mid-1970s, it was also forced to tolerate open dissidence; the military coup of December 1981 not only changed nothing essential in this regard but it even ended several years later with recognition of a political opposition.

A parallel path was clearly followed by Hungary, especially beginning in 1965; it led to the appearance of open dissidence. An analogous development began to appear in Czechoslovakia in the 1960s. Halted by the repression following the Prague Spring, it would slowly become active again in the second half of the 1970s. But the GDR, Bulgaria, Romania, and especially Albania seemed to retain longer, if not totalitarian regimes in their entirety, at least certain elements, especially very strong repressive institutions capable of keeping the masses fearful and obedient without having recourse to mass terrorism.

The abandonment of the idea of a "Communist regime" that was everywhere identical in favor of a form of Communist domination that was itself undergoing a transition from totalitarianism to a weaker authoritarianism—

all behind a self-imposed façade of immobility—raises several important questions. What factors encouraged leaving totalitarianism behind? The death of the leader? But Stalin had succeeded very well in taking the place of Lenin and reinforcing the totalitarian nature of the regime. Why were those who succeeded Stalin ignorant of how to renew this accomplishment themselves? Or, if they had the know-how, why were they incapable of maintaining the status quo?

Was it due to the economic inefficiency of the repressive system; to the conflicts between the different branches of the ruling group; to the pressures of international rivalry; to the resistance of the masses who wanted tranquility and well being, even if only of a minimal kind; to profound changes in outlook, which made measures unacceptable that had formerly been considered justified; or all of this combined? In this case the weight of each of these factors would have to be determined. The same questions need to be asked of authoritarian Communist regimes and of their slow disintegration. Here the circumstances are better understood because of the regimes' increasing transparency with time and of their growing difficulties in hiding the manifestations of discontent in the population, including, as of a certain point, in stifling the voice of dissidence.

Two Stages of Transition

Accepting the idea of a transition in the forms of Communist domination from the exercise of totalitarian power to the exercise of authoritarian power allows us to understand the peaceful emergence from Communist domination itself. Seen from this perspective, it becomes part of the normal paradigm of the decomposition of authoritarian regimes, either as a result of a military defeat (the Greece of the generals, post-Salazar Portugal, and the Argentina of Videla and his cronies) or by way of a transition toward democracy desired by an increasingly less-silent majority but in the end given final impetus from above (the Spain of Juan Carlos). The USSR falls into the first category, with the loss of the military race with the United States and also the war in Afghanistan; this set off a series of reforms that ended in erasing all Communist domination. The demise of authoritarianism in the face of a popular impetus toward democracy is evident too in the case of Poland and Hungary of 1989.

We thus are led to ask why the change in the nature of the political regime has not been perceived as such either by the populations concerned or by outside observers, which means that still today we speak of a "Communist regime" as if it formed a period on which history has no hold. Certainly the inadequacy of the term and what it implies is already evident in the Soviet Union from the end of 1953; Ehrenbourg's *The Thaw*, which gave its name to the period between the liquidation of Beria and the Twentieth Congress of the Communist Party of the USSR, appeared in 1954. Other terms were used in other countries to express the feeling of an improvement of living conditions; around 1956 in Poland, one spoke of a *renewal*, and the Hungarians called the Kadar regime after 1965 a *goulash socialism*. It is nevertheless true that no one seems to have diagnosed the departure of totalitarianism and the replacement of one political regime by another. Why?

The response is simple: because there was no one to do it. And there was a reason not to. In the eyes of the Communists, there could have been no change in the regime's nature since the "socialist regime" was still at work. Institutional continuity was preserved: industry was nationalized, agriculture collectivized, the economy planned, and the Communist Party, in the guise of its leaders, still exercised full power and was active in every area. Continuity was assured by the maintenance of the same people at their posts—with the exception of a few sectors—especially in the security services. Official rhetoric for its part loudly repudiated the very idea of a rupture with the Leninist and Stalinist past: the Party was supposed to have always followed a straight line; it was admitted certainly that there had been errors and misrepresentations, even crimes, but all of that had been corrected by the Party itself, and things had gotten back to normal. This is to say that the Party leaders, obsessed by the appearance of stability and by their ideological convictions, did not realize the depth of the changes that were taking place and of their possible long-term effects. They did not even have the words to describe them.

Now let us consider the dissidents. Even in a country as advanced on the road to change as Poland after 1956, the takeover by Gomulka and his team in the early 1960s raised fears of a return to practices that no one had yet forgotten. And also the "revisionists" who, immediately after 1956, counted on an evolution of the "socialist regime" toward more liberty and an efficient economy came to believe ten years later that it would not allow reforms but was by its nature unchangeable, that it kept its original nature—more and more it was called *totalitarian*—and that only fluctuating factors prevented it from going back to the methods of government it had formerly used. The events of March 1968, followed by the military intervention in Czechoslovakia and the end of hopes awakened by the Prague Spring, only reinforced revisionists in this conviction.

It was around the same time that a turning point took place in the attitude of Western Communists and "fellow travelers." The anticipation of what the Czechs called "socialism with a human face," which had filled the period following 1956 and allowed people to close their eyes to the bloody repression of the Hungarian Revolution, then began to give way to an increasingly critical position regarding the USSR, fed by the appearance of dissension, the work of Alexander Solzhenitsyn, and the workers revolting in Poland. The workers were joined, even though timidly and with some reservations, by the dissidence of lifelong Communists convinced that nothing truly important had been produced in the USSR since Stalin's death and that it was the same totalitarian regime in power, a "Communist regime" being totalitarian by definition. Also, all of them logically foresaw that the "Communist regime" would only be destroyed by a bloody uprising or, even more likely, by a third world war. Although this corollary was disproved by history, it seems the obvious conclusion was not drawn from this, that the "Communist regime" in its terminal stage was different in principle from what it had been in its youthful years. It was no longer totalitarian; it was authoritarian.

The idea that Communist domination went from a totalitarian regime to an authoritarian one threatens to be, in the countries that endured it, badly received by a fraction of public opinion. In fact, in all of these countries, political life from then on was organized around a division between forces coming out of the former anti-Communist opposition, or those who presented themselves as such, and the Communist parties, or those who came out of them, claiming to be adherents to a social democracy. The first group used references to the past as a weapon in the struggle that pitted them against the second group. And they have tried to impose a total condemnation of the "Communist regime," identified with the "evil empire." Certain extremists have even gone so far as to rehabilitate local brands of fascism or Nazism through their anti-Communism or by asking if a Nazi victory would not have been better than a Stalinist one in World War II.

At the opposite pole the Communist Party, which kept its former name, has done well not only in Russia but also in the western Czech Republic. At the present in several countries, certain former Communist leaders enjoy a positive image in the eyes of voters; the first secretary of the Lithuanian Communist Party was elected president of the republic, defeating a former dissident, and his Slovenian homologue is still head of state. General Jaruzelski, whom the Poles were supposed to have covered with shame, is ahead of Lech Walesa in the polls. These are the facts that the idea of a "Communist regime," invariably totalitarian, is incapable of explaining, but that become comprehensible in the perspective offered here, whose interest, as a consequence, is not just retrospective.

Translated by Lucy B. Golsan

Index